CULT OF THE IRRELEVANT

Princeton Studies in International History and Politics

G. John Ikenberry, Marc Trachtenberg,
and William C. Wohlforth, Series Editors

For a full list of books in this series see https://press.princeton.edu/catalogs
/series/title/princeton-studies-in-international-history-and-politics.html

Recent Titles

Cult of the Irrelevant

The Waning Influence of Social Science on National Security

Michael C. Desch

PRINCETON UNIVERSITY PRESS

PRINCETON AND OXFORD

Copyright © 2019 by Princeton University Press

Published by Princeton University Press
41 William Street, Princeton, New Jersey 08540
6 Oxford Street, Woodstock, Oxfordshire OX20 1TR

press.princeton.edu

All Rights Reserved

Library of Congress Control Number 2018935645
ISBN 978-0-691-18121-9

British Library Cataloging-in-Publication Data is available

Editorial: Eric Crahan and Pamela Weidman
Production Editorial: Jill Harris
Jacket Design: Carmina Alvarez
Jacket Image: Operations Research game with Milton Weiner and Olaf
    Helmer, 1966. Courtesy of the RAND Corporate Archives.
Production: Erin Suydam
Copyeditor: Jack Rummel

This book has been composed in Adobe Text Pro

Printed on acid-free paper. ∞

Printed in the United States of America

10 9 8 7 6 5 4 3 2 1

CONTENTS

ACKNOWLEDGMENTS

I am grateful for comments on this project to participants in the various seminars at the Notre Dame Institute for Advanced Study; the Buffet Center for International Studies at Northwestern University; the Lone Star National Security Forum (Texas A&M, University of Texas Austin, and Southern Methodist University); the University of Virginia's International Security Colloquium; the Program on International Security Policy (PISP) at the University of Chicago; the Jack Wright Series at George Washington University; the Notre Dame International Security Program seminar series; MIRTH at the University of California, Berkeley; the Department of Political Science at Baylor University; and especially for two seminars at the Security Studies Program at MIT. I also thank Etuna Maass, Gustavo Gari, Michael Rangel, Eddie Linczer, Mackenzie Nolan, Sienna Wdowik, Aidan Dore, Anne Vesser, Monica Montgomery, Owen FitzGerald, John Linczer, Cassandra Anzalone, and Ji Hye Shin for terrific research assistance. For extensive discussions on the topic, I thank Sonja Amadae, Robert Art, Paul Avey, Richard Betts, Peter Campbell, John Cisternino, Daniel Drezner, David Engerman, Tanisha Fazal, Francis Gavin, Gary Goertz, George Herring, Jeffrey Isaac, Sean Lynn-Jones, Thomas Mahnken, John Mearsheimer, Vipin Narang, Barry Posen, Harvey Sapolsky, Todd Sechser, Rogers Smith, Marc Trachtenberg, Stephen Walt, and especially Stephen Van Evera.

Parts of chapter 1 were published as "Technique Trumps Relevance: The Professionalization of Political Science and the Marginalization of Security Studies," *Perspectives on Politics* 13, no. 2 (June 2015): 377–93 (reprinted by permission of Cambridge University Press); and chapter 5 draws from my contribution to a larger piece cowritten with Paul C. Avey, which was presented at two workshops organized by the "Strengthening the Links" Project of the Teaching, Research, and International Policy Program at the College of William and Mary in Washington, DC, in August 2014 and in Williamsburg in January 2015.

I am grateful to the staffs of the National Archives and Record Administration, College Park, MD; the Rockefeller Foundation; the Dwight

D. Eisenhower Presidential Library; the John F. Kennedy Presidential Library; the Lyndon Baines Johnson Presidential Library; and the Archives of Dartmouth College; and Harvard University. Paul Avey, Peter Campbell, and Marc Trachtenberg generously shared unpublished materials with me that they came across in the course of their own research. Alexander McNaughton, the son of the late John McNaughton, graciously allowed me to consult his father's diaries and date planners. Erin Fitzgerald provided me with documents and information from her time running the Minerva Initiative. I appreciate the correspondence, discussions, and formal interviews I had with Ann Dreazon, Eric Edelman, Robert M. Gates, Morton Halperin, and Tom Mahnken.

Of course, none of these colleagues who commented on various parts of this book, nor those who consented to be interviewed or provided information, bear any responsibility for any remaining errors of facts or interpretation here.

Finally, I am grateful for time off and financial support from the Notre Dame Institute for Advanced Studies Faculty fellowship (fall 2012), the Richard Lounsbury and Earhart foundations, and especially the Carnegie Corporation of New York.

I dedicate this book to Samuel Huntington (*requiescat in pace*) who to my mind gave the most compelling answer to social science's relevance question I have ever heard: pick substantively important questions of broad concern and answer them in the most rigorous way you can.

CULT OF THE IRRELEVANT

1

The Relevance Question

PROFESSIONAL SOCIAL SCIENCE AND THE FATE OF SECURITY STUDIES

In his April 14, 2008, speech to the Association of American Universities, former Texas A&M University president and then secretary of defense Robert M. Gates declared that "we must again embrace eggheads and ideas." What he meant was that "throughout the Cold War, universities were vital centers of new research" and that at one time U.S. national security policymakers successfully tapped intellectual "resources outside of government" to help them formulate policy.[1] One of the most influential civilian academic strategic theorists, the late Harvard Nobel laureate Thomas Schelling, confirmed that there once was "a wholly unprecedented 'demand' for the results of theoretical work: scholars had an audience and scholars had access to classified information. Unlike any other country . . . the United States had a government permeable not only by academic ideas but by academic people."[2]

While not all scholars and policymakers agree that the two sides of what many now see as a yawning chasm have had, or could have, much useful to say to each other in the realm of national security affairs, the vast majority do. Former ambassador David Newsom, for example, thought that of all the various groups in American society that could shape U.S. foreign policy, "the free realm of academia—the 3,638 institutions of higher education and the persons associated with them—should have the most knowledge and insight to offer to policymakers."[3] MIT professor and long-term U.S. government consultant Ithiel de Sola Pool agreed that training in the social sciences constituted a useful tool for policymakers.[4]

Despite this general optimism and the best of intentions among both scholars and policymakers "the relationship between the federal government and the social sciences generally and historically, while substantial in scope, has not been altogether harmonious," to put it mildly.[5] According to a Teaching and Research in International Politics (TRIP) survey, a regular poll of international relations scholars, very few believe they should not contribute to policy making in some way. Yet the majority also recognize that the state-of-the-art approaches of academic social science constitute precisely those approaches that policymakers find least helpful.[6] A related poll of senior national security decision makers confirmed that for the most part academic social science is not giving them what they want.[7] The problem, in a nutshell, is that scholars increasingly equate rigor with the use of particular techniques (mathematics and universal models) and ignore broader criteria of relevance.

Gates's efforts to bridge the Beltway and Ivory Tower gap thus came at a time when it seemed to be growing wider. In April 2009, Harvard professor (and former high-level State Department, Defense Department, and intelligence community official) Joseph Nye opined in a widely discussed article in the *Washington Post* that "the walls surrounding the ivory tower never have seemed so high."[8] The gap between scholars and policymakers has widened in recent years, particularly in the realm of national security affairs, once a model of collaboration.[9] And there is hard data undergirding this concern. As figure 1.1 shows, the willingness of leading international relations scholars to offer such policy recommendations has declined in absolute terms, at least since 1980 (and I will show well before then).[10] In the view of many on either side of the chasm, the bridge between the Ivory Tower and the Beltway has become an increasingly rickety one, particularly as the discipline of political science has striven to become more scientific.

This development is puzzling: it flies in the face of a widespread and long-standing optimism about the compatibility of rigorous social science and policy relevance that goes back to the Progressive Era and the very dawn of modern American social science.[11] As historian Barry Karl remarked apropos Charles Merriam, one of the founders of the modern discipline of political science, he "was an American activist of his generation before he was a political scientist; it was his reason for becoming a political scientist. He saw no conflict between activism and science. Indeed, he saw science as

FIGURE 1.1. Quantitative methods, formal modeling, and policy prescriptions in top IR journals since 1980. (The TRIP journal data from which I generated this and subsequent figures are available at http://www3.nd.edu/~carnrank/.)

the essential precondition of a useful activism."[12] And early in the Cold War at the height of the Behavioral Revolution in the social sciences, his student Harold Lasswell sought to craft a "policy science" that would apply cutting edge social science to the pressing policy problems of the day. Indeed, there is confidence that the effort to make the social sciences more "scientific" is not incompatible with relevance.[13] Some scholars go so far as to argue that it is the sine qua non of real relevance.[14] This confidence persists today.[15]

I suggest that this growing scholarly/policy gap is the result of the professionalization of the discipline of political science. While the professionalization of a discipline and its increasing irrelevance to concrete policy issues is not inevitable, there nonetheless seems to be an elective affinity between these two trends.[16] Rigor and relevance are not necessarily incompatible but they are often in tension, which is why social science's relevance question endures. Figure 1.1 demonstrates this point clearly: as the number of scholarly articles using sophisticated quantitative or formal methods increased since 1980, the percentage of them offering concrete policy recommendations—the core of policy relevance—has declined.

Second, many proponents of the scientific study of politics now eschew advocacy of particular policies on the grounds that doing so is incompatible with scientific objectivity.[17] This is the widely embraced, but frequently mischaracterized, value-neutrality concern that the early twentieth-century

German social scientist Max Weber first raised.[18] Third, many pressing policy questions are not readily amenable to the preferred methodological tools of social scientists. Fourth, even when the results of these approaches are relevant to policy questions, they are often not accessible to policymakers or the broader public.

Finally, many scholars are overly optimistic that despite these other problems the pursuit of basic research will nevertheless produce applied knowledge via a "trickle-down" (or bubble-up) process.[19] Adherents of this view believe that normal progress of science naturally confers policy benefits in much the same way that some economists are sanguine that economic growth will increase the wealth of the poorest, even if wealth is quite unevenly distributed.[20] As F. A. Lindemann, Winston Churchill's wartime science adviser put it, "Every addition to our knowledge re-acts upon industrial problems and either suggests improvements in technical processes or at any rate prevents the waste of time entailed in attempting impossibilities."[21] This reinforces the inclination of social scientists not to worry about whether their own work is directly relevant.[22]

These factors explain why the more "scientific" approaches to international relations scholarship seem to be the least relevant, at least as measured by their practitioner's willingness to offer policy recommendations. The problem, in my view, is not so much that "scientific" approaches to national security policy are irrelevant by definition; rather, their current dominance is a symptom of a larger trend among the social sciences to privilege sophisticated method and universal models over substance with a resulting decline in policy relevance. As Kenneth Waltz warned, methods-driven work is likely to be at best only "accidently relevant."[23] Method-driven and model-driven research do not cause identical pathologies but both can inhibit "problem-driven" research, the sine qua non of policy relevance.[24]

This is by no means an argument against the importance of theory in security studies. Social science theories matter because they can serve as analytical models, rhetorical instruments, and cognitive frameworks for policymakers as they make and implement policy.[25] The key is that scholars try to address problems of concern to the policy community and in a way that informs action. Rather, it echoes the caution expressed by participants in the Rockefeller Foundation Conference on International Politics, held on May 7–8, 1954, such as Reinhold Niebuhr who maintained that "the theorist's contribution would be very irrelevant if he thought that the only rational theory was one based on constants and general laws. Theory must be built into the knowledge of what the statesman faces."[26]

This book seeks to answer social science's larger relevance question: How can it be both a rigorous scholarly enterprise while also engaging with society's practical problems? To do so, it engages four specific questions: First, what do I mean by policy relevance? Second, what has been the influence of academic social science on policy historically? Third, what explains variation in its influence over time? Finally, what, if anything, should be done to close any gaps between scholars and policymakers?

In general, policy-relevant scholarship limns the range of possibilities open to policymakers and assesses the consequences of the particular policy choices they make.[27] While such work does not have to be produced directly for policymakers, it should offer concrete policy recommendations derived from systematic investigation aimed at shaping government action, directly or indirectly. The best metaphor for describing policy-relevant scholarship is that it provides policymakers (or journalists or citizens) with a mental map to help them navigate the real world.[28]

Expectations for what sort of influence scholars can have need to be reasonable. The notion that to matter academic social science must regularly shape high-level national security decisions on a consistent basis is too demanding a standard. As RAND Corporation historian Bruce Smith noted, "The end product of most planning and research activities is not an agenda of mechanical policy moves for every contingency—plainly an impossible task—but rather a more sophisticated map of reality carried in the minds of the policy makers."[29] Relevance, of course, is not identical with influence. A scholar can offer concrete policy recommendations but policymakers may not adopt them. Moreover, even if policymakers adopt these recommendations, that is no guarantee that good or effective policy will result. So relevance, in my view, is a necessary, if not sufficient, condition for influence. And I will offer logical arguments and historical evidence to suggest that scholarly input into policy is more often than not beneficial and its absence detrimental to good policy.

Ascertaining the extent to which academic social scientists had influence on policymakers is challenging:[30] As political scientist John Kingdon warned, the influence of academics on policy debates is often "hidden," and the secrecy surrounding national security decision making makes their role in national security strategy even more opaque.[31] An internal State Department report highlighted the problem of measuring the impact of external research: "Actual utilization of this information is difficult to measure. Reports and written memoranda are distributed to approximately 500 officers in the Department and other agencies concerned with foreign policy and national security matters. The external research division answers some 35 telephonic queries per day. The continuing demand for this kind of information indicates a felt need on the part of policy and intelligence officers, but it is not known exactly how or to what extent this information is put to use in the actual formulation of policy or analysis of issues."[32] Indeed, such an exercise shares the more general challenge of tracing the influence of ideas—the currency of academics—on policy outcomes.[33]

To answer this second question about the influence of social science on policy, I explore the changing relationship between the discipline of political science and its subfield of international security from the early years of the twentieth century through the post–Cold War era. Most security scholars share Columbia political scientist Robert Jervis's view that there was a "golden age,"[34] during which "there were significant links between theory and U.S. policy."[35] International security has long been among the most policy relevant of subfields within the discipline of political science. This is still the case today, at least as measured by the willingness of authors in top international relations journals to offer explicit policy recommendations. There is a significant difference in this regard, as figure 1.2 shows, between articles since 1980 dealing with security issues (i.e., weapons of mass destruction, weapons acquisition, terrorism, and military intervention) and other issue areas in the field of international relations.

Admittedly, this view of an academic-policy golden age is not universally shared.[36] After serving in the Second World War, U.S. Navy anthropologist Alexander Leighton reported that the conventional wisdom among social scientists in government during the war was that "the administrator uses social science the way the drunk uses a lamppost, for support rather than illumination."[37] More recently, highlighting the difference between U.S. nuclear declaratory policy (in which civilian defense intellectuals apparently had influence) and actual operational doctrine and war plans (where they did not), historian Bruce Kuklick presented the most sustained critique of the Golden Age nostalgia.[38] One basis for pessimism that policymakers and scholars could have much to say to each other is that the former operate in a very different environment from the latter. Policymakers need good enough answers in a short period of time while scholars are hesitant to say anything about an issue until they are highly certain of their answer.[39] Former director of the State Department Policy Planning Staff during the George W. Bush administration and Stanford professor Steve Krasner also blamed the "complexity" of the policymaking process for the inability of scholars to intervene effectively in it.[40] Given this, so the pessimists maintain, it is futile to think that it can mesh with the academic enterprise.

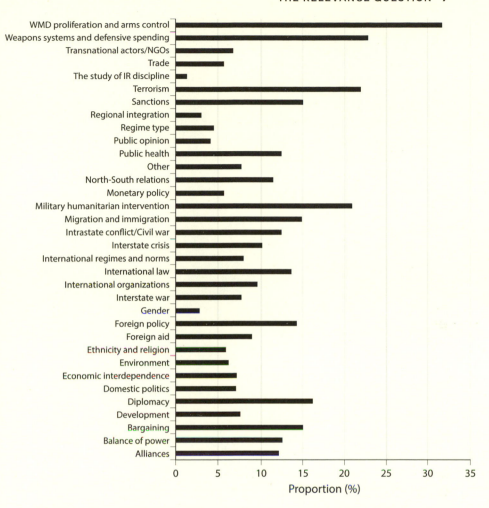

FIGURE 1.2. Articles providing policy prescriptions by topic. (Source: TRIP.)

Another objective of this book, therefore, is to look at a broader swath of history and a wider array of national security issues. Doing so reveals that, despite waxing and waning, there were periods in which social scientists had significant policy influence. Indeed, few people outside the subfield of international security are aware of the extent to which the U.S. government routinely reached out to academic social scientists to meet these challenges in the past. The history of the last hundred years shows that the scholarship of some social scientists did have real impact on presidential and senior poli-cymakers' decision making at certain junctures, particularly during wartime and periods of crisis. Table 1.1 highlights some of these particular national security issues.

TABLE 1.1. Social Science and National Security Issues

World War I
The Inquiry and postwar settlement
Public information and morale
Psychological testing of soldiers
Economic mobilization of the economy

World War II
Military job assignment and training
Morale studies
Psychological health of troops
Race relations
Enemy military assessments
Managing U.S. war production
Price controls and rationing
Foreign area and language training
Bombing strategy
Propaganda

Cold War
Nuclear strategy
Political development and modernization theory
Psychological warfare
Human performance
Manpower retention and training
      Human factor engineering
      Foreign security environments
      Policy planning strategies
      Effect of civilian morale on military capabilities
      Social effects of fallout
      Strategies for undermining Communist rule
      The psychology of bombing strategies
      Propaganda
      Counterinsurgency
      The operational code of the Bolsheviks
      Arms control and stability
      Limited war
      Coercive bargaining

Post–Cold War
Ethnic conflict and civil war
Nuclear proliferation

Post-9/11
Terrorism
Counterinsurgency
Foreign imposed regime change

This book seeks to trace and explain this influence in national security policymaking, much as political scientist Robert Gilpin did for the role of natural scientists in U.S. nuclear weapons policy.[41] The late Stanford political scientist Gabriel Almond pointed out that many of his colleagues ignored the history of the discipline, save for occasionally dismissing it as a prescientific dark age. In his view, this was part of an intentional strategy to shape the future of the discipline by ignoring its past.[42] If the policy-relevant past was a period of methodological and intellectual stagnation, then moving forward, political science ought to eschew policy relevance in the interest of scientific progress. I want to reintroduce this history to challenge the facile view that policy-relevant security studies is an artifact of the discipline's prescientific era and also highlight the downsides for relevance of previous efforts to modernize and professionalize the discipline.

Another model for this book is historian Peter Novick's history of history. In it, he tells the story of his discipline through the waxing and waning of the notion of "objectivity"; I aim to shed light on the development of political science through changing notions of "relevance."[43] Both "objectivity" and "relevance" define the core of these disciplines but also connect them with issues outside of the guild. Changes in them shape both the discipline and its relationship with the rest of society. And they remain deeply contested, which is why both the "objectivity" and "relevance" questions remain open today.

My third question, then, is when and under what conditions do social scientists do work that matters for policymakers? An answer to it matters for two reasons: as we saw already, there is some debate about whether and if it has really affected U.S. national security policy. This debate about the extent of the influence of academic social scientists calls for further historical investigation to ascertain, in the words of a National Research Council study, whether there is any "relationship . . . between basic [social science] research and programmatically useful results."[44] I share Elizabeth Crawford's hunch that "a more widespread knowledge of the 'history' of the relationship of government and social science may also make the discussants realize that whatever happens to be the particular controversy of the moment, it is not likely to be unique."[45]

In the literature on the role of the ideas of "policy experts," there is now a trend toward moving beyond general characterizations (they matter or they don't) to establishing more nuanced propositions about when and under what conditions experts influence policies.[46] An answer to this

question requires me to provide a more general explanation—a theory—
for the variation in their willingness to do so. I will show that academic
social scientists did have some influence on national security policy but
that the so-called Golden Age of strategy (1945 to 1961, according to
economist Thomas Schelling) exerted an influence that was both earlier
and shorter than we have generally recognized. The waxing and waning
of policy relevance among the social sciences has two components to it:
the relationship between academic disciplines and the policy realm and
the dynamics within those disciplines themselves. A complete account
of this relationship would also have to consider developments in government (the increasing internalization of social science research) and
public opinion (the decline in confidence in academic expertise).[47] I focus
here primarily on developments within social science as the heart of the
relevance question.[48]

Concern about how the professionalization of social science disciplines
has led to a disengagement from practical affairs is long standing, manifesting itself in books from Robert Lynd's 1939 *Knowledge for What?* to Ian
Shapiro's 2005 *Flight From Reality in the Human Sciences*.[49] My explanation
for social science's enduring relevance question is that social science, at least
as it has developed in the United States since the early twentieth century,
contains two contradictory impulses: to be a rigorous science and a more
broadly relevant social enterprise.[50] Initially, there was optimism among
social scientists about the compatibility of these two goals.[51] But there are
also tensions between them.[52] Historically the most useful policy-relevant
social science work in the area of national security affairs has often been
interdisciplinary in nature, and this cuts against increasingly rigid disciplinary boundaries in the academy. There are also widely recognized tensions between "basic" and "applied" research more generally, which not
surprisingly manifest themselves in the social sciences as well.[53] In essence,
the professionalization of the social sciences sparked a process of goal dis-
placement in which steps taken to make them more rigorous so as to enable
them better contribute to policy had the unintended result of eventually
making them less relevant.[54]

This pattern has been evident in the changing relationship between political science, its subfield international security, and the policy world over
the past century.[55] I begin with this observation but add to it exploration
of the specific mechanisms that lead to this retreat from relevance and a
detailed historical account of the field of security studies that illustrates it
in action.

War Builds the Bridges between the
Ivory Tower and the Beltway . . .

During wartime, the tensions between these two impulses have been generally muted; in peacetime, they intensify and there are powerful institutional incentives within academe to resolve them in favor of rigor rather than relevance.[56] The international security environment—among the most intense of external stimuli—can restrain internal disciplinary tendencies to retreat from relevance during periods of war or heightened threat and foster cooperation between academia and government.[57] My explanation for this recurring pattern follows from the substantial literature on the effect of war on the state and domestic politics.[58] War solidifies relations between the government and other elements in society.[59] As Gene Lyons explained, "War is a moment of crisis which compresses time and illuminates needs that less dramatic environments obscure or never force to the surface. War also involves the entire society and gives the central government new powers, for the exercise of which it needs new sources of information and expertise."[60]

Two specific mechanisms lead to higher levels of wartime cooperation between government and academia. First, the need for expertise leads policymakers and the public to look to universities for natural and social science knowledge that could contribute to the war effort.[61] Second, a common sense of threat fosters a general rally-around-the-flag effect and stimulates increased patriotic sentiment, which affects even professors.[62] This sentiment helps tilt the balance of opinion within the disciplines in favor of a broader definition of rigor that does not exclude relevance and increases scholars' willingness to balance the tensions between rigor and relevance.[63] In other words, war fosters, paraphrasing philosopher of science Thomas Kuhn, a "revolutionary" approach to science.

And Peace Weakens Them as Disciplinary
Dynamics Come to the Fore

Left to their own devices, however, academic disciplines tend to resolve these tensions between rigor and relevance by favoring the former.[64] While a variety of different factors play some role in the peacetime decline in policy relevance among social scientists,[65] I focus on the process of what Kuhn famously termed "normal science" and the impact of institutional dynamics—both vested interests and institutional self-image. Normal science and

organizational interest explain why the social sciences tend to isolate themselves from the rest of society and the culture of "science" accounts for the
particular way in which they do so.[66] The tragedy of the professionalization
of social science is that it is both the engine of scientific progress but also
contains the seeds of its own irrelevance.

The first logic for the decreasing relevance of social science flows from
the dynamics of the scholarly enterprise itself. The French sociologist Emile
Durkheim famously argued that the division of labor is a fundamental fact of
modern life because it is an efficient way to accomplish a variety of complex
tasks.[67] Given the limits of individual human cognition, it is only through an
intellectual division of labor that science can progress.[68] This growing specialization advances normal science through deeper investigations focused
on increasingly narrow questions.[69] Kuhn explained that "normal research,
which is cumulative, owes its success to the ability of scientists regularly to
select problems that can be solved with conceptual and instrumental techniques close to those already in existence."[70]

Such progress, however, comes at the cost of the increasing isolation
of the various specialties from each other and from society as a whole. As
Friedrich Nietzsche colorfully put it, "A specialist in science gets to resem-
ble nothing so much as a factory workman who spends his whole life in
turning one particular screw or handle on a certain instrument or machine,
at which occupation he acquires the most consummate skill."[71] The result
is a hyper-fragmentation of knowledge that now makes it difficult for even
scholars in different disciplines to understand each other, much less policymakers and the general public.[72] The result of this narrowing of focus is that
many academics no longer deal with issues of interest to broader society.[73]

Max Weber famously lamented that the ethos of modern rationalism was
ushering in the "iron cage" of modern bureaucracy.[74] I fear that in a similar
fashion the process of normal science has fostered an intellectual withdrawal
from policy relevance among the social sciences. Sociologist Andrew Abbott
explained that "specialists in knowledge tend to withdraw into pure work
because the complexity of the thing known eventually tends to get in the
way of the knowledge system itself. So the object of knowledge is gradually
disregarded."[75] In other words, the advancement of modern science ironically makes it less directly applicable to concrete problems as it becomes
more specialized.[76]

Second, one of the hallmarks of professionalism is "corporateness,"
which Samuel Huntington defined as "a sense of organic unity and consciousness of themselves as a group apart from laymen."[77] Explaining the

paradox that the public holds greater esteem for their personal physicians while the medical establishment favors leading medical researchers, Abbott attributed this process to a desire to maintain professional "purity," which can only be done through a withdrawal "from precisely those problems for which the public gives them status."[78] Traditional theories of organizational behavior would also attribute the decreasing relevance of academic social science to the fact that universities, like most other complex organizations, seek autonomy, reduction of uncertainty, and more resources.[79] When these goals conflict, organizations almost always prefer the first.

One means by which disciplinary organizational interest encourages scholars to separate themselves from nonspecialists is by using jargon and other modes of discourse that are incomprehensible to the laity.[80] Economist John Kenneth Galbraith recounted that economists regard this as "the filter by which scholars are separated from charlatans and wind-bags."[81] Such a screen is even more attractive to social science disciplines such as political science, which deal with issues that are not otherwise inherently difficult for educated laypersons to engage. To maintain their autonomy and protect their monopoly on expertise they need to construct higher barriers to entry. Sophisticated social science methods (models, statistics, or abstruse jargon) offer an ideal barrier to entry for the nonprofessional because they take considerable investment in time and effort to learn. Speaking within the guild makes it possible to maximize autonomy by making the university more distinct from, and hence independent of, the rest of society.[82] In short, one does not have to be as cynical as George Bernard Shaw, who famously quipped that "all professions are conspiracies against the laity," to believe that the increasing withdrawal from relevance within the social sciences is in part fostered by disciplinary vested interest.[83]

A reinforcing set of organizational incentives are "sunk costs" and the resulting "law of the instrument" mind-set, which lead many scholars who invest the time and intellectual capital in learning particularly sophisticated research techniques to amortize their investment by either choosing only questions amenable to them or forcing questions which are not into their template.[84] Such an approach may occasionally address policy issues, but only in the way a broken clock tells the correct time twice a day. This trend may also be reinforced by another bureaucratic rationale: failure while pursuing normal science is punished far less often in the academy than failure operating outside the reigning paradigm. Finally, eschewing policy engagement is also a way for social scientists to avoid political controversy that might bring unwanted government and public scrutiny.[85]

A somewhat different, but complementary, organizational interest explanation for the retreat from relevance in academic social science involves how disciplines define rigor and the incentives the individual members of a discipline have to adopt similar approaches to each other. Harold Wilensky explained that "in modern societies, where science enjoys extraordinary prestige, occupations which shine with its light are in a good position to achieve professional authority."[86] One of the hallmarks of science is its ability to measure causes and effects precisely, ideally in mathematical terms.[87] In order to comport with the canons of modern science, scholars increasingly believe they should pursue only those research questions with variables that they can quantify.[88]

To square this circle, many have embraced the distinction between "basic" and "applied" research. Basic research, according to the National Research Council's Study Group on Opportunities in Basic Research in the Behavioral and Social Sciences for the U.S. Military, "is defined as systematic study directed toward fuller knowledge or understanding of the fundamental aspects of phenomena" while "applied research is defined as systematic study to gain knowledge or understanding necessary to determine the means by which a recognized and specific need may be met."[89] The former pursues knowledge for its own sake while the latter seeks solutions to specific problems.[90]

Today, among American universities, an "ideology of basic research" now defines their mission.[91] As the late Donald Stokes put it, "In academic research circles . . . the ideal of pure inquiry still burns brightly."[92] Such an approach is necessarily driven by its own internal agendas and criteria so as not to contaminate the process of science with normative or practical considerations.[93] Lord Acton had outlined that mind-set many years earlier: "I think our studies ought to be all but purposeless. They want to be pursued with chastity, like mathematics."[94] More recently, Abraham Flexner, the founding director of Princeton's Institute for Advanced Study, reportedly preemptively declined an invitation to his colleague Albert Einstein from President Franklin Roosevelt on the grounds that "Professor Einstein has come to Princeton for the purpose of carrying on his scientific work in seclusion, and it is absolutely impossible to make any exception which would inevitably bring him into public notice."[95] It should therefore not be surprising that as the social sciences increasingly emphasized their "scientific" character, they became more disengaged from practical affairs.[96] Many scholars seek to salve their relevance consciences by assuming that basic research's results will nonetheless trickle down (or bubble-up) to policymakers.

John Gunnell confirmed in his history of the American Political Science Association, that despite its desire to have its cake (be relevant) and eat it too (be highly rigorous), as the discipline professionalized it became less committed to practical reform.[97] During the 1950s and 1960s the "technification" or "scientification" of political science increased under the banner of the Behavioral Revolution. Since then, "method" has become the defining feature of its claim to being a "science."[98] The result is that political science is increasingly dominated by the belief that the systematic study of politics can only be conducted with a set of "prescribed techniques."[99]

There are good reasons for believing that the effort to make political science more "scientific" would tend to make it less policy-relevant. "Technification" often leads political scientists to use research methods for their own sake, rather than based on their appropriateness for the research questions at hand; privilege technique over in-depth knowledge of the issue; and in general, steer the research enterprise away from doing work of broader interest.[100] Pursuit of rigor defined narrowly as technique means that less and less of political science is relevant to practical problems.[101]

Increasingly, if one wants to be a "good" political scientist, one emulates the approaches and practices of the leading scholars, institutions, and disciplines. Homogenization is thus a rational response to competition with other organizations for status and legitimacy.[102] One key mechanism through which disciplines become homogenous is through faculty hiring in which universities compete for the same group of leading scholars.[103] Another mechanism is the process of academic peer review, which can foster "the homogenization of opinion."[104] The initiation of peer review in the *American Political Science Review* (*APSR*) in the early 1960s clearly had this result.[105] Former editor Lee Sigelman explained that this process made "it more likely that a given paper will be selected for publication because it passes muster among a narrow range of specialists rather than because it is considered to be of potentially great interest and importance to a broad range of readers. Thus, the end product may be a wider array of narrower articles—greater diversity at the price of even greater fragmentation."[106] Also, most of the professional incentives academics face today lead them to write for each other and pursue disciplinary agendas, rather than write more accessibly and address issues of broader import.[107] In this way, even a small group of scholars committed to a narrow definition of rigor can have a disproportionate influence on the development of the discipline.[108]

Figure 1.3 shows that the policy relevance of articles published in the *APSR* (measured in terms of whether they offered "policy prescription")

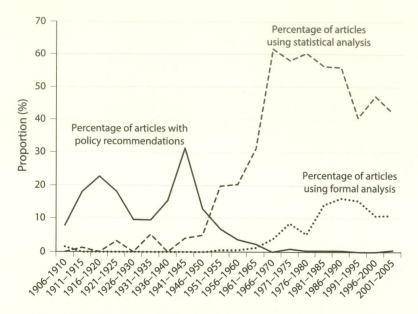

FIGURE 1.3. Percentage of policy-relevant articles in *APSR* from 1906 to 2006. (The data for this graph were compiled by the late Lee Sigelman. Chris Deering of George Washington University kindly shared it with me, and Luis Schenon used it to produce this graph. The data are also available at http://www3.nd.edu/~carnrank/.)

has declined precipitously.[109] As Sigelman put it, "By the early 1960s, prescription had almost entirely vanished from the *Review*. If 'speaking truth to power' and contributing directly to public dialogue about the merits and demerits of various courses of action were still numbered among the functions of the profession, one would not have known it from leafing through its leading journal."[110]

While one might question Sigelman's codings of the policy relevance of articles in the journal, there are three reasons to still regard them as reflective of real trends: as the editor of the discipline's flagship journal he was intimately familiar with the trends within its pages. Since he did not code them to support my argument, we can be confident that his judgment was not biased in favor of finding the pattern I predict. Finally, they track well with assessments of trends in other scholarly journals. Figure 1.1, as we saw, shows the results of a similar analysis of leading international relations journals (including the *APSR*) from 1980 through 2011, which demonstrates the same decline as in the Sigelman data.

The final question, then, is how to strike a better balance between rigor and relevance. Despite doubts about when and how academic social science influences national security policy, much time and money has been devoted to trying to connect these two realms, both inside and outside the Beltway. It would thus seem worthwhile to figure out how to ensure that these resources are well spent.[111] There are also good reasons for thinking that more policy-relevant social science would contribute to better policy. Finally, there is abundant evidence that the relationship between practical problems and basic science is reciprocal. Rather than the findings of the former trickling down to the latter, a growing number of historians of science have shown that the solution of practical problems at least as often contributes to theoretical advances.[112]

Finding such a balance between rigor and relevance, I argue, also flows in part from the moral obligations of scholars not only to "science," but also to "politics," in an effort to combine and reconcile Max Weber's discussion of these two distinct vocations. I am also inspired in this effort by C. P. Snow's incisive limning of the "two cultures" of science and literature and his related concern that a new cultural divide between academic social science and policy was emerging, with similarly deleterious consequences for both.[113] Policy engagement ought to be viewed not so much as an avocation for social scientists but as a core component of the scholarly enterprise.

Tracing and explaining the changing influence of social science on policymakers is too large an undertaking for one book.[114] Therefore, I propose to focus primarily on the changing nature of one social science discipline—political science—and its policy-relevant subfield, security studies, as a window into this larger question. The stories of the development of political science as a separate social science discipline and the subfield of security studies have been told elsewhere; in this book I focus on telling the story of their changing relationship, emphasizing its closeness in wartime and its estrangement in peace.

Many political scientists today believe the discipline of economics has answered the relevance question once and for all, managing simultaneously to be both the most rigorous of the social sciences and also the most influential in terms of broader policy.[115] According to this view, if security studies would only more vigorously embrace cutting-edge methodologies, it would be better integrated into the discipline of political science.[116] It is precisely the effort of some political scientists to push an exclusively method-driven, rather than a problem-oriented, approach to security studies that lies at the root of the discipline's relevance question today. Security studies embraced cutting-edge social science methods such as operations research, systems analysis, econometrics, and game theory early on, significantly contributed to their development, but soon discovered their limitations, well before the rest of the discipline.[117] Moreover, two of the most prominent economists in security studies—Thomas Schelling and Walt Rostow—highlight both the promise and the peril of pursuing a science of strategy, suggesting that remaking political science and security studies in economics' image is no shortcut to settling the relevance question.

Let me be clear, this book is by no means an argument against the use of models and sophisticated research methods in security studies. Indeed, one of its arguments is that theory is one of the most important contributions that scholars can make to policy analysis.[118] Likewise, and all other things being equal, if substantively important national security policy questions can be answered using statistical or formal methods, these approaches certainly ought to be employed. What it does argue against, however, is the conflation of "rigor" with the exclusive use of such techniques and its privileging over relevance. The cost of such a mind-set is to ignore many important policy issues because we cannot engage them "scientifically." It also challenges the notion that disciplinary professionalization will put to rest social science's relevance question.

Finally, political science and security studies are excellent cases for a variety of reasons. First, while national security studies has been an inter- and multidisciplinary enterprise for much of this period, political science has been its most consistent home.[119] Although the place of security studies in political science over the years has been uncertain, it has been even more "tenuous" and "precarious" in other disciplines such as history, sociology, or economics. These cases offer variation over this period of time in terms of both the causes (threat environment and professionalization) and also the consequences (the engagement or disengagement of scholars with national security affairs).[120] They also cover much of the period in which political science was developing into a separate and distinct social science discipline and security studies was becoming an important part of its subfield of international relations.

The following seven chapters trace this pattern of wartime social science relevance and peace-time irrelevance across American history in the twentieth century from the First World War through the Global War on Terror. In each, I explore how cutting edge social science was applied initially with great optimism as a tool to answer social science's relevance question from the First World War to the present for issues such as nuclear deterrence, political development and nation building, and coercive bargaining, only to find in each case, that the effort to craft a science of strategy led to intellectual dead ends and policy debacles as disciplinary dynamics increasingly privileged narrowly defined scientific rigor over broader policy relevance, particularly in peacetime. Chapter 9 summarizes the argument, anticipates the most likely objections to it, and offers some concrete suggestions for how to reestablish the balance between rigor and relevance in the years to come.

2

How War Opened the Door to the Ivory Tower during the First World War and Peace Closed It Again

America's twentieth-century wars mobilized large segments of the academic world as part of the war effort.[1] As Harvard professor and regular government consultant Philip Mosely observed, "The national effort at foreign policy research has been most strongly stimulated, or prodded into being, in two periods, those of the two world wars."[2] Reflecting that, historians have characterized the First World War as the "chemists' war" in recognition of that discipline's contributions to certain military technologies. They have called the Second World War the "physicists' war," not only in acknowledgement of that discipline's most significant contribution—the atom bomb—but also for other less-heralded, but equally important, technologies such as radar. According to lore, it was only during the Cold War that the many contributions of social scientists to national security policymaking were finally recognized with the application of the sobriquet "the social scientists' war."[3] While there is more than an element of truth in this conventional wisdom, it obscures the fact that the social sciences have made important contributions to all of America's wars during this period.

Still, the course of scholarly involvement in policy-relevant national security affairs has also waxed and waned over the years. It regularly began with initial optimism that the basic and applied elements of social science research could be reconciled, as the tensions between these two objectives were largely submerged during the war or the period of heightened international security competition. Once the threat receded, however, tensions between scientific rigor and practical relevance reemerged and the inclination within the Ivory Tower was to favor the interests of the former at the expense of the latter.[4]

This chapter begins with an examination of the emergence of distinct social science disciplines, including political science, within American universities, emphasizing in particular how they increasingly modeled themselves on the approaches and methods of the natural sciences as they professionalized. I highlight how the professionalization of the social sciences tended to disconnect them with practical policy engagement for four reasons: First, the "scientization" of the social sciences privileged "how" you know something (method) over "what" you know (substance). Second, the process of normal science in the social sciences produced a division of labor with the result that social science questions became narrower and more abstruse. Third, the demand for "objectivity" in social science research led to a widespread conviction that practical engagement invariably injected "values," and thereby bias, into scholarly work. Finally, social scientists drew a distinction between "basic" (or "pure") and "applied" research and maintained that science dealt only with the former. This exclusive focus on basic research did not worry many social scientists as they were confident that somehow their results would still find their way to practical applications. This was rarely the case, however, and so the pursuit of knowledge for knowledge's sake would increasingly disconnect academic social science from the practical concerns of policymakers.

Next, it explains how war or a prolonged and sustained period of international threat can overcome these disciplinary dynamics that work against relevance, at least for a while. It does so by sweeping up scholars in the more general "rally around the flag" mentality that pervades wartime politics. This leads to a weakening of disciplinary boundaries and a heightened awareness of scholarly obligations not only to their profession but also to the rest of society. Further, government and the public increasingly demand the academy's contribution to the war effort. Finally, scholars discover advantages to such participation, including greater resources and also reciprocal intellectual benefits to their scholarship from direct engagement in applied research in support of the war effort.

I then illustrate these dynamics by looking at the relationship between the social sciences and national security policymaking in two periods, one of total war and one of relative peace: the First World War and the interwar era. The outcomes and processes in each accord with the dynamics of my theory, which anticipates greater scholarly relevance in wartime but lesser in peacetime.

TABLE 2.1. The Pattern of the Waxing and Waning of Security Studies from the First World War through the Interwar Era

Period	Threat environment	Status of security studies
World War I	↑	Inaugural Inquiry
Interwar	↓	New science of politics leaves it behind

The Professionalization of the Social Sciences Raises the Relevance Question

Today, as historian Peter Novick noted, "no aspect of academic life is as taken for granted as the division of inquiry into separate disciplines—institutionally embodied as learned societies at the national or international level, as departments on individual campuses."[5] But American social science as we know it is a recent development, emerging only in the late nineteenth century.[6] The disciplines of economics, political science, and even history and philosophy for that matter, were largely components of the same amorphous field until the early 1900s.[7] It was only then that America saw the rise of the "research university" as a distinct component of the academic world. Its models were the German university system and the natural sciences.[8] From the former, it inherited an emphasis on research, as opposed to teaching or practical application, as its core mission.[9] It also developed the inclination toward ever-increasing specialization into distinct disciplines such as sociology, economics, psychology, anthropology, and political science from the Teutonic model.[10] The social science disciplines we recognize today in American universities are thus a relatively recent development.[11]

The paradox of disciplinary specialization was that it was justified initially to make the social sciences more relevant.[12] It was political controversy resulting from concrete political engagement that reinforced professional disciplinary inclinations to leave "reform" to the dilettantes.[13] Thus the practical effect of disciplinary professionalization has ironically been to make scholars less likely to address questions of broader interest to the rest of society.[14] These professional developments cut against two countercurrents in American postsecondary education. First, the notion that the federal government needed to support "useful" scholarship was already well-established after the Civil War with the Morrill acts (1862 and 1890) and the Hatch Act (1887), which together established the so-called land-grant universities and tasked them with helping to achieve various practical goals in the states in which they were established, particularly in the areas of agricultural science and engineering. Second, the Progressive Era, epitomized by Governor Robert La Follette's "Wisconsin Idea" of state government–university cooperation, reinforced the land-grant era ethos that the role of universities should be to produce useful knowledge in the social and economic realms.[15] From the beginning, the pressure for universities to conduct "relevant" research largely came from outside the Ivory Tower.[16]

These dynamics were clearly evident in the development of the new discipline of political science. Constitutional scholar John Burgess established the first distinct program in that discipline at Columbia in 1880. Reflecting his legal background, it was truly interdisciplinary, combining law, history, philosophy, and government.[17] Political science as a separate discipline began to emerge in the late nineteenth century and came of age only in 1904 with the founding of the American Political Science Association (APSA).[18] Its first four presidents—Frank Goodnow, James Bryce, A. Lawrence Lowell, and Woodrow Wilson—all remained committed to fostering a relevant political science.[19] Reflecting a dual commitment to scholarly rigor and practical relevance, its subfield of public administration received a boost from America's newfound colonial mission and would become the intellectual center of gravity of the discipline in its formative years.[20] Indeed, the majority of early APSA members were not academics, though that would eventually change dramatically.[21]

In the early days there was widespread optimism among American social scientists that scientific rigor and practical relevance would go hand-in-hand.[22] This view was reinforced by America's liberal tradition, which engendered optimism about the capacity of human reason to ameliorate the human condition.[23] One of the most important figures in the early development of the discipline was the University of Chicago's Charles Merriam, who epitomized the ambivalence among political scientists as to whether what they did was "social science as activism or technique."[24] Merriam would ultimately choose the latter, becoming not only the father of the "New Science of Politics" movement in the 1920s but also the grandfather of the behavioralist movement in political science after the Second World War, the second major effort to refashion the discipline as a real "science."[25]

From the natural sciences, the social sciences adopted the increasingly rigid distinction between "basic" and "applied" research, which was becoming more deeply entrenched at about the same time.[26] Chicago sociologist William Fielding Ogburn typified this emerging professional view, arguing that a scholar had "to give up social action and dedicate [himself] to science."[27] Science increasingly was equated with pure research, knowledge for its own sake. Social science's relevance question flows largely from the distinction between basic and applied research.

Science was increasingly defined by the methods used. Sociologist Alexander Leighton gave voice to the widespread sentiment that "the one substantial thing which social science has to offer is the element that is common to all sciences—the scientific method."[28] Central to it was precise mathematical measurement of variables and formal specification of the relationship among them.[29] Sociologist Leslie White captured the ethos well: "We may thus gauge the 'scientific-ness' of a study by observing the extent to which it employs mathematics—the more mathematics the more scientific the study. Physics is the most mature of the sciences, and it is also the most mathematical. Sociology is the least mature of the sciences and uses very little mathematics. To make sociology scientific, therefore, we should make it mathematical."[30] Manifesting an extreme version of this attitude, Ogburn insisted that the University of Chicago's new Social Science Building on campus bear Lord Kelvin's famous dictum: "When you cannot measure . . . your knowledge is . . . meagre . . . and . . . unsatisfactory."[31] If the natural scientists were the model for the newly emerging social sciences, economics quickly came to be seen as the most successful adopter of that model.[32]

However, not all social scientists agreed that the dismal science represented the best approach to studying social life. Lynd was typical of those who were not bedazzled by it. He objected not to the attempt to use mathematics in social science per se, but rather to its use simply to imitate the natural sciences.[33] The problem, in political scientist Charles Beard's estimation, was that "research under scientific formulas in things mathematically measureable or logically describable leaves untouched a vast array of driving social forces."[34]

As the social sciences sought to professionalize on the model of the natural sciences, research in the various disciplines became narrower and focused on smaller and more arcane questions.[35] The problem, however, with this increasing division of scholarly labor was that it isolated scholarship from the social forces policymakers sought to understand and control. In his APSA Presidential Address in 1926, Beard lamented that the typical political scientist of his era increasingly lived "in mortal fright lest he should be wrong about something, [so] he shrinks from any interpretation—from the task of seeking any clue to what William James called the big, buzzing, booming confusion of this universe."[36] As a result of the normal scientific division of labor, many social scientists pursued only narrow disciplinary agendas with a constrained set of approved tools, which increasingly hindered solving the important social problems that were less amenable to them.[37]

A final element in the emergence of the modern social sciences was the requirement that their practitioners be "objective." Objectivity meant that the conduct of social science research had to be "value-free," concerning itself only with establishing and analyzing the facts about what "is" and eschewing any discussion of what "ought" to be.[38] Consensus among professional social scientists quickly crystalized around the proposition that objectivity precluded policy engagement.[39] Its core premise was the widespread belief in the incompatibility between "social advocacy and scientific neutrality."[40] Economist Wesley Mitchell succinctly laid out the rationale in his American Association for the Advancement of Science Presidential Address in January 1939: "The investigator who tries to persuade men that they should choose one course of action rather than another may be drawing sensible conclusions from his scientific findings, but he is certainly not doing scientific work when he does so. . . . For the man who has a cause at heart, however fine that cause may be, is likely to prove a biased observer and a sophisticated reasoner."[41] This mandate for value-free social science was part and parcel of the larger debate about whether the social sciences could be policy relevant without sacrificing their claim to be scientific, the nub of the relevance question.[42] In other words, there was a tension between rigor and relevance in the new social science disciplines almost from their beginnings.[43]

So from the beginning of the twentieth century, there has been a tension between the two objectives of the evolving research university system. Science and practical application were in tension generally, but the social sciences experienced it particularly acutely.[44] Part of this had to do with social science's more tenuous claim to being a "science" and part of it had to do with the more political, and hence contested, focus of much social science research. This tension between these twin objectives would lead to what political scientist David Ricci termed the "tragedy of political science": as the discipline sought to become more scientific, in part to better address society's ills, it became less practically relevant.[45] While the notion that science and reform were incompatible did not become deeply entrenched in political science until after the Second World War, that was clearly the trajectory of professional thinking in the discipline as it developed.[46] And political science was by no means unique in this respect among the social sciences.[47]

If the dynamics of professionalization would lead the social sciences to increasingly eschew policy relevance, forces outside of the profession could counter them, at least temporarily.[48] The most important of these was war. Why would war lead to greater involvement by academic social scientists in policy? To begin with, disciplinary boundaries seem much more fluid in wartime than they do in peacetime.[49] In the face of such a crisis, broader national "problems" understandably seem far more important than mere disciplinary considerations.[50] That is why "scientism"—the belief the social sciences should mimic the natural sciences—waxed after the First World War and then again after the Second.[51]

And during wartime, scholars, like other citizens, feel an ethical obligation to contribute to the war effort. As the members of the World War II–era APSA Committee on War-time Services rhetorically asked their colleagues, "If the college professor will not plunge into community life and join the discussion of the things that challenge the existence of the community, what right have we to expect others to do so?"[52] In wartime, value considerations therefore seemed more compatible with "objectivity" among social scientists, or at least became more important to them than scientific purity.[53] This was the case for other disciplines aside from political science.[54]

It was not just altruism that led social scientists to become more engaged during wartime; they also perceived practical benefits from doing so. One obvious benefit was that it enhanced their disciplines' standing in society.[55] And if the social sciences could not demonstrate their usefulness, contemporary scholars cautioned that its standing in society would suffer.[56] Therefore, the APSA committee members warned "that the customary individualism of the profession is a luxury that cannot be unimpaired in wartime; political scientists must not go through the war with a business-as-usual attitude toward research and critical writing. The crises upon the nation and awaiting the nation demand that the profession recognize priorities in its scholarly work."[57]

Another self-interested rationale for greater scholarly engagement with practical issues was that wartime brings into bolder relief the reciprocal relationship between practice and the development of theory. As Lynd suggested in the late 1930s, "However great a part 'pure curiosity' and 'the *disinterested* desire to know' may have played in the acquisition of scholarly knowledge and natural science, it has been the *interested* desire to know in order to do something about problems that has predominantly motivated social science, from the *Wealth of Nations* down to the present."[58] This realization was more widely shared among social scientists in wartime, even those committed to crafting a new science of politics.[59]

The First World War Galvanizes the Progressive
Ideal of Rigor *and* Relevance

The Great War was the first sustained effort to apply academic social science knowledge to national security policy in the United States.[60] It was a watershed in its effect on the rest of American life, comparable only to that of the Civil War.[61] Naturally, it dramatically affected academics and universities as well.[62] Indeed, they were among the war's greatest boosters and many professors were eager to serve the war effort. The war, for example, reinforced the inclination of social scientists to engage in policy-relevant research. The chair of San Francisco Federal Reserve Bank complained that the program for the 1916 American Economic Association (AEA) annual meeting contained nothing related to the war, but by 1917 AEA had the highest member participation rate in government of any professional association.[63]

One important source of this willingness was social scientists' wartime embrace of the Progressive Era "service ideal."[64] The primary intellectual approach to social science early in the war was Pragmatism, the view that the purpose of knowledge was action, and it undergirded the Progressive commitment to scientifically guided reform. Logical Positivism, one of the reigning philosophy of science canons, held that only knowledge derived from science was valid.[65] But Positivism would not come to the fore until after the war.[66] While participation in the war effort discomfited some Progressive scholars, most found a way to reconcile their ideals with the war effort.[67] Columbia philosopher John Dewey, a leading scholarly light in the movement, played an important role in persuading his fellow Progressives that the war could advance their larger cause.[68] In addition, Progressive publicists such as Walter Lippmann called from outside of the Ivory Tower for academic political scientists to sally forth and engage in the war effort.[69] The wartime Progressive agenda brought a "new class of university-trained intellectuals" to power, including President Wilson himself.[70] Even skeptics like Randolph S. Bourne grudgingly admitted the war's magnetic effect between intellectuals and government.[71] Self-interest was another potent rationale for the increasingly deep engagement of the academy in the war effort.[72] Contribution to the war effort increased social science's standing within American society more generally, which conferred many benefits on engaged scholars, including greater prestige and more resources.

Recognizing that it was becoming a total war, and that the United States could no longer remain aloof from it, the Wilson administration took steps to mobilize academia along with the rest of American society. As part of that process, the government encouraged the establishment of a variety of other institutions to foster connections with academe. One example was the National Research Council, an offshoot of the National Academy of Sciences, which was designed to mobilize science for wartime service.[73] Harvard chemist, and later president of Harvard, James B. Conant joined the Cleveland Project, a "low-tech preview" of the Manhattan Project, which conducted chemical warfare research on college campuses, including American University in Washington, DC.[74] Such arrangements were not particularly attractive to scientists because they had to accept military commissions and work in government facilities on government-directed projects.[75] This experience would shape thinking about how to mobilize the natural sciences for future wars, particularly the Cold War.

Along with the natural sciences, the social sciences and some parts of the humanities were also conscripted for the war effort. Archeologist William Buckler, serving during the war as a special assistant in the U.S. Embassy in London, conceived a novel program of academic cooperation with the government. He persuaded White House advisor, Colonel Edward House, to set up what came to be known as the Inquiry.[76] Established in the fall of 1917, it was comprised largely of academic social scientists who served as a brain trust for the Wilson administration as it planned for the postwar European settlement.[77] Columbia University historian James Shotwell recalled his time with it nostalgically, "for never before had universities been mobilized for such a service."[78]

While the Inquiry also included nonacademics such as journalist Walter Lippmann, it was overwhelmingly an academic undertaking. Indeed, it came to include a veritable who's who of American academic figures. Led by Sidney Menzes, House's brother-in-law, and the president of the City College of New York, it enlisted within its ranks such distinguished scholars as Shotwell, Yale geographer Isaiah Bowman, and Harvard historians Archibald Cary Coolidge and Samuel Eliot Morison, along with many other leading scholars from America's top universities and learned societies such as the Geographical Society.[79] The 150 scholars participating in the Inquiry ultimately produced almost 2,000 reports and drafted nearly 1,200 maps. Some of them even traveled to Paris after the Armistice to serve directly as advisors to the American delegation during the postwar negotiations. Table 2.2 provides an overview of the other projects the Inquiry undertook and the relative allocation of resources to each. The Inquiry's most important contribution was to provide the intellectual foundation for Wilson's postwar vision for the European settlement, his Fourteen Points.[80]

The influence of the Inquiry is hard to gauge inasmuch as most of its reports were of a factual or informational nature as opposed to offering specific policy advice.[81] Nor were all of the Inquiry's recommendations accepted and acted on by the American delegation. To the extent that the Inquiry did not live up to expectations, it was a function of two factors: First, given the exigencies of wartime mobilization, not all of the top intellectual talent on these topics was available to it. Second, the Progressive Era faith that scientific planning could solve the world's most intractable problems was bound to be shaken by the realities of world politics.[82] Still, it is fair to credit the Inquiry with shaping American policy toward postwar Europe. Shotwell confirmed that the work of some of these academics was actually used by the negotiators.[83] Moreover, it was precisely in those instances in which policymakers ignored the Inquiry's advice (i.e., its members' opposition to the settlement's harsh treatment of Germany) that it is evident that the wisdom of its experts would have produced a better outcome had they been heeded more fully.[84]

TABLE 2.2. The Work of the Inquiry

Project	Staff Size
Cartography	17
Russia and Eastern Europe	15
Diplomatic history	14
Latin America	12
Reference/archives	11
General research	10
International law	8
Austria-Hungary	6.5
Economics	6
Western Europe	5
Western Asia	5
Balkans	4.5
Africa	4
Far East	3
Executives	3
Pacific Islands	1
Italy	1

Source: Gelfand, *The Inquiry*, 46.

The Inquiry was undoubtedly the most prominent example of how social science, in particular, and American universities more generally, were mobilized for the war effort, but it was by no means the only such effort to marshal scholars. In February 1918, the Committee on Education and Special Training was established to link universities with the war effort in a more direct way. With roots in the Morrill Act, and formalizing the Plattsburgh system of informal military training, this program produced the Students Army Training Corps, the forerunner of the modern Reserve Officer Training Corps (ROTC). This experience with wartime education had reciprocal effects on universities such as sparking concern with "problems of the contemporary world" and fostering an interdisciplinary approach to dealing with them.[85]

Another important point of academic engagement with the war effort was through the Committee on Public Information (CPI), more commonly referred to as the Creel Committee, which similarly "brought about a veritable mobilization of the country's scholarly resources, and made schools, colleges, and various non-educational groups among the 'strong-points' in the inner lines" of the war effort.[86] Key players in this effort to mobilize domestic public support for the war effort and maintain morale included the dean of the Graduate School at the University of Minnesota Guy Stanton Ford, Samuel B. Harding of Indiana University, and James W. Searson of Kansas State. The CPI also worked very closely with the private National Board for Historical Service led by Inquiry member James Shotwell, which connected it with some 150 other scholars.[87]

Finally, two other areas of wartime social science mobilization, which would establish precedents for the future, were in psychology and economics. Psychologists helped develop aptitude tests for potential soldiers.[88] And economists devised some of the principal tools of modern economics, including statistical methods, which not only served the war effort though managing the national economy but also set the stage for important intellectual advances in the discipline in the postwar era.[89]

Woodrow Wilson's own background as a political scientist and former university president, combined with the abiding Progressive Era enthusiasm for the scientific administration of politics, gave the effort to marshal political science for the war effort a road map. Progressivism rejected the classical view that knowledge and practice were distinct and mutually incompatible realms. Instead, during the Progressive Era, scholars sought to link the two. The war fostered an optimistic intellectual climate in which science and practical application could be seamlessly interwoven.[90] Many social scientists came away from their war experiences confident that social science could continue to guide policy in peacetime.[91] Economist Wesley Mitchell, for example, regarded his wartime experience as a harbinger of a bright future in which "economists and other social scientists would soon assume their rightful roles in an intelligently planned society."[92] Even those who took a darker view of the wartime experience admitted that the Progressive quest for "scientific control" of politics was even more essential then in order to prevent a repeat of that calamity.[93] In other words, one intellectual legacy of the First World War was to buttress the belief that science and policy were mutually compatible.

The Interwar Retreat from Relevance

Despite this optimism, with the end of the war, the U.S. Senate's failure to ratify Wilson's League of Nations, and the country's more general retreat into isolationism, the role for academics, or anyone else for that matter, in foreign and defense policymaking, shrank dramatically.[94] As Richard Hofstadter colorfully put it, "the *rapprochement* between the intellectuals and the people dissolved even more quickly than it had been made. The public turned on the intellectuals as the prophets of false and needless reforms, as architects of the administrative state, as supporters of the war, even as ur-Bolsheviks; the intellectuals turned on America as a nation of boobs, Babbits, and fanatics."[95]

To be sure, the wartime experience of cooperation between Washington and the Ivory Tower was not totally discredited by the failure of Wilson's postwar vision of the League of Nations. Continuing the land-grant tradition, the U.S. Department of Agriculture became the largest government sponsor of social science research.[96] One of the most ambitious of these interwar efforts to keep social science at work on national issues was President Herbert Hoover's Research Committee on Social Trends, which brought together a number of academic social scientists to conduct a national survey of American social needs in anticipation of a major federal government initiative for social reform.[97] In peacetime, though, Hoover had to walk a fine line between his desire to continue government utilization of the nation's social science resources and the opposition of many in Congress to his further enhancing executive power. This opposition to the expansion of executive authority would ultimately stymie further efforts to utilize academic social science expertise in a significant way until the outbreak of the Second World War.[98]

What interwar support there was for relevant social science research was increasingly underwritten by nongovernmental organizations. This reflected the general pattern during this period of most universities refocusing primarily on basic research and limiting their acceptance of outside funding to private foundations.[99] Indeed, this dovetailed with the strategy preferred by leading scientists to ensure continuing postwar support free from government control. The optimal way to accomplish this, in their view, was private support of basic research in universities.[100] The philanthropic world, for example, became deeply engaged in the effort with foundations such as Rockefeller and Carnegie making major investments.[101] They stepped into the fiscal breach left by the retreat of the federal government.[102] As Gene Lyons explained, there was a pressing need to establish these bodies precisely because "social science in the universities . . . was apt to be fragmented, narrow, and parochial."[103]

These foundations tended to be more "problem" than "discipline" focused in their grant making, however.[104] And a result of their investments, new institutions linking academic social science and the policy world emerged, including the National Bureau of Economic Research, the Social Science Research Council (SSRC), and the Brookings Institution. Merriam, a key player in the establishment of the SSRC and an active New Dealer, epitomized the early optimism that viewed rigorous social science methods and policy relevance as compatible, confident that rigor and relevance were mutually reinforcing.

Some scholars blame the war itself for aggravating the tensions between the Progressive ideal and the reality of power politics, thereby dashing its optimism about the compatibility of science and reform.[105] But this view neglects the tensions between these objectives that had been evident in the Progressive project from the very beginning. Their source was not the war but rather the continuing professionalization of the social sciences. We can trace the beginnings of the "scientific" approach to politics—what would later be called behavioralism—to the 1920s. Challenging the Progressives, the Neopositivists of the 1920s believed that social science needed to measure its variables mathematically and explain their relations using universal models.[106] "By the 1930s," Hamilton Cravens reported, "quantification and statistical methods came to the social sciences and helped nourish a virtual religion of scientific positivism among many social scientists coming of age in the profession in the 1930s and 1940s."[107] Hand in hand with this professional evolution dawned the realization that science and practical politics were no longer compatible.[108] As early as the mid-1920s, even optimists like Mitchell were growing pessimistic that they could manage the tensions between rigor and relevance.[109]

Once the war ended, two particular factors emerged that reopened the supposedly settled relevance question. The first was a sense of insecurity about the "scientific" standing of the social sciences, which encouraged scholars to eschew any activity that seemed to compromise it. For many scholars, policy engagement smacked of engineering at best, or amateur tinkering at worst, and those committed to science increasingly avoided it. Second, in the polarized political climate of the immediate postwar years, scholars sought to steer clear of political controversy.[110] "Pure" science, rather than "applied" social engineering, appealed to many social scientists as the best way to sidestep unwanted controversy and the inevitable meddling by outside actors it would provoke. To be sure, a significant number of social scientists still believed they were addressing broader social problems through their research and teaching, but the model was now one in which their theoretical and conceptual results would trickle down to inform policymakers.[111] However, the reality was that the interwar era would see a decline in the use of social science research by policymakers.[112]

Despite the encouragement of private foundations and other institutions and the crisis of the Great Depression, tensions between a certain image of science and policy relevance festered, both among social scientists themselves and between them and government officials.[113] These trends were fully evident in the discipline of political science, which "came of age" as a science between 1920 and 1940. Its maturation involved recognizing the "conflicts" between the twin objectives of rigor and relevance. As a result, according to disciplinary historians Albert Somit and Joseph Tanenhaus, after World War I, "for the first time there emerged a school of thought [in political science] which argued that the discipline should abandon its extra-scientific activities and concentrate on building the systematic body of knowledge implicit in the term 'science.'"[114]

The watershed year for this shift in emphasis was 1920, and it was directly connected with the end of the First World War.[115] The harbinger of this postwar sea change was Merriam's call for "new science of politics" at the American Political Science Association annual meeting that year.[116] Three national conferences followed devoted to planning how to professionalize the discipline.[117] The first step was Merriam's appointment as head of the APSA Committee on the Organization of Political Research in 1923. In addition to APSA, the new Social Science Research Council, another of Merriam's projects, emerged as an important source of funding for social science research with a particular orientation toward supporting the more scientific approaches.[118]

Given Merriam's leadership of the new science of politics movement, it is ironic that he was not himself particularly methodologically sophisticated in his own work.[119] Merriam also remained committed to an engaged and activist agenda for the discipline. However, his disciplinary allies A. B. Hall and R. T. Crane would take a much less methodologically pluralist view. At their September 1923 conference on the Science of Politics at the University of Wisconsin Madison, they adopted a much harder line on the proposition that "science" meant the model of the natural sciences, particularly the use of mathematics. They were also far less interested in reform than Merriam, primarily on the grounds that direct involvement with it was incompatible with the scientific approach.[120] The link between a scientific approach to the study of politics and a particular focus on American politics also dates from this period. That subfield, with its growing interest in voting and other easily quantifiable social phenomena, represented low-hanging fruit for the discipline's new science of politics movement.[121]

To be sure, not all political scientists were willing to give up on policy. Beard's 1926 Presidential Address led to the establishment of an APSA Committee on Policy to consider the discipline's broader role in society.[122] Thomas Reed, the chair of the APSA Committee on Policy between 1927 and 1935, struggled to preserve a more relevant discipline with support from the Carnegie Corporation. Even Merriam, with his commitment to both rigor and relevance, would have second thoughts about the effort to fashion a science of politics.[123] Still, this increasingly desperate interwar rearguard relevance action failed.[124] Almost twenty years later, the APSA Committee on War-time Services deplored political science's "failure" to be broadly useful to the war effort.[125] Disciplinary historian Bernard Crick lamented that "the education of the American teacher of politics in the 'thirties became more and more a training in research techniques and less and less an education in history and philosophy. His gains in sociological techniques were all too often at the expense of cutting away the very foundations . . . of any genuine sociological knowledge."[126]

This failure would also manifest itself in the virtual absence of political scientists in government service. The APSA Committee on the Civil Service would report that "only since 1939 have political scientists, as such, had much chance to gain entrance into the permanent Federal civil service."[127] Tellingly, the committee thought that the discipline's problems were the result of insufficient training in mathematics and methods. But a careful reading of the committee's report makes clear that the real problem was not that the discipline had failed to emulate physics, but rather that academic political scientists were not researching and teaching about relevant problems. And those few who did demonstrated little practical knowledge about them.[128]

The interwar period brought into focus the peacetime limits of the compatibility between science and policy, and exposed the proclivity among scholars when push came to shove, to favor rigor ("science") over relevance ("reform"). Reflecting this shift, public administration, once a major subfield in political science—it constituted about a fifth of the discipline and was regarded as among its most prestigious subfields—began its precipitous decline, the result, in part, of the reemergence of tensions between rigor and relevance, and the discipline's collective decision to emphasize the former.[129]

Not even the Great Depression, the greatest economic crisis of the twentieth century, could reconcile the tensions inherent in the desire of social scientists to craft a rigorous science while also contributing to concrete reform policies. They would not reconnect the halls of power with the groves of academe, as some have maintained.[130] Illustrative of this was that Harvard's three-hundred-year anniversary celebration in 1936 treated direct engagement with contemporary problems with disdain. The Harvard overseers were reluctant to even invite its most famous alum, President Roosevelt, to participate. Historian Jeremi Suri explained that "influencing the White House was not on the agenda for this glamorous showcase of Harvard's accomplishments. Cambridge was a long way from Washington, DC, and the university sought to maximize the independence reinforced by distance. Harvard, like its counterparts in New Haven and Princeton, sheltered itself from the society around its gates."[131] Indeed, more than anything else the Great Depression demonstrated the failure of the trickle-down theory that basic social science research would produce relevant and useable applied knowledge without any additional effort to identify its applied implications.[132]

Ironically, Republican Herbert Hoover (who had extensive experience in wartime Europe) had done more than any other U.S. government official, both as secretary of commerce and later as president, to bring more social scientists, particularly economists, into government.[133] In fact, the Depression demonstrated the impotence of social science at one of the most critical points in American history.[134] Tellingly, an increasingly desperate Franklin Roosevelt would employ a military metaphor in his March 1933 speech to try to justify the steps he would have to take to deal with the crisis.[135]

Sociologist Robert Lynd's *Knowledge for What?* represented the late interwar era's most influential public jeremiad decrying the growing irrelevance of academic social "science." More systematic evidence that the tensions between rigor and relevance were resolved in favor of the former was educational psychologist Charles H. Judd's 1938 report for the National Resources Committee, "Research—A National Resource." In it, he noted that "members of governmental research agencies . . . point out that there is a certain sterility in much of the academic treatment of social problems in courses given in universities because of the lack of contact on the part of students and members of the faculty with the problems which research must solve. It is frequently stated by those who are responsible for the appointment of university graduates in the bureaus of the Government that these graduates are lacking in realistic understanding of the problems of social organization."

Judd's report highlighted the lack of commitment among colleges and universities to conducting relevant research. He concluded that was one reason why "governmental agencies do not utilize as fully as they might the intellectual resources of the nation." His explanation for this was that "scientific men are in the habit of writing for their colleagues rather than for the general public. Furthermore, the refinements of scientific reports often depend on the use of mathematical formulas and technical terminology which are not readily understood by the non-technical reader." This led him to end on a pessimistic note: "The needs of the Nation will not be met nor will the ordinary citizens be satisfied until far more readable information on the social sciences than is now published by the Government is made available. . . . The social scientists of the country ought to realize that any exclusiveness or aloofness on the part of social scientists is sure to operate to the disadvantage of social science itself."[136]

In sum, significant progress in institutionalizing the wartime cooperation between academic social science and government policymakers did not occur in the interwar period. Left to their own devices, the social science disciplines increasingly looked inward, pursuing rigor rather than relevance, and thereby reopening the relevance question.

THE (NEAR) STILLBIRTH OF SECURITY STUDIES DURING THE INTERWAR ERA

The academic study of national security affairs was affected by this general waning in interest in policy-relevant social science, admittedly also reinforced by liberalism's general skepticism about military affairs. As William T. R. Fox noted, "The men most influential in giving shape to college, university, and research organization work in the field of international relations between the two World Wars grew up under the influence" of the early twentieth century peace movement supported by philanthropists like Andrew Carnegie. In his view, political scientists of this era tended to extrapolate from American domestic politics, believing that only the global spread of democracy and world government could keep the peace. They also focused on aspects of politics for which large amounts of quantitative data were available. Thus, liberalism and "traditional definitions of political science" combined to retard the study of international relations as a separate discipline, slowing the development of academic national security affairs during this period.[137]

Still there was some interest in policy-relevant social science—particularly in the area of security studies—prior to the Second World War.[138] Reflecting that, professional programs in international affairs were established at Chicago (1928), Johns Hopkins (1930), and Tufts (1933) and geographer Nicholas Spykman established Yale's Institute of International Studies (IIS) at about the same time (1935). IIS would subsequently play an important role in fostering policy-relevant national security research during the Second World War. Its new journal *World Politics* for a time becoming the subfield's leading journal.[139] In addition, Princeton's Institute for Advanced Study under the leadership of historian Edward Meade Earle also supported some early work in the subfield.

As will become clear, however, these programs were exceptions to the general trends in the social sciences. They were interdisciplinary in orientation and focused as much on policy as scholarship. Moreover, their eventual fates prove the rule of about the tenuous standing of national security affairs in academe. As international relations scholar Hans Morgenthau noted, "With the end of the first World War there began what can properly be called the age of the scientific approach to international affairs." In his view, this "scientific era of international relations produced as its inevitable result the substitution of scientific standards for political evaluations and, ultimately, the destruction of the ability to make intelligent political decisions at all."[140] This is illustrated by the early career struggles of Bernard Brodie, one of America's most distinguished scholars of strategic studies.

BERNARD BRODIE'S BRIEF AND UNHAPPY PREWAR TENURE AT DARTMOUTH

Brodie completed his Ph.D. at the University of Chicago in 1940 under the supervision of Quincy Wright, one of the leading American scholars of international relations, who regarded him as one of his "star" students.[141] He spent the next year at Princeton at the Institute for Advanced Studies working under Earle, who was instrumental in Brodie's being hired by Dartmouth College as an instructor on a one-year contract beginning in 1941.[142] Brodie was paid a flat fee of $2,500, rather than "a pro rata salary" based on the number of courses he taught, though in addition to his year-long course on "Military Strategy," he seemed amenable to teaching whatever else the college needed.[143]

Brodie taught at Dartmouth from 1941 to 1943 and really seemed to be thriving there. He and his wife Fawn loved Hanover, New Hampshire. His regular correspondence with Dartmouth dean E. Gordon Bill was sprinkled with effusive and apparently sincere praise for the town along the lines of "there is no other spot on earth we would rather be in."[144] His research and writing was also flourishing. In addition to the publication of his first book *Sea Power in the Machine Age*, which received good notices in the *New York Times* and *Time* magazine,[145] he was invited by the War Department to give lectures in the Army Orientation course at various installations in the New England region and was quickly establishing himself as a leading public intellectual in the national security realm.[146]

Unfortunately, winter came early to Hanover in the summer of 1942 for the Brodies: in August, Brodie accepted a position with the navy that would keep him away from Dartmouth for a third of each year.[147] Initially, this was to be a civilian position but it soon transitioned into a commission as a lieutenant. His first assignment was to write a history of the Ordnance Bureau, but it eventually became something much more important, writing up confidential analyses of battles and campaigns for the Chief of Naval Operations and even something very "hush-hush."[148] But as a March 8, 1943, letter from Bill to Brodie informing him that his contract at Dartmouth would not be renewed made clear, Brodie's situation in Hanover was tenuous for other reasons as well.

First, his public visibility seemed to engender some resentment among his less distinguished colleagues (who felt he "was too big a man in [his] field"). Second, Brodie's scholarly productivity seemed to call into question his commitment to the liberal arts teaching enterprise. Finally, and apparently most important, the political science department did not regard the work he did as real political science, but rather something more appropriate for a "department of foreign relations or some such thing."[149] This sentiment was apparently more widespread among American college and university faculty as evidenced by a column Walter Lippmann wrote on October 30,

1943, making the case to include military affairs in the curricula of America's institutions of higher education.[150]

Brodie had seen the handwriting on the wall at Dartmouth for some time, understanding both that as an active research scholar he was swimming against the currents of local small college academic culture but also that there was a body of professional opinion in his discipline that regarded national security affairs as lying "outside the field of political science."[151] Brodie clung to his hope of coming back to Dartmouth after the war, at one point turning down an offer from his alma mater the University of Chicago, but eventually accepted a position at Yale's Institute for International Studies in early 1945.[152] Yale would turn out to be hardly more hospitable to his subfield after the end of the Second World War.

THE RISE OF YALE'S INSTITUTE FOR INTERNATIONAL STUDIES

The rise of Yale's Institute for International Studies (IIS) illustrates both the promise and the peril of policy-relevant national security scholarship in an academic setting before, during, and immediately after the Second World War. In the period between its establishment in 1935 and its collapse in the early 1950s and subsequent relocation to Princeton, IIS for the first time in American history assembled an impressive group of scholars of international affairs who produced some of the most influential research of its era.[153] It also demonstrates the pattern of the "new science of politics" optimism about the reconcilability of science and practical engagement running aground on the shoals of peacetime tensions between these two objectives.[154]

At Yale, a cluster of distinguished scholars, including Percy Corbett, Frederick S. Dunn, Jacob Viner, Grayson Kirk, Arnold Wolfers, Nicholas J. Spykman, Richard Bissell, William T. R. Fox, Klaus Knorr, Gabriel Almond, Harold Lasswell, and William Kaufmann, among others, coalesced around IIS now led by Arnold Wolfers. Among the influential books and monographs the institute produced were Spykman's *America's Strategy in World Politics*, Samuel Flagg Bemis's *Latin American Policy of the United States*, and Bernard Brodie's edited volume *The Absolute Weapon*.[155]

The rocky course of IIS's short career is comprehensively told in the archives of the Rockefeller Foundation, which was the institute's major benefactor during its more than fifteen-year existence. Yale's initial effort to secure Rockefeller Foundation support for a program in international law and international relations in 1931 did not pan out.[156] Law School dean Charles E. Clark seemed concerned that the program was tainted with an "isolationist" and "realist" hue, which would make it unattractive to Rockefeller.[157] While Rockefeller Foundation program officer Edmund Day reassured him that these would not be factors in the ultimate decision, Rockefeller ultimately declined to fund the Yale proposal.[158] Another factor that seemed to play a role in the foundation's lack of enthusiasm for the original Yale program was the perception that it, in the words of a later IIS document, "was generally non-scientific and was concerned more with the description of unique events than with revealing the common elements in classes of events."[159]

A subsequent Yale proposal sought to balance a more systematic social scientific approach with direct policy relevance and met with more success. In May 1934, Spykman, then the chairman of Yale's International Relations Program, proposed a program in international relations under the auspices of ISS to "conduct studies of national polices aiming at the preservation of peace."[160] In May 1935, Rockefeller approved a five-year, $100,000 grant for the IIS that supported Spykman and other Yale international relations faculty including Wolfers and Dunn. Despite an ambitious research agenda, the institute was not as productive as Spykman hoped. Part of the problem was Spykman's poor health, but part of it was attributable to other issues, not the least of which was an unrealistic set of objectives.[161] Despite falling short of its initial goals, Rockefeller program officers seemed satisfied with IIS's progress. In a handwritten note, program officer Sydnor Walker pointed out that "Yale seems to be our greatest hope for an integrated research program in international relations at an Amer. Univ."[162]

In May 1941, on the eve of America's entrance into the Second World War, Rockefeller approved an additional three-year grant of $51,500 for the institute.[163] By now, the work of its members was beginning to bear fruit. IIS's highest impact publication was Spykman's book *The United States and the Balance of Power*, which came out after Pearl Harbor in early 1942 to much critical acclaim.[164] The institute took stock of its role, and that of other university-based research centers, in doing policy relevant scholarship. Dunn, who replaced Spykman as director of the institute, wrote a ten-page memorandum on the topic in 1943 that made this case in some detail.[165] But by January 1944, he had become more pessimistic about the prospects, pointing out that within universities "the conditions sometimes found inhibit rather than encourage creative activity" in this area.[166] Rockefeller Foundation staff realized at about the same time that the problems were not only intellectual but also financial. Whereas the foundation had seen its support to IIS as seed-corn to start a program that the university would eventually fully fund, the university was unwilling or unable to assume full financial responsibility for it, particularly once the war ended.[167] We will return to this story of how IIS's rise and fall tracked with periods of war and peace and disciplinary trends in a subsequent chapter.

Conclusions

This chapter illustrates the results of the intersection of disciplinary and international security dynamics through exploring the relationship between social science and policymaking in war- and peacetime. The former suppresses disciplinary inclinations to favor internal disciplinary agendas that lead social scientists to eschew policy relevance. However, during peacetime, social science disciplinary dynamics led them to disengage with practical policy issues. This was the direct result of the effort to make the discipline more scientific, as the distinction between "basic" and "applied" research had become one of the most important ways of distinguishing whether a scholar was doing science or not.

Of course, many social scientists remained eager to find a way to square the circle between professionalization and practical relevance. To do so, they reassured themselves with the notion that the results of pure research will just trickle down and inform concrete policy decisions without their directly engaging with policy issues. The experiences of the First World War and the interwar suggest that such confidence is overdrawn. Social scientists cannot expect disciplinary business-as-usual to regularly produce more broadly useful results. Active engagement with policy—in terms of the topics chosen, the methods employed, and how the results are reported—is essential to effectively translate social science scholarship into practical results. Scholars cannot simply sit back and wait for their results to sprinkle down on policymakers like rain from the clouds.[168]

3

World War II

SOCIAL SCIENTISTS IN THE PHYSICISTS' WAR

As with so many other aspects of American society, the mobilization of the country's intellectual resources for the Second World War was even more extensive than it had been in the First. Bernard Brodie later reflected that during World War II a revolution occurred in terms of both innovative new military technologies (especially the atomic bomb) but also the new role of civilian experts in developing them and devising strategies for how to employ them.[1] At the behest of President Roosevelt, MIT engineer Vannevar Bush established the National Defense Research Committee (NDRC) in 1940 to harness American scientists to the war effort.[2] The NDRC later morphed into the Office of Scientific Research and Development (OSRD), "the most powerful and highly centralized organization for the sciences."[3] In David Engerman's words, "World War II was the watershed moment for the involvement of federal agencies in university-based research. Indeed, the impact of World War II on postwar academic life is hard to overestimate."[4] The extent of this cooperation is striking because "prior to World War II, the research and development activities of the Army and the Navy were at an extremely low level," according to the Second Hoover Commission.[5] For that reason, some regard it as the true golden age of government and university cooperation.[6]

The role of physical scientists in the war effort was substantial and has been widely acknowledged.[7] A small sample of their contributions included the development of radar, ballistic missiles, and atomic weapons.[8] Moreover, a key NDRC organizational innovation, which would become important in the postwar establishment of the National Science Foundation, was to contract research projects out to universities or other private research facilities instead of drafting scientists into government service as had been done in the last war.[9] Scientists regarded this shift as a great improvement over the First World War approach of putting scientists in uniform and directing their research through military discipline.[10]

Less well known or widely acknowledged was the role of social scientists and other scholars in the war effort. Office of Strategic Services (OSS) historian Barry Katz chronicled how the social sciences were called to the colors in a major way: "World War II has been called the physicists' war in deference to the unprecedented recruitment of the scientific community to government service and the historic pooling of intellectual effort that followed. . . . It was also, however, the economists' war—and the sociologists', the historians', the philosophers' war—even if, viewed from the perspective of the human sciences, it ended less with a bang than a whimper. The social sciences and the humanities were called to arms in an intellectual mobilization that pressed into government service a community of academic scholars that was no less extraordinary than that of their scientific counterparts."[11] Scholar-cum-naval officer Alexander Leighton confirmed that "during the war, there was extensive use of social science."[12]

Why are social science's contributions to the war effort not as well recognized as those of other scholars? Part of the explanation is that some of those who participated in it came away from the experience with mixed feelings about their contributions.[13] Others were even more negatively affected by their experiences. Anthropologist Geoffrey Bateson, for example, returned from overseas service with the OSS a broken and embittered man.[14] While it is not surprising that the experience of government service in wartime would not live up to some social scientists' lofty expectations, this does not mean that they made no significant contribution to the war effort. Indeed, the pattern we see in participants' autobiographical reflections about their service is that they often judge their lack of influence based on their failure to affect major change, ignoring their more modest but real impact on policy. Also, they downplay the fact that even when they were ignored on specific issues, they often turned out to be right about them.

TABLE 3.1. The Pattern of the Waxing of Security Studies during the Second World War

Period	Threat environment	Status of security studies
World War II	↑	Total mobilization of the Academy

According to a postwar Russell Sage Foundation study, "Much of the contribution of the social sciences to the prosecution of World War II consisted not of new research but of the application of already existing knowledge to practical problems."[15] Among the areas in which extant social science contributed to the war effort were (1) military job assignments; (2) morale studies (both domestically and internationally); (3) psychological health of soldiers; (4) race relations in the armed forces; (5) propaganda; (6) assessing the enemy; (7) U.S. war production; (8) effects of price controls and rationing; and (9) foreign area and culture training.[16] The National Resources Planning Board and the Civil Service Commission established a National Roster of Scientific and Specialized Personnel to identify qualified social scientists for government service in 1940.[17] And it had a significant impact: in 1938, about 7,830 of the 75,000 federal employees were social scientists; by 1943, I estimate that 313,346 of the more than 3 million federal employees came from that professional background.[18] While the ratio of social scientists in government hardly changes, their absolute numbers exploded. Given that, it is hardly an exaggeration to conclude that World War II "was a god-send for the social sciences."[19]

The reason that social scientists decamped from their interwar ivory towers and marched back toward practical engagement was that the growing danger of war overcame many of the disciplinary obstacles to it. In the interwar period social scientists became more interested in methodological techniques and statistics. This broader sense of threat helped a "purposivist" critique of academic social science to take hold in the late 1930s, which marked a shift in interest from basic to applied research among social scientists.[20] It did so, in part, by convincing scholars that relevance was as important as rigor.[21] Indeed, the looming Nazi threat was the context of Lynd's cri de coeur deploring interwar social science's growing irrelevance.[22] Peter Mandler noted that the "period [from 1939 through 1953] uncoincidentally spans the years of international crisis leading to the Second World War, the war itself and the renewed crises of the early Cold War. It represents one of the peak periods of social scientists' involvement in public policy and a peak period, too, in their engagement with the popular imagination."[23]

The war also inculcated among the social scientists and other scholars who served in it an ethos emphasizing the obligation of their intellectual disciplines to the larger community.[24] At its core was the notion that scholars held "dual citizenship in the civic republic and the republic of letters, they had acquired during the war an immediate sense not only of the social relevance of ideas but of the social responsibility of the intellectual."[25] Indeed, even before Pearl Harbor many prominent social scientists joined prointerventionist voluntary organizations such as the Council for Democracy's Committee for National Morale.[26] Civic-mindedness was reinforced by necessity for the social sciences, as Julian Woodward of the Office of War Information emphasized, because unlike the natural sciences, which would continue to enjoy significant funding for "basic research," government support for the social sciences depended on "their data [being] relevant to immediate or near-immediate operational problems."[27]

The Disciplines at War

The need to be relevant in wartime was widely felt among the social sciences. For example, psychology was put to work in the service of the U.S. Army to assist in such areas as the classification of new recruits for subsequent assignments, their training, ensuring their physical and mental health, and especially maintaining their morale once in uniform.[28] As testimony to the contribution that social science could make to this last effort, Fredrick Osborn, a brigadier general, author of two social science texts, member of the Social Science Research Council, and trustee of the Carnegie Corporation was assigned responsibility for the U.S. Army's various morale activities. His efforts to maintain troop morale leaned heavily on two forms of social science research—surveys and field experiments—to ensure that proposed policies had their intended effects.[29]

The academy also marched off to war through the contributions to the management of the war effort by faculty in business schools and related disciplines like economics, both within the U.S. armed forces and also in the more general mobilization of the American economy. Indeed, the United States' entrance in the Second World War coincided with the emergence of a new field of study called "statistical control." A large number of graduate students and young faculty entered this new field but the most influential among them in the national security realm was a junior faculty member at the Harvard Business School by the name of Robert S. McNamara. After the war, he would apply what was then called "operations research" (OR) and subsequently "systems analysis" to the Ford Motor Company and later the Pentagon.[30]

The first defense applications of OR were in air defense and antisubmarine warfare, but its most direct impact was felt in two facets of air war strategy.[31] First, the B-29 Special Bombardment project concluded that it would be more efficient for these heavy bombers to shed their cumbersome armor making them faster than Japanese interceptors.[32] Second, analysts working in the Enemy Objectives Unit (EOU) of the Economic Warfare Division of the American Embassy in London led by Chandler Morse and then Charles Kindleberger, included a veritable who's who of leading academic economists. Charles Hitch, Henry Rowen, Carl Kaysen, and Walt Rostow, who would later assume senior positions in the Kennedy administration, got their start in strategic analysis in Britain analyzing the effectiveness of the Allied bombing campaign against Nazi Germany. Their task, as Rostow described it, was "to develop and apply criteria for the selection of one target system versus another, one target within a system versus another, and if the target was large enough and bombing precise enough, one aiming point versus another."[33]

By late 1943 and early 1944, three distinct theories of airpower were competing to guide Allied bombing strategy. The British Royal Air Force advocated bombing the German civilian population to terrorize and turn them against the Nazi regime.[34] A related theory held that attacks on Germany's industrial base would undermine popular support for the regime. Conversely, EOU advocated precision bombing against critical target systems in the German military machine.[35] As Rostow later explained, "We sought target systems where the destruction of the minimum number of targets would have the greatest, most prompt, and most long-lasting direct military effect on the battlefield."[36] These competing theories directly defined targeting debates.[37]

In late 1943, the RAF and the U.S. Eighth Air Force squared off over area bombing versus more precise targeting of German aircraft production. In early 1944, the debate shifted to what were the best targets to cripple the German war economy. This discussion pitted the commander of U.S. Strategic Air Forces in Europe, Lieutenant General Carl Spaatz, who advocated striking the Nazi petroleum, oil, and lubricants (POL) industry, against marshal of the Royal Air Force Arthur William Tedder and his science advisor

Professor Solly Zuckerman, who maintained that attacks against railway marshaling yards would most decisively cripple the German war machine. After D Day in June 1944, Tedder and Zuckerman continued to advocate the marshaling yards strategy while the United States, led by EOU, argued for attacking bridges around the Allied lodgment in France combined with continuing POL strikes.[38] After the war, subsequent analysis concluded that oil had been the most lucrative target.[39] The EOU was also instrumental in calling into question the RAF theory that terror bombing would undermine German civilian morale.[40] This experience undoubtedly reinforced the former EOU-cum-New Frontiersmen's skeptical view of uniformed military expertise when they discovered that despite the ineffectiveness of counter-city attacks, military bureaucratic momentum nonetheless led the Allied Air Forces to intensify them.[41]

Yet another example of applied wartime social science was sociologists Edward Shils and Morris Janowitz's study for the Intelligence Section of the Psychological Warfare Division of Supreme Headquarters Allied Expeditionary Forces (SHAEF) of why German soldiers continued to fight so doggedly and effectively even after it was clear that Germany would lose the war. Their answer was that it was not, as widely thought, Nazi ideology, but rather the durability of the primary groups of the Wehrmacht, which provided strong psychological support for soldiers' continued resistance. Shils and Janowitz's theory of combat motives directly shaped Allied strategy and subsequently had lasting intellectual influence on both academic and military sociology.[42]

Shils and Janowitz were not the only leading sociologists to contribute intellectually through their wartime service. In addition to his voluntary work, Talcott Parson's served briefly in the Foreign Economic Administration's Enemy Branch where among other things he opposed Secretary of the Treasury Henry Morgenthau's plan to deindustrialize postwar Germany.[43] University of Chicago professor Samuel Stouffer's leadership of the Research Branch of the Information and Education Division of the Army Service Forces not only made a direct contribution during wartime but also had a longer-term impact on the postwar discipline of sociology. Stouffer's unit played an important role in systematically surveying soldiers' opinions. Among other things, Research Branch survey results assisted the military in designing a strategy to encourage soldiers to regularly take antimalarial medicine in the South Pacific, helped it to craft a post–VE Day point-based system to demobilize some combat troops without disrupting the morale of other soldiers heading to the Pacific Theater, and conducted the assessments that highlighted the critical role that unit cohesion had on individual combat performance.[44]

Research Branch's most enduring studies were connected to wartime racial integration in the U.S. Army. In the fall of 1944, its staff administered a series of opinion surveys to officers and soldiers to gauge the effects of the emergency integration of African-Americans on combat units in Europe during the Battle of the Bulge. Their results were striking: despite initial skepticism, white officers and noncommissioned officers very quickly concluded that African-American soldiers performed as well as other American soldiers and reported that their integration did not cause insuperable damage to the morale and good order of the units to which they were assigned. The results came to the attention of the War Department's Gillem Board, which was charged with formulating policy on the postwar utilization of African American soldiers. While one participant characterized the study as a "failure" because there was not an immediate change in policy, others see it as having been more successful over the longer term.[45] Given that the postwar U.S. armed forces would in many respects lead the country in racial integration, this latter more optimistic assessment seems justified.[46]

Despite being one of the first generation of social scientists to utilize quantitative research methods, Stouffer's approach in government was primarily problem, rather than method or theory, oriented.[47] Indeed, he was methodologically plural in his approach to army research. He was also thoroughly interdisciplinary in his perspective on the branch's work.[48] Even before the war, he had grown concerned about a gap between scholars and policymakers and vowed not to let it develop in his organization. As he recounted, "A vicious circle develops—I have seen it happen several times in Washington. The research men, frustrated because their stuff is not being sought or used, become more 'academic,' satisfying their desire for expression by doing what may be good work from a scientific standpoint, but useless from a standpoint of policy determination. This must not happen here."[49] The key, in Stouffer's view was to balance method and real-world applicability: "The techniques of research largely used in our studies of nearly half a million soldiers throughout the world, were not particularly sophisticated and were not techniques primarily developed by academicians."[50]

Many regard anthropologist Ruth Benedict's work on Japanese political culture as one of the most influential examples of applied social science. It supposedly shaped both wartime strategy and postwar political reconstruction.[51] Other members of the Foreign Morale and Analysis Division (FMAD) of the Office of War Information (OWI) regretted that they did not gain much traction among policymakers with their prescient conclusions that Japanese military and civilian morale was not unshakeable.[52] Parsing the impact of their work nicely illustrates the challenges of gauging social science's influence on policymaking in wartime.

The role of anthropology in the war effort is striking given that prior to the war leading anthropologists strongly opposed any such collaboration. After the First World War, Franz Boas, the founder of the school of "cultural anthropology," became embroiled in an ugly public controversy when he criticized some of his colleagues for aiding the American war effort under the guise of doing field research in Central America.[53] This led his students Benedict and Margaret Mead to agonize about government service early in the Second World War. Two related factors finally persuaded them to throw in their scholarly lots with the war effort: First, the U.S. government and the American public appreciated that anthropologists' unique linguistic and cultural expertise could advance the war effort by helping the U.S. policymakers to better understand their allies and adversaries.[54] Second, anthropologists themselves acutely felt the Nazi threat given that their discipline had professionalized, in part, in repudiation of race-based theories of culture not unlike those animating the Third Reich. Given that, "objectivity" concerns paled before Hitler's existential threat to the culturalist approach dominant in mid-twentieth-century anthropology.[55] As an indication of how dramatic this reversal was, estimates are that more than half of professional anthropologists served in government during the war.[56] The appendix to this chapter provides a list of some of the most prominent among them.

Despite Boas's chariness about government service, a handful of anthropologists had served even before the war in the New Deal–era Applied Anthropology Unit established in the Bureau of Indian Affairs (BIA).[57] This beachhead improbably opened the door for wartime service after the War Relocation Authority (WRA) placed its first internment camp for Japanese-Americans on BIA land. Appreciating the potential contribution anthropologists could make to ensuring stability in the camps, WRA brought them on staff.[58] This experience with Japanese-American culture, in turn, provided them with the opportunity to study Japanese culture as well. When the OWI—the organization set up to analyze and shape morale both at home and abroad—was established, it was natural that WRA anthropologists would be tapped to join the effort to monitor and try to influence Japanese military and civilian morale.[59] Benedict herself signed on to conduct "national character" studies on Japan.[60] As a unit of OWI, FMAD was initially established to study civilian morale. A separate section worked with the Sociological Division of Military Intelligence Service on the Joint Morale Survey (JMS) focused on Japanese military. Work by the JMS would eventually be distributed to the OSS, the Department of State, the Department of the Navy, the British liaison unit, and even the White House.[61]

It is important to understand the political context in which JMS operated. The conventional wisdom among the public and throughout much of the U.S. government was that Japanese soldiers and civilians were mindless fanatics who would fight to the death.[62] If that view was correct, there would not be much point in conducting propaganda operations against them as only a war of extermination could end the conflict. Personnel in FMAD questioned that assumption and designed propaganda campaigns to encourage Japanese soldiers to surrender and civilians to press to end the war. They found, for example that the morale and combat effectiveness of Japanese soldiers varied widely. Deriving lessons from the fighting on New Guinea, they successfully applied them to the campaign in the Philippines. Analysts of the FMAD also correctly concluded that under the right circumstances, Japanese POWs would cooperate and give useful intelligence to Allied forces. And in terms of the morale of the Japanese public, FMAD and JMS identified the central role of the emperor in public consciousness, arguing that employing the right propaganda strategy could leverage this public esteem to end the war without an invasion of the home islands by promising to preserve the monarchy.[63] After the war, the United States Strategic Bombing Survey, a systematic effort to assess the effects of the U.S. bombing campaign against the Axis, largely validated JMS's findings about Japanese morale.[64]

Nor did anthropologists have to serve directly in government to have significant influence in wartime America. Some also did so as public intellectuals, among the most influential of whom was another of Boas's students: Margaret Mead.[65] Before Pearl Harbor, Mead and her colleagues founded a private organization—the Committee on National Morale—to help mobilize social scientists for the good fight. During the war, she served on the National Research Council's Committee on Food Habits, which sought to anticipate wartime nutrition issues that might arise.[66] She also conducted research on intra-allied relations for the Council on Intercultural Relations, a private group funded by OWI to coordinate studies of strategically important regions.[67] She further contributed to the war effort through her scholarship, particularly by developing the approach of studying "culture at a distance."[68] Analysts from the OSS reportedly found it quite useful given their limited access to enemy territory.[69] Finally, Mead was instrumental in facilitating U.S. government's promotion of area studies through a series of meetings organized under the auspices of the Office of the U.S. Provost Marshal, the War Department organization charged with postwar occupation responsibilities.[70] Anthropology thus had a modest, but nonetheless real, impact on various aspects of U.S. wartime policy.[71]

Of all of the disciplines, political science's wartime experience was most mixed. On the one hand, as Somit and Tanenhaus explained, "remaining doubts [about policy engagement] were resolved by the events of December 7, 1941. Not long thereafter, the Committee on War-time Changes in Political Science Curriculum frankly accepted the profession's obligation to assist in the war effort."[72] Illustrative of this shift in mind-set, was Merriam, who was prompted to reengage with policy by the deteriorating world situation and to do so with far less preoccupation with using only "specific techniques of investigation."[73] During the war, a few political scientists such as John Herz joined the Frankfurt School at war in the OSS's Central European Section.[74] Other political scientists with area expertise contributed in a variety of ways from providing intelligence analysis to training military officers for postwar civil affairs assignments in occupied countries.[75] Harvard's Carl Friedrich not only taught American soldiers destined for occupation duty but also served himself as political advisor to the deputy governor of the U.S. Military Zone, General Lucius Clay. In that capacity, he played an important role in planning for the establishment of the constitutional system of the Federal Republic of Germany.[76] Indeed, there were so many political scientists serving in Washington during the Second World War that from 1942 through 1945 the American Political Science Association held its annual meeting there.[77]

On the other hand, relatively fewer political scientists than historians, economists, sociologists, or anthropologists directly participated in the war effort.[78] This was in part the result of negative attitudes about the discipline among policymakers. Few were convinced that political science was "a necessary, or even a highly desired, background of knowledge for any of their research positions."[79] Leaders of the discipline were of two minds about why this was the case. Given the relatively greater success of economics, many inclined to the view that political science needed to follow the dismal science's professional trajectory and become more theoretical and quantitative. This view dovetailed nicely with the new science of politics agenda of the interwar era. However, the APSA Committee on War-time Services also heard from policymakers that a big part of the discipline's problem was that political scientists lacked substantive knowledge and practical experience, things that had little to do with the discipline's level of methodological development. And the two parts of the discipline that seemed most useful to wartime policymakers—public opinion and international relations/comparative politics—taught very different lessons about the direction the field needed to go. The former was more fully compatible with the new science of politics approach than was the latter. And in any case, there was broad agreement that "something more than the customary political science curriculum is needed if ready ingress to the federal service is to be provided for undergraduate and graduate students."[80] Just what that approach needed to be was not clear, ensuring that the interwar debate about the professionalization of political science would reignite after the war.

The Challenge of Assessing Wartime Policy Influence

Discerning OWI/FMAD/JMS's influence on policymakers illustrates the difficulty of tracing the influence of social scientists more generally.[81] The major challenge FMAD faced was getting its heterodox policy recommendations to policymakers. Many of them were unaware of what social scientists were doing in this area (and many other areas) of the war effort. Others knew but were still skeptical of the utility of social science. Finally, a few policymakers genuinely interested in using social science research findings did so mostly because they liked the particular conclusions it reached.[82] Closely examining the role of social science in the propaganda war against Japan illustrates both its potential and limits.

The primary U.S. policymaker for Japan in the later part of the war was Under Secretary of State Joseph Grew. Capping a long career in the U.S. Foreign Service, he served for a decade as ambassador to Japan. Upon his release in 1942 from internment, Grew was appointed a special assistant to the secretary of state and sent on a tour of the United States on behalf of OWI to explain the war against Japan to the public. He was subsequently named director of the Office of Far Eastern Affairs at the State Department on May 1, 1944, and then became under secretary of state on December

20, 1944, acting as Secretary of State Edward Stettinius's alter ego through September 1945.[83]

Grew clearly shared OWI/FMAD/JMS's more nuanced view of Japanese morale vulnerabilities.[84] He no doubt came to this perspective based in part on his own extensive experience in Japan. But it is also clear that OWI/FMAD/JMS reinforced his views and played an important role in shaping U.S. strategy against Japan, largely for the better. Planning for postwar Japan began in December 1943.[85] One of the most contentious issues was what to do with the emperor. It was first discussed in February 1944.[86] As Grew and OWI knew, U.S. public opinion was running strongly against allowing the emperor to remain on the Chrysanthemum Throne after the war.[87] There were also widespread doubts about, and even outright opposition to, doing so within government, including from presidents Roosevelt and Truman.[88]

Facing broad anti-Japanese public sentiment and entrenched government opposition, Grew and some of his State Department colleagues, along with OWI/FMAD/JMS, fought military efforts to target the emperor with propaganda and even airstrikes.[89] Going on the bureaucratic offensive, the Inter-Divisional Area Committee on the Far East at the Department of State recommended keeping the emperor in place in a March 1944 position paper, which it further elaborated on in May.[90] Grew himself went on a one-man campaign, discussing the emperor issue with the commander-in-chief, U.S. Pacific Fleet and Pacific Ocean Areas, Chester W. Nimitz "and his psychological warfare officers" and reported that they "were in complete agreement that for the present we had better let the Emperor alone, as he might be found to be an important, if not essential asset, both in bringing Japan to unconditional surrender and in avoiding chaos and guerrilla warfare after our eventual occupation of Tokyo."[91]

On the eve of Potsdam Conference, Grew met with President Truman to convey to him his opinion that "the greatest obstacle to unconditional surrender by the Japanese is their belief that this would entail the destruction or permanent removal of the Emperor and the institution of the Throne." He went on to propose that "if some indication can now be given the Japanese that they themselves, when once thoroughly defeated and rendered impotent to wage war in the future, will be permitted to determine their own political future, they will be afforded a method of saving face without which surrender will be highly unlikely."[92] Grew later reflected that had retention of the emperor been included in the Potsdam Declaration, the Japanese would likely have surrendered before the two atomic bombs were dropped on Hiroshima and Nagasaki.[93]

At that moment, Truman was unwilling to commit to leaving Hirohito in place, though he did instruct Grew to meet with Secretary of War Henry Stimson, Secretary of the Navy James Forrestal, Army Chief of Staff General George Marshall, and Elmer Davis, the director of OWI to brief them on this policy. While all were sympathetic to Grew's argument, they decided to hold off on making a decision about the emperor in view of the ongoing fighting on Okinawa.[94] What broke the ice-jam freezing a decision about the emperor for Secretary of War Stimson was a report written by OSS Colonel Deforest Van Slyck, "Observations on Post Hostilities Policy Toward Japan." In what Stimson called a "remarkably good paper," Van Slyck made the case for retaining the emperor.[95] Prior to his service in the OSS, Van Slyck had been an Army Air Force intelligence officer and before the war a Yale history professor.[96] In both wartime billets, Van Slyck would have been privy to OWI/FMAD/JMS products.[97]

But there are even more direct links between OWI/FMAD/JMS and Under Secretary Grew. While the former ambassador had a wealth of first-hand experience with Japan, he nonetheless reported consulting "many students of Japan" as he made policy decisions. Moreover, it is clear that he, like other senior decision makers dealing with Japan, was dependent on the POW interrogation reports and the public opinion polls of Japanese civilians for assessments of their morale. Again, these materials most likely originated from OWI/FMAD/JMS. Finally, and perhaps most persuasively, Grew cited by name OWI/FMAD/JMS codirector Alexander Leighton's book recounting his wartime service in connection with these arguments about retaining the emperor.[98]

British historian and OWI deputy director for the Far East George Taylor would later boast to an interviewer that OWI/FMAD/JMS's study of the role of the emperor in Japanese society helped him convince Roosevelt and Truman to leave Emperor Hirohito in place after the war.[99] This claim seems overdrawn. However, Leighton's more nuanced assessment is persuasive: "It seems probable that the Division served to substantiate some of the OWI and War Department policies together with their underlying assumptions, and acted as a brake on others. Toward the end of the war it was very likely instrumental in a number of policy changes." Concrete examples of this influence include shaping psychological warfare strategy against the Japanese military; imposing the policy of "truthfulness" in propaganda broadcasts directed toward the Japanese home front; opposing any effort to engage in wholesale postwar overhaul of Japanese culture and institutions, particularly deposing the emperor; and tailoring of propaganda directed toward the

Japanese home front based on the realization that morale was crumbling already by late 1944.

Like Grew, Leighton lamented that OWI/FMAD/JMS had failed to defuse the A-bomb decision on grounds that it was unnecessary in light of crumbling Japanese morale. But it was unrealistic of him to expect that an organization headed by a middle-ranking navy officer would have such influence on high-level decision making. And despite regretting this failure, Leighton did not come away from his wartime experience thinking that there was no role for social science in government. Indeed, he drew the exact opposite conclusion: "That social science has potentialities for development and use in human welfare that are comparable with what has been realized in other fields where the scientific method has been employed for several hundred years."

This evidence raises the question of how and why anthropology had the influence it did. One reason is that the discipline balanced internal concerns like methodology with the need to engage substantively important policy problems. Despite his hyperpositivist rhetoric, Leighton's wartime experience, like Stauffer's, led him to a much more catholic view of methods: "Controlled observations were impossible and statistical methods could be used only to a limited degree. In consequence, the [Foreign Moral Analysis] Division employed its basic assumptions as a paleontologist uses his concepts in reconstructing an extinct animal from a few teeth and a piece of bone."[100] Or as Mead herself put it, "We can carry out innumerable carefully controlled experiments with university students and still know nothing about the kind of thing studying peoples in different living cultures can teach us. But most people prefer to carry out the kinds of experiments that allow the scientist to feel he is in full control of the situation rather than surrendering himself to the situation, as one must in studying human beings as they actually live."[101] Finally, in addition to their methodological pluralism, anthropologists bucked the trend in social science of focusing on smaller and smaller questions. As Carlton Mabee pointed out, "Mead prided herself on being willing to tackle big problems, in big units, using broad, swift, interdisciplinary, cultural and cross-cultural methods even though it went against the long-term trend in behavioral science toward specialization and quantification."[102] In other words, the Second World War wartime climate suppressed disciplinary tendencies that otherwise would have undermined anthropology's contributions to wartime policy.

Historians versus Economists in the OSS Methods War

Even before the war, in December 1941, President Roosevelt had established the Office of the Coordinator of Information under Colonel William J. Donovan to, in the words of Harvard diplomatic historian and OSS veteran William L. Langer, "draw on the universities for experts with long foreign experience and specialized knowledge of the history, languages, and general conditions of various countries."[103] After Pearl Harbor, the Coordinator of War Information (CWI) was established to focus on purely intelligence matters.

The key vehicle for this was the CWI's Research and Analysis Branch (R&A), which subsequently would become the analytical heart of the OSS. Langer recalled that "when General William J. Donovan in August 1941 organized what later became the Office of Strategic Services, his chief aim was to bring into government service scholars who, in addition to their specialized knowledge of foreign countries, were trained in particular disciplines and thoroughly grounded in the methods of assembling, selecting, evaluating, and presenting evidence."[104] By the end of the war, the Research and Analysis Branch of the OSS—"something like a huge social science research institute"—would employ nearly seven hundred people in Washington and around the world, most of whom were scholars drawn from social science fields like political science, economics, geography, history, psychology, and even archeology. Indeed, in recognition of its contributions to the war effort, R&A was only half in jest designated the "Chairborne Division."[105] In addition to the EOU's work in London, OSS economists in Washington, DC, undertook related studies of the logistics of German invasion of French North Africa, which contributed to Allied planning for Operation Torch; German ground operations in Southern Russia in 1943; and Japanese capability to invade Australia.[106] Langer emphasized the value of this effort to the U.S. government by pointing out that despite the postwar disbanding of the OSS, the Research and Analysis Branch survived intact, later becoming the analytical core of the Cold War Central Intelligence Agency.[107]

This wartime experience was so extensive that it set the stage for the postwar patterns of cooperation between academic social scientists and the U.S. government.[108] One president of a major American university that contributed disproportionately to the OSS—Charles Seymour of Yale—served in the Inquiry during the First World War, thereby constituting a direct link between the two efforts.[109] In fact many leading scholars were OSS veterans.[110]

Langer noted that "no other nation during the war was, or so far as I know, has since been able to bring such concentrated intellectual power to bear on wartime problems as did Donovan's R and A."[111] Given the eminence of the scholars who served in R&A, its impact on American social science would be felt long after the war.[112]

As an intelligence organization OSS was remarkable for its ideological diversity, including some famous Marxists among its analysts including Herbert Marcuse, Franz Neumann, and Otto Kirchheimer.[113] According to Raffaele Laudani, Marcuse, Neumann, and Kirchheimer, "proudly defended their participation as one of the few attempts to make the Frankfurt School's Critical Theory a practical tool in the fight against fascism."[114] Not surprisingly, they did not achieve all of their most ambitious goals such as persuading U.S. policymakers to de-Nazify postwar Germany through a working-class based "revolution through legal means" instead of the moderate "social democratic compromise" the Allies actually pursued. But such ambitious policy aspirations were unrealistic for mid-level intelligence analysts, and their failure should not obscure their less spectacular, but real, successes in the areas of occupation policy and postwar war-crimes trials.[115]

Intelligence historian Robin Winks highlighted the compatibility between academia and the OSS: "In any academic community there are scholars of whom it is said that they have twenty fresh ideas a day, ten of them quite mad, five naïve or stupid, three without point, and two exciting and potentially of great value. Most bureaucracies, seeking to homogenize their members, would not tolerate so low-level a return; any sound university will bear with eighteen expressions of madness, stupidity, and nonproductivity in exchange for two of great value."[116] R&A took a similar view. Another factor that made for a natural complementarity between the Ivory Tower and the intelligence community was the fact that the vast majority of the information necessary for the war effort—somewhere on the order of 90 to 95 percent—came from open sources, the natural purview of academicians.[117] Donovan was a believer in using academics for intelligence work because he had a "hunch" that most of the useful information the government would need would come from unclassified sources that scholars produced in the normal course of business.[118]

Not surprisingly, given the participation of academic social scientists in R&A research, scholarly debates about the epistemology and methodology of social science intruded into the process of wartime intelligence analysis. Like their civilian counterparts, some analysts maintained that only through establishing R&A's work as "professional" and "objective," would it be taken seriously among policymakers. Their epistemological standard was very much in line with the reigning positivism of the interwar era and the most vociferous, but by no means exclusive, advocates of this position were OSS economists.[119] An R&A *methodenstreit* (epistemological debate) erupted in the middle of the actual war, pitting the economists against the political and historical analysts in the European Branch.

What settled the debate were each side's respective analytical performances. The generally qualitative analysts in the European Branch proved quite prescient about German morale and the sources of civilian support for the Nazi regime; even if they were slow to recognize the Holocaust, they nonetheless provided useful information about civil affairs and postwar governing issues in Germany. Conversely, the economists in R&A, who had little use for the nonmathematical social science approaches of the historians and area specialists of the European branch, dropped the ball on major questions such as the level of the mobilization of the German economy. The root of this mistake was that they ignored their noneconomist colleagues who would have told them that the Nazis did not fully mobilize in 1941 because they expected to win the war quickly.[120]

In 1943 R&A underwent a major reorganization prompted by the need to temper the economists' "methodological imperialism."[121] The result of the subsequent reorganization was to elevate a cohort of economists who were less wedded to methods than empirical reality and more interested in public engagement. As Katz noted: "In the interdisciplinary crucible of the Research and Analysis Branch, the economists—*qua* economists—learned about history and about values."[122] And it was this broader perspective, rather than their use of sophisticated analytical techniques, which explains their subsequent policy influence.[123] Toward the end of the war, the USSR Division of R&A produced a report entitled "The Capabilities and Intentions of the USSR in the Postwar Period," which shaped the debate about U.S.-Soviet policy well into the postwar era.[124]

The Wartime Acme of Area Studies

The wartime R&A experience demonstrated two further things: First, that area studies were of most "value in strategic planning and military operations."[125] Social Science Research Council (SSRC) president Pendleton Herring later testified that "the war probably had a good part in enlisting the interest of such individuals. In many cases young men who went off to strange lands as soldiers returned to them as scholars, not to libraries but to villages, slums, or ministries and offices, trying to get at a better understanding of what was happening."[126] Even before the end of the war, representatives of the Carnegie Corporation approached Langer to explore postwar cooperation between R&A and universities.[127] The R&A Branch of OSS was hardly the only element of the U.S. government that embraced the area studies approach.[128] Area studies and language training were also integral to the Army Specialized Training (AST) and Army Civil Affairs Training (ACAT) programs, which were established early in the war and housed on 227 colleges and universities. Army Specialized Training was intended for enlisted personnel while the ACAT was designed exclusively for officers. The flagship for these programs was the School of Military Government at the University of Virginia.[129] Over the longer term, however, neither this nor the R&A experience fundamentally changed academia, particularly in peacetime.

Second, interdisciplinary work was essential to producing useful intelligence information.[130] Policymakers were indifferent to disciplinary concerns; all they cared about was whether they could get useful policy advice.[131] These lessons reflected the practical purposes to which the research was to be put.[132] Langer hoped that this R&A wartime experience would constitute a "challenge to the cloistered scholasticism of academic thought."[133] In the short term, it seems to have had this effect.[134] As we will see, however, both these lessons learned would meet with resistance among academic social scientists after the war, highlighting the resurgent postwar tensions between scholars and policymakers.

Conclusions

As the Second World War demonstrated, sophisticated social science methods are certainly sometimes applicable to policy. In particular, economists demonstrated that they could employ these tools yet remain directly relevant in some realms. However, the failure of the OSS to employ them successfully on noneconomic issues constitutes a cautionary tale for those who think that discipline ought to serve as a model for the rest of the social sciences. Moreover, the natural sciences still defined "science" for many social scientists.[135] Many social scientists were content to focus on doing "pure" research, confident that policy-relevant results would flow from it with no additional effort on their part. These cases show that such confidence was unjustified.[136] Professional disciplinary incentives, unchecked by extradisciplinary forces, encourage preoccupation with general models and cutting-edge methods, which pursued for their own sakes can disconnect scholarship from practical affairs. To be sure, this was not always the case, but exceptions were more "accidental" than anything else.[137] While war resolved the relevance question for a time; peace would reopen it again.

Strikingly, even social scientists themselves who served in government came to realize that disciplinary dynamics worked against policy relevance. Looking back on his time in government, Stouffer reflected that

> the more I have seen of the problems of putting research into action the more sympathy I have had with the policy makers who sometimes are resistant to research. The research man has a tendency to fall between two stools. Either (a) he will not translate his results into an idiom which the policy maker understands and state briefly and lucidly the implications for policy, or (b) he will recommend a policy which must be based not along on variable x dealt with in his research, but also on variables y and z which he does not know any more about than the policy maker. This is only in part the policy maker's fault in demanding recommendations which go far beyond the data. It is also the researcher's fault, for it is all too easy for the researcher either to retreat from the field or to become so entranced with his special data that he overlooks other factors which the policy maker must take into account.[138]

The problem, as sociologist, psychiatrist, and wartime naval officer Alexander Leighton explained, is that

> from the very beginning of science there has been a tendency for scientific activities to revert to scholasticism and dogma, like cleared land becoming overgrown. . . . Statistical and mathematical procedures . . . carry with them some of the aura and prestige of the physical sciences. They, too, impress laymen and give those who employ these techniques a sense of dealing with "hard facts." Without wishing to detract from their great intrinsic value, it is evident that they can be exceedingly treacherous because of the false sense of accomplishment that comes from unerringly following out the approved procedures, and from the ease with which interpretation can be made to appear factually demonstrated by figures.[139]

Stouffer's and Leighton's experiences provide evidence of the enduring tension between scholarly rigor and applied research during World War II.

These cases also demonstrate that other approaches to social science are as, if not more, useful than those preferred by academic social scientists. For example, area studies—the study of what is unique about particular areas of the world based on deep knowledge of their language and culture—proved to be invaluable to policymakers during the war. Unfortunately, this approach cut against the professional grain of many of the social sciences and so its tenuous wartime standing would not long survive the peace. Another lesson these cases teach is that scholars needed to understand the policymaker's needs as they think about how they conduct their scholarship. It is abundantly clear that scholars just doing their thing is no guarantee that they will produce useful knowledge beyond the academy. Finally, social scientists need to balance methods and theory with the policy "context of applied work."[140] Leighton drew the logical conclusion for scholars who want to influence policymaking: "The *problem* is the center of concern and all methods are brought to bear that may be fruitful."[141]

Moreover, these cases also highlight the unrealistic expectations that scholars sometime have about how their work can influence policy. As we saw, some social scientists hoped that their work would spur major decisions such as the promotion of social revolution in postwar Germany, the immediate racial integration of armed forces, or the prevention of the use of the atomic bomb. Not only was their expectation of being able to shape policy at that level unrealistic, but such ambitions may have prompted wartime social scientists to overlook the more modest, but real, contribution they actually made to the war effort.[142]

Finally, the social sciences' wartime experience had a positive impact on them. What spurred their postwar progress was the interdisciplinary nature of the tasks it addressed, its problem orientation, and the enormous amounts of data that government service made available to social scientists.[143] To list just a few examples of such reciprocal benefits, recall that the first draft of Ruth Benedict's pathbreaking *The Chrysanthemum and the Sword* was FMAD Report No. 25 "Japanese Behavior Patterns."[144] Shils and Janowitz's wartime study of the Wehrmacht almost single-handedly established the field of military sociology.[145] Stouffer's *American Soldier* became the model for much early Cold War social science research underwritten by the Pentagon.[146] Neumann's wartime service with the OSS led to a major postwar revision of his classic *Behemoth: The Structure and Practice of National Socialism*.[147] This list could include other disciplines.[148] This wartime experience had effects across the social sciences, but it was particularly evident in the areas relevant to national security. In other words, not only did the social sciences contribute to the war effort, but that experience, in turn, changed them, often for the better.

Appendix. Anthropologists in the Office of War Information and the Office of Strategic Services

Anthropologist	Institution
E. Wyllys Andrews IV	Harvard University (Ph.D.); Tulane University
William Bascom	Northwestern, Cambridge University, and the University of California–Berkeley
Gregory Bateson	University of Cambridge (M.A.); University of Cambridge, Columbia University, New School for Social Research, Harvard University, University of California–San Francisco, Stanford University, and University of California–Santa Cruz
Lloyd Cabot Briggs	Harvard University (Ph.D.); Peabody Museum, Franklin Pierce College, and University of Paris
Carleton Coon	Harvard University (Ph.D.); Harvard University and University of Pennsylvania
Cora DuBois	University of California–Berkeley (Ph.D.); University of California–Berkeley, Hunter College, Harvard University, and Cornell University
Anne Fuller	Harvard University (Ph.D.)
Nelson Glueck	University of Jena (Ph.D.); Hebrew Union College
Gordon Hewes	University of California–Berkeley (Ph.D.); University of North Dakota, University of Southern California, and University of Colorado–Boulder
Frederick Hulse	Harvard University (Ph.D.); University of Washington, Colgate University, and University of Arizona
Janse Olov (Robert Ture Olov)	Uppsala University (Ph.D.); National Archaeological Museum (France), Ecole du Louvre, Sorbonne, University of Paris, Harvard University, and UNESCO
Felix Maxwell Keesing	University of New Zealand (Litt.D.); London School of Economics, University of Hawaii, and Stanford University
Alexander Lesser	Columbia University (Ph.D.); Columbia University, Brooklyn College, Brandeis University, and Hofstra University
Edwin Loeb	Yale University (Ph.D.); University of California–Berkeley
Leonard Edward Mason	Yale University (Ph.D.); University of Hawaii–Manoa

Anthropologist	Institution
Mark Arthur May	Columbia University (Ph.D.); Syracuse University, Columbia University, and Yale University
Alfred Métraux	Sorbonne (Litt.D.); University of Tucuman, Bishop Museum of Honolulu, Yale University, Smithsonian Institution, and UNESCO
George Peter Murdock	Yale University (Ph.D.); Yale University, University of Pittsburgh
David Rodnick	University of Pennsylvania (Ph.D.); Air University, University of Oslo, Columbia University, Princeton University, Inter-American University, Iowa Wesleyan College, Texas Technological University, and University of Hamburg
Morris Siegel	Columbia University (Ph.D.); Columbia University, Boston University, Atlanta University, University of Puerto Rico, University of Illinois, and Oklahoma State University–Stillwater
Richard Francis Strong Starr	Princeton University (Ph.D.); Fogg Museum and Institute for Advanced Study
David Bond Stout	Columbia University (Ph.D.); Vanderbilt University, Syracuse University, University of Iowa, and State University of New York–Buffalo
Morris Swadesh	Yale University (Ph.D.); University of Wisconsin–Madison, City College of New York, Universidad Nacional Autonoma de Mexico, and University of Alberta
T. Cuyler Young	Princeton University (M.A.); University of Chicago, University of Toronto, and Princeton University
Clyde Kluckhohn	Harvard University (Ph.D.); University of New Mexico, Harvard University
Florence Kluckhohn	Harvard University (Ph.D.); Wellesley College, Harvard University
Alexander H. Leighton	Johns Hopkins University (M.D.); Cornell University, Harvard University, Dalhousie University
Dorothea Leighton	Johns Hopkins University (M.D.); Cornell University, University of North Carolina, University of California–San Francisco, and University of California–Berkeley

Continued on next page

Anthropologist	Institution
Geoffrey Edgar Solomon Gorer	University of Cambridge (B.A.), Sorbonne, and University of Berlin; Rockefeller Institute and Yale University
Ruth Benedict	Columbia University (Ph.D.); Barnard College, Bryn Mawr College, Columbia University
Morris Edward Opler	University of Chicago (Ph.D.); Reed College, Cornell University, and University of Oklahoma
John Embree	University of Chicago (Ph.D.); University of Hawaii, University of Chicago, and Yale University
Royal Brown Hassrick	Dartmouth College (B.A.), Harvard University, and University of Pennsylvania; South Plains Indian Museum (Oklahoma), Denver Art Museum, Regis College, and University of Denver
Katherine Spencer Halpern	University of Chicago (Ph.D.); American University

Source: Compiled from Price, "Gregory Bateson and the OSS," 379, and other sources in this chapter.

4

Social Science's Cold War

THE BEHAVIORAL REVOLUTION'S QUIXOTIC EFFORT TO CONSTRUCT A "POLICY SCIENCE"

As Dorothy Ross noted, the immediate post–World War II era was an important juncture for the social sciences. They experienced something of a "golden age," in which they reached "their highest point of self-confidence and of intellectual and popular authority in the United States and around the world."[1] Tracing and explaining the waxing and waning of their policy relevance is important not only for understanding the social sciences' professional development but also as a window into the larger intellectual and political milieu of these dark times in Cold War American history, which were brightened by the hope that wartime cooperation between the social sciences and policymakers could continue and even deepen as the former continued their efforts to catch up with the natural sciences.

This and the following chapter treat two parallel yet distinct postwar developments in the role of academic social science in national security policymaking. This chapter explores developments tied to the relevance question on the Ivory Tower side of the bridge connecting academe with the postwar national security policymaking community. The next looks at the situation on the other side of the bridge in Washington, DC.

Both sides of the bridge were profoundly affected by the experience of the Second World War. At the broadest level, each side came away from the experience concurring that social science, much like the natural sciences, had made an important and positive contribution to the war effort. There was broad agreement on the need to find a way to institutionalize that cooperation in anticipation of the prolonged period of neither war nor peace that was likely to emerge as the wartime alliance with the Soviet Union collapsed.[2] This broad consensus, however, glossed over some very different understandings of exactly how social science had done so during the war. The two sides learned very different lessons about how to institutionalize this cooperation in the emerging Cold War era.

Wartime experience should have taught scholars that social science proved most useful when it was interdisciplinary, focused on applied rather than basic research, and executed in teams within government organizations rather than undertaken by individual researchers outside of government.[3] But many came to share Harvard sociologist Talcott Parsons's view that the social sciences, further professionalized on the model of the natural sciences, should confine themselves to "basic" research. They salved any twinge in their relevance consciences with the expectation that these results would eventually trickle down to policymakers with little additional effort on their part.[4]

This academic view no doubt reflected the complex threat environment the United States faced in the immediate postwar period. To be sure, relations with the Soviet Union were fraught as a result of the imbalance of conventional forces in Europe and the growing Soviet nuclear arsenal. It is not surprising then that Russian area studies would prosper, at least initially, with U.S. government support. Unlike the periods of total war between 1917 and 1918 and 1941 through 1945, the Cold War threat waxed and waned, however, over time and across regions. Cold War historian John Lewis Gaddis recounted that President Roosevelt did not anticipate the intense rivalry with the Soviet Union that eventually developed. He was less concerned than others about the pernicious effects of Communist ideology and confident that a postwar balance of power scheme could mitigate its effects.

The sense that the Soviet Union might present a serious threat to the United States only began to change with the crises in Greece, Turkey, and Iran, which led to the proclamation of the Truman Doctrine in March 1947. The subsequent Soviet acquisition of atomic weapons and the "loss" of China to communism led to the promulgation of NSC-68 in 1950, marking the point at which the Cold War really got hot for most Americans, a sense of threat that the outbreak of the Korean War reinforced.[5] Indeed, some historians of the American university system mark the beginning of the "postwar era" on campus with the 1957 Sputnik launch, which decisively made the case for federal support of academic research on national security grounds.[6] Only a few years later, psychologist Charles Bray fretted that "interest in the military aspects is dying out as the sense of need and urgency created in World II and the Korean War lessens."[7] Moreover, some developments—particularly the spread of nuclear weapons—had mixed effects on the security environment. For some analysts, mutual assured destruction (MAD) had a stabilizing, rather than destabilizing effect, on great power relations.[8] And despite some early crises directly involving the two superpowers, much of the Cold War would be waged in the developing world where the stakes were far less clear and therefore highly contested. Area studies focusing on those regions would not prosper to the same extent as Soviet studies.

The effect of this shifting threat environment on the relationship between national security policymakers and academic social scientists was less consistent in dampening the tensions between rigor and relevance than it had been during the previous periods of total war.[9] The end of the Second World War also coincided with a new wave of interest in professionalizing the social sciences.[10] Among the earliest casualties of the resulting Behavioral Revolution was the area studies approach. This was felt first in other areas of the world but eventually came to affect even Soviet studies.[11] The "scientization" of social science and a gradual loosening of the tight wartime links between the Ivory Tower and the Beltway have not gone unnoticed. Some scholars indict Cold War government support of social science for its "scientistic" turn.[12] Others blame the war in Vietnam for weakening the bridges between academe and the national security policy community. I maintain that the heart of social science's postwar relevance question is found at the intersection of disciplinary professionalization and the complex international security environment of the early Cold War.

This chapter explores the causes and consequences of the evolving academic social science model for squaring the circle between continued professionalization of the discipline and fostering its ongoing contribution to policymaking. It begins with a discussion of the debate about the establishment of the postwar National Science Foundation (NSF)—the proposed U.S. government agency that would continue wartime support of science—and how the problematic place of the social sciences in that effort shaped social scientists' thinking about the future directions of their disciplines. Next, it considers the Behavioral Revolution in social science, which continued ongoing professional trends and reinforced the lessons of the NSF debate that if the social sciences wanted to be regarded as legitimate among the natural sciences, they needed to look more like them in their approaches and methods.

To be sure, many social scientists were not content to disconnect themselves completely from the policy world; their effort to have their rigor cake and eat it too with relevance was to try to develop what came to be called "policy science." But the policy science approach ultimately failed to answer the relevance question once and for all. Indeed, the Behavioral Revolution encouraged most social scientists to favor rigor over relevance when the tensions between the two inevitably reemerged. The consequence of that tilt was to undermine what from the perspective of national security policymakers was one of the most useful contributions of social science: area studies. As area studies was replaced by universal approaches to comparative politics and development and modernization theories, its usefulness to policymakers declined with deleterious consequences for U.S. national security policymaking. I conclude with an assessment of how the Behavioral Revolution affected the discipline of political science, demonstrating that its result was to disengage academia from the policy world and driving those political scientists who remained committed to it off campus.

The Postwar National Science Foundation Leaves Social Science Out in the Cold War

World War II marked a sea change that connected government support for science to national security in a major way for the first time.[13] Prior to that, save for a brief period during the First World War, the dominant German notion of the "research university" generally mandated a strict separation of science and policy, with scholars eschewing the latter in the interest of preserving their scientific integrity and objectivity.[14] The World War II experience with government support for science was in fact mixed: scientists appreciated the money and other resources it provided but continued to chafe at the restrictions on their intellectual freedom to choose what to work on, security restrictions which limited when and where they could publish their findings, and the "endless red tape" of dealing with the government, particularly when working for it directly.[15] The challenge for the scientific community was to find a way to continue to garner large-scale federal support while maximizing scientists' intellectual freedom and disciplinary autonomy.

Even before the end of the Second World War, the debate about post-war government support of science—largely shaped by President Franklin Delano Roosevelt's science adviser Vannevar Bush's July 1945 report "Science: The Endless Frontier"—began to break down along the "basic" versus "applied" fault line.[16] Articulating the optimistic view of the relationship between basic and applied research, Bush envisioned that basic research would produce useful practical results without the need for scientists to concern themselves with the latter. He established what would become the "dominant paradigm" for thinking about the relationship between the two. He sought, on the one hand, to preserve a pure vision of science, but on the other to ensure that it continued to receive generous federal support, which would only come if it was somehow useful to policymakers. Bush's vision was that government would support basic research by arguing its benefits would trickle down to the applied realm.[17]

This tension between "basic" and "applied" research played itself out in the debate about the establishment of the National Science Foundation (NSF), the peacetime successor to the wartime Office of Scientific Research and Development (OSRD).[18] On one side, West Virginia senator Harley M. Kilgore advocated an NSF that would support research addressed directly to national needs, the results of which would be made widely available to the public, which benefitted a range of universities beyond the elite few, and that received input from a broad spectrum of interest groups outside of academia. Kilgore's ideal reflected the late president Roosevelt's vision and was widely shared among congressional supporters of the NSF.[19] Even more conservative members sympathized with this view based more on the argument that basic research funding was a "public good" that only the federal government could provide.[20]

Bush, in contrast, led the intellectual charge for an NSF that maximized scientific freedom with continued federal support for research.[21] His vision was an NSF thoroughly infused with the ideology of basic research.[22] He proposed a structure for it that protected scientific freedom of inquiry, gave a handful of elite universities substantial control over the funding, privileged the intellectual property rights of the researcher, and went to great lengths to shield federal research support from outside political influence.[23] He and his fellow scientists regarded basic research as incompatible with applied research directed at concrete problems.[24] American scientists wanted government support while also maintaining their professional autonomy. Their challenge was to find a way to square the circle between congressionally mandated relevance and their own desire to preserve their

disciplines' autonomy.[25] Harvard president James Conant also strongly supported the notion that the NSF should fund "uncommitted" research in the
belief that it would not only produce better scholarship but that its applied
benefits would also eventually trickle down from it.[26] Echoing Conant's
optimism on this score, a Russell Sage Foundation study confidently concluded that "pure research proves in the end to be the most valuable of
all."[27] The winning argument for the natural scientists was that the NSF
should fund basic research in the expectation that it would eventually have
applied results.[28]

This debate explains why the establishment of the NSF was delayed by
more than five years and significant social science funding did not come until
after the Sputnik crisis.[29] It was stymied for a number of reasons ranging
from ideology to turf.[30] The two primary stumbling blocks, though, were
administrative control—would it reside with the scientific community or the
government?—and would it include the social sciences?[31] On the latter, leading natural scientists like Bush had opposed making social scientists eligible
for NSF support on three grounds: that the Second World War had shown
that it was the natural sciences that were most critical to the country and
thus most deserving of federal support; the social sciences were not really
"sciences"; and the supposed association of many social scientists with the
New Deal meant that these disciplines were dangerously politicized.[32] Other
natural scientists feared that the limited involvement of the social sciences in
the New Deal would make their inclusion in the NSF politically controversial.[33] This objection was not at all trivial. As Mark Solovey recounted, "For
the [natural] scientists . . . the alleged contamination of the social sciences
by values not only disqualified them as a 'science'; such contamination, as
evidenced by their involvement with 'planning' or 'labor,' threatened to
provoke destructive partisan controversy and thus jeopardize the main goal
of creating a central agency for the natural sciences."[34] At root, though, Bush
was virulently opposed to the inclusion of the social sciences on the grounds
they were not "sciences."[35]

The political mood in Congress was hardly friendly toward social science either.[36] Many of the issues social scientists dealt with seemed to be
amenable to "common sense" and therefore not in need of specialized study.
Members of Congress were put off by the jargon and other inaccessible
aspects of much social science research. They also expected a clear and
immediate payoff for the research they funded. Representative Clarence J.
Brown (R—Ohio) pithily summarized the larger political vulnerability of
the NSF on this issue: "If the impression becomes prevalent in Congress

that this legislation is to establish some sort of an organization in which there would be a lot of short-haired women and long-haired men messing into everybody's personal affairs and lives, inquiring whether they love their wives or do not love them and so forth, you [scientists] are not going to get your legislation."[37]

An initial Senate vote on July 3, 1946, excised the social sciences by 46 to 26.[38] A later compromise solution did not formally exclude the social sciences but also did not make them a priority either. The subtle distinction proponents crafted was that their funding would be "permissive but not mandatory."[39] And those few social science projects NSF did support were carefully chosen to emphasize their "scientific" (and hence nonpolitical) character. Harry Alpert, an NSF consultant, advised the staff to focus on "hard-core" social science that would be methodologically rigorous and highly theoretical.[40] That was the strategy they adopted.[41] The burden of proof was thus placed on social science to demonstrate that it was a "science" worth supporting under the compromise language for NSF funding priorities drafted in 1950. Even then, it was not until 1953 that NSF began formally reviewing social science programs and only in 1959, in the wake of the Sputnik crisis, that it established the Office of Social Sciences, but only on the understanding that its support would be limited to "basic research."[42] Once established, NSF staff would actively discourage proposals for support of applied research in the social sciences.[43] As Henry Riecken, NSF's assistant director for social science, explained, "At the National Science Foundation we think that the most important thing we can do at present is to provide continuous—not intermittent—but steady, continuous support to fundamental research, especially on methodological problems: problems of measurement, problems of data analysis, problems of doing experiments as well."[44]

Given these strictures, social scientists had only two options. They could push for a separate National Social Science Foundation or they could become "scientists" by using the approaches of the natural sciences and engaging in basic, rather than applied, research. In the context of the initial debate about the NSF, the Social Science Research Council advocated the latter course.[45] Many social scientists followed suit, increasingly employing natural science methods and models and downplaying any effort to directly engage with policy.[46] In the late 1960s, Congress again tried to establish a separate social science foundation to reduce Department of Defense's (DoD) influence and garner more support for the social sciences.[47] By then many social scientists were committed to staying with NSF.[48]

Some prescient critics of this trend among social scientists feared that it would lead to "irrelevance."[49] NSF board member and University of Notre Dame president Fr. Theodore Hesburgh, for example, unsuccessfully lobbied for a broader, more engaged, indeed a more catholic, vision of what constituted legitimate social science.[50] Ironically, one of the original natural science proponents of the NSF, Harvard's James Conant, also became a skeptic of the NSF, arguing that "anyone who claimed that the solution to social, political, or economic ills lay in something known as the 'scientific method' would have a 'very dubious' hypothesis to defend."[51] Unfortunately, Hesburgh and Conant were among the few university administrators who allowed such intellectual doubts to get in the way of the prestige and large "overhead" rate NSF support of basic research bestowed on their campuses.[52]

The majority view was articulated by Talcott Parsons who advocated an alternative social science strategy of "'riding in on the coattails' of natural scientists" to the NSF.[53] Seconding this view, the Russell Sage Foundation advanced the notion of the "unity of science": "The social sciences apply to learning about man and his behavior, in all its various aspects, the same kinds of reasoning, and even many of the same techniques of inquiry, that are employed by scientists who study inanimate nature or nonhuman biology."[54] The result, in Mark Solovey's words, was that "mid-century American social scientists commonly emphasized technical rigor rather than critical analysis."[55] Gaining NSF support for social science thus set the stage for the subsequent estrangement between social science and practical affairs.[56] In other words, the NSF debate reopened the relevance question for postwar social science.

Talcott Parsons Designates "Basic" Social Science Research as a National Resource

No scholar more actively tried to shape postwar social science than Talcott Parsons. The Harvard sociologist (and one of the early translators of Max Weber into English) was among the many social scientists who had rallied to the colors during the Second World War. That experience convinced him that social science had been an important, if underappreciated, weapon in the arsenal of democracy. Moreover, the development of the atomic bomb instilled in him a sense of urgency about clarifying the role that social sciences could play in guiding postwar policy.[57] Parsons waged this campaign across a variety of fronts, from the letters-to-the-editor column of the *New*

York Times to the pages of scholarly journals. The main effort of this battle, however, was his massive 1948 report to the Social Science Research Council: "Social Science—A Basic National Resource."[58]

In it, Parsons outlined a detailed campaign plan for making the social sciences more scientific while ensuring that they would continue to aid policymakers as they waged the Cold War. Sounding familiar themes about the applicability of the approaches and methods of the natural sciences to the social sciences, he sought to distance them from the humanities, which were "orientated much more to appreciation than to analysis, prediction, and control." Science, in his view, proceeded though a division of labor among disciplines balkanized into "minute specializations." The hallmark of science, and its unifying element for Parsons, was theory: "The critical basis of the organization and generalization of knowledge lies in 'conceptual schemes' or 'theory.' It may therefore be said that the most important single index of the scientific status of a body of knowledge lies in the degree of technicality and scope of empirical applicability of the generalized conceptual schemes, of 'theory' in the field." As Parsons explained, "specific orientation to theoretical problems makes possible a speed and decisiveness of advance to generalized levels of knowledge not possible without it. Valuable as are the other types of work, it is the theoretically oriented type which should spearhead the advance of social science."[59]

Theory, in turn, was inextricably linked, in Parsons's mind, with basic, rather than applied, research. Indeed, Parsons recognized a fundamental tension between science and policy: "The kind of simplification which is essential, especially in the early stages of a scientific development, seems unrealistic and useless to practical men. It does not promise help in their immediate problems." Moreover, he opposed social scientists doing policy-relevant work because he feared it would undermine social science by raising unrealistic expectations and siphoning off the best minds into policy analysis. But he added there was "another set of reasons for emphasizing 'pure' or basic research. Important as continuing liaison with the active empirical world may be, the nonscientific pressure impinges more directly and powerfully on the social scientist active in practical application. In maintaining a balanced and steadfast orientation to technical standards, the social scientist must hold a model of purely scientific work continually before him."[60]

Parsons was in many respects the Charles Merriam of the early Cold War. While not a particularly methodologically sophisticated social scientist himself, he was nevertheless adamant that the only hope for the future of social science was for it to be dominated by "key" men committed to the scientific enterprise.[61] As he boasted, "Those who still argue whether the scientific study of social life is possible are far behind the times. It is here, and that fact ends the argument."[62] Indeed, he feared that the forces for the status quo within the social sciences were so powerful that he was willing to see the rest of the field remain ineligible for support from the NSF if he could not guarantee that it would go exclusively to social "scientists."[63] A revised, coauthored, draft of Parsons's report was to have been published as a monograph under the SSRC's imprint, but multiple revisions were rejected because the council's reviewers remained unpersuaded by Parsons's views of the unity of the natural and the social sciences and his confidence that basic research would eventually produce practical results.[64] Still, Parsons's personal failure with SSRC should not mask the larger success that he and like-minded colleagues enjoyed in remaking social science in his preferred image through the Behavioral Revolution.

The Behavioral Revolution Tries to Have Its Science While Remaining Policy Relevant Too

James Conant's skepticism about making the social sciences "scientific" in the natural science sense notwithstanding, that is exactly the route that some social scientists took during the Cold War under the flag of behavioralism, the most recent scientific approach to studying social phenomena.[65] Behavioralists believed in the unity of the scientific method, which they maintained was equally applicable to physics or politics.[66] Their approach combined elements of biology, psychology, and economics, and subjected them to formal and mathematical analysis to analyze human behavior.[67] Quantitative methods were the preferred tool of the behavioral approach to the study of politics.[68]

As important as this positive definition was the contrast with the alternative approach. A 1962 President's Science Advisory Committee report, *Strengthening the Behavioral Sciences*, implicitly excluded "those social science investigations in which more qualitative and historical approaches were employed—unless they were included under 'good, hard thinking.'"[69] Capturing the intellectual euphoria of the movement, some behavioralists enthused that their approach "represent[ed] the last stage of the enlightenment."[70] Indeed, it constituted the high point in their "scientific aspiration."[71]

The Behavioral Revolution's "creed" consisted of eight theses: First, social science could be made into a science in the sense that it could be both predictive and explanatory. Second, it limited its focus to such "observable" phenomena as individual political or social behavior.[72] Third, values and norms were excluded because they could not be scientifically analyzed. This reinforced objective analysis, rather than "advocacy," as the only legitimate task for science.[73] Fourth, it limited "empirical" data exclusively to that which was measureable or quantifiable.[74] That is why behavioralists were skeptical of qualitative evidence.[75] Fifth, they were adamant that general models should guide research. Sixth, they were strongly committed to the natural science distinction between pure and applied research, sharing its preference for the former.[76] Seventh, while the Behavioral Revolution was interdisciplinary in rhetoric, its vision was one in which the different disciplines all shared the same natural science methods.[77] Finally, and not surprisingly, research methods were the central concern of the Behavioral Revolution.[78] Behavioralists aspired to employ the most rigorous approaches available.[79] The roots of behaviorism extend back to Logical Positivism, but its immediate predecessor, at least in political science, was Merriam's interwar New Science of Politics movement.[80] The Behavioral Revolution in political science was a microcosm of the broader changes in post–World War II social sciences.[81]

It would be a mistake to ignore the political and other extra-intellectual factors shaping behavioralism. One rationale for hopping on the behavioralist bandwagon was that "science" enjoyed enormous prestige after the Second World War and any discipline that could wrap itself in that mantle enjoyed great benefits, particularly in prestige and resources.[82] Behavioralism also enjoyed some decided rhetorical advantages: social science sounded dangerously like socialism in the superheated political climate of the early 1950s while behavioralism seemed less politically charged.[83]

The Behavioral Revolution crested in two distinct waves after the Second World War. The first was characterized by a broad, interdisciplinary approach committed to providing policymakers with useful knowledge.[84] Initial work in it was funded by major foundations including Ford, Rockefeller, and Carnegie, encouraged by interdisciplinary bodies like the Social Science Research Council, and even for a time by various agencies of the U.S. government. Stepping into the breach opened by Congress's delay in establishing the NSF, the Office of Naval Research (ONR) funded basic social science research for anthropologists such as Ruth Benedict and Clyde Kluckhohn.[85] This wave had hardly crested when another one rolled in. This latter was more disciplinarily oriented and explicitly committed to basic research and pure science.[86] While it also enjoyed support from diverse sources, its primary patron would be the NSF.[87] Indeed, as Hunter Crowther-Heyck recounted,

> The program officers at these agencies consciously sought to promote research that would advance several social sciences as disciplines, especially work that would lead to methodological or instrumental advance. As a group, they held no brief for or against any particular conceptual scheme, problem area, or philosophical stance, so long as the research being proposed was methodologically sophisticated. The interest of these patrons in the advancement of technique was best expressed in their support for the development of computer modeling and simulation, the advancement of statistical techniques, and the expansion and elaboration of survey research.[88]

The first wave of behavioralism's dual commitments to methodological pluralism and policy relevance were inextricably linked.[89] As University of Chicago political scientist Hans Morgenthau attested, "The great majority of social scientists will try to satisfy society and scientific conscience at the same time."[90] It is not surprising that these twin aspirations would be combined in a new movement to create a "policy science."[91] The policy scientist sought to translate basic research findings and apply them to concrete policy problems.[92] Policy science sprouted from the barren soil of the Great Depression and took root in the rich loam of the Second World War and the Cold War.[93] It enjoyed generous support from the Ford Foundation's Behavioral Sciences Program (BSP).[94] While the names most closely associated with this movement were Merriam and his student Harold Lasswell, it was in the latter's view an interdisciplinary enterprise.[95] With the cresting of this first wave, the time was widely thought ripe for development of social science disciplines that could be both rigorous and relevant.[96]

The early behavioralists did not believe they would be irrelevant to policy; in fact, many engaged in what they regarded as policy-relevant basic research. Lasswell himself had served as chief of the Experimental Division for the Study of War-Time Communication at the Library of Congress during World War II.[97] Indeed, it is striking that Lasswell's interest in moving beyond "a purely scientific, objective science of politics" during the interwar period coincided with the outbreak of the Second World War.[98] Still, at the heart of behavioralist project lay a profound paradox: in order to bolster social science's credibility to offer policy advice, it had to become more removed from contact from real-world politics and narrower in its theoretical and empirical focus.[99] As Lasswell explained, "The policy approach is not to be confounded with the superficial idea that social scientists ought to desert science and engage full time in practical politics. Nor should it be confused with the suggestion that social scientists ought to spend most of their time advising policymakers on immediate questions. . . . The basic emphasis of the policy approach, therefore, is upon the fundamental problems of man in society, rather than upon topical issues of the moment."[100] Ironically, the Behavioral Revolution's commitment to science was in part animated by the belief that this would give the disciplines the credibility necessary to influence policy.[101] But when the tensions between rigor and relevance arose, as they invariably did, and scholars were forced to choose one or the other, many ultimately choose science and irrelevance.[102] Indeed, they eschewed "premature policy science" that might slight "pure science," which should remain the highest priority.[103]

Lasswell himself seemed blissfully unaware of the paradox inherent in his belief that science was defined by method but which would encourage its disconnect from practical affairs.[104] In his optimism, he also failed to see that his policy science program was swimming against powerful currents in the social sciences, including increasingly rigid disciplinary borders, growing concerns that policy-relevant scholarship was blurring the distinction between facts and values, and an increasingly widespread preference for the production of pure theory instead of practical application.[105]

While it is not clear that Lasswell ever admitted defeat, he and some of the main foundation supporters such as Ford and Rockefeller did begin to have second thoughts.[106] For example, Lasswell himself went from a firm commitment to value-free social science early in his career to an explicit recognition that value commitments were part and parcel of policy engagement.[107] In 1952, former Rockefeller president Raymond Fosdick admitted that "beyond the questions of social fact lie the questions of social value, or morals and ethics." When "the problems of mankind [are] calling for perspective and vision, our social scientists cannot be merely analyzers and computers."[108] In response, Rockefeller created a Program in Legal and Political Philosophy explicitly to "counterbalance" the major investments in behavioralism from other foundations.[109] Despite Rockefeller's interwar support for the Social Science Research Council, a leading new science of politics center, by the Cold War it was more inclined to sail against the behavioralist wind and underwrite more humanistic approaches that focused on practical problems.[110] Tellingly, the nadir of Ford Foundation enthusiasm for the Behavioral Science coincided with the Sputnik crisis.[111]

The Behavioral Revolution had begun with great optimism about achieving rigor and relevance but ultimately failed to reconcile the two.[112] "The proud announcement in the early fifties of the policy sciences has given way to a profound skepticism of such a concept in the sixties," Irving Louis Horowitz sadly conceded.[113] An important cause was the enduring tensions between science and relevance, the heart of the relevance question.[114] To be sure, the policy sciences were not completely discredited, but there is no doubt that as had happened in most revolutions, euphoria quickly gave way to an intellectual Thermidor.[115]

Since the apogee of the policy science movement came around the mid-1960s, there has been a tendency to attribute its demise to the more general political reaction against campus collaboration with the government during the Vietnam War era. While there is no doubt that its death was in part collateral damage from that increasingly unpopular conflict, deeper disciplinary factors were also at work.[116] As political scientist Charles Lindblom explained, "In drawing practitioners' attention to a careful choice of methods of inquiry—that is *how* to study—[the Behavioral Revolution] may have drawn their attention away (though it was already far away) from a careful choice of *what* to study."[117] It was this postwar generation of social scientists who most acutely felt the tensions between rigor and relevance that the war had papered over for their teachers.[118]

What were the roots of these tensions between science and policy? Robert Proctor attributed them to the "legacy of positivism," particularly its "detached indifference" to the phenomena it studies.[119] It did so because it privileged research methods over concrete results.[120] Critics may overstate their case when they suggest that behavioralism favors technique over substance.[121] But Lasswell was surely correct in his observation that after the Behavioral Revolution "the disciplines which possessed quantitative methods were the ones that rose most rapidly in influence."[122] This is why even otherwise committed behavioral revolutionaries like Gabriel Almond gradually came to worry that "for many of us in the camp of the behavioralists, the intoxication of new research technologies, and the explanatory power of insights from other disciplines has obscured this mission" to improve the human condition.[123] This epistemological legacy led later behavioral social scientists to try to reduce their disciplines to "mere technique."[124] Anxiety among social scientists that technique trumped relevance as the Behavioral Revolution matured was more widely shared, particularly among national security scholars.[125]

A final word about social science and relevance: the relevance question actually has two distinct facets, both of which were evident in the policy science movement. The clearest manifestation of it is when as a result of the tensions between rigor and relevance, scholars increasingly eschew the latter. But there is another facet as well. When scholars privilege method and abstract models to such an extent they force concrete policy problems into them like a bed of Procrustes. Doing so, however, often leads to policy failure, which in turn, further discredits the effort to use social science to inform policymaking among both scholars and policymakers, further widening the gap. Subsequent chapters will explore this latter pathology through two unsuccessful efforts to create a science of strategy.

The Behavioral Revolution Sweeps Political Science . . .

The behavioral approach affected all of the social sciences, but it had a particular resonance among political scientists who believed that their discipline had fallen behind the others in terms of methodology precisely because it was overly preoccupied with influencing policy.[126] Political science seemed to behavioralists like Parsons woefully backward, especially compared with economics.[127] Almond spoke for many when he enthused that political science was developing "in the age of the scientific revolution—indeed, it is an integral part of this revolution. There is hardly a major center of graduate training in the United States where scientific methods have not been accepted, or are in the process of being accepted, and where the components of the scientific approach are not acknowledged to be important parts of graduate training. The use of quantitative methods, the use of the new research technology, sample surveys, rigorous logical methods, sociological, psychological, and anthropological theory, large-scale research undertakings, research grants, team research, surely are here to stay."[128] The Behavioral Revolution sparked rising expectations and instilled great optimism among many of the foot soldiers in political science, as it had done with many social scientists in other fields.[129]

To "move political science from a pre-paradigmatic (or literally non-scientific) condition to a paradigmatic stage," the Behavioral Revolution pushed the discipline away from its historic orientation toward the study of the formal institutions of government and its heavily normative commitments.[130] It had its first, and deepest, impact on the subfield of American politics, but would eventually affect other subfields such as comparative politics and international relations.[131] Perhaps its greatest effect on the discipline was through its undermining of the once dominant subfield of public administration, which was closely linked with American politics.[132] In addition to Lasswell and Almond, the leading figure in the Behavioral Revolution in political science was David Easton, whose influential systems theory of political behavior represented for many the acme in the study of politics.[133]

The behavioralist approach got a major boost from the Social Science Research Council's Committee on Political Behavior, which in 1951 and 1952 supported efforts to promote a more "'systematic' study of politics."[134] The Behavioral Revolution in political science established beachheads at the University of Michigan's Inter-university Consortium for Political Research and Yale University's political science department.[135] There were also important interdisciplinary centers that had significant impact on political science, such as Stanford's Center for Advanced Study of the Behavioral Sciences and the University of Chicago's Committee on Behavioral Sciences.[136] Ironically, the University of Chicago of the late 1940s and early 1950s not only hosted some of the leading behavioralists in the discipline but also some of their most important critics including political theorist Leo Strauss and international relations scholar Hans Morgenthau.[137]

As with the Behavioral Revolution in social science more generally, the first wave in political science was sanguine about the discipline's ability to maintain the balance between rigor and relevance. In fact, early proponents explicitly recognized the potential tensions between rigor and relevance yet remained committed to balancing them: "Because the political behavior orientation implies a major emphasis upon systematic research and upon empirical method, it aims at being quantitative whenever possible. But it cannot be limited by such possibilities. The political scientist cannot escape the obligation and must not deny himself the opportunity to ask important questions, important in the description of political process, simply because his answers must be more or less qualitative."[138] Unfortunately, this optimism would soon turn to pessimism and the first wave's commitment to balance rigor and relevance would not characterize the second.

The father of the New Science of Politics movement in the 1920s, Charles Merriam, eventually experienced doubts about it on the grounds that its preoccupation with research methods was distancing the discipline from the policy engagement to which he was also committed.[139] While Merriam was a methodological "pluralist," justifying the particular research approach on the grounds of what was best suited to answering substantively important questions, his students and other followers were not.[140] Almost forty years later, another avatar for the scientific study of politics, Easton, would admit to similar disillusionment that the Behavioral Revolution had finally settled the relevance question.[141]

This same pattern of early optimism about the discipline balancing its scientific and practical inclinations followed by disappointment was also evident in the more contentious reception of behavioralism among political scientists specializing in international relations.

Also Affecting the Subfield of International Relations . . .

The Ford Foundation played a major role in supporting much of the most prominent early behavioralist work in political science's subfield of international relations.[142] The pivotal moment came when RAND Corporation president H. Rowan Gaither chaired the Study Committee on Policy and Program for the Ford Foundation in 1948, which concluded that the Cold War and the nuclear revolution had made it essential that America have a better understanding of world affairs.[143] Pioneering interwar quantitative scholar of war Quincy Wright, largely forgotten during the Second World War, experienced a renaissance of interest in his work among behaviorally oriented international relations scholars in the mid-1960s.[144] The philosophy behind such support was very much animated by the belief that a more professional and scientific subfield of international relations would ultimately prove to be a more reliable source of policy advice.[145] The initial Ford approach to promoting behavioral international relations was both interdisciplinary and practically focused.[146] But both would eventually run aground on the rocks of political science's disciplinary interests.

The seeds of trouble were planted early among the most enthusiastic proponents of the behavioral approach to international relations. University of Illinois professor Dina Zinnes confessed to feeling "a seductive security in mathematics that" she "found impossible to resist."[147] Among those whose commitment to science was, in part, psychological, it is not surprising that they would be intolerant of other approaches more willing to balance rigor and relevance. The University of Michigan's J. David Singer, for example, conceded that in principle "tolerance of diversity is clearly a virtue, but just as phlogiston theorists in chemistry or creationists in biology would constitute a misuse of public resources entrusted to our care, rejection of an epistemology that has demonstrated its superiority over and over for centuries would be a violation of public trust. Alchemists and astrologers would be anachronistic on any serious university faculty today, and I trust that in due course the antiscientific mentality in world politics will be equally out of place."[148] Finally, he and Yale's Bruce Russett would articulate two other key tenets of the behavioralist persuasion in international relations. Singer would deny any tension between science and values.[149] Perhaps he was insouciant on this score because he shared Russett's confidence that the behavioralist exclusive focus on basic research would nonetheless produce findings that "in the long run" would trickle down to policymakers?[150]

Other international relations scholars resisted the Behavioral Revolution in political science on the grounds that the subject matter of the subfield (state behavior) was less amenable to the behavioral approach than the core phenomena of other subfields like American politics (which increasingly focused on individual voting behavior) and due to their greater commitment to produce policy-relevant scholarship.[151] The most articulate critics of the Behavioral Revolution in political science from the perspective of academic international relations and national security studies were Morgenthau and other realist scholars and policymakers. Since most leading scholars of international relations were animated by real-world problems, rather than puzzles in models or cutting-edge methods, it is not surprising that Morgenthau's critique of behavioralism would resonate more broadly.[152] Even some early proponents of the Behavioral Revolution in international relations like Chicago's Morton Kaplan lost their enthusiasm for it.[153]

Morgenthau captured the inconsistency in the early Cold War mood: "Confidence in the power of reason, as represented by modern science, to solve the social problems of our age and despair at the ever renewed failure of scientific reason to solve them."[154] Unlike other critics of behavioralism in political science, Morgenthau and the realists were not in principle opposed to a scientific approach to the study of these issues. They argued that theory, rather than quantification and other methods, was a hallmark of science.[155] Of course, an exclusive preoccupation with universal theory can also lead to a disconnect between social science and the world of practical affairs. Parsons, for example, advocated a strict separation between "theory" and "policy." Explicitly identifying himself with Oran Young's critique of behavioralism in international relations, Albert O. Hirschman deplored how "*compulsive and mindless theorizing*" has hindered our understanding of other parts of the world.[156] Realists also embraced an interdisciplinary approach to studying international relations, combining political science, history, and philosophy. Finally, Morgenthau and his allies objected that the behavioral approach's value-free exterior concealed a normative agenda to remake international relations in a liberal fashion.

With support from the Rockefeller Foundation, Morgenthau was able for a time to paddle against the disciplinary currents in political science. But his and other realists' efforts to resist behavioralism in international relations by steering a "middle course" between previous legal and historical approaches that had dominated the subfield and the new scientific approaches eventually failed.[157] With the triumph of behavioralism generally in the discipline, and its growing inroads in the subfield of international relations, by the 1960s the notion that rigor and relevance were mutually exclusive had become the conventional wisdom among most political scientists.[158]

By Leaving Security Studies Out in the Cold

The period between the end of the Second World War and the mid-1960s illustrates both the widespread desire to foster academic security studies but also the challenges it faced. The Social Science Research Council sponsored three task forces on "Military Problems and Social Research" (1945–46), "Civil-Military Relations Research" (1952–56), and "National Security Policy Research" (1956–64) and awarded numerous research grants related to security studies. The first task force began with great enthusiasm based on the recent wartime experience but sputtered and did little more than change its name during its short two-year existence.[159] The second was set up in 1952 with a broad mandate for promoting civil-military relations scholarship. In 1953 it held a series of meetings on the vulnerability of the United States to bomber attack but found that not much current social science work focused on the topic. The committee thus commissioned a paper on the topic by Harvard economist Carl Kaysen, which was subsequently published in *World Politics*.[160] Concluding that the academy was unlikely to produce the desired research on its own, the committee applied for a series of grants from the Carnegie Corporation of New York and began awarding them to scholars willing to engage in broad historical studies of U.S. national security policy. Table 4.1 shows the number of these grants by year.

Continuing the work of the second task force, a third was established in 1956 with a more explicit policy focus. It continued the previous task forces' grants program but narrowed their focus to current defense policy and also began supporting conferences. The first of the latter was held at Dartmouth College in June 1958. In that same year, the committee took up a proposal by Princeton economist Klaus Knorr to attract more economists to national security affairs through grants and a conference. This was followed in June 1959 with a major conference bringing together scholars and military officers at the U.S. Military Academy. In 1962, Princeton political scientist Robert Gilpin organized a conference at Dobbs Ferry, New York, on the role of scientists in making public policy, followed the next June by another on the military and American society at Princeton. Despite these many activities, by 1964, SSRC president Pendleton Herring announced the termination of this last task force for lack of funds.[161] Strikingly, the SSRC initiative to foster policy-relevant national security affairs in the academy collapsed well before Vietnam convulsed the Ivory Tower.

To be sure, some behaviorally oriented academic social science would reach national security policymakers. The military, for example, collaborated with behaviorally oriented social scientists on occasion to their mutual benefit.[162] MIT political scientist Ithiel da Sola Pool was among the most prominent of them, and we will consider his role further in the next chapter. In addition to the substantive contributions this scholarship may have made, policymakers were undoubtedly also attracted to it because partnership with nongovernmental institutions such as universities dovetailed with liberal America's preferred way of mobilizing for war with as little reliance on the state as possible.[163]

TABLE 4.1. SSRC National Security–Related Research Awards (1945 through 1963)

Years	#s
1944–45	0
1945–46	0
1946–47	0
1947–48	0
1948–49	0
1949–50	0
1950–51	0
1951–52	0
1952–53	0
1953–54	2
1954–55	12
1955–56	6
1956–57	7
1957–58	10
1958–59	0
1959–60	3
1960–61	6
1961–62	4
1962–63	6

In the final analysis, however, the growing hegemony of behavioralism in political science undermined policy-relevant security studies because it eschewed prescriptive analysis and privileged basic over applied research.[164] Behavioralism hindered relevance in security-related social science research because it led scholars to ignore factors that could not be quantified or otherwise easily integrated into formal models.[165] RAND staffer Paul Kecskemeti attested that for contemporary behaviorally oriented work in national security affairs, "the emphasis must be on the perfection of the tool rather than upon the delivery of the final goods. Methodological self-examination necessarily claims a great deal of attention."[166] And reflecting doubts that basic research was trickling down (or bubbling up to policymakers from methodologically sophisticated staff) to practical application, the National Research Council's Advisory Committee on the Management of Behavioral Research in the Department of Defense chaired by William Kaufmann in 1971 called for studies "to establish the relationship, *if any*, between basic research and programmatically useful results."[167]

Loyalty and Exit: The Behavioral Revolution and the Cult of the Irrelevant in Political Science

How were all of these developments viewed within the discipline of political science? Most academic political scientists recognized the tensions between rigor and relevance that the Behavioral Revolution had exposed. Henry Reining, dean of the School of Public Administration at the University of Southern California and president of the American Society of Public Administration, was candid in recognizing their existence and blunt in denying that they could be eliminated: "We have a basic problem which will continue to be a problem and should continue. The Government wants answers. The scholar wants the opportunity to raise questions. The scholar wants freedom. The Government, for foreign policy and other reasons, cannot give him complete freedom. And so this conflict is built in. And there is no way to answer it. This is one of those situations that we have got to live with, we have got to accommodate to."[168] Given that a choice had to be made, most academic political scientists enthusiastically embraced rigor, and did so recognizing that it came at the expense of relevance.

Indeed, an increasing number began to make a virtue of this necessity by becoming vocally critical of efforts to bridge the growing gap between the academic and policy worlds, thereby remaining loyal to science. Typical was American Political Science Association president and Stanford political scientist Gabriel Almond who testified to his growing doubts that Defense Department support for academic social science was a good thing. Almond was also critical of the State Department, which he dismissed as "a conservative, humanistic institution, dominated by a foreign service which is trained largely in the law, in history, in the humanistic disciplines. They believe in making policy through some kind of intuitive and antenna-like process." In his view, the only intellectually legitimate source of government funding for scholars was that provided by the NSF to support basic social science research.[169]

But other political scientists inside and outside of the Ivory Tower, found the effect of the Behavioral Revolution and the policy sciences movement to be largely pernicious. It led prominent political scientists within the discipline such as Henry Kissinger and Zbigniew Brzezinski to exit the Ivory Tower and cross over the bridge to the beltway permanently. Both were Harvard products who studied in Cambridge at a time in which it seemed as if it was still possible to be both a scholar and deeply engaged with policy. In both cases, however, the tensions between scholarly rigor and policy influence forced them to make a choice. Both ultimately chose relevance and left the Ivory Tower permanently in order to pursue their passion for policy.

Kissinger attended Harvard in the immediate post–World War II era, having returned from the European theater and postwar occupation duties with substantial policy experience for a relatively young man. Harvard of the late 1940s, with its "Saturday afternoon seminars" in which faculty enthusiastically engaged foreign policy issues with an eye toward offering constructive policy advice was his métier. Historian Jeremi Suri noted that post–World War II Harvard's ambiance, in contrast to the late 1930s, constituted an "abnormal Cold War merging of intellectual and policy worlds."[170]

Even during these halcyon days at Harvard, however, Kissinger faced an uphill struggle to maintain a balance between rigor and relevance. The more general trends in the discipline of political science in favor of an exclusive pursuit of rigor were starting to take root even within Harvard's ivy-covered walls. Kissinger's mentor William Yandell Elliot encouraged him to eschew these "impersonal 'scientific' approaches to human behavior (emphasizing social structure and economic calculation)" and so he "shunned the traditional paths for academic recognition through scholarly specialization and disciplinary politics" in favor of policy engagement.[171] Upon completing his doctorate, Kissinger turned down faculty positions at Chicago and Pennsylvania and in 1955 went to the New York Council on Foreign Relations

(CRF), an establishment think tank. Kissinger's time there was reportedly pivotal in terms of his eventual turn from academia.[172]

Despite his return to Harvard after his stint at the CFR, Kissinger remained a marginal academic figure who shunned the Government Department in favor of the Center for International Affairs and his International Seminar. The latter was Kissinger's invention, to which he "invited promising young leaders from around the world to spend the summer at Harvard," the majority of whom were not scholars.[173] Illustrative of his tenuous situation was the fact that his tenure case was a close-run thing as his colleagues regarded him as more interested in policy than scholarship. His publically acclaimed CFR nuclear weapons book found a less receptive audience on campus, as his Government Department colleagues did not regard it as appropriately scholarly.[174] Dean McGeorge Bundy saved his case only by intervening in the process, rolling a log with potential opponents by establishing a position divided between Kissinger and another junior faculty member—Stanley Hoffmann—about whom others in the Government Department were more enthusiastic.[175] Despite squeaking through to tenure with Bundy's heavy thumb on the scale, Kissinger remained a marginal figure. As Suri observed, "Although he was a professor at Harvard, Kissinger was never an integral part of the institution."[176] When Kissinger left his tenured professorship to serve in the Nixon administration, few of his colleagues were surprised that he did not return after Harvard's statutory two-year leave for government service expired.

No doubt, some of Kissinger's colleagues thought that his controversial involvement in the Nixon administration's escalation of the Vietnam War, which made him radioactive on the banks of the Charles River (or on any other university campus), led him not to return. Others who knew him personally no doubt suspected that his time in the White House had inflated his already ample ego to the point where being a mere Harvard professor would no longer suffice to serve his unbounded ambition. His biographer Walter Isaacson quoted him as asking friends while flying on an Air Force 707, "What university would give me an airplane like this?" Also, the salary and the prestige of such a modest position were no longer sufficient for him. He reportedly informed Bundy's successor as Harvard dean, Henry Rosovsky, in the course of discussions about his possible return that "I'm a world historical figure . . . I can't just lead a normal life."[177]

While Vietnam and Kissinger's ego undoubtedly influenced his decision to give up on academia, there is evidence that the changes that had taken place there while he was in government played a role as well. It became clear to Kissinger that he could no longer balance policy and scholarship in the late 1970s the way he had in the 1940s and 1950s. This situation led Henry Kissinger to warn that "one of the challenges of the contemporary situation is to demonstrate the overwhelming importance of purpose over technique."[178] He would later bemoan to another biographer the "loss of intimacy between scholars and practitioners" today.[179] Historian Jeremi Suri agreed that given these changes in academia we could never have another Kissinger today.[180]

Kissinger's younger colleague Zbigniew Brzezinski had a similar career trajectory. A few years behind Kissinger, Brzezinski could have had a quite successful academic career at Columbia despite being denied tenure at Harvard. But by the 1960s, academia no longer seemed hospitable to someone like him for whom "the highest form of attainment is to combine thought with action."[181] Indeed, among his students Brzezinski was disparaging about trends in the discipline of political science: "If you look at the [*American*] *Political Science Review*, it is very hard to discern how you apply that to real life."[182]

He increasingly came to realize that the only way to combine thought and action was to associate himself with some sort of non- or para-academic institution such as a think tank or a policy school.[183] After his term of service as special assistant to the president for National Security Affairs to Jimmy Carter ended, rather than return to Columbia or Harvard, Brzezinski chose to remain inside the Beltway at a policy school. And upon being offered positions at both Johns Hopkins School of Advanced International Studies (SAIS) and Georgetown, he chose an untenured position at SAIS because he feared Georgetown was so academically oriented that it would preclude him from doing serious policy work.[184]

The Behavioral Revolution also prompted political scientists in the policy world, or other policymakers who might have used academic political science in their work, to become skeptical of it. This is a topic we will explore in depth in the next chapter, but typical of the view in government were those of RAND political scientist Bernard Brodie. Already in the mid-1950s, he complained that "the political scientist worries much more about the slowness of development in his own field than about the possibly dangerous impact of the relatively simple-minded findings he has made thus far." Warming to the topic, Brodie explained that "political science, like most other social science, is made of prose. It has been charged, I think justly, that it is usually bad prose, and I will not attempt to argue that the badness of the prose is necessary. But certainly the few attempts I have seen to introduce the symbolic language of mathematics into political science discourse have seemed forced, perverse, and usually ludicrous."[185]

Brodie's RAND colleague Paul Kecskemeti added that the "fundamental problems" central to basic research are not what policymakers care about.[186] Moreover, he also complained that a preoccupation with methods over substance was inherent in the policy science enterprise.[187] And challenging the growing optimism that political science basic research results would trickle down to the policy world, Carl Pfaffmann, vice president of the Rockefeller University and former chairman of the Division of Behavioral Sciences of the National Academy of Science, lamented that the "behavioral and social sciences, as academic disciplines, have not developed the tradition of applied sciences, as in engineering."[188] Finally, Kecskemeti highlighted what he saw as the paradox of policy sciences: it can only deliver the policy goods when it becomes a full-blown science.[189] But as was widely recognized among social scientists, rigor and relevance were condemned to remain in tension with each other.

Conclusions

This chapter has recounted how with the end of the Second World War, social science disciplines were pulled in two diametrically opposed directions. The general intellectual climate of the post–World War II/early Cold War era was one of great optimism about professionalizing and modernizing the social sciences on the model of the natural sciences. This impulse affected all of the social sciences to one extent or another, but especially political science. This optimism quickly gave way to disillusionment, however. The inherent tensions between "rigor" and "relevance" reasserted themselves once again, and it became clear that a peacetime choice between them might have to be made. On the one hand, the experience of the war, and the growing realization that the country faced a protracted period of rivalry with the Soviet Union, encouraged the disciplines to try to remain relevant to policy. On the other hand, the mixed security environment and desire to remake the social sciences in the image of the natural sciences eventually pushed them away from it. For a time, the chimera of a "policy science" seemed to hold out the possibility of squaring that circle. But eventually, the tensions between rigor and relevance became acute and social scientists were forced to choose between them. Henry Kissinger and Zbigniew Brzezinski, two of the most famous political scientists who served in high-level positions in government and sought to keep a foot firmly planted on both sides of the bridge, eventually gave up and left academia.

As we will see in the following chapter, postwar national security policy-makers quickly grew pessimistic that university-based social scientists would produce the sort of research that would be helpful to them. They therefore began to explore alternative models, which they hoped would effectively produce it. This gloomy assessment was based on their interpretation of the wartime experience and on their concerns with the trajectory of postwar academic social science.

5

Summer Studies, Centers, and a Governmentwide Clearinghouse

FEDERAL EFFORTS TO MOBILIZE SOCIAL SCIENCE FOR THE COLD WAR

If the Second World War saw the mobilization of large numbers of physical scientists, the Cold War would finally explicitly include many social scientists from the get go as well. In only a slight overstatement, briefers to Secretary of Defense Robert McNamara would refer to the Cold War as the "Social Scientists' War" in recognition of how the Kennedy administration tried to marshal those disciplines in the same way that government officials during the Second World War had brought physical scientists into the war effort.[1] As RAND executive Warren Weaver put it at a seminal conference in 1947, "Since the last war there has been a change in the character of war, a change in the character of the inevitable amalgamation of all intellectual and material resources of the country which are necessary to maintain our position in peace and enable us to defend ourselves if the need arises, a complete change in the attitude on the part of the military toward accepting civilians into partnership, no less, in the ownership of the United States."[2] Thus, as with the First and the Second World wars, the Cold War witnessed continuing government interest in drawing on social science as a resource for national security policymaking.[3]

Two elements of the early Cold War security environment seemed to open the door for civilian national security expertise. The first was the nuclear revolution, which had been ushered in largely through the work of civilian natural scientists.[4] Given the revolutionary nature of these weapons, and the fact that military officers had themselves never fought a nuclear war and so could not claim a monopoly on strategic expertise with those new weapons, there also appeared to be a significant role for civilian social scientists to contribute to nuclear strategy. In addition, the rise of insurgencies in the less-developed world, and the general acceptance of the notion that understanding their causes and consequences involved far more civilian than military expertise, gave social scientists an opening in that realm as well. A secret memorandum from MIT provost J. A. Stratton outlining the terms of reference for the institute's new Center for International Studies' (CENIS) relationship with the U.S. intelligence community confirmed that "it is imperative that we mobilize our resources for research in the broad field of political warfare as has been done rather successfully in connection with the development of more conventional weapons of war; and we must do this on the assumption of a long pull rather than for a series of crisis operations."[5]

Indeed, the experience of the Second World War prompted widespread optimism about the potential role for social science in national security policymaking. Weaver admitted that as a result of the war and the revolutionary postwar changes in military technology, "the military has come to realize (and, I think, to realize completely and honestly) that they have to accept and want to accept a type of partnership with civilians and a type of partnership with competence wherever they may find it, such as they have not been interested in accepting in the past. . . . They were quite willing to accept civilians on a certain service level in the past. They used to say, 'We like to have you around, and if you are awfully smart we will ask you questions and you will answer them as well as you can; but then we will go into another room and shut the door and make our decisions.' That, in the past, they were quite willing to do. Now, however, they want us in the back room with them."[6] In this spirit, the U.S. government became a major user of social science as well as employer of social scientists.[7]

Such public optimism, however, concealed a vigorous in-house debate among national security policymakers about whether academic social science, particularly as it was developing after the war, would really prove useful. For example, in December 1950 and January 1951 the State Department's Bureau of Intelligence and Research (INR) cosponsored a conference with the Social Science Research Council called Social Science and Point IV, President Truman's early Cold War initiative in the developing world. Afterward, Samuel Bayes, director of programming planning and advisory staff of the Technical Cooperation Administration, sent SSRC president Pendleton Herring a polite letter of thanks.[8] Behind the scenes, however, INR's internal assessment of the event was scathing: in a March 6, 1951 memo, INR staffer Edward W. Doherty dismissed the academic social science contribution as "drivel" and shuddered "to think that [U.S. economic development programs] might be answered in any substantial way in terms of providing our social scientists with an experimental approach to their subject."[9] Despite rhetorical euphoria, early Cold War relations between policymakers and social scientists were clearly mixed as the U.S. government, unlike academic social science, was less in the thrall of the ideology of basic research that increasingly came to dominate the Academy.[10]

This chapter offers a different take on the changing relationship between academic social science and national security policymaking during the early Cold War: first, while initial U.S. government support for social sciences did include some basic research, the driving force behind this trend among the social scientists was their internal processes of disciplinary professionalization. Government funders eventually concluded that basic social science research was of little use to them and shifted to funding almost exclusively applied work. In fact, they increasingly complained that basic social science research was couched in excessive jargon and deplored the unwillingness of scholars to provide policy relevant findings unless they could meet very high standards of scientific proof.[11]

On the former, RAND analyst Herbert Goldhamer complained that "much of social science impresses one as being modern more by virtue of various stylistic traits than by demonstrable additions to, or modifications of, our stock of substantive (or methodological) knowledge. . . . This seems attributable in large measure to an excessive preoccupation with the apparatus and language of social science rather than with the social world."[12] On the latter, his colleague Franklin Collbohm elaborated that policymakers believe that "to get a neat answer to the wrong question may be worse than to get an incomplete answer to the right question."[13] The root problem was that social scientists wanted to do pure science while policymakers demanded useful research.[14] In looking for it on campus, they soon realized that they were increasingly buffeted by the disciplinary winds.

Second, while Vietnam helped discredit academic social science involvement in policymaking, the disciplinary trends that would undermine it manifested themselves well before the war became controversial. A National Research Council study on the relationship between social science and national security cryptically hinted at deeper problems: "Even before the Vietnamese war and the reactions against it, which intensified problems of the relationship between academic researchers and government agencies, efforts were under way from both sides to attempt to improve the fruitfulness of those relationships."[15] But as we shall see, professional developments within academic social science made such cooperation increasingly difficult.

This chapter first explores the debate about Department of Defense support for science, highlighting how early U.S. government willingness to support basic research among university faculty soon gave way to an overwhelming focus on applied research once policymakers concluded that results of the former were unlikely to trickle down to the latter. It next chronicles the various internal U.S. government efforts to grapple with organizing and utilizing policy-relevant social science research related to national security affairs. Here it considers a variety of different external efforts government officials designed to better utilize this research: ad hoc summer studies, university research centers, and federally funded research and development centers (FFRDCs). The general trend we see is one in which national security policymakers came to increasingly rely on in-house in place of "private" research conducted by university-based scholars.[16] It concludes by highlighting what policymakers wanted from social science and distilling some lessons from these efforts.

The Pentagon's Use of Science

SCIENCE IN GENERAL

In the interregnum before the establishment of the National Science Foundation (NSF) in 1950, the military services continued their wartime programs of supporting science, including the social sciences, though Cold War defense-related research did not really take off until after the beginning of the Korean War in June 1950.[17] Ironically, the Department of Defense was the largest federal supporter of scientific research by the U.S. government early in the Cold War. About two-thirds of DoD research was conducted outside of the department.[18] Most of this research was in the natural sciences and engineering, but a considerable amount of it involved the social and behavioral sciences as well.[19] In fact, the Department of Defense was the major supporter of social science research at that time, far outstripping the Department of State and most other civilian agencies.[20] As Gene Lyons explained, "In none of the civilian agencies was there the built-in drive and momentum that was generated in the military, the ability to mobilize resources and develop an operational base for supporting research. It was this concentration on operations, bolstered by a 'systems' approach, that made the military the most substantial supporter of foreign area research in the federal government."[21]

Mirroring the wartime debate about the future of postwar federal support for science that eventually produced the NSF, the DoD and the services also debated the relative merits of funding basic or applied research. To be sure, there were some proponents of supporting basic research. Their rationales reflected those of civilian scientists who thought support for basic research should be NSF's exclusive mission. For instance, the Office of Naval Research (ONR) played the key role in supporting basic science during the five-year gap in funding for science caused by the debate about NSF.[22] In fact, ONR would establish the funding pattern later embraced by NSF.[23] While most scientists supported the establishment of the NSF because they were wary of military control of science, in many respects, ONR's earlier years represented something of a "golden age" for them because it supported basic research with few actual strings attached.[24] ONR would, though, be the exception that proved the rule of the U.S. government's general preference for applied over basic research.[25]

From the very beginning of this debate, there were many skeptics of the value of basic research. Eisenhower's secretary of defense, Charles Wilson, for example, set the tone, opining that "basic research is when you don't know what you are doing."[26] As Harvard professor and deputy chair of the Defense Department's Research and Development Board Don Price elaborated, "[The military] stands firmly on its cardinal principle: it does not make research contracts for the purpose of supporting science, but only in order to get results that will strengthen the national defense. . . . American scientists are still struggling to reconcile their eighteenth-century devotion to science as a system of objective and dispassionate search for knowledge and as a means for furthering the welfare of mankind in general, with twentieth-century necessity of using science as a means of strengthening the military power of the United States."[27] As a result of this mind-set, defenders of external research in the Defense Department and the services came to support only applied research.

What seems to have settled the issue once and for all were the growing doubts among senior civilian and military leaders about the trickle-down rationale for supporting basic research. According to a 1962 report of the Behavioral Sciences Subpanel of the President's Science Advisory Committee, the U.S. government demand for applied policy research "has been largely unmet, or met in piecemeal, after-the-fact ways."[28] The last nail in the coffin of this argument was a mid-1960s DoD study Project Hindsight, which sought to determine whether basic research had in fact produced much useable military technology. Using a combination of process tracing and reverse engineering on major weapons systems to trace where the core technology had originally come from, it concluded that basic research only contributed militarily useful technology in one out of a hundred cases.[29] The policy implications of this finding for DoD support of basic research were damning.[30] Hindsight marked the endpoint of the Department of Defense's gradual shift from support of basic to applied research.[31] This is undoubtedly why Vincent Rock, the U.S. government's leading expert in the late 1950s on the use of research by senior national security policymakers, concluded that rather than utilizing basic research, "the whole history of the federal government's involvement in science is a record of pragmatic response to particular problems."[32]

This shift was reflected also in the institutional evolution of DoD and service support for research. The wartime Office of Scientific Research and Development was demobilized in 1946 and the individual services took responsibility for contract research activities. With the 1947 National Security Act, a Research and Development Board was established in the Office of the Secretary of Defense.[33] But early efforts to impose a coherent framework on defense-related research failed. Not surprisingly, a proposal from the National Research Council of the National Academy of Sciences to set up a Research Board for National Security outside of government went nowhere.[34] Internal efforts to establish a unified Defense Research and Development Board within the Pentagon toward the end of the 1940s also failed, largely due to the opposition of the services. Part of this failure is attributable to interservice rivalry and bureaucratic resistance but there were also larger philosophical issues at stake: the services were more interested in applied research and wanted to maintain control of their own programs to ensure that they were supporting what they regarded as useful research.[35]

THE SOCIAL SCIENCES

As we saw, the idea of mobilizing behavioral science for the Cold War had been raised first by Carnegie Trustee (and former Army general) Frederick Osborn in 1946.[36] The Department of Defense was receptive to supporting such research because various officials saw having its results as an asset in conducting operations and developing strategy for the emerging post–World

War II world.[37] This effort took place in an intellectual environment characterized by initial optimism about the compatibility of modern science and
the needs of policymakers. As Social Science Research Council president
Pendleton Herring later reflected, "Now we have reached the point where
the military are using the social science disciplines and this is a very great
advance."[38]

Overall, the Department of Defense funded social science research in
five areas: (1) human performance; (2) manpower selection and training;
(3) human factors engineering; (4) foreign military security environments;
and (5) policy-planning studies.[39] From the very earliest days of the Cold
War, the DoD and the military services sought to utilize social science research not only for prosaic issues such as human performance and military
organization but also for grander efforts such as the formulation of strategy
for winning the Cold War.[40]

Cold War service support for social science began during the Second
World War. The first, and most important, sponsor was the U.S. Navy, particularly its ONR. From 1943 to 1953, ONR was the major sponsor of Yale's
Cross-cultural Survey and Human Relations Area files, a U.S. government
effort to compile useful area studies information about various parts of the
world. In October 1946, an ONR panel report recommended supporting
research in following areas: (1) comparative studies of different cultures;
(2) the structure and function of groups; (3) communication of ideas and
values; (4) leadership; and (5) growth and development of the individual.

Perhaps the navy's most relevant social science research directed at guiding high-level national security policy was Project Michelson. Established
in 1960 at the China Lake Test station with a small staff including a director
and three assistants,[41] and funded through the Polaris submarine-launched
ballistic missile (SLBM) program,[42] it sought to tap the "great wealth of
information within the body of knowledge represented by the social and
behavioral sciences that would be of great value to policymakers, if only this
information were available to them in useful form."[43] Michelson represented
an early effort to "bridge the gap" between state-of-the-art social science
and the needs of national security policymakers. As its first status report
noted, "Project Michelson has attempted to develop a systematic program
to identify and apply the techniques and findings of the behavioral and social
sciences that are relevant to the problems of international conflict. It has
sought to focus the empirical and conceptual resources of these sciences on
such problems in a way that would provide the navy and other governmental
agencies with evidence-based inputs to the selection of alternative policies,

postures, strategies, and weapons systems, while simultaneously developing the capability of these resources to increase the evidential base of such inputs."[44] It epitomized the contemporary optimism that rigor and relevance were mutually compatible and sought to bring to bear "hard" social science to the study of policy issues like deterrence.

Despite its promising beginnings, Michelson staff had to admit that among their fellow social scientists, "certainty and precision of measurement are often valued more than relevancy."[45] Given that, they were honest in admitting that the ultimate "relevance" of the project was uncertain.[46] Their modesty was well-founded: the leading chronicler of the navy's early Cold War role in sponsoring external research did not regard Michelson as important enough to cover it in his book on the period and an early participant came away from his experience with little confidence in its organization and administration.[47]

In June 1948, the U.S. Army established its General Research Office, subsequently renamed the Operations Research Organization (ORO), in conjunction with Johns Hopkins University.[48] The ORO's main mission was to conduct operations research (OR) for the army, but it took on broader projects as well. It sponsored, for example, a major postwar study of the role of economic aid in American foreign policy.[49] In support of President Truman's postwar efforts to integrate the army, ORO managed Project Clear, a continuation of the World War II studies of racial integration.[50] During the Korean War, ORO dabbled in operational issues, for example, persuading the Air Force to use B-29s for tactical bombing at night. But from the start, ORO and the army had a "troubled relationship" because ORO personnel wanted to go beyond their tactical OR brief and engage strategic-level and even policy issues. In June 1961, ORO broke with Johns Hopkins and reconstituted itself independently as the Research Analysis Corporation.[51] For a time George Washington University hosted the U.S. Army's Human Resources Research Organization (HumRRO). From its beginning in 1951, HumRRO's focused on military manpower issues.[52] In many respects, it represented a continuation of the World War II–era the American Soldier project.[53] In Korea, HumRRO was deployed to study North Korean and Chinese POWs.[54] The most famous, or perhaps infamous, of these army programs was the Special Operations Research Organization (SORO), of which more below.

Harvard's prestigious Russian Research Center (RRC) was established thanks to an Air Force's Human Resources Research Institute (HRRI) grant to study the psychological effects on Russia of nuclear strikes as part of Air

Force targeting.[55] Despite generating controversy on Capitol Hill, the RRC émigré interview program proved quite successful both outside and inside government.[56] A Behavioral Sciences Laboratory was also established at Wright Patterson AFB, but the most important Air Force Cold War social science research effort was Project RAND.[57]

Following the 1958 Defense Reorganization Act, the Directorate of Defense Research and Engineering (DDR&E) opened a social science office. DDR&E was another post-Sputnik DoD organizational innovation designed to promote research and development for the DoD and the services. While primarily focused on promoting and coordinating natural science and engineering research and development, DDR&E also sponsored social science research. One early example was the 1959 "Pool Report" (chaired by MIT political scientist Ithiel de Sola Pool) on "Research on Psychological and Political Effects of Military Postures." The DDR&E also sponsored reports on "limited warfare," written by among others Klaus Knorr, Pool, and Max Millikan. The Smithsonian Report, "Technology of Human Behavior," of July 1960 was also a DDR&E-sponsored effort, as was a 1963 follow-up to Pool's first report.[58] Finally, DDR&E also sponsored much of early national security research on arms control.

As we will discuss later, the fact that important elements of DoD's social science research were overseen by the engineers and physical scientists from DDR&E in part explains DoD's initial openness to the behaviorally oriented approach to social science in contrast to other parts of the U.S. government such as the State Department. As University of Chicago sociologist Morris Janowitz complained, "I believe the research and development structure of the U.S. government within the military establishment still reflects the necessities of the natural science and not the peculiar characteristics of the so-called 'soft' sciences."[59]

These efforts began as individual initiatives by the various services and offices in the Pentagon but soon grew into larger and more coordinated efforts to mobilize the disciplines for the "social scientists' war." In the fall of 1957, for example, the Advisory Panel on Psychology and the Social Sciences under DDR&E inaugurated a behavioral research program to respond to needs of DoD. This effort was transferred to Smithsonian Institution as part of its Research Group in Psychology in May 1959. In 1958 the Soviet Sputnik satellite launch led to action on this front at the apex of government when Vice President Richard Nixon pushed for a Temporary Group on National Support for Behavioral Science as part of the President's Science Advisory Committee (PSAC).[60]

The Advanced Research Projects Agency (ARPA), subsequently renamed the Defense Advanced Research Projects Agency (DARPA), was also a creature of the post-Sputnik era of national anxiety about the United States falling behind the Soviet Union in terms of science and technology. Whereas DDR&E focused on research and development more directly linked to defense applications, ARPA was established to foster longer-term and even more basic research that may or may not have direct defense application. ARPA's most famous innovation was a computer linked communication system called ARPAnet that morphed into today's Internet.

Like DDR&E, ARPA's main focus was the natural sciences and engineering but it also came to include some social science research, largely focused on defense personnel and organizational management issues.[61] Nuclear physicist and ARPA chief scientist Herbert York's study, "Toward a Technology of Human Behavior for Defense Use," led to the establishment of a Behavioral Sciences office in ARPA directed by J.C.R. Licklider, a psychologist and computer scientist who later taught at MIT.[62] Early ARPA social science work focused more on technical issues such as man-machine interface but also would engage broader policy-related efforts such as Project Agile, which dealt with "remote area conflict."

Personifying the fluid boundaries between DDR&E and ARPA social science research was Seymour Deitchman. An engineer, he began his government career at the Institute for Defense Analyses (IDA), a Federally Funded Research and Development Center (FFRDC) working for the Office of the Secretary of Defense (OSD) and the Joint Chiefs of Staff (JCS). Later he joined DDR&E to serve as executive secretary on a limited war project headed by Harold Brown. He stayed on to serve as special assistant for counterinsurgency to Brown's deputy for tactical warfare, Dr. John Lucas. These two projects convinced Deitchman that social science would have a major role in the Cold War. He would later direct Project Agile and chaired an ad hoc committee in 1964 to coordinate social science research between DDR&E, the Services, and ARPA. This committee identified four areas as "relevant" to DoD's mission: (1) political studies; (2) operations research, system analysis, and economics; (3) psychological operations; and (4) manpower selection and training. In addition to DDR&E and ARPA, the Office of the Assistant Secretary of Defense for International Security Affairs also sponsored social science research related to arms control and counterinsurgency.[63] Figure 5.1 reproduces a contemporary organization chart that traces how these various DoD research efforts fit together.

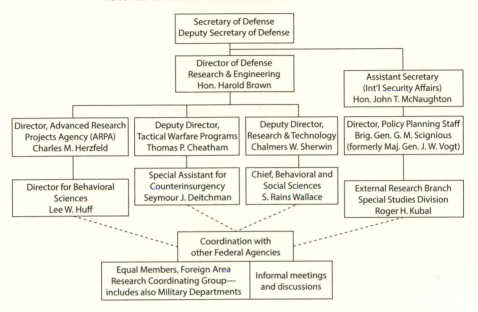

Department of Defense
Personnel Concerned with Behavioral & Social Sciences

FIGURE 5.1. Department of Defense research offices. (Figure arrangement follows "Statement of Lt. Gen. W. W. Dick, Jr., Chief of Research and Development, Department of the Army," "Behavioral Sciences and the National Security," Subcommittee on International Organizations and Movements, Committee on Foreign Affairs, U.S. House, December 6, 1965, 66.)

This same rationale applied to some of the other civilian national security agencies of the U.S. government.[64] For example, on January 15, 1951, the Joint Chiefs of Staff "Review of the Current World Situation" called for a social science Manhattan Project to set up a program of psychological warfare against communism. This paper led to the establishment of the Psychological Strategy Board in April (which failed) but then was succeeded in 1954 by the Operations Coordinating Board. Both were civilian agencies charged with, among other things, mobilizing social science research for the Cold War.[65]

By the early 1960s, well before the Vietnam War, two challenges to effectively mobilizing social science were already evident to national security policymakers. One was organizational: a wide variety of organizations in the U.S. government were trying to do so, but often with very little coordination. The solution to this problem was reasonably clear: the government needed a plan to harness "social scientific capabilities for more effective national security policy planning and action."[66]

The other, less tractable, problem was more philosophical. In 1964 the U.S. government was spending around $210 million annually on social science research (with $62,000 going to national security research at CIA, DoD, or the Department of State), but of this only 10 percent was spent on "educational institutions."[67] In other words, the majority of federal government spending on social science research supported in-house rather than university or other nongovernment scholars.[68] The problem, according to Charles E. Hutchinson, the chief of the Behavioral Sciences Division in the Air Force Office of Scientific Research, was that absent DoD funding, university social scientists paid more attention to "improved methodologies and generalizable knowledge" than concrete policy.[69]

The tensions between basic and applied research were evident in the U.S. government's research effort and particularly affected social science. These programs began by funding basic research in academia in the hope that its applied applications would trickle down to policymakers. For example, initial U.S. Air Force funding for Soviet Studies was similarly oriented more toward basic than applied research.[70] But disillusionment with the results of basic research soon set in, and by the Korean War the emphasis in Department of Defense and service research support had shifted decidedly in the direction of applied research. By 1954, for example, DoD was spending only $20 million (1.3 percent) on basic research out of a total research budget of $1.5 billion dollars.[71]

Federal Efforts to Coordinate Social Science

A SOCIAL SCIENCE CLEARINGHOUSE

While the Department of Defense was the primary source of federal government support for national security-related research, interest in a broader governmentwide program also manifested itself at the National Security Council and in the Department of State. This interest arose from concerns about "a gap between academic research and foreign policy," already apparent before the Vietnam War became controversial on campus.[72] This problem would come to be widely recognized but never fully resolved. In 1965 the National Research Council of the National Academy of Sciences assembled a study group on DoD's use of social science, which issued reports in 1968 and 1973 that in turn constituted the basis of Gene Lyon's classic study of government use of social science *The Uneasy Partnership*.[73] Its title speaks volumes about the continuing unresolved relevance question. This and the next section review the solutions government officials explored to try to address each of them.

Concern about how to marshal scientific expertise for national security policymakers percolated up from lower-level White House discussions as early as 1956. NSC staffers Robert H. Johnson and George Weber were engaged in this topic by an Office of Defense Mobilization Science Advisory Committee report urging the NSC to develop a more robust scientific advisory body to keep national security policymakers abreast of the latest scientific developments.[74] By July 1958, the NSC had zeroed in on the narrower question of the "adequacy of Government Research Programs in Non-military Defense" raised in a study by the Advisory Committee on Civil Defense of the National Academy of Sciences—National Research Council. This time the Office of Defense and Civilian Mobilization (ODCM) was tasked with responding to it.[75] In January 1960, Gordon Gray, Eisenhower's special assistant for national security affairs, asked Vincent P. Rock of the ODCM[76] to join the NSC Planning Board to "(1) study the general character of such research and the way it is originated and carried out by the several departments and agencies either directly or through private facilities and (2) to appraise the extent and adequacy of the coordination of national security policy research within the Government."[77]

As his first step in this project, Rock drafted a form letter for Gray's signature to be sent to senior officials at Treasury, the National Aeronautics and Space Administration (NASA), the Office of Science and Technology, the United States Information Agency (USIA), the Central Intelligence Agency (CIA), the Council for Foreign Economic Policy, the Bureau of the Budget, the Office for Coordination of Defense Mobilization, the Joint Staff, the White House, Justice, the Atomic Energy Commission (AEC), State, the Office of the Secretary of Defense (OSD), Commerce, and the National Science Foundation.[78] He attached a series of questions about the "scope and character" of its "national security policy research"; how such research was "initiated and utilized," including what role "policy officials and planning staff" play, how the former kept apprised of research-relevant developments, and if and how the agency tried to shape policy; whether "outside agencies or institutions" were contracted with to perform the research, and if so, how security was maintained and could its results be published; did NSC agencies make use of nongovernment-sponsored research; did they "maintain a clearing house of information on research carried out by other departments of the Government"; was agency supported research "coordinated with other departments and agencies"; how much was budgeted for research in the social sciences compared with "the natural sciences and technology"; was there a need for better coordination of such research among government agencies;

and, finally, did it make sense to set up a separate governmentwide Federally Funded Research and Development Center (FFRDC) to conduct such research along the lines of RAND or the Institute for Defense Analyses?[79]

Later in the month, Rock received a response from one agency, which reported that most of the national security research used by its employees came from "personal contacts and through normal reading of scholarly journals." Nonetheless it went on to endorse the idea of having access to such information in anticipation of consideration of NSC documents and plans. On the question of whether to achieve this objective the U.S. government needed to establish a new FFRDC or if some other less formal arrangement might suffice, the memo endorsed establishing a more limited research "clearinghouse" in the NSC instead of a "full-blown research organization."[80]

On the basis of this and other responses, Rock submitted his draft report to National Security Advisor Gray on March 3, 1960. His assessment was that "the field of national security policy research is only partially organized and is fragmentary in character," problems he thought needed to be addressed by the NSC staff. "Noteworthy is the relative lack of research, as such, dealing with problems of national security at the highest level of synthesis and generalization. Moreover, there are research gaps in a number of important areas affecting national security." His conclusion was that "there must be a means of correlating departmental research in support of Presidential decision making. There must also be a means of initiating research on problems that do not fall neatly into the primary responsibility of any single department or agency."

Rock saw this problem as having two distinct components: one was internal to the U.S. government and involved the reorganization of the NSC and national security agencies; the other was broader, involving the "intimate relationship between the process of national security policy formulation and the initiation and feed-back of research to support the policy maker." His solution was to more closely connect the policy planning offices of the various parts of the national security bureaucracy with a new NSC organization he proposed to establish.

This Office of Special Studies was "to communicate with, and stimulate creatively, the research community on the one hand, and to communicate with the policy maker and to respond creatively to his needs on the other hand." This new office was to be staffed by "men who have one foot in policy and one in research . . . to broaden and sharpen the communication between the two." Its objective was to bridge the gap between the two realms: "The problems of the policy maker must be made known. The research questions must be clearly framed. The relevant findings must be clearly and precisely presented. Thus the policy maker and the researcher can acquire a mutual awareness of each other's problems and perplexities so that a fruitful flow of research will enrich the capability of the policy maker to make wise decisions."[81]

Rock's report went on to survey the policy relevant national security research commissioned by various parts of the U.S. government. Defense was by far the largest sponsor of such research, both through the Office of the Secretary of Defense as well as the various services. Illustrative of the interface between natural science and engineering research, on the one hand, and social science on the other, were the various studies the Joint Chiefs of Staff Weapons System Evaluation Group (WSEG) conducted on such topics as the effects of civilian morale on military capabilities or the social effects of nuclear fallout. In addition to WSEG, defense-related external research was commissioned through the Office of the Secretary of Defense's contract with IDA; the Air Force's Project RAND; the Army's Operations Research Office (ORO) at Johns Hopkins University, the Human Resources Research Office (HumRRO) at George Washington University, the Special Operations Research Office (SORO) at American University; the Navy 's Naval Warfare Analysis Group (NWAG) and Operations Evaluation Group (OEG), which were both located at MIT; and projects sponsored by all three services at the Stanford Research Institute (SRI).

Rock's report then turned to the policy research process itself. Here he concluded that the advisors to senior policymakers were the key pillars on which to build a bridge between policymakers and the external research community. One important obstacle to effective cooperation was time: senior policymakers had very little of it while researchers were too slow in producing results. But time was not the only challenge; the nature of academic research was also a hindrance: "Private research, particularly in the social sciences, tends to deal with past problems or with problems that may have been current at the time the research was undertaken, but are no longer current by the time the project is finished." Finally, organizational obstacles needed to be overcome. Research was communicated well internally within same organization but "limitations on interagency access to research results limit their use. Research 'thinking' is well communicated among the various research organizations, but research results are not well communicated among policy makers." He attributed this problem to that motivational heart of bureaucratic politics: protection of turf.

Finally, Rock considered four avenues for promoting external research: (1) consultants; (2) one-time contracts; (3) support for basic research; and

(4) ongoing research by "special organizations." He concluded that this last, which included both FFRDCs but also academic organizations like MIT's CENIS, was probably optimal given that conducting research in such organizations was more attractive to academic and other private researchers, involved less government red tape, and made it possible to pay higher salaries.

The initial reaction to Rock's efforts was not wildly enthusiastic on either side of the academic/policy divide. The National Science Foundation, while technically a U.S. government body, probably spoke for most private academics in thinking that "the coordination of national security research is preeminently a government function."[82] Conversely, National Security Advisor Gray confessed to an aide that "I have had this report on my desk for a week and have not had a chance to read it. May I have your recommendations; first, as to whether it is necessary for me to read it, and second, as to what we do next."[83] Only Vice President Richard Nixon seems to have maintained an independent interest in the topic of federal support for the social sciences, but he appears to have been something of an outlier within the administration.

Nonetheless, on April 5, 1960, the NSC Planning Board discussed Rock's report and agreed to have him draw up "terms of reference" for an NSC National Security Policy Research "clearinghouse."[84] This body, which would consist of one to three detailees from other NSC agencies, was to perform only research coordination. The terms of reference were drafted on April 13[85] and submitted to the president by Johnson.[86] The NSC approved "A Research Clearing House Within the NSC Staff," which was tasked with keeping "components of the NSC Staff informed of research being done within and outside the Government which has significant bearing upon their responsibilities for national security policy-making or operations coordination, placing emphasis upon a high degree of selectivity. . . . [And also] facilitating appropriate access within the Government to such research."[87] However the Planning Board deferred until the next administration Rock's proposal that it also sponsor new research.[88]

Not surprisingly given the greater number of academics in government, interest in "External Research and National Security Policy" was greater in the Kennedy administration. Deputy National Security Advisor Walt W. Rostow, for example, circulated multiple copies of Rock's report to other senior national security officials including his old Yale economics tutor Richard Bissell then at CIA and Deputy Assistant Secretary of Defense for International Security Affairs Paul Nitze.[89] In a March 1961 memorandum, Johnson conveyed to Rostow a report he had written, noting that it built on Rock's previous report.[90] In it, Johnson focused on three narrower issues: how to "best keep track of research going on outside the government"; "spot able analysts" of national security affairs; and identify significant government national security research concerns and encourage research on them. Johnson suggested that the most useful work would be done in three areas: "broad politico-military strategy and related questions of weapons systems and arms control"; area studies; and studies of "economic and political change in the developing countries." Policymakers would find three things of particular use: theories or concepts "about the character of the phenomena with which the policy-maker deals"; analysis of concrete policies; and finally what he called "policy ideas," which he defined as the "seeds" of "fully formulated policy proposals."[91]

Building on Rock's findings, Johnson suggested that "further awareness of research and some effort to fill research gaps and to meet the now unfilled research needs of the national security policy planners" would constitute an "advance." His solution was a research-policy broker "who will, as a member of the NSC Staff working under the direction of the Deputy Special Assistant, serve as a broker between individuals concerned with research on national security problems and those concerned with national security policy planning." He envisioned this research officer "circulat[ing] freely" through the national security bureaucracy, including not only the NSC but also Defense, State, and the CIA. This individual was not to be a researcher, but would rather "serve as a focus and catalyst for this activity rather than a substitute for it."

Johnson sought to assemble a research group chaired by the deputy national security advisor and including representatives from State, Defense, and the Central Intelligence Agency. The group would identify research topics of interest and then coordinate external research so as to avoid duplication, foster the "wider utility" of the work done, and ensure that "scarce research talents" were not overtaxed. By the time the Kennedy administration took office there was little support for establishing a separate governmentwide FFRDC to handle the task, and Johnson thus focused primarily on how to utilize existing staff at RAND and IDA or how to engage individual scholars in policy-relevant research either directly by contract to the NSC or indirectly through university organizations like MIT's CENIS. Finally, this individual was to develop a list of both topics and potential researchers who could undertake them and also organize a major conference bringing together U.S. government national security policymakers, higher education leaders, and foundation officers to ascertain what current research might be of interest to the former and how government officials could encourage and keep abreast of work on topics of interest to them.

Johnson inventoried current U.S. government efforts along these lines. The closest analog to his proposal was the activities of the INR's External Research (XR) Division, which initially had confined itself to the particular research needs of the intelligence community but now, as a result of Rock's previous efforts, was looking more broadly at foreign policy–related research outside of government. At the Department of Defense, and again in response to Rock's initial efforts, the somewhat episodic reporting on defense-related research by the Office of Defense Research and Engineering was supplemented by an effort to get the individual services to regularly report on their research efforts to the secretary and the deputy secretary of defense, as well as the deputy assistant secretary of defense of international security affairs. The primary obstacle to this effort was not only organizational but also bureaucratic: the services were loath to share such proprietary information broadly even within the U.S. government.

Johnson reported that he ran an experiment in which he tried to compare the content of extant research lists produced by defense and state with "a list of national security planning problems" produced at a February 17, 1961, meeting of the NSC. Only one piece of research—RAND's famous "Nth Country Problem" study of the consequences of nuclear proliferation—overlapped with that list. He drew a number of conclusions from the exercise: The current lists of nongovernment research were so skimpy—in terms of both numbers and also descriptions of the work—as to be of "very limited utility for our purposes"; private library and bibliographic resources were likely to prove more useful; and extant lists of "government-sponsored research" proved most useful. In Johnson's view, such lists did not constitute a viable solution to the problem of inventorying research; only "personal contact" by a research broker would suffice. The challenge this broker would face would be to "get across to the busy policy planner . . . the kind of research that deals in broad concepts or hypotheses." This was not a challenge he was confident could be fully solved.

Johnson tried to anticipate what each of the agencies would do. The NSC, he thought, would be interested in developing both direct research support for the NSA, his deputy, and the NSC staff and also having a mechanism to coordinate national security policy planning research across government. The State Department proposed having INR collate proposals from the various bureaus, which the secretary's Policy Planning staff would then vet, with the top proposals being farmed out and managed by INR's External Research Division. Defense planned to increase and better coordinate the use of their "existing contractual arrangements" summarized in table 5.1.

TABLE 5.1. Current DoD External Research Contracts

Component	Contractor	Amount
OSD/ARPA	RAND	$1 million/yr. "retainer"
OSD/ARPA	IDA	$2.5 million
OSD/WSEG	IDA	$2.7 million
USAF	RAND	$13.5 million/yr.
USA	ORO/JHU	$4.5 million/yr.
USA	HumRRO/GWU	?
USA	SORO/AU	?
USN	OEG/MIT	$1.5 million/yr.
ARPA/USAF, USA, USN	SRI/Stanford	?

Johnson explored two approaches to the problem: First, the U.S. government could contract for the research it needed with individuals, either as consultants or drafters of one-off papers; assemble groups of researchers; or utilize the personnel of existing research bodies inside or outside government. One idea he floated was to set up a social science version of IDA's JASON Division—a collection of nongovernmental natural scientists who met regularly to consult on defense issues—to regularly bring to bear those disciplines' expertise onto pressing national security problems. But a recurrent concern was whether outside researchers needed to have U.S. government security clearances and whether having them would raise as many problems as it would solve.

Johnson's other solution was better coordination of the existing U.S. government research programs. Here, he recommended an "informal and flexible" approach that would, on the one hand, ensure that there was broader awareness of what research was being done by various parts of the national security community, but would, on the other hand, not stymie research with too much central control and recognize the limits of the influence the NSC was likely to have on the various research bodies inside and outside of government.

The final topic Johnson considered was whether the government could encourage and guide nongovernmental research. He was quite pessimistic about its prospects for doing so:

In general, one cannot be too sanguine about the possibilities of great influence on private research. Much of the research talent on national security policy problems—particularly problems of strategy—is already employed by the operations research organizations which are under contract to the government. Individual researchers may hesitate to enter the field. It is interesting in this connection to note that one of the members of the Social Science Research Council committee that reviews research proposals in the national security policy area reported a year or so ago that few acceptable proposals were submitted to the committee.[92]

He concluded by suggesting that if a separate organization along the lines of the NSF were established to fund social science research, it might be able to encourage more nongovernmental work on national security related issues. But the effort to establish a separate National Social Science Foundation would founder in the later 1960s, making this option moot.

FOREIGN AREA RESEARCH COORDINATION GROUP

The other major government supporter of social science research was the Department of State, which maintained a much smaller but longer-standing external research program under its Bureau of Intelligence and Research's External Research office (INR/XR). It also attempted to play the central clearinghouse role.[93] This effort had begun in 1948 with INR/XR efforts "to identify and acquire foreign area research materials that complement the government's own in-house studies and/or meet policy needs."[94] Indeed, until the Rock initiative at NSC, INR/XR was the only such effort in the U.S. government.[95] In theory, it "became the clearing house of information on such contract research."[96] In reality, its coverage was limited mostly to State Department activities: "Most of the other 99 per cent of contract research on foreign areas and international affairs is being planned and carried out with little or no guidance and involvement from the Department of State."[97]

For intellectual culture reasons, State came late to the social science research game. George Kennan, a Foreign Service officer and the first director of the Policy Planning staff, epitomized his department's negative attitudes about scholarly research: "The judgment and instinct of a single wise and experienced man, whose knowledge of the world rests on the experience of personal, emotional, and intellectual participation in a wide cross-section of human effort, are something we hold to be more valuable than the most elaborate synthetic structure of demonstrable fact and logical deduction."[98] A reinforcing element in State's jaundiced attitude toward social science was epistemological and methodological: in the early Cold War years, the

Department took its intellectual orientation from the realist approach to international relations, and so it was less inclined to embrace the current trends in behavioral social science research.[99] In fact, State's research customers had a decided "area bias," which was by then already on the wane in the academy.[100]

INR/XR came to play a larger role during the Kennedy administration in contracting with scholars and universities for research but still on a very modest level compared with Defense.[101] And what modest research State did sponsor focused more on substantive topics and area studies than on disciplinary agendas, as table 5.2 shows.

TABLE 5.2. INR/XR Group Research Projects in Foreign Affairs and the Social Sciences

Ongoing

Social science research on international affairs	I. Foreign policy and international relations
	II. International legal studies
	III. Overseas business and administration
	IV. International economics and economic development
	V. Economic theory
	VI. Political theory and political behavior
	VII. International communication
	VIII. Cross-cultural studies
	IX. Demographic analysis
	X. Military affairs
	XI. Education and aids to research
Studies of foreign areas	I. Area studies—general
	II. Africa
	III. Far East
	IV. Latin America
	V. Near East
	VI. South Asia
	VII. Southeast Asia
	VIII. USSR and Eastern Europe
	IX. Western Europe and British Commonwealth

Continued on next page

Canceled or suspended research

I. Psychological and unconventional warfare	A. Psychological warfare:
	Attitudes
	Communications theory, systems and media evaluation
	General
	Broadcasting
	International exchange program
	Libraries and exhibits
	Methods and techniques
	Motion picture activity
	Press and publication
	Handbooks and manuals
	Public opinion, reactions to specific issues
	Public opinion, troop-civilian relations
	Training
	Vulnerabilities
	B. Unconventional warfare
	C. Military government
II. Geography	General
	Regional
	Coasts and beaches
	Weather and climate
	Topography
	Urban areas
III. Transportation and telecommunications	General
	Railway
	Highway
	Inland waterways
	Ports and naval facilities
	Civil aviation transportation
	Telecommunications
IV. Sociological	General
	Population
	Religion, education and public information
	Manpower
	Health and sanitation
V. Political	General
	Structure of government
	Political dynamics
	Public order and safety
	National policies
	Intelligence and security

VI. Economics	General
	Agriculture, fisheries and forestry
	Fuels and power
	Minerals and metals
	Manufacturing and construction
	Trade and finance
VII. Scientific	General
	Electronics
	Air, ground and naval weapons
	Atomic energy
	Miscellaneous
VIII. Armed forces	General
	Ground forces
	Naval forces
	Air forces

Source: Furnas to Lay, attachments 1 and 2.

Small external research programs were also established in the Arms Control and Disarmament Agency and in the intelligence community.[102] The CIA, however, relied "heavily on the external research functions of the State Department to keep itself advised of private research activities concerned with foreign areas."[103] And in general there was really no coordinated effort by the government outside of Defense to promote national security-related research until the mid-1960s. Overall, as table 5.3 makes clear, State was the most junior partner by a large margin in the federal effort to sponsor internationally focused social science research.[104]

TABLE 5.3. Federal Funds Obligated for Social Science Research Related to Foreign Areas and International Affairs, FY 1963

Agency	Funds obligated
AID	$6,000,000
ACDA	$2,800,000
State	$147,000
Army	$2,000,000
Air Force (with RAND)	$3,300,000
Health, Education and Welfare	$1,000,000
National Science Foundation	$500,000
USIA	$400,000
Total	$16,147,000

Source: "Federal Agency Support of Social Science Research Related to Foreign Areas and International Affairs," 1.

A major step in this effort to consolidate U.S. government national security research was the establishment of the Foreign Area Research Group
(FARG), which was set up in April 1964 in response to the secretary of
state's desire for better coordination of research in this area across the U.S.
government. It stated purpose was "to exchange information about their
plans for contract research, to discuss these proposals when necessary to
improve their relevance to more than one agency, and to take full account of
these considerations in the final shaping of their programs."[105] "Having tried
an independent contract research program for 3 years," an anonymous INR
staffer explained, "we have decided that we can make better use of our limited funds for external research. By combining our long established contacts
with the academic community and our special knowledge of, and informal
coordination of, government contracting for foreign affairs research, we can
bring some rhyme and reason to the present chaos of government contract
research while at the same time meet the Department's research needs."[106]
FARG endeavored to synchronize government research contracts "with
the independent character of American institutions of higher education."[107]

Undeniably, FARG received an organizational boost from the Project
Camelot controversy, a SORO-sponsored study of political instability in
the developing world that leaked and caused widespread concern about
the militarization of social science, but that was hardly its origin.[108] And
despite the Camelot crisis FARG never achieved its most ambitious objectives. This was in part because it was a voluntary association comprised of
twenty-two different U.S. government agencies, all with their own interests
and agendas.[109] Given that, it was not very effective. NSC staffer Charles E.
Johnson cursorily dismissed it: "Most of the time the meetings are not worth
attending."[110] FARG continued to struggle into the 1970s.[111] The internal government reorganization solution to more effectively utilizing social science
research was no panacea.

The challenge, therefore, remained how to tap social science expertise
in a way that produced useful results and avoided the academic social
science pathologies that manifested themselves early on. Policymakers
explored a variety of external options, including drafting scientists, developing in-house expertise, and tapping universities before settling on a
combination of these approaches and adding two others: expanding the
use of individual and organizational contracts for directed research projects and establishing dedicated organizations to tap scientific expertise for
national security purposes.[112] None of these solutions fully satisfied either
scholars or policymakers.

Ad Hoc Summer Studies

The initial approach national security policymakers employed to tap out-side expertise was to commission ad hoc individual and group directed research via the famous "summer studies," meetings which brought together mostly academic researchers to tackle specific defense questions between semesters. In the summer of 1950, for example, MIT hosted Project Troy, a major research effort involving physicist Edward Purcell, anthropologist Clyde Kluckhohn, and social scientists Samuel Stouffer and Jerome Bruner to explore the technical and nontechnical aspects of broadcasting behind the Iron Curtain.[113] This was in important respects the inaugural effort to mobilize social science for the Cold War. Despite its conclusion that there was no "psywar" silver-bullet, the Department of Defense commissioned a follow-on project.[114] Project Troy Plus, also known as the "Soviet Vulnerability Project," was led by MIT economist Walt Rostow. It sought to strategize about how to erode Communist rule in peacetime and during war.[115] At roughly the same time, the University of Michigan Survey Research Center did related work for the Air Force on the psychological aspects of various targeting strategies.[116]

Another prominent summer study was Project Charles, an MIT-based interdisciplinary study that determined that the continental United States was defensible against Soviet bombers.[117] In 1951, Cal Tech hosted the army's Project Vista on "military priorities."[118] One recommendation was the use of tactical nuclear weapons to defend Western Europe.[119] Other projects included a Defense and Early Warning (DEW) Line summer study in 1952; Project Nobska, which led to the Polaris missile program;[120] Project Revere, a Korean War–era project to study the effect of air-dropped propaganda materials undertaken by the Johns Hopkins-based ORO;[121] Project Agile, in which SRI researchers studied counterinsurgency operations;[122] and finally Project Themis, a 1967 DoD project to support broader and higher-quality research at American universities.[123] Table 5.4 summarizes these various studies.

In looking at these studies, we can see two trends: first, a growing desire to integrate social and behavioral sciences along with natural sciences and engineering in the growing Defense Department research network; second, a marked decline in external summer studies and increasing reliance on in-house government research.[124]

TABLE 5.4. Defense-Related Summer Studies, 1948–65

Name	Sponsor	Institution	Year	Topic	Impact
Lexington	AEC	MIT	1948	Nuclear aircraft	↓
Hartwell	ONR	MIT	1950	ASW/SLOC security	↑
Metcalf	ONR	Harvard	1951	Radar	↑
Michael	Navy/ONR?	MIT?	1951	Undersea warfare	↑
Charles	Air Force	MIT	1951	Air defense	↑[1]
East River	Army		1951	Civil defense	↑[2]
Vista	Army, Navy, Air Force	Cal Tech	1951	Limited war in nuclear age	↓↑[3]
Lamp Light	Navy	MIT	1954	Navy role in air defense	↑
Nobska	Navy	NAS	1956	Nuclear submarine	↑
Monte	Navy	NPGS	1957	Mine countermeasures	↑
White Oak	Navy	Naval Ordinance Lab	1958	SLOCs	↑
Atlantis	Navy	Lincoln Lab	1959	Ocean surveillance	↑
Sorento	Navy	Scripps	1959	Nonacoustic submarine detection	↑
Walrus	Navy	NAS	1960	Merchant shipping	↑
South Lincoln	Navy	NAS	1962	Polaris communications	↑
Star Light	Navy	NAS	1962	Use of space	↑
Monte Plus 5	Navy	NPGS	1962	Mine countermeasures	↑
Sonar Signal Study	Navy	IDA	1963	Sonar	↑
Seabed	Navy	In-house	1964	Future of sea-based deterrence	↑
Pebble	Navy	NPGS	1965	Mine countermeasures	↑

Source: J. R. Marvin and F. J. Weyl, "The Summer Study," *Naval Research Reviews* 19, no. 8 (1966): 1–7, 24–28.
1 Led to establishment of Lincoln Lab and DEW Line.
2 Led to establishment of Michael.
3 Predated Maxwell Taylor's *Uncertain Trumpet*.

Academic Centers

AREA STUDIES CENTERS

The second route the U.S. government national security community took to promote policy-relevant social science research dealing with national security was to try to establish more permanent centers and institutions on university campuses. There were two types: First, the wartime cooperation of area specialists with the intelligence community and other arms of the U.S. government continued well into the Cold War, when OSS connections were replaced by those with the new Central Intelligence Agency.[125] The key lesson from the World War II experience was that the deep historical, cultural, and linguistic expertise necessary for the U.S. government as it faced the looming Cold War could only come from universities.[126]

Building on this wartime experience, DoD and the services established programs, centers, and other institutions on university campuses. This was made possible through the postwar return of regional specialists to the groves of academe where they populated these newly established "area studies" research centers.[127] An early effort was Yale professor G. P. Murdock's "cross-cultural survey," which produced the Human Relations Area Files (HRAF) to "accumulated a vast stock of ethnographic information, expanding its scope from forty cultures in 1938 to 150 in 1949."[128] Government sponsorship of HRAF was intended to marshal academic area expertise to produce country handbooks for the Department of Defense and the services.[129] This effort to subcontract the job to academics was not at all satisfactory, however, and so there was a continuing search for more well-institutionalized mechanisms to tap area expertise for national security policymakers.[130]

The most successful postwar area studies programs focused on the United States' primary Cold War adversaries, particularly the Soviet Union. Indeed, Soviet Studies would become the model for all subsequent area studies programs in important respects.[131] The Carnegie Corporation of New York underwrote the establishment of the Russian Institute at Columbia and the Russian Research Center (RRC) at Harvard.[132] The Rockefeller Foundation also played a significant role in supporting area studies, ensuring its humanistic bent by making "language and culture" its centerpiece.[133] In doing so, Rockefeller explicitly embraced the OSS area studies approach.[134]

While the area studies centers like the RRC constitute the most sustained and successful examples of DoD support for social science (and humanistic) scholarship, the story was not a completely happy one. On the one hand, particularly after Sputnik and the 1958 National Defense Education Act, which supported language and cultural training more broadly, area studies centers proliferated and seemed to flourish.[135] On the other hand, already by the mid-1950s the RRC and other area studies centers increasingly felt disciplinary pressures to choose between scholarly rigor and policy relevance. And as Soviet Studies became more "disciplinary," its ties with government "loosened." "The early experts, who were rooted as much in area as in discipline, trained students who were increasingly responsive to the siren song of disciplines—in part because they would be hired, promoted, and tenured in departments, not area studies programs," in historian David Engerman's account.[136] A few choose the former and survived; most inclined toward the latter and became marginal in the various social science disciplines. Thus a big part of the story of the decline of area studies and the growing disconnect between social science and policymaking toward various regions of the world has to be told in terms of such disciplinary developments.

NATIONAL SECURITY STUDIES CENTERS

The sad fate of Yale's storied Institute for International Studies (IIS) was typical of independent national security research centers. The trend was for these centers to briefly prosper in balancing social science rigor and policy relevance, particularly in wartime or other periods of international threat, but soon sink from view under the tide of disciplinary trends and antiwar ideology. Given that, the government also established a number of more general centers of international affairs with substantial equities in the defense realm and some dedicated security studies centers. But even the most successful and durable—MIT's CENIS—proved to be a mixed bag. The fate of these academic programs illustrated the larger problem of relying on universities and disciplines to devote sustained attention to national security affairs.

As during the interwar period, IIS's standing became precarious again after the war even though its research output was steadily increasing in terms of both quantity and influence. Indicative of the latter was the report from an institute conference, A Security Policy for Postwar America. To be sure, the group, which included Frederick Dunn, Arnold Wolfers, William T. R. Fox, and David Rowe from Yale, along with Edward Mead Earle and Harold Sprout from Princeton and Grayson Kirk from Columbia, did not get everything right about the emerging postwar world. But their overall conclusions and recommendations seem remarkably prescient almost seventy years later. Steering a middle course between the extremes of a return to isolationism and the widespread "utopianism" of world federalism, the IIS group outlined a realist vision in which the United States would have to contend with Russia as a peer competitor, but should not assume that its former wartime ally would necessarily become an implacable adversary either. Pointing to the common interest between the two superpowers in avoiding World War III and preventing the reemergence of "the German problem," the group anticipated an enduring superpower rivalry, but one that if managed adroitly did not inevitably have to lead to war.[137] Not surprisingly given Yale's role during the war, IIS was also the postwar locus for thinking about the implications of the "nuclear revolution," a topic explored in depth in the next chapter.

Why, despite these successes, did the institute fail to establish a firm post–World War II beachhead at Yale? Part of the reason was undoubtedly attributable to personalities: the favorable winds behind security studies in New Haven shifted abruptly when President Charles Seymour was replaced by A. Whitney Griswold, an early IIS member who had grown disenchanted with the institute's intellectual trajectory due to the increasing amount of defense policy research it was conducting. When he became president of Yale in 1951, one of his first moves was to close it down.[138] But it would be a mistake to blame IIS's demise solely on personalities.

Griswold's opposition to the institute also reflected academic institutional concerns.[139] Recall that the core philosophy of the institute's work was, in Dunn's words, "the development of a more disciplined type of policy analysis."[140] But IIS still tried to sail against the winds of both the traditional scholarly approach to research (the institute sponsored a lot of team projects as opposed to supporting the work of individual scholars) and it paid scant attention to traditional academic disciplinary boundaries. In contrast, Griswold "sought academic purity and took steps to attain it."[141] Rejecting what he characterized as the "'service-station' concept of the university," Griswold emphasized disciplinary agendas and approaches to scholarship and eschewed federal support of research that tended to encourage applied, rather than basic, research. And it was not just Griswold who had reservations about IIS; Yale's political science department also launched a post–World War II campaign to deemphasize international relations on campus in favor of "'domestic' political science."[142]

With the support of the Rockefeller and Milbank foundations, many of the IIS principals decamped to Princeton and set up shop again, bringing with them the leading scholarly international relations journal *World Politics*.[143] The institute's director Arnold Wolfers remained at Yale and tried to make the best of the situation. Even his optimistic gloss on these developments to the Rockefeller Foundation conceded that policy-relevant research had been severely curtailed at Yale as a result.[144] For a brief time, Princeton became the key link between the government national security community and those academics still interested in doing policy relevant research.[145] But the Princeton Center for International Studies proved not to be a model of successful integration of national security studies into the disciplinary departments either.[146]

It is true that by 1968 surveys identified university-based "national security" centers at a number of institutions such as Berkeley, UCLA, Chicago, Columbia, Cornell, Harvard, MIT, Indiana, Michigan, Michigan State,

Stanford, Ohio State, Washington, Princeton, Johns Hopkins, Dartmouth, and Wisconsin.[147] This hardly indicates that the field was well-ensconced in the Ivory Tower, however. Today many of these programs no longer exist (Berkeley, Cornell, Harvard, Michigan, Michigan State, Washington, Princeton, and Wisconsin) or have broadened their focus so much that they bear little resemblance to the original programs (UCLA and Ohio State), as table 5.5 shows.

Many universities were hesitant to embrace national security programs because they lacked "professional respectability."[148] And in general, the place of national security studies in the academy has always been tenuous: It is not well integrated into the social science disciplines, even in its natural home political science. Moreover, its survival has been heavily dependent on outside resources, whether from private foundations like Carnegie, Ford, and Rockefeller or the U.S. government.[149] Such dependence on external founding placed these centers at the mercy of changing foundation agendas.[150] Rockefeller and Ford eventually moved away from supporting private national security research, which further weakened the standing of these centers. Those few exceptions like MIT that survived relatively intact prove the rule about the tenuous standing of national security on campus as their success was due to continuing relationships with government funders committed to supporting policy-relevant social science.[151]

As its official history noted, MIT's CENIS "was created in response to a renewed sense of national crisis, at a time when that spirit of collaboration with the nation's government was at its peak."[152] Its raison d'être, therefore, was to bring together scholars and policymakers and focus them on solving important real world foreign policy and national security "problems."[153] Founding member Walt Rostow explained that he and his colleagues "believed that a portion of academic talent should be devoted to generating these concepts, and, as individuals, we were prepared to make that allocation. We hoped that we could do more by remaining in academic life than by returning to Washington as public servants, as I was asked to do and seriously considered doing. We also believed that, if high standards of academic professionalism and integrity were sustained, work on contemporary and foreseeable problems of the active world could add to the body of scientific knowledge."[154] CENIS had three overarching and interrelated research foci: "The dynamics of the Communist world, the dynamics of the developing world, and the evolution of American society."[155] Radical historian Michael Klare observed with ill-concealed disapproval that CENIS was so successful that it became "fixed in the popular imagination as the very paradigm of university-military collaboration."[156]

TABLE 5.5. The Fate of University National Security Programs

Institution/program	Current status
University of Chicago	Morgenthau's Center for Foreign Policy Research replaced by Program on International Security Policy in late 1990s
Yale	Institute for International Studies—closed. Eventually replaced by International Security program
Princeton	Center for International Studies merged into Center for International and Regional Studies
Columbia	Institute for War and Peace Studies still active
Harvard	Kissinger's Defense Studies Program did not survive nor Huntington's Olin Institute. Only Belfer Center for Science and International Affairs at Kennedy School remains
MIT	CENIS survives but Security Studies Program takes over defense-related programming
Wisconsin	National Security Studies Group now defunct
University of California–Berkeley	Defunct
University of California–Los Angeles	Defunct
Duke/UNC	Triangle Institute for Security Studies still extant
Ohio State	Mershon Center still extant but focus broader than security studies
Pennsylvania	Foreign Policy Research Institute split off
Georgetown	Center for Strategic and International Studies split off
Stanford	Center for International Security and Arms Control still extant
Michigan	Defunct
Michigan St.	Defunct
Indiana	Defunct, new program established in 2000s
Cornell	Defunct, now Peace Studies?
Johns Hopkins	Defunct
Dartmouth	Now Dickey Center

CENIS grew out of the series of ad hoc projects and summer studies run by MIT faculty for various national security agencies of the U.S. government, the most important of which was Project Troy. Follow-on efforts to Project Troy led to a proposal within the U.S. intelligence community to set up a "Cambridge Institute."[157] Its rationale was that "part of the contribution of an academic group is the identification of problems and proposals beyond those contemplated by Government operators or Intelligence agencies."[158]

Rather than a more traditional university like Harvard, MIT was logical place for such an institution given that the engineers who dominated the institute were more inclined toward an applied research orientation than academic natural scientists who preferred basic research. The institute's extensive World War II experience with government-sponsored defense research and MIT's continuing natural science and technical collaboration with the Pentagon on defense research such as aeronautical engineering conducted at the Draper Lab also worked in the institute's favor.[159] With the dawn of the Cold War, the senior administration at MIT once again answered the call of duty. As Provost Stratton proudly recounted, "Through-out every past period of crisis the Department of State and the Department of Defense have drawn heavily upon the academic staffs of Harvard and M.I.T., and the Central Intelligence Agency may count on the loyal support of this academic community." The challenge was how to best tap this expertise. "The problem," in Stratton's view, was "to invent a mechanism whereby our outstanding experts in the various fields of political, social, and natural science, represented here principally by Harvard and M.I.T., can apply their knowledge and talent in the national interest without abandoning completely their obligations to the education of students or their particular fields of professional specialization." The solution he proposed was a national security version of Princeton's Institute for Advanced Studies that could provide as much help to the government as possible without compromising scholarly integrity.

As initially conceived, the center's tasks would (1) develop "principles and methods for the conduct of political warfare"; (2) "determine likely targets of political warfare in terms of sensitive areas and sensitive subjects"; (3) "contribute to a formulation of the ideals and objectives of the Western World in statements that may be clear and comprehensible to such peoples as are designated to receive them"; (4) "conduct technical investigations of the several media for the dissemination of information throughout the Soviet Union and Satellite States"; (5) "devise and develop technical methods of minimizing the effectiveness of Soviet countermeasure programs";

(6) "more broadly, formulate plans and programs that may enable the U.S. to take the initiative in an undeclared electromagnetic warfare disclosed by the apparently deliberate and intensive jamming of American and British point-to-point, intercontinental transmission"; and (7) "investigate in further detail various objectives of political warfare outlined in the Troy report specifically directed against the supreme Soviet governing body; among these are measures to cause deterioration in the Soviet Administrative structure, to incite defection, to undermine faith in the dependability of satellites, and in general to detach the Russian population from the grip of their leaders."[160]

A significant amount of CENIS's initial funding came from the new Central Intelligence Agency; in fact, CENIS's founding Director Max Millikan had been an analyst there. But this covert sponsorship engendered political controversy on campus, even before the Vietnam War poisoned MIT's campus climate after 1968, leading CENIS to seek funding from other U.S. government agencies.[161] The equally new National Security Council stepped in to fill the looming fiscal breach.[162] But funding shortages and political controversy would ultimately prove to be less of a challenge to CENIS than disciplinary parochialism.[163]

In addition to a critical mass of like-minded faculty, and a supportive university administration, CENIS flourished with its singular policy focus and interdisciplinary orientation because MIT had no social science departments. This meant that the center did not run afoul of the disciplinary vested interests that afflicted other institutions. MIT's political science department, for example, was only opened in 1965.[164] But with the establishment of this and other disciplinary social science departments came unanticipated challenges. Donald Blackmer reported that "the most important factor [in CENIS's decline], however, was the Center's very success in incorporating most of its senior staff into academic departments. This was causing long-term members to lose some of 'their sense of identification with the Center and their commitment to it, as other obligations and loyalties intervened.'"[165]

Federally Funded Research and Development Centers: The RAND Case

Given the dissatisfaction with summer studies and individual contracts, and the tenuous place of university-based area and national security centers and programs, it is not surprising that Department of Defense and service supporters of national security policy-relevant research would move to establish separate nonacademic entities to conduct this sort of work. The impetus for the establishment of what were initially called Federal Contract Research Corporations (FCRCs), and later designated Federally Funded Research and Development Centers (FFRDCs), was the desire to regularize and replace the summer studies.[166] There were three broad types of these organizations: labs, system engineering and technical direction centers, and study and analysis centers. The last of these was most relevant to social science.

The FFRDC was supposed to provide the best of both worlds of academia and in-house government research, serving as a bridge and a transmission belt between the two realms. They were also to provide objective assessments of government programs while avoiding the conflicts of interest that private companies might face.[167] To attract top-flight scholars, they tried to foster a quasi-academic work environment and pay salaries above the Civil-Service scale. Reflecting an already jaundiced view of the prospects for a more direct relationship with academics, the most attractive element of these organizations for national security policymakers was that they were not subject to the vagaries of academic institutions.[168] Such organizations also appealed to U.S. government sponsors because their employees could work with classified materials and were subject to much more effective intellectual direction than independent scholars in universities.[169]

FFRDCs had wartime precedents in "ad hoc, not-for-profit, university-based organizations created during World War II to address specific technological problems."[170] The archetypical example on the natural science/engineering side was MIT's famous wartime Radiation Laboratory (the Rad Lab), which would become the peacetime Lincoln Laboratory. Some organizations also did social science-type research such as the "study and analysis centers" like the Operations Evaluation Group (OEG).[171] While most national security-focused FFRDCs were more operationally oriented, the key exception was RAND, which had a broader intellectual mandate.[172]

Some see the growth in the number FFRDCs, and their initial connections with universities, as indications of a robust pattern of early cooperation between academic social science and national security policymaking.[173] The conventional wisdom is that these relationships only frayed over concerns that classified research might be incompatible with academic freedom and culture and the turmoil of the anti–Vietnam War movement.[174] But a close reading of the history of the relationship between these organizations and the universities tells a more complex story. The more important factor was the fundamental incompatibility between the philosophies of the academy (which favored basic research) and the government (which increasingly wanted only applied research). Nor were the social scientists working in them immune to the methodological pathologies that were pushing their academic brethren toward irrelevance. This will become evident through the history of two of the most important of these defense-related FFRDCs.

Of course, the most prominent of the national security FFRDCs was the RAND Corporation. RAND's charter defined its mission as "a continuing program of scientific study and research on the broad subject of air warfare with the object of recommending to the Air Force preferred methods, techniques, and instrumentalities for this purpose."[175] Despite modeling itself on a university, it was never affiliated with one.[176] Its initial sponsor was a private company, the Douglas Aircraft Corporation, though later it would become an independent nonprofit organization.[177] While RAND had a much broader intellectual mandate than did these other FFRDCs, it still struggled to balance scholarly integrity with the demands of the Pentagon bureaucracy.[178]

Douglas approached the U.S. Air Force in the summer of 1945 with the original RAND concept. The newest of the U.S. military services would be among the first to embrace the FFRDC concept because it was less wedded to bureaucratic interests and highly dependent on nonmilitary areas of scientific expertise to execute its military operations.[179] Air Force chief of staff General H. H. "Hap" Arnold, who had worked closely with a number of the World War II–era proto-FFRDCs, was enthusiastic about the project, setting aside $30 million for three studies of intercontinental warfare.[180] His experience working with physical scientists at MIT during the war on projects such as radar had convinced him that the government ought to find a way to institutionalize this cooperation.[181] In September 1945 Arnold convened a meeting at Henderson Field in California with, among others, the head of Douglass Aircraft Corporation, and announced a $30 million contract for Project RAND.[182]

When, in May 1947, RAND separated itself from Douglas there was a brief discussion of whether it should affiliate with a university or pursue an independent course.[183] It chose the latter. RAND vice president J. R. Goldstein explained that "universities in peacetime seemed inappropriate to house a group dedicated to problems of the military."[184] A postwar Department of State study elaborated that "one factor in its decision was 'the near absence of a well-developed body of thought and community of scholars dedicated to the study of national security as an analytic field.'"[185] Even had they been so-inclined, RAND's founders had no other choice than to go it alone as universities were hardly lining up outside the gates to engage with this new national security research organization. Cal Tech president Lee DuBridge and University of Illinois dean Louis Ridenour both turned down the opportunity to direct it.[186] As historian Gregg Herken explained, "There was an early tension . . . between the scientists at Rand and their counterparts at colleges and universities," which he attributed to the political differences between the two groups.[187] These tensions went well beyond partisanship.

Unlike academic social science departments, RAND was a thoroughly interdisciplinary research organization. As Goldstein recounted, "RAND's work necessarily crosses such arbitrary lines drawn to match professional skills. Our problems don't fall into such neat categories as physics or economics, and typical analyses cut across departmental lines."[188] His colleague mathematician Robert Specht agreed: "We try to avoid the compartmentalization of skills, where the physicist must know some political science, the political scientist must know some physics, and where a worker on one project may find stimulus for an idea coming from work in another and apparently unrelated project."[189] RAND's social science projects also unapologetically engaged research topics that involved political "value judgments," which most modern scientists assiduously avoided.[190]

While RAND's intellectual center of gravity was in the natural sciences and engineering—its first two major defense studies were of satellites and intercontinental ballistic missiles—discussion of a possible role for social sciences commenced almost immediately.[191] The Air Force's first chief for research and development, General Curtis LeMay, would later become a vociferous critic of RAND. But after some initial hesitation, he was for a time a proponent in the Air Force of giving social scientists a major role in RAND.[192] The majority of social scientists hired by RAND were economists, but by 1947 it began to reach out to other disciplines as well.[193] At one point, staffer Nathan Leites even enlisted anthropologist Margaret Mead to work on various RAND projects. Eventually, almost all of the social sciences would be represented on its staff.[194]

The founder of RAND's social science division was a former student of University of Chicago economist Jacob Viner, a polymath by the name of Leo Rosten. In addition to writing Hollywood screenplays and books on Yiddish, Rosten had taken an advanced degree from the London School of Economics and earned a fellowship from the Social Science Research

Council before serving in the Office of War Information during the Second World War. Rosten was charged with recruiting "bright young professors from Columbia, Princeton, Yale and other top-notch universities" to work at RAND.[195] Rosten would be succeeded by Hans Speier, an OSS veteran and devotee of Harold Lasswell's "policy science" movement.[196]

A seminal event in the development of the social sciences at RAND was the conference RAND organized in New York from September 14 to 19, 1947, which brought together a veritable who's who of leading social scientists with the twin objectives of introducing them to RAND and also helping its staff "judge the nature and extent of the contribution which the human sciences can make" to RAND's mission.[197] Among the participants were Columbia University anthropologist Ruth Benedict, Yale political scientist Bernard Brodie, Chicago sociologist Herbert Goldhamer, Oxford don Charles J. Hitch, UCLA philosophy professor Abraham Kaplan, Yale Law professor Harold Lasswell, Columbia political scientist Franz Neumann, Chicago sociologist William Ogburn, Samuel Stouffer of the Harvard School of Social Relations, and Chicago economist Jacob Viner. Table 5.6 lists the various projects they discussed.

TABLE 5.6. Issues at 1947 RAND NYC Conference

Discipline	Topic
Psychology and sociology	Psychological warfare and morale
	Crisis disaster and situations
	American goals and values
Political science	Decision-making and the social structure of the USSR
	Civilian and military policy
	American foreign policy
Economics	Economic war potential of Russia and the United States
	Economic conditions of international friction
	Economic preparedness: stockpiling and reduction of vulnerability
	Foreign economic assistance
Studies in intelligence and military affairs	Content analysis and intelligence
	Secrecy and disclosure
Research methods and organization	Techniques of attitude measurement
	Composition of research teams
	Reliability of prediction

Source: *Conference of Social Scientists, September 14 to 19, 1947*, viii–xvi.

RAND was in many respects the ideal intellectual environment for social scientists interested in national security policy. It attracted some of the
brightest minds in the national security field, gave them access to classified
information without imposing military discipline, and best of all, imposed
on them no teaching obligations. While RAND was by no means the first
"think tank," its success in the national security realm in the early Cold War
led to their proliferation in number and growth in influence.[198] Most importantly, RAND offered a venue for policy-relevant security work even before
Vietnam made it increasingly less welcome in the academy.

In its early years, RAND social scientists made a number of contributions
to policymaking spanning the gamut from "softer" to the "harder" social
science analyses. A good example of the former is Leites's seminal work on
Soviet strategic culture and the "operational code" of the Bolshevik leadership, which reportedly influenced Paul Nitze's thinking in drafting National
Security Council Memorandum 68. RAND also developed much more
"scientific" social science approaches that combined cutting edge concepts
from mathematics and economics and applied them to defense problems.
RAND's substantive areas of research included strategic theory; Soviet studies; missile and satellite technology; as well as such esoteric topics such
as linear programming, systems analysis, and game theory.[199] At the peak
of its influence, RAND was widely heralded as the wave of the future and
the accolades about its performance in bridging social science and defense
policymaking led one analyst to conclude that "RAND appears to be one
of the best investments the United States government has made since the
Louisiana Purchase."[200]

Beneath its placid public surface, however, the terms of debate about
social science at RAND were strikingly similar to those roiling academic
social science disciplines at the time.[201] Those social scientists who most
closely approximated the methods and approaches of the natural sciences—
particularly the economists—prospered. But other RAND social scientists
felt they were treated like second-class citizens. In fact, RAND consigned
them to a separate division.[202] The initial exclusion of the noneconomists
from the high-profile work on nuclear strategy led them to focus on other
issues like unconventional war.[203]

As the intellectual tone was set by the natural scientists and the economists, RAND social science work came to be dominated by Systems Analysis, an off-shoot of Operations Research (OR). "Operations research,"
in RAND staffer and later Harvard economist Thomas Schelling's view,
"was not then the application of *science* to military operations, but the

application of *scientists* to new problems unrelated to the content of their original training and experience."[204] Proponents embraced OR for its precision and helpfulness in clarifying alternative policy choices and sought to apply these virtues to higher-level problems under the guise of Systems Analysis.[205] Some RAND analysts such as economist Charles Hitch were modest about its limits, particularly the application of OR techniques to higher-order policy assessments. As he explained, "It is intrinsically harder (for an operations researcher or anyone else) to decide between, say, two bomber development projects which may bear fruit in 1965 or 1970 than to find a good tactic for known bombers to use in penetrating known defenses." He was also cognizant of social scientists' inability to meaningfully quantify concepts like "military power" or strategic value.[206] Rather than more complex mathematical models, what Hitch thought were necessary for better strategic analysis was simply a firmer grounding in theory.[207]

Another early enthusiast for economic and quantitative approaches to the study of defense issues was RAND analyst and later secretary of defense James Schlesinger. Ironically, Schlesinger maintained that the influence of quantitative analysis on policymaking was exaggerated in the popular imagination. The source of confusion, in his view, was the conflation of Operations Research, which had proven very effective at the tactical level because "the solution is embodied in the available data," with Systems Analysis, which tried, inappropriately in his estimation, to apply those tools to policy choices, which are "not amenable to the same type of treatment."[208] He concluded that, "the great danger in systems analysis is that it may result in an attempt to transform problems of optimal choice into measureable problems of efficiency, a possibility that disappears when one moves outside the framework of a given weapons system."[209] As with Hitch, he argued that the higher the level of strategic decision, "the less quantitative and the less systematic becomes the analysis."[210]

Such intellectual modesty was in short supply at RAND. Most social scientists there were initially bullish about what cutting-edge social science methods and approaches could bring to the study of strategy: "In the old war game, professional opinion and subjective qualitative information are supreme," an anonymous RAND staffer enthused, "[Now,] analysis and objective quantitative data tell the tale."[211] As Alex Abella reported, the head of RAND's Mathematics Division—John D. Williams—was among the true believers: "From the start, one of his pet projects at RAND was developing a theory of war along the lines of Einstein's grand unified theory of physics."[212]

RAND mathematician R. D. Specht confessed that "in our youth we looked more scientific; that is to say, we attached more importance, years ago, to the business of representing by a single analytical model that part of the real world with which we were dealing. With the context chosen, the assumptions determined, the criterion selected, we could turn our attention to the more intriguing questions of how best to apply modern mathematical techniques and high-speed computers to produce a neat solution from which conclusions and recommendations could be drawn."[213] The development of RAND social science was joined at the hip from the beginning with the Behavioral Revolution through the Ford Foundation, which played a central role in promoting both.[214]

As before, social scientists were initially optimistic about the compatibility of modern social science and the needs of policymakers. RAND political scientist Bernard Brodie, for example, thought that economics would offer the optimal foundation for building a science of strategy.[215] In that confident frame of mind, he heralded the emergence of what he termed the "scientific strategists" who substituted "numbers" for history.[216] But the tensions between social scientific rigor and policy relevance soon brought Brodie back down to earth, dampening his early enthusiasm for the cutting-edge tools of economics.[217] He came to realize that "the usual training in economics has its own characteristic limitations, among which are the tendency to make the possessor insensitive to and often intolerant of political considerations which get in the way of his theory and calculations." "We have learned too," Brodie conceded, "that in analyses aimed at policymaking, it is far more important to consider carefully all the many factors and contingencies which may influence or change our problem than it is to achieve a high degree of mathematical or economic sophistication of the analytic techniques applied to solve it for any one set of assumptions."[218]

Brodie's growing disenchantment with economics led to skepticism that strategic problems could be analyzed using its tools.[219] He went on to lament that "one is sometimes amazed at how little some of the best-known strategic analysts of our times may know about conflicts no more remote in time than World War I, let alone earlier wars (the same is, however, true of professional military officers). It is not that they have no time for history but rather that the devotees of any highly developed science—and economics is clearly the most highly developed of the social sciences—tend to develop a certain disdain and even arrogance concerning other fields. It is a grave intellectual fault, but a very common one." Brodie concluded that "it is unfortunately true that the most profound issues in strategy, those likely to affect most deeply the fates of nations and even of mankind, are precisely those which do not lend themselves to scientific analysis, usually because they are so laden with value judgments."[220] Given his intellectual evolution away from economics toward history and other "softer" approaches to social science, and his realization that policymaking and value judgments were inseparably joined, it is not surprising that he would adopt the nineteenth-century Prussian military thinker Carl von Clausewitz as the model for strategic analysis in his later years.[221]

Mathematician and RAND founding father Warren Weaver agreed: "I am not one of those who happen to think that all you need to do to solve the problems of social science is to obtain a few sufficiently smart engineers, or a few sufficiently smart mathematicians, or, indeed, a few sufficiently smart anybodies. Indeed, I am not overly optimistic about the contribution that, say, mathematical analytical thinking can make in solving problems of social science." As he had noted at the 1947 New York conference, the task a social scientist faces "comprises a thousand factors, some of which are quantitative; but most of the important ones are not quantitative. . . . It depends on all sorts of things that you can't weigh or measure."[222] In a similar vein, Specht elaborated that "the stability of the thermonuclear balance or the composition of a strategic deterrent force or the character of the next generation of tactical weapons—these are not questions that may be attacked usefully in this manner." Contemporary econometric techniques could not model such complex problems because there was too much uncertainty in the measures of variables to quantify them.[223] "We have learned," he added, "that new tools—high-speed computers, war gaming, game theory, linear and dynamic programming, Monte Carlo, and others—often find important application and are often powerful aids to intuition and understanding. Nevertheless, we have learned to be more interested in the real world than in the idealized model that we prepare for analysis, more interested in the practical problem that demands solution than in the intellectual and mechanical gadgets that we use in the solution."[224] So as RAND social scientists moved beyond simple World War II–type OR problems, the role of the social sciences expanded and broadened in the 1950s.[225]

Camelot's Failure to Craft a Policy Science of National Security

To be sure, not all university-based social scientists were hors de combat. A handful answered the call of duty, among the most active of them was political scientist Ithiel de Sola Pool. Perhaps not coincidentally, Pool was a University of Chicago graduate who had studied with Charles Merriam. During the Second World War, Pool served in Washington, DC, with Harold Lasswell and Nathan Leites, two other comrades in the "policy sciences" vanguard. After the war, Pool taught for a time at Stanford before settling at MIT, where he helped found its political science department.[226]

Pool was among those early optimists who thought that the Behavioral Revolution had answered social science's relevance question once and for all by marrying sophisticated social science research techniques to the needs of policymakers. He was very active in many of the early limited war research efforts, including leading the 1963 Second Smithson Report on insurgency, counterinsurgency, and U.S. Cold war national security strategy. Deitchman noted that this report did not have as great an impact he had hoped it would because it was written in "sometimes abstruse language that . . . would make it difficult for the action-oriented parts of the defense bureaucracy to understand, accept, and implement."[227] It was nonetheless influential in a negative way as it was the genesis of a major, yet ill-starred effort, to bring to bear social science on pressing policy issues, the Special Operations Research Organization's (SORO) Project Camelot.[228]

SORO was established at American University in Washington, DC, in 1957.[229] The army had approached other Washington-area schools including Maryland, Georgetown, and Catholic University, but all declined to host it. American was not the first choice as it was hardly a leading academic institution at the time. From the very beginning, SORO was to be an intellectual chimera designed to bring together scholars and army officers in collaborative research efforts.

SORO's initial impetus was the army's less-than-satisfactory experience with contracting out to universities for the production of its Human Relations Area Files handbooks.[230] SORO's brush with infamy came from its connection with Project Camelot, a U.S. Army sponsored study of political and social dynamics in the developing world to support counterinsurgency operations there.[231] It had its origin in a 1961 study by MIT's Pool.[232] As a December 4, 1964, letter from SORO explained, "Project Camelot is a study whose objective is to determine the feasibility of developing a general social systems model which would make it possible to predict and influence politically significant aspects of social change in the developing nations of the world."[233] Its objectives were to identify "indicators and causes" of insurgency; assess possible policy responses by host governments; and construct a general model of insurgency.[234] It would become the single "largest integrated social science research project ever undertaken," with $3 to $5 million budgeted over three to four years for just the pilot project piece of it.[235] Camelot's directors envisioned it as an interdisciplinary and multimethod project.[236] Proponents of Camelot like Pool considered it "basic" research effort and so had little concern that it would prove controversial.[237] It would prove to be anything but uncontroversial, with long-lasting negative repercussions for the effort to bridge the gap between academic social science and the policy community.

A University of Pittsburgh anthropologist peripherally involved in it misrepresented the source of Camelot's funding in discussions with colleagues in Chile. When it became clear that the sponsor was, in fact, the U.S. military, a firestorm of outrage swept the developing world.[238] Coming in the midst of growing discontent about the Vietnam War, many regarded Camelot as the "crucial turning point" in academic-DoD relations.[239] Domestic controversy led Secretary of Defense McNamara to cancel it on July 8, 1965.[240] Its demise disheartened those who hoped it might provide a template for sustained and harmonious collaboration between social scientists and policymakers. After the Camelot controversy, SORO rechristened itself the Center for Research in Social Systems (CRESS) in 1966 and moved off the AU campus in 1969.[241] It continued to conduct research, even securing an ARPA contract to study quantitative political science in the post-Camelot era.[242] However, the consensus is that SORO/CRESS was largely a failure. The quality of its research declined further and the organization became even more dependent on its military patrons.[243]

The two most common explanations for Camelot's spectacular failure are bureaucratic warfare between the departments of Defense and State for control of foreign policymaking[244] and political opposition to campus collaboration due to the highly charged political climate of the Vietnam War.[245] While these factors played a role in the controversy over Camelot, they hardly constitute a complete explanation for why that effort to answer the relevance question had the opposite effect of keeping it open for years to come.

On the former, bureaucratic opposition from the State Department was constant.[246] Thomas Hughes, director of the INR, testified that State Department efforts to "coordinate" policy-relevant research in the U.S. government started well before Camelot erupted into public controversy.[247] Such a constant factor cannot account for a change in policy. On the latter, even before Vietnam poisoned the atmosphere for government/university collaboration on campus, challenges to the effort had already emerged. SORO, for example, was never successful in bridging the gap between the national security policy community and academia. It was on, but never of, its campus host, American University. An IDA study of DoD use of social science pointed out that "although SORO operates under an Army contract with the American University, it is not a part of the campus organization and its participation is only incidental to the educational function of the university."[248] Camelot, in fact, epitomized the tensions between scholarship and the needs of policy.[249] These were rooted, in turn, in the tension between basic and applied research.[250]

As Irving Louis Horowitz noted, "The notion of basic science requires a distinct separation of its functions from policy-making functions."[251] One result of this belief that basic science was incompatible with applied social science research projects like Camelot was that few leading academic social scientists would agree to participate in them. While it did engage a few top academic social scientists such as Lucien Pye and Pool (MIT), Morris Janowitz (Chicago), and Klaus Knorr (Princeton), in general its staff did not consist of leading academic social scientists. They were instead, in Joy Rohde's characterization, "middling scholars, the rank-and-file of the military-industrial-academic complex."[252] Just over a quarter of them had Ph.D.s and less than 20 percent came to SORO from a traditional academic background.[253] That, in turn, would ensure that the quality of such efforts would be low. University of Chicago historian and State Department Policy Planning Staff member William Polk agreed that "when the best minds in the academic community turn aside, we get poorly conceived projects like Camelot."[254]

The Camelot debacle is explicable in terms of the threat environment and the dynamics of the professionalization of academic social science. The many academics who eschewed Camelot did so, in part, because they did not regard what was happening in Vietnam or the rest of the developing world as a threat to U.S. national security.[255] This view was reinforced by what one SORON (the organization's self-deprecating nickname for its employees) disparaged as the "dogmas" of science (especially the preoccupation with methods), which in his view accounted for the lack of scholarly engagement with these issues.[256]

SORO's failure was rooted in the originally flawed conception of the organization, which could satisfy neither the academic nor policy worlds.[257] It had an interdisciplinary staff, of whom the majority were political scientists. Indeed, the tension between the competing objectives of academic rigor and policy relevance was evident well before the Camelot controversy exploded. With "the Manhattan Project for the social sciences" thus managed by "consultants" rather than regular faculty from its inception, it is clear that the gap between government and academic social science predated Vietnam.[258] Camelot, though, certainly further undermined the behavioralist consensus that value-free social science and policy relevance were mutually compatible.[259]

In important respects, SORO demonstrates that the original conception of the FFRDC constituted a tacit admission that direct cooperation between the academy and the Pentagon was fraught with deep tensions. This observation holds more generally for the rest of the FFRDCs and the other government-funded national security research organizations.[260] The trend was for FFRDCs associated with universities eventually to break with them. In 1968, 63 percent (10 of 16 programs) of DoD FFRDCs were university administered; by the mid-1990s, that dropped to 10 percent (2 of 20 programs).[261] FFRDCs had simply never constituted reliable bridges between academic social science and the policy world.

Despite the second thoughts among early proponents of highly sophisticated social science approaches to national security affairs at places like RAND, these approaches remained common in academia. This had two effects: "Scholarship in the field became more academic" among later generations of Cold War strategists.[262] Strategist Roman Kolkowicz, for example, lamented that "over-abstraction, scientism, numerology, and technical jargon are all part of the legacy" of the early Cold War defense intellectuals.[263] And in those few instances in which academic social science did influence policy, the privileging of models and methods over appropriateness, often produced counterproductive policies.[264] For example, critics like Colin Gray indicted the economic approach to Vietnam strategy as contributing to the failure of United States efforts there, a case we will consider in-depth in chapters 6 and 7.[265] The fate of these scientific strategists epitomizes the tensions between policy relevance and a narrow definition of scholarly rigor.

What Did Early Cold War National Security Policymakers Want from Social Science?

This section considers what national security policymakers in the legislative and executive branches of government wanted from social science and explains why they were not satisfied with what they were getting.

Social science, as we saw in the last chapter, was not popular in Congress and could be politically controversial, no doubt reinforcing the growing caution among national security policymakers about the type of work they commissioned. For example, the Air Force's Human Resources Research Institute (HRRI) support for Harvard's Russian Research Center (RRC) raised anti-Communist hackles when some members of Congress objected that the government's sponsoring of the study of Marxism could have the perverse effect of promoting it. Similarly, a RAND study of "strategic surrender" was excoriated as defeatist by Capitol Hill opponents of government support for social science early in the Cold War.[266] Subsequently, the political attack on DoD support for social science would come from the other end of the political spectrum in the wake of the Project Camelot controversy. But political problems were of a second order compared to the epistemological and methodological gap that was growing between academic social scientists and national security policymakers.

One of the most consequential legislative aftershocks of the Camelot controversy was an amendment that Senator Mike Mansfield (D-Montana) added to the 1969 Defense Authorization Bill. The year prior, Mansfield and his colleague William Fulbright (D-Arkansas) had begun a sustained attack on DoD social science research.[267] As Mansfield explained his amendment, "Congress . . . is giving clear notice to the Defense Department and to university scientists who now rely upon military support and to Members of Congress responsible for funding of academic research by other agencies *that the function of the military is not to support academic research, but rather is to obtain only that research which in the eye of a prudent and reasonable man relates to known requirements of the military for advances in science.*"[268] The thrust of the Mansfield Amendment was that all defense research be directly relevant to national security policy. It was particularly critical of DoD support for basic research.[269]

Some regard the Mansfield Amendment as yet another manifestation of post-Vietnam political opposition to university/government collaboration, particularly in the area of national security. To be sure, there were some congressional concerns about the propriety of the Defense Department sponsoring academic research, particularly in foreign countries.[270] But the problem for this political argument is that if the Mansfield Amendment is only about Vietnam (or Camelot), why did it continue to allow funding for military research on campus if it was directly relevant to DoD's mission, including that connected with the continuing U.S. war in Southeast Asia? The answer is that the Mansfield Amendment was in reality intended to foster a "national science policy" aimed at promoting applied, instead of basic, research.[271] This effectively curtailed DoD support for basic research for a time and also had an important secondary effect on another government agency that supported basic research, the National Science Foundation.[272] Support for NSF has long been controversial, particularly as it relates to the social sciences. It has only increased during periods of threat such as Sputnik or the reinvigorated Cold War of the 1980s and otherwise declined during other periods such as the waning days of the war in Vietnam.[273]

Congress, it seems, had grown increasingly dubious of the trickle-down theory that basic research would produce applied results.[274] South Dakota Republican senator Karl Mundt forcefully articulated this skepticism in an exchange with Harold Brown's successor as head of DDR&E John S. Foster: "Those kinds of applied research projects I can understand a lot better than just the whimsical desire to see whether or not settlers in a Latin American country are successful or unsuccessful when you are transplanting them. It seems to me here we have got an immediate problem. Your shop is eminently well set up to handle money to meet the problem, and you have done some work in areas where the urgency is much less; to wit, Latin America, than Vietnam."[275]

Mundt and his colleagues were also not fans of the Department of Defense supporting university research. Mississippi Democratic senator John Stennis warned that "I consider that [social and behavioral sciences] to be the softest spot in all the [DoD] research and development program."[276] Congressman H. R. Gross (Iowa-R) pushed Deitchman hard on this in a hearing:

> MR. GROSS: Who does let those negotiated contracts with the
> universities to provide the brain power to run the military
> departments?
> MR. DEITCHMAN: Contracts with universities are let by the military
> departments and ARPA. . . .
> MR. GROSS: . . . why [has] the Pentagon hired a private contractor with
> some so-called civilian smart boys to go over and tell the military
> how to fight the war in Vietnam.[277]

There was more to congressional skepticism than just political concerns. New Jersey Republican Peter H. B. Frelinghuysen Jr., sensing the trends in academic social science that were marginalizing area studies, remarked that "I would think you are not going to make much sense unless you go overseas to get an understanding of some of the problems you are talking about. Unless you are in Vietnam or unless you are in some of these locations you are likely to come up with a very academic, bookish kind of analysis, I should think."[278] These views reflected a growing sense that the primary questions members of Congress should ask when they considered government support for social science is what national security policymakers wanted from it.[279]

What executive branch national security policymakers wanted were answers to concrete policy questions, including specific recommendations about what to do about them. Director of the State Department's Bureau of Intelligence and Research (and former Columbia University political scientist) Roger Hilsman explained that "the Secretary wants what he calls 'policy-oriented' research. By this term we mean research which not only contributes to foreign policy formulation but which provides a systematic exploration of policy alternatives."[280] Phillip Mosely, another academic who spent a substantial amount of time working in government, confirmed that the key is for scholars to offer policy recommendations.[281] There was, of course, some early optimism that social science could deliver this. Irwin Altman of SORO, for instance, opined "that political science, history, and international relations have tackled questions very close to military needs. Their typical approach has been to deal with '*big issues*' and to seek *solutions* to problems, even when '*hard*' scientific data was missing or when rigorous techniques were unavailable to collect data."[282] Such optimism was not universally shared, however, and in any case quickly dissipated.

The director of MIT's CENIS, and former CIA analyst, Max Millikan lamented the "excessive division of labor between specialists in action and specialists in knowledge" that was emerging already in the early 1960s.[283] His Cambridge neighbor Phillip Mosely agreed that "the response of the scholarly community to the vast need is far from adequate."[284] The root of the problem, in the view of political scientist and frequent government consultant Alfred de Grazia, was that most policymakers simply do not accept "the behavioral sciences as a tool of government."[285] To be sure, there was some variation within the U.S. government on this score, with the State Department and the intelligence community being more hostile to the behavioralist approach than the Department of Defense, at least initially.[286] But eventually even proponents of more modern approaches to social science in DDR&E and DARPA had second thoughts about its usefulness.[287]

The reason that policymakers thought that they were not getting what they needed from social science was that they believed that it was increasingly shaped by internal disciplinary considerations rather than the needs of policymakers. According to E. K. Karcher of the Army's Office for Research and Development, "It has long been a matter of discussion whether military research achieves maximum effectiveness when organized strictly in accordance with the content of the research from a disciplinary aspect, or organized around major military operational problems."[288] His preference, and that of many other policymakers, was the latter.

The root of the problem, from their perspective, was that rigor and relevance were often in tension.[289] As their disciplines professionalized, academic social scientists preferred to conduct basic research, confident that its applied implications would trickle down to policymakers without any additional effort on their part. But policymakers were not sanguine about this happening. Indeed, William C. Johnston, an academic who served in the Foreign Service and the United States Information Agency, remarked that "I do not object to what my friends in both the natural sciences and the social sciences call 'pure' research." But he cautioned that "on the other hand, it seems to me that maybe we cannot afford quite as much of it."[290] Millikan rejected the entire distinction between basic and applied research on the grounds that the two are inextricably linked.[291]

Lurking behind academic social science's fixation on basic research was its preoccupation with employing the methods of the natural sciences. This effort to ape the natural sciences undermined their usefulness to policymakers. As Polk observed, "In the social sciences today, particularly in political science, a great deal of attention is being given to methodology. From the perspective of the administrator, this is an 'in-house' problem, as useful to him as is his thought on governmental organization to the scholar."[292] Retired Air Force colonel George Croker agreed, noting that "in altogether too many instances researchers have foreclosed on the possibility of effective utilization of their efforts by attempting overrefined analysis."[293] Max Millikan elaborated at length about how preoccupation with research design and other methodological concerns among academic social scientists widened the gap between them and policymakers: *"All this is complicated by the operator's impression that the researcher is playing with complex intellectual machinery for its own sake. There seems an unnecessary amount of special language, a wearisome spinning-out of definitions, subtle distinctions, and elaborate classifications, and a ponderous amassing of documentation."*[294]

In addition to a preference for the research techniques of the natural science, Millikan also faulted his academic colleagues' commitment to a value-free social science for their estrangement from policy relevance.[295]

After the brief halcyon days of the ONR basic research interregnum, the thrust of DoD social science support became increasingly applied. Initially, much of this research was conducted by behaviorally oriented social scientists.[296] But policymakers' dissatisfaction with their approach to research grew quickly, the result of the very different agendas of the disciplinary social scientists and their erstwhile Defense and service patrons. As an NRC study of DoD support for social science explained, "High-level officials, both in the Department of Defense and in the former Bureau of the Budget, believe that research should be more useful to them than it is. Nonmission-oriented basic research is considered to have lacked policy payoffs and to have constituted both a subsidy to producers and a source of difficulty and irritation with the Congress. Research producers are sometimes viewed as being more interested in furthering their academic disciplines than providing operational help to the Department of Defense. . . . Hypotheses seem to be those generated by their relevance to the discipline rather than to consumers of research and the Department of Defense." The report concluded that "the user-producer relationship has been much less happy. There is substantial evidence . . . that users are very dissatisfied with social science contributions to the solution of policy-planning problems."[297]

Two specific differences, according to the NRC study, were that "social scientists speak in a jargon incomprehensible to layment [*sic*]" and the tendency of "social scientists, 'when faced with a specific problem that has no ready-made conceptual answer . . . frequently [to] retreat to the laboratory for more research and more facts . . . [when] the client would ordinarily settle for less than a scientifically adequate answer."[298] The larger problem was that academic disciplinary agendas were driving the social sciences to embrace quantitative research approaches that many policymakers thought inappropriate on the grounds that they were simply not applicable to high-level policy decisions.[299] Also, increasing disciplinarity among the social sciences undermined the interdisciplinary approaches that many policymakers regarded as essential for answering the questions they posed.[300] The net effect was to produce social science research that national security policymakers thought was "often irrelevant."[301]

Conclusions

In sum, this chapter makes three points: First, the Cold War saw continuing, if uneven, interest among U.S. national security policymakers in using social science. Second, despite this continuing interest, there was just below the surface an undercurrent of dissatisfaction with academic social science as it became more oriented to producing basic, as opposed to applied, research. Finally, this led to an ongoing search by national security policymakers for alternative arrangements through which to tap social science expertise. What early Cold War national security policymakers wanted was social science that was accessible to the layman, struck a balance of theory and practice, and engaged the key policy problems they were grappling with.[302]

In the next two chapters we will look more closely at two of the most important national security policy areas in which government officials sought to tap social science expertise: nuclear strategy and statecraft, and political development and counterinsurgency. Each illustrates how war or international crisis leads to greater interest on both ends of the bridge between the Ivory Tower and the Beltway in marshaling social science in support of national security policymaking. They also reveal, though, that disciplinary dynamics invariably reassert themselves when the threat seems to wane with the consequence of encouraging scholars to privilege models and methods over practical application. This often leads to a disengagement with practical policy, as scholars pursue basic, rather than applied, research. Sometimes such scholarship can also produce suboptimal (nuclear war-fighting doctrines) or even catastrophic (coercive bombing and counterinsurgency) policies. Not coincidentally, the two central figures in these chapters—Thomas Schelling and Walt Rostow—were both economists. In their quest to craft a science of strategy they would in different ways reopen both aspects of the relevance question.

TABLE 5.7. The Pattern of the Waxing and Waning of Security Studies during the Cold War

Period	Threat environment	Status of security studies
The nuclear revolution	↑↓	Dead end of strategy
The Vietnam War	↑↓	Quagmire

Appendix. An Inventory of Federal Research in the Behavioral Sciences: National Security Social Science Funders

Executive Office of the President[303]
CIA (mostly through DoS/INR/XR)
Office of Emergency Planning ($200–500k = $200k annually to NAS)

DoD
ASD for Civil Defense ($800k)
Systems Evaluation Division
ASD Installations and Logistics
Logistics Management Institute
Defense Documentation Center

Department of the Army
Continental Army Command, Deputy CoS for Combat Development, Combat Operations Group
Chief of Military History
Defense Logistics Studies Information Exchange
Office of the Chief of Research and development, Director of Plans and Management, Management Division
Director of Plans and Management, Manpower and Personnel Division
Director of Plans and Management, Programs and Analysis Division
Director of Army Research, Human Resources Research Office ($2.3 million/yr.)
Mathematics Research Center
Research Analysis Corporation ($1 million/year)
Special Operations Research Office ($400k/year)
U.S. Army Personnel Research Office ($1 million/year)
U.S. Army Personnel Research Office, Combat Systems Research Laboratory
U.S. Army Personnel Research Office, Evaluation Research Laboratory
U.S. Army Personnel Research Office, Military Selection Research Laboratory
U.S. Army Personnel Research Office, Support Systems Research Laboratory

Army Material Command, Neuropsychiatry and Psychophysiology
    Research Branch
Programs and Management Office
Neuropsychiatry and Psychophysiology Research Branch, Walter
    Reed Army Medical Research Laboratory
Quartermaster Corps, Institute of Heraldry

Department of the Air Force
USAF total ($7.2 million/year)
Air Training Command
Office of Aerospace research, Office of Scientific Research, Directorate
    of Life Sciences, Behavioral Sciences Division ($1.2 million/year)
Deputy Chief of Staff for Research and Technology, Director of
    Development Planning ($13.8 million including RAND)
Systems Command ($3.2 million)
Systems Command, Aeronautical Systems Division
Field Stations, USAF Special Weapons Center
Deputy Chief of Staff for Systems and Logistics, Assistant for Logistic
    Planning

Department of the Navy
U.S. Navy, Bureau of Medicine and Surgery, U.S. Naval Medical
    Neuropsychiatric Research Unit
Bureau of Naval Personnel, Personnel Analysis Division
Bureau of Supplies and Accounts, Assistant Chief of Research and
    Development, Systems Research Division
Marine Corps, Operational Research and Development Program
Office of Naval Research ($9 million/year)

DoS
Department of State, Bureau of Educational and Cultural Affairs, Plans
    and Development Staff ($13 million/year)
Foreign Social Science Research Program
Bureau of Intelligence and Research ($3.4 million/year)
INR/XR ($100k/year)
ACDA ($1 million/year)

Nondepartmental Federal Agencies
Selective Service System

U.S. Congress
House Foreign Affairs Committee
Senate Foreign Relations Committee
Legislative Reference Service

6

The Scientific Strategists Follow the Economists to an Intellectual Dead End

Since nuclear strategy first opened the door for the civilian Cold War defense intellectuals to peddle their policy wares in the halls of power, this issue is a good one to explore when and under what conditions academic social science influences policy. "Academic strategists" such as Bernard Brodie, Albert Wohlstetter, Herman Kahn, William Kaufman, and especially Thomas Schelling reputedly exercised such influence that the period between 1945 and 1961 is regarded as the "golden age" of academic national security studies.[1] Brodie himself boasted that "it is no exaggeration to say that all the distinctively modern concepts of military strategy, most of which have been embraced by the military services themselves, have evolved out of [the] ranks [of the 'scientific strategists']."[2] Former RAND staffer Roman Kolkowicz claimed that "the deterrence paradigm, developed by the defense intellectuals in the 1950s and 1960s, provided the central methodological concept for the management of nuclear strategy."[3] Even Air Force Chief of Staff general Thomas White, a skeptic of civilian defense intellectuals in general, grudgingly conceded that some of them knew more than he did about nuclear policy issues.[4]

Many later scholars agree. "All the fundamental ideas about nuclear strategy came from civilians," in Robert Jervis's estimate.[5] Retired army general and former University of Pittsburgh provost Wesley Posvar cautioned that "the impact of this work [by academic strategists] is so great that any serious new study which treats of the present military situation in international politics, including the whole fields of deterrence and arms control, must take account of it."[6] Even a root-and-branch critic of American academic strategists such as British scientist P.M.S. Blackett ruefully admitted that their "writings have had a rather big influence."[7]

To be sure, not everyone is convinced that there really was such a Golden Age. Pointing to the divergence between U.S. nuclear declaratory policy (in which defense intellectuals apparently had influence through the theory of mutual assured destruction) and actual operational doctrine and war plans (where in his view they did not because operational doctrine continually emphasized nuclear war fighting), historian Bruce Kuklick presented the most sustained critique of this conventional wisdom.[8] According to his account, "The men who actually made decisions were least concerned with *scientific* ideas of any sort" and the ideas of strategists had "little causal impact," save perhaps as *ex post facto* rationalizations for policymakers' decisions.[9]

This chapter shows that the Golden Age theorists did in fact have some influence but that it waxed and then waned during the Cold War.[10] Further, it began to decline even before the Vietnam War, which most people blame for the estrangement of scholars and policymakers. Rather than just political conflict over Vietnam (which certainly reinforced this trend of scholarly disengagement from policy), the growing Beltway–Ivory Tower gap was deeply rooted in intellectual developments within the academy—the privileging of complex methods and universal models over engaging substantive issues—which reduced the policy relevance of the work of many academic defense intellectuals. Two factors favor that explanation: the first is timing. The estrangement began well before the Vietnam War became a major sore spot on campus. The second is process: policymakers complained that social scientists' increasing preoccupation with abstract models and sophisticated methods undermined their usefulness.[11] What led to that, I maintain, was their growing embrace of economic approaches to nuclear strategy in an effort to turn it into a "science."

The increasingly abstract and methodologically fixated character of late Golden Age "scientific" theories of nuclear strategy would eventually lead to what historian Marc Trachtenberg characterized as an intellectual "dead end": nuclear theory had lost contact with concerns of policymakers and became increasingly driven by internal academic concerns. This resulted, in his view, from the fact that "the most basic issues were [at that point] analyzed on a very abstract level. One could work out in general terms the argument for 'strategic stability,' or for various nuclear war-fighting strategies. But at this level of abstraction there were no final answers—at this highly abstract level of conceptualization the most basic intellectual tensions could not be resolved."[12]

The end of the Golden Age is thus a cautionary tale for subsequent generations of nuclear scholars, some of whom in their effort to recreate a "science" of strategy seem once again to be emulating the methods and approaches of economics that brought academic nuclear strategy to a dead end.[13] To be sure, sophisticated social scientific methods and universal models are not necessarily incompatible with policy-relevant scholarship; rather, when they are employed without attention to their appropriateness for the concrete question at hand and pursued for internal disciplinary reasons such as theoretical elegance or congruence with our preferred image of what a "science" should be, they are not very helpful to policymakers. Further, when such approaches on occasion influence policy, their effects can be pernicious, which then further exacerbates the tensions between rigor and relevance.

This chapter proceeds in four sections: its first task is to establish whether nuclear strategists in fact had any influence on nuclear strategy. Having established that they did, at least early on, it attributes their waning influence to their effort to craft a "science of strategy" modeled on economics. Scientific strategists, particularly Thomas Schelling, reached a dead end by privileging internal disciplinary concerns like logical rigor and the use of sophisticated methods over addressing concrete policy problems. Moreover, it then argues that Schelling's effort to craft a general science of nuclear strategy led him to overreach and apply it to conventional coercive bombing operations in Vietnam. The failure of policies based on his models played a significant role in discrediting the whole enterprise of academic strategy. I conclude with some lessons from the Golden Age about how to avoid ending up in an intellectual cul-de-sac for today's aspiring scientific nuclear strategists.

The Waxing of the Golden Age of Civilian Nuclear Strategists

Two related events at the end of the Second World War set the stage for the longest peacetime period of national security policy cooperation between social scientists and the U.S. government. These were the invention of the atomic bomb and its use against Japan in the last weeks of the war and then the outbreak of the Cold War two years later. Not surprisingly given Yale University's role in producing policy-relevant defense analysis during the Second World War, the initial locus for thinking about the implications of the "nuclear revolution" was at its Institute for International Studies (IIS).[14] There, political scientist Bernard Brodie first argued that the development of these weapons would fundamentally change the nature of international relations.

For much of history, in Brodie's view, military force had been a *useful* instrument of statecraft. But with the advent of nuclear weapons and their proliferation among a number of great powers, only the *threat* of force remained available to statesmen because the actual use of nuclear weapons by two nuclear armed states would be mutually catastrophic. "Thus far the chief purpose of our military establishment has been to win wars," he explained, but "from now on its chief purpose must be to avert them. It can have almost no other useful purpose."[15] Brodie anticipated that the development of the H-bomb would permanently tilt the cost/benefit ratio against war.[16] It was, in fact, Brodie's mentor University of Chicago economist Jacob Viner who drew the logical implication of his student's argument that nuclear weapons were only useful for deterrence.[17] All these ideas crystalized in a volume of essays Brodie edited for IIS entitled *The Absolute Weapon* which established the contributors as the country's leading experts on nuclear strategy, their services much in demand in government and the military.[18]

Because they were so revolutionary, nuclear weapons would not remain the exclusive purview of the uniformed military. It was, after all, natural scientists, many with academic affiliations, who had invented the bomb in the first place. It was therefore not surprising that civilian social scientists, some of whom remained in the academy while others migrated to intellectual halfway houses like the new RAND Corporation, played the key role in clarifying their effects on statecraft.[19] Civilians could stake their claim in the nuclear realm because, as RAND economist and later Department of Defense comptroller Alain Enthoven told one Air Force general, "I have fought just as many nuclear wars as you have."[20] Brodie added a second rationale: in a world of MAD (mutual assured destruction), only prewar political decisions really mattered, which were squarely in the area of civilian expertise.[21]

In addition to Yale, social scientists at other universities were consulted by policymakers about nuclear strategy. The staff of the Weapon System Evaluation Group, for example, an organization established in 1948 to advise the Secretary of Defense and the Joint Chiefs of Staff on the various technical aspects of weapons systems, reached out to MIT professor Max Millikan and a group of eight other social scientists to solicit their views on how many casualties the United States would have to inflict in order to break the Soviets' will to continue to wage war. Not surprisingly, they concluded that this was not a question that could be answered with mathematical precision.[22] From December 1950 throughout 1951, Brodie himself served directly as an advisor to Air Force Chief of Staff general Hoyt Vandenberg helping the Air Force select Soviet targets. He was, in fact, the first civilian to review the U.S. emergency war plan.[23]

To be sure, all was not sweetness and light in the groves of post–World War II academe. Dissension among the defense intellectuals themselves undercut their influence on nuclear strategy.[24] Brodie was slated to conduct a major study of nuclear targeting for Vandenberg but was "abruptly terminated" before it was completed after Edward Mead Earle reportedly blackballed him with Secretary of the Air Force Thomas Finletter.[25] But it was the reemerging postwar intellectual tensions between scholarly rigor and policy relevance that were the major obstacle to sustained cooperation. As a result of more widespread lack of enthusiasm among universities for doing policy-relevant national security research, interest grew in finding an alternative way to marshal civilian intellectual resources for the Cold War.[26] One of the most important mechanisms policymakers created to do so was the Federally-Funded Research and Development Center (FFRDC), of which the RAND Corporation was the acme in the national security realm.

Perhaps RAND's most important national security research involved how the United States ought to think about nuclear strategy once the Soviet Union developed its own nuclear capability. While a number of RAND analysts studied this issue, the most influential was Albert Wohlstetter, later a professor of political science at the University of Chicago.[27] A trained mathematician, Wohlstetter was a man of broad interests, ranging from business to the philosophy of science. During the Second World War, he served in diverse branches of the U.S. government from the War Production Board to the National Housing Agency. Wohlstetter's first project for RAND was his famous "basing study" which analyzed how the Strategic Air Command's (SAC) dependence on a small number of air bases might make it vulnerable to a Soviet first strike, thus eliminating a large part of the United States' nuclear arsenal. While he struggled to get SAC to concede this vulnerability, Fred Kaplan concluded that in the end Wohlstetter's study "finally led SAC to reduce its dependency on elaborate overseas bases. . . . There is no question that the Wohlstetter study helped reduce this reliance."[28] RAND historian Bruce Smith concurred that the basing study eventually led to Air Force policy shifts after an Air Staff committee signed off on its recommendations.[29]

Wohlstetter's second contribution to U.S. nuclear strategy was the research that led up to his famous January 1959 *Foreign Affairs* article "The Delicate Balance of Terror," in which he argued that the United States could not depend on the continuing invulnerability of its nuclear deterrent.[30] Wohlstetter's analysis of the vulnerability of U.S. intercontinental ballistic missiles overcame Air Force skepticism that "hardening" them in concrete silos would serve to mitigate their vulnerability.[31] It not only addressed a pressing policy problem, but the general RAND approach to defense analysis (quantitative data analyzed using sophisticated methods such as operations research or systems analysis), which Wohlstetter epitomized, also raised the bar for strategic analysis both inside and outside of the U.S. government.[32] Still, as Wohlstetter's RAND colleague E. S. Quade cautioned, "In an analysis aimed at policy making, the relevance of the many factors and contingencies affecting the problem is more important than sophisticated analytical technique."[33]

While a number of academics including Henry Kissinger and Robert Osgood questioned the Eisenhower administration's policy of "massive retaliation," the most trenchant critic of the strategy of relying solely on nuclear weapons to deter a conventional Soviet attack was Princeton University (and later MIT) political scientist William Kaufmann.[34] Like Wohlstetter, Kaufmann had an eclectic background that included Yale, Wall Street, and wartime service in the U.S. Army. His Princeton Center for International Studies report "The Requirements of Deterrence" landed the "critical blow" in the public debate about whether to rely exclusively on the threat of nuclear retaliation to deter a Soviet conventional attack on Western Europe.[35] It attracted the attention of Hans Speier, the new head of the RAND social science division, for whom Kaufmann began doing summer consulting. His recommendation that the United States engage in a build-up of its conventional forces not only appealed to the bureaucratic interest of the U.S. Army but also became a major plank in Senator John F. Kennedy's Presidential campaign platform.[36]

The other result of Kaufmann's work was to spur interest in the use of strategic nuclear forces to limit damage from the Soviets' nuclear arsenal. Counterforce was a response not only to the growing problem of the credibility of the United States' extended deterrent in Europe, but also represented a possible means for limiting damage and avoiding bloody countervalue exchanges against cities and population centers.[37] Kaufmann's work was influential not only among defense intellectuals, but also in the U.S. Air Force, where it was viewed as a potent bureaucratic weapon in its war against the

U.S. Navy, whose Submarine Launched Ballistic Missiles (SLBMs) were not yet accurate enough to conduct such strikes.[38] The peak of his influence would come when Secretary of Defense Robert McNamara would announce his "no cities" doctrine in two speeches, one in Athens, Greece, and the other Ann Arbor, Michigan, in 1962.[39]

So what can we conclude about the influence of these civilian strategists during the Golden Age? Kuklick observed concerning the irrelevance of civilian theories of the nuclear revolution and MAD that they were not reflected in the military's actual war plans and operational doctrine. But some writings of defense intellectuals, such as Wohlstetter's, did have a direct impact there. Also, the neat distinction between military/nuclear war fighting and civilians/MAD breaks down as some civilians like Kaufmann and Thomas Schelling also came to advocate war-fighting strategies subsequently evident in these plans. But most importantly, evidence that academic notions of MAD were not reflected in actual war plans and military doctrine hardly constitutes proof that these ideas were irrelevant.

To begin with, some policymakers and later scholars find evidence that MAD was a significant part of U.S. doctrine at least between 1960 and 1974.[40] Moreover, looking at doctrine, war plans, and force posture for evidence of civilian influence is seductive because these things are concrete and relatively clear. But doing so ignores the many nonstrategic factors that shape them.[41] In addition, it overlooks the possibility that even though the ideas of the civilian strategists did not influence the military, they could influence presidents' understandings of the impact of the nuclear revolution.[42] Jervis, for example, conceded that for "most of the history of American doctrine and war planning has been the attempt to design substitutes for damage limitation." But he went on to suggest that "the influence of the fear of war on political leaders is not sensitive to the details of doctrine and war planning that preoccupy the specialists . . . [because] mutual vulnerability exists and casts an enormous shadow. This condition is not subtle nor does it depend on the details of the strategic balance or targeting that may loom large to academics or war planners; such details are dwarfed in the eyes of decision makers by the danger of overwhelming destruction."[43]

Even President Eisenhower, the architect of massive retaliation, rejected the notion that the United States could fight a nuclear war, once remarking that "you can't have this kind of war. There just aren't enough bulldozers to scrape the bodies off the streets." Endorsing a version of MAD, Eisenhower believed that, "until an enemy [has] enough operational capability to destroy most of our bases simultaneously and thus prevent retaliation by us, our deterrence remains effective."[44] He took this position at a time during which the United States had for all practical purposes a nuclear monopoly, at least in terms of deliverable weapons. And the U.S. military's preferred strategy at the time was SAC's "air-atomic strategy," which envisioned fighting and winning a nuclear war.[45]

This attitude persisted into the Kennedy and Johnson administrations. As the Soviet ability to inflict damage on the United States grew, the Kennedy administration flirted with counterforce, war-fighting strategies. To be sure, Trachtenberg and others have documented that U.S. policymakers were never completely comfortable with MAD and they continually explored doctrines and force postures to escape it, or at least provide an alternative to all-out nuclear war should one occur.[46] These experiments included flexible response and "no cities."[47] Despite these strategic dalliances, Kennedy and other senior national security policymakers eventually gravitated back to MAD.[48] Indeed, at a time when the United States still enjoyed massive if not complete nuclear superiority, the Joint Chiefs of Staff, told the president that a U.S. first strike was unlikely to eliminate the Soviet Union's ability to "strike back hard."[49] Deputy National Security Advisor Carl Kaysen confirmed that by "'61 Kennedy had already come to the conclusion that McNamara had come to by '63, namely that 'superiority' really didn't mean anything and the difference between superiority and parity or near parity was not significant; that you could never get a force that would do anything much for you beyond deterrence."[50] Or as McNamara himself reported, *"nuclear weapons serve no military purpose whatsoever. They are totally useless—except only to deter one's opponent from using them.* This is my view today. It was my view in the early 1960s. At that time, in long private conversations with successive Presidents—Kennedy and Johnson—I recommended, without qualification, that they never initiate, under any circumstances, the use of nuclear weapons. I believe they accepted my recommendation."[51] McNamara informed Paul Nitze in 1962 that "the concept of a 'worsened relative military position after a general nuclear war' is not a meaningful one to me when each side has the capacity to destroy each other's civilization."[52] This no doubt explains why, in the words of former Kennedy White House staffer Marcus Raskin, "most of the people who actually made high policy thought that planning for nuclear war was merely an exercise in the theory of annihilation, that it could have no practical consequences."[53] In other words, there is good evidence that MAD provided the theoretical compass and mental map that guided policymakers through the forest of the nuclear age even if they did not always follow it consistently.

Air Force historian Edward Kaplan reminded us that a "committed executive opposition can slow, stop, or even reverse the bureaucratic momentum behind military policy."[54] And nuclear analyst Desmond Ball identified twenty instances since 1945 when U.S. policymakers considered using nuclear weapons but did not despite the existence of these rigid war plans and offensive nuclear doctrines.[55] The reason, in his view, was that "that the pre-planned options in the SIOP are too idealized, that they are a-strategic in the sense that they would be of little relevance in real-life situations."[56] In other words, just because civilian decision makers did not shape the arcane details of the SIOP does not mean that their ideas about nuclear war were by any means irrelevant.

How can we tell if the ideas of the civilian strategists shaped presidential thinking about the nuclear revolution? Could they have not figured out the meaning of the nuclear revolution on their own?[57] There are grounds for believing that some of the civilian strategists provided policymakers with their mental maps for the nuclear age. First, it is widely recognized that the ideas of the civilian strategists were "in the air" during policy debates—both in internal U.S. government discussions but also in many public fora such as popular magazines like *Look, Esquire, The Atlantic Monthly*, and the *Saturday Evening Post*—so there are reasonable grounds for thinking they influenced presidents to think differently from military leaders about nuclear strategy.[58] Second, while we cannot rule out completely the possibility that policymakers came to their understanding of the nuclear revolution independent of both the military and the civilian defense intellectuals, that does not seem like the most likely explanation for how high-level civilian decision makers with little expertise in the issue and lots of other items on their plates came to think about the nuclear revolution.[59] Deputy Assistant Secretary of Defense John McNaughton told his Cambridge colleagues after joining the Kennedy administration that "political decision makers seldom think in extremely sophisticated terms."[60] Some of them already knew that. Reflecting back on his White House years, Kissinger agreed that "the convictions that leaders have formed before reaching high office are the intellectual capital they will consume as long as they continue in office. There is little time for leaders to reflect."[61] It is not unreasonable, therefore, to suppose that the ideas of the civilian defense intellectuals about the nuclear revolution provided the mental roadmap that guided policymakers as they thought about how, or how not, to use them.

Finally, it is true that the U.S. military's nuclear war plans and doctrines did not always reflect civilian theories of mutual assured destruction for much of the Cold War. However, historian David Alan Rosenberg cautioned against making too much of these war plans, pointing out that "through the Truman years, the only basic policy with respect to atomic warfare was NSC-30, 'U.S. Policy on Atomic Warfare,' adopted by the National Security Council (NSC) on September 16, 1948. That policy formally recognized the military's need to plan for the use of nuclear weapons 'in the event of hostilities,' but ultimately left the decision as to how and when such weapons would be employed to the President himself."[62] Kaysen recounted a September 1961 White House meeting on the Single Integrated Operational Plan (SIOP) for nuclear weapons in which the president lambasted Chairman of the Joint Chiefs of staff General Lyman Lemnitzer about the military's hide-bound commitment to a few rigid and prepackaged war plans.[63]

Thomas Schelling: The Laureate of the Scientific Strategists

Among all of the scientific strategists, none is more prominent, at least among his fellow academics, than economist and Nobel laureate Thomas Schelling.[64] His direct involvement in policymaking began with his brief stint at the Bureau of the Budget during the Second World War before attending graduate school in economics at Harvard. After graduating he spent 1948 through 1951 working for the Marshall Plan, largely on foreign aid and economic reform matters. Schelling also spent a year on the staff of RAND Corporation during 1958 and 1959, where he worked largely on national security issues but also devoted some time to thinking and writing about social science methodology, particularly game theory. He spent most of the intervening and subsequent years in academia, first at Yale, next at Harvard, and finally at the University of Maryland, for a time continuing to serve as a consultant to various offices in the U.S. government. This relationship formally ended in the late 1960s, with the most active and influential period of Schelling's consulting in the national security realm having been in the late 1950s and the early 1960s.[65]

While at RAND or serving as a consultant, Schelling's national security-related work focused on four issues: surprise attack and ensuring the survivability of the U.S. nuclear arsenal as Soviet capability grew, arms control and strategic stability, and two related facets of bargaining in war—limited nuclear war and the coercive use of military force. The first two issues were clearly aimed at reinforcing mutual assured destruction;[66] the latter two took him beyond that to explore elements of nuclear war fighting.[67] Indeed,

Schelling saw these two sets of issues as linked: "We usually think of arms control or deterrence as having failed if war breaks out; and so it has, but it can fail worse if we give up at that point. It is not entirely clear that a general war—a war between the USA and the USSR, involving their strategic forces on a large scale—would necessarily be unlimited either in the way it would be fought or in the way it would be concluded."[68] Privately, Schelling told colleagues he did not think a nuclear war would necessarily be an all-out "spasm" war and that "general war needn't be an all out [sic] orgy of destruction."[69] In his view of the state of strategic thinking, the "stability approach" was over and now the most pressing intellectual problem for social science was how to think about "controlled strategic war."[70]

The core of Schelling's approach to the use of military force as an instrument of statecraft was to conceive of it as a subset in the larger process of "bargaining," which he came to, and never left, as a result of his early academic training in economics and his initial policy experience with European economic recovery.[71] In a seminal 1956 essay in *The American Economic Review*, Schelling made two assumptions about bargaining between actors, whether individuals in the market or states in the international system: (1) They would rather strike a deal that gives them something they would not otherwise gain than reach no deal whatsoever; and (2) the key to successful bargaining resides in the ability of one actor to make the other believe that such a deal can only be struck on terms favorable to the former.[72]

While both of these assumptions would prove powerful and productive in the analysis of domestic, economic bargaining, they would not be as successful in analyzing issues in international security affairs.[73] The failure of the first assumption would explain why the application of Schelling's bargaining theories in the coercive air campaign against North Vietnam in 1965 would not persuade Hanoi to cease its support for the Vietcong in South Vietnam. This was clearly a case in which one side—North Vietnam—preferred no deal and war to the one on offer from the United States.

The second assumption would ultimately lead Schelling beyond mutual assured destruction and toward a position that bargaining in the nuclear realm could continue beyond the threshold of nuclear war. As he explained in *The Strategy of Conflict*, "If war to the finish has become inevitable, there is nothing left but pure conflict; but if there is any possibility of avoiding a mutually damaging war, of conducting warfare in a way that minimizes damage, or of coercing an adversary by threatening war rather than waging it, the possibility of mutual accommodation [bargaining] is as important and dramatic as the element of conflict."[74] He would claim that there was far more room for bargaining, even in the midst of a nuclear war, than most people realized.

As Schelling posed it in his later book, *Arms and Influence*, "the problem is to make [a threat] persuasive, to keep it from sounding like a bluff."[75] In his view the key to success for one nuclear actor facing another was for the former to establish a "reputation" such that the credibility of his or her commitment to a preferred position was greater than that of the other side. Whereas in the past, it was the balance of material military capabilities that mattered in explaining which side prevailed in a conflict, Schelling argued that in the nuclear age, when it was likely that both sides could suffer catastrophic damage in an all-out nuclear war, it was the side that demonstrated greater credibility of commitment to its position by showing greater willingness to manipulate risk to gain it that would prevail.

Schelling suggested that actors might need to take some counterintuitive steps to establish such credibility. One of these was to restrict one's own ability to do anything other than what one wants to do. As he later reflected, "I suppose the most elementary and pervasive concept, the one I began playing with before I left graduate school, is that binding oneself, eliminating or penalizing certain options available to oneself, can change another's expectation of what one will do and change that other's decision what to do, to one's own benefit."[76] Schelling chided his dovish Harvard Law School colleague Roger Fisher that "in a world that gets 'more sport out of risk and violence' than we do, there is no effective substitute for the 'willingness of someone concerned to take a risk himself—to take sheer political guts in a difficult problem.'"[77]

Concretely, Schelling recommended that "if national representatives can arrange to be charged with appeasement for every small concession, they place concession visibly beyond their own reach."[78] One example of this was the stationing of a "token" military force as a "plate glass window" that once broken would inexorably draw the United States into a limited war as a means to make credible the threat of waging a larger war in Europe's defense despite the danger of escalation to general nuclear war. Such a symbolic deployment would leave the Soviet Union with "the last clear chance" to avoid disaster and so bolster the credibility of the U.S. commitment to defend NATO.

This paradoxical approach was one in which "bargaining 'strength' inheres in what is weakness by other standards."[79] Stated another way, "the supreme objective may not be to *assure* that [war with another superpower] stays limited, but rather to keep the risk of all-out war within moderate limits *above zero.*"[80] This was his logic of the manipulation of risk, "not the risk that the United States will *decide* on all-out war, but the risk that war will occur whether intended or not."[81] Watching President Kennedy's October 22, 1962, Cuban Missile Crisis address with his Harvard and MIT colleagues, Schelling mused that "the Alliance as a whole is stronger when the US is less flexible."[82]

Another approach Schelling advocated to solve the credibility problem in an era of mutual vulnerability was for one side to take a series of actions in other areas or issues to bolster its credibility to defend a major commitment. In *Arms and Influence*, he asserted that "we cannot afford to let the Soviets or Communist Chinese learn by experience that they can grab large chunks of the earth and its population without a genuine risk of violent Western reaction."[83] Schelling's rationale for a global vision of commitment was his assumption of their interdependence: "Essentially we tell the Soviets that we have to react here [Vietnam] because, if we did not, they would not believe us when we say that we will react there [Europe]."[84] By taking military action in third areas, and with lower levels of force, "there is an opportunity to demonstrate [to the adversary] on the first few transgressions that the threat will be carried out on the rest."[85]

How did Schelling initially manage to be so influential among policymakers, particularly given his commitments to cutting-edge social science methods and abstract models? First, he focused on issues that policymakers were already engaged with. One such issue was how to ensure the viability of our nuclear deterrent given the growing Soviet nuclear arsenal of the late 1950s and early 1960s. "It is not the 'balance'—the sheer equality or symmetry in the situation—that constitutes mutual deterrence," he pointed out, but rather "it is the *stability* of the balance. The balance is stable only when neither, in striking first, can destroy the other's ability to strike back."[86] The challenge, given this vulnerability, was how to configure and use our forces so as to be able to withstand a surprise attack and still threaten a robust second strike. Schelling also explored how to credibly extend America's nuclear umbrella over its allies given its growing vulnerability to a Soviet second strike. As he framed the problem, "There is a large 'third area' in which we wish to deter Russian aggression by a threat more credible than that of mutual suicide."[87] Whether his proposed solutions to this credibility problem are convincing is another matter, but there can be little doubt that he touched on a pressing concern to national security policymakers.

In 1957 he took up a suggestion, first floated two years earlier in the *Manchester Guardian*, that NATO eschew nuclear first use against the Warsaw Pact's cities in the interest of encouraging the Soviets to do the same.

Schelling believed that it was *"possible* to find limits to [nuclear] war" and recommended a "no cities" doctrine as unilateral policy for the United States.[88] This proposal was briefed to incoming Secretary of Defense Robert McNamara by Schelling's RAND colleague Kaufmann on February 10, 1961. McNamara's biographer Deborah Shapley maintained that it was "clearly derived from the theories of bargaining and escalation, which economists and mathematicians at Rand and elsewhere had developed in the previous decade."[89] Since in his otherwise incisive and influential critique of the Eisenhower strategy of "massive retaliation," Kaufmann did not offer the "no cities" option as a potential solution to the credibility problem with extended deterrence in an era of mutual vulnerability (focusing instead on conventional deterrence and demonstrating credibility of commitment by opposing Communist encroachments wherever they occurred around the world), it seems highly likely that he picked up the "no cities" idea from other RAND colleagues, particularly Schelling.[90] Historian Campbell Craig reasonably concluded that "McNamara was imposing upon the military policy of the West Schelling's thesis that a direct war with the Soviet Union, even a nuclear war, could be controlled, restrained, manipulated, and eventually won."[91]

Schelling himself applied his bargaining theory to the Berlin Crisis in a five-page memorandum that made its way with President Kennedy to his weekend retreat in Hyannis Port, Massachusetts, in the summer of 1961. In it, he argued that "the role of nuclears in Europe should not be to win a grand nuclear campaign, but to pose a higher level of risk to the enemy. . . . We should plan for a war of nerve, of demonstration, and of bargaining, not of tactical target destruction." This was, in his view, "an argument for a selective and threatening use of nuclears rather than large-scale tactical use." National Security Advisor McGeorge Bundy subsequently reported that it made a "deep impression" on the president.[92]

Another key to Schelling's initial influence was his close association with individuals who "bridge[d] the gap" between the worlds of ideas and policymaking. He had many contacts with Kennedy national security officials, including McGeorge Bundy and Walt Rostow. In the McNamara Pentagon, his main contact was his Harvard colleague McNaughton, an expert on the law of evidence, who served successively as deputy assistant secretary of defense for International Security Affairs (Arms Control), general counsel for the Department of Defense, and prior to his death in the summer of 1967 as assistant secretary of defense for International Security Affairs where for a time he was McNamara's point man on Vietnam.[93] Schelling and McNaughton's professional and personal association went back at least to 1949. In his diary, McNaughton noted that he met Schelling and his wife at a seminar on "Structural Disequilibrium" at the Economic Cooperation Administration in Paris on November 30, 1949. They would subsequently see each other professionally and socially almost every week for the next year while working at the ECA and living in Paris.[94]

During the late 1950s and early 1960s, they were colleagues at Harvard and participated together in the Harvard-MIT Joint Seminar on Arms Control (JSAC). JSAC had its origins in a 1960 American Academy summer study on arms control held at MIT's Endicott House. Following up JSAC's success, the Rockefeller Foundation agreed to support an ongoing seminar series on the subject.[95] JSAC was not just a typical faculty seminar. It aimed to bridge the gap between the academic and policy worlds, with seminar members carrying "out an increasing regime of consultation with government bodies and public speeches and appearances at panels and forums."[96] A number of its members in addition to McNaughton would also find their way down to Washington. These included McGeorge Bundy (national security adviser), Abram Chayes (State Department legal adviser), Lincoln Gordon (ambassador to Brazil), Walt Rostow (deputy national security advisor, director of the State Department's Policy Planning Staff, and then national security advisor), Henry Rowen (DASD/ISA), Jerome Wiesner (special assistant to the president for Science and Technology), Arthur Barber (deputy assistant secretary of defense for Arms Control), and Richard Barnet (Arms Control and Disarmament Agency).[97] Table 6.1 records McNaughton's JSAC attendance, the topics discussed, and his position at the time.

According to their mutual friend and colleague Morton Halperin, Schelling first suggested to Paul Nitze, the assistant secretary of defense for International Security Affairs, that he take on McNaughton as an arms control expert during the latter's sabbatical year 1961–62.[98] During McNaughton's time in U.S. government, he and Schelling met almost seventy times, mostly in the Pentagon. McNaughton got Schelling a security clearance and brought him on as a consultant for several projects between 1962 and 1966.[99] One of the most important was a major study Schelling did for ISA (McNaughton) and the Policy Planning Council (Rostow) on "Strategic Developments Over the Next Decade." Schelling presented it to an interagency group meeting in Quantico, Virginia, and it was subsequently slated to be the subject of a White House conference at Camp David in October 1962.[100] Ironically, the real world Cuban Missile Crisis would preempt this theoretical discussion of nuclear strategy.

TABLE 6.1. John McNaughton's Attendance at Joint Seminar on Arms Control (1961–66)

Date	Topic/Readings	Position
2/6/61	Arms control/Thomas Schelling, Fred Iklé, and Morton Halperin	Harvard Law
2/20/61	First- vs. second-strike/Herman Kahn and Jeremey Rivkin	Harvard Law
3/20/61	Disarmament/Grenville Clark and Herman Kahn	Harvard Law (discussant)
4/10/61	Soviet attitudes toward arms control/ Richard Barnet	Harvard Law
5/8/61	Stability of total disarmament/Thomas Schelling	Harvard Law
5/22/61	Influence of civilian arms control theory on U.S. defense policy/ Kennedy FY 1962 budget message	Harvard Law
10/16/61	Disengagement of U.S. from Europe/ various plans	DASD/ISA/AC
11/19/62	No Cities/Thorton Read and Morton Halperin	GC/DoD: Just prior to 12/18 speech at Michigan which would subsequently be published in *JCR*
4/8/63	Dual-use nuclear technology/no reading	GC/DoD
10/14/63	Limited Test Ban Treaty/no reading	GC/DoD (McNaughton and Carl Kaysen presented)
1/12/66	Vietnam/no reading	ASD/ISA (Discussion led by Henry Kissinger)*

Source: Rapporteurs' Reports for JSAC for the years 1961 through 1966 at UAV 462.1142.3, Harvard University Archives.

* The Rapporteur's report for that session notes that McNaughton was in attendance but records no remarks by him. In his Diary, however, he later recorded that "At the *Arms Control Seminar* that night, the main lesson was that most of the brethren assume that a compromise must be reached. No one argues that we should drive the VC 'back to North Vietnam.'" Asheley Smith, transcriber, "Unclassified Personal Diary of John T. McNaughton," January 1, 1966–April 22, 1967, 7.

A concrete example of Schelling's influence was his role in shaping McNaughton's thinking about not targeting cities with nuclear weapons. Admittedly, Schelling's conception of a "no cities" nuclear strategy was not identical with the counterforce aspects of Flexible Response.[101] He emphasized unilateral restraint leading both sides to spare cities in war; in contrast, the counterforce strategy in Flexible Response came to be more oriented toward reducing civilian damage by degrading the adversary's nuclear capability.[102] Still, the similarities between the two are greater than the differences, making credible the attribution of Schelling's intellectual influence on it. Indeed, being perhaps less than fully candid about his significant role in McNaughton's 1963 essay in the *Journal of Conflict Resolution*, Schelling subsequently cited it as evidence that at least some Kennedy administration officials fully shared his version of "no cities."[103] While the piece has no footnotes, phrases such as the "reciprocal fear of surprise attack," the title of chapter 9 of Schelling's *The Strategy of Conflict*, are in quotation marks and the essay clearly reflects Schelling's influence.[104] This should not be surprising given that Schelling served as a consultant to McNaughton's office, visiting at least thirty times in 1962 alone.[105] As table 6.1 indicates, McNaughton was thoroughly familiar with Schelling's work from JSAC.

Second, while Schelling was an early innovator in the development and application of game theory to policy issues, he tended not to employ its most abstruse and highly mathematical versions in his national security work.[106] He would later reflect "that some of the very best game theory I ever did didn't use any paraphernalia—no matrices or anything of the sort. It was just a way of thinking about a problem."[107] When he was recognized in 2005 with the Bank of Sweden Prize in Memory of Alfred Nobel "for having deepened our understanding of conflict and cooperation through game-theoretic analysis," he confessed to being "surprised and somewhat perplexed" given that "what I did was not recognizable as game theory."[108] His explanation for why the science of strategy was "retarded" was not its lack of quantification. "My own view is that the present deficiencies are not in the mathematics, and that the theory of strategy has suffered from too great a willingness of social scientists to treat the subject as though it were, or should be, solely a branch of mathematics."[109]

Finally, Schelling saw theory and policy as inextricably linked. His objective was to produce "theory mainly inspired by the need to understand actual situations and problems and aimed at developing unifying interpretations of conflict behavior." In fact, he foresaw "no great division between those who develop theory and those who hope to use it in its applications."[110] He confirmed in the preface to *The Strategy of Conflict* that his "motivation for the purer theory came almost exclusively from preoccupation with (and fascination with) 'applied' problems; and the clarification of theoretical ideas was absolutely dependent on an identification of live examples."[111] He was naturally drawn to the concerns of policymakers, even though his primary focus was on theory. Schelling sought to develop theory that was "easily accessible and readily communicated once it had been developed [rather] than an esoteric theory that requires specialized technical skills and a large investment in learning before it yields up its treasure."[112] He was also willing to present it to policymakers in short, jargon-free memoranda and was comfortable with other traditional modes of government communication such as policy briefings.

Economics Led Nuclear Strategy to an Intellectual Dead End

Many analysts agree that the Golden Age came to an end roughly coincident with the Vietnam War.[113] Most also think that this was no coincidence. The political fallout from the war thus seems a sufficient explanation for the demise of the scientific strategists. But was Vietnam the only reason for the estrangement of academics from policy relevant issues like nuclear strategy? As we saw previously, there was evidence of increasing intellectual tensions between academia and government well before Vietnam. The establishment of RAND and other FFRDCs was in fact a response to the growing difficulty in working with social scientists at universities directly.

One cause of this was the increasing influence of the economic approach to social science in general and strategy in particular. As Trachtenberg explained, "There was an intellectual vacuum in the whole national security area. The economists, and people heavily influenced by their style of thinking, were for a variety of reasons drawn to this vacuum. What they had was something very general, a way of approaching issues, rather than anything that in itself suggested substantive answers that went right to the heart of the strategic problem."[114] "What was new," Eliot Cohen agreed, "was not the use of numbers or equations to help solve military problems but rather the coronation of one social science—Economics—as the rightful queen of war planning and strategy."[115]

Brodie had initially believed that strategy could become a "science" and that economics provided the model for it.[116] And as economics came to dominate strategic analysis, method and theory became increasingly more important than substance. Reviewing Kaufmann's book *The McNamara Strategy*, Brodie enthused that "what is novel about the modern type of [defense] analysis is the marvelous development and refinement of the *method* and also the conscious and open dedication to the effort."[117]

This early confidence among civilian strategists about their ability to forge a "science" of strategy eventually gave way to second thoughts, however.[118] In a 1966 letter to James Holland of the Army War College, Brodie confessed that he was a "trifle uneasy" about his early call to make strategy a science modeled on the methods of economics: "I must tell you," he wrote, "that I am not so disposed today as I was then to toss so many bouquets to the economists. It is not the substance of what I say in that paper that bothers me so much as the tone. I am concerned with the fact that the relevant political issues tend to be automatically de-emphasized by giving so much emphasis to the comparability of strategy with economics."[119] As Brodie later reflected, "Elegance of *method* is indeed marvelously seductive, even when it is irrelevant or inappropriate to the major problems."[120] Moreover, there was growing recognition that whereas economics dealt with easily quantifiable measures such as money, international relations and national security affairs did not.[121] While some of the material elements of "power" could be quantified, many of the other nonmaterial aspects of it could not. By the early-1960s there was growing evidence that the economic approach to strategic thought in the United States had reached something of an intellectual dead end.

Specifically, as they succumbed to the seduction of elegant models and sophisticated methods, many of the Golden Age nuclear strategists also lost touch with the practical concerns of policymakers.[122] Typical of their responses to this increasingly academic approach to strategy was Bundy's lament that "there is enough, and perhaps too much, analysis aimed at scholarly rigor and scientific validity. There is enough and perhaps too much system-building in which models of this or that political process are constructed. . . . What there is not enough of yet, and what I come to praise, is the kind of academic work which proceeds from the same center of concern as that of the man who is himself committed to an active part in government."[123] The policymakers "center of concern" was the concrete policy problems they faced. But the increasing dominance of economic approaches to nuclear strategy led the field to privilege academic concerns.

No single individual better epitomizes the promise and the limits of the effort to make strategy a science through the application of economic theories and methods than Schelling. Given his deep engagement with national security affairs during the 1950s and early 1960s, Schelling seems to contradict my argument about the tension between theoretical elegance and methodological rigor, on the one side, and policy relevance on the other. He was simultaneously theoretically oriented; methodologically rigorous, at least on the model of economics; and he was, at least initially, quite policy relevant and sometimes influential. But as often had been the case in the past, the tension between theoretical elegance and methodological rigor and policy relevance could be managed, at least for a time, but never fully resolved. And when push came to shove, Schelling the economist prevailed over Schelling the policy analyst. The result was that his policy recommendations became less and less persuasive to policymakers and some of those they actually applied turned out to be catastrophic failures because the assumptions they made about bargaining behavior were not universally applicable in the security realm.

Schelling could not permanently suppress the tensions among theoretical elegance, methodological rigor, and policy relevance for three reasons: first, he came to the study of strategy (and every other issue he considered) first and foremost as an economist. And as with most of his academic colleagues, he preferred to apply economic approaches and methods to the problems he engaged, believing them to be more elegant than the alternatives.[124] Echoing Milton Friedman's famous defense of the assumption that individuals and firms behaved "as if" they were rational actors in the market even if they really did not, Schelling cited "the advantage of studying 'strategy' with an eye to theoretical development" not because it was an accurate description of reality but because "the assumption of rational behavior is a productive one. It provides a grip on the subject that is peculiarly conducive to the development of theory."[125]

While Schelling conceded that most economic issues amenable to bargaining needed to "involve divisible objects and compensable activities," the *gestalt* of his presentation was that this approach to bargaining was broadly applicable to many, if not most, national security issues.[126] As he put in the preface to his seminal book *The Strategy of Conflict*, "In the strategy of conflict there are enlightening similarities between, say, maneuvering in limited war and jockeying in a traffic jam, between deterring the Russians and deterring one's own children."[127] Elsewhere he suggested that "it is not only criminals . . . but our own children that have to be deterred."[128] The link, both for good and ill, between Schelling's economic worldview and his policy engagement (not to mention his family life), runs like a red thread throughout his career.

When the tensions between models and methods on the one hand, and practical problems on the other, eventually manifested themselves, he ultimately resolved them in favor of the former. Indeed, in Schelling's view, what had retarded the study of strategy was its exclusive policy focus. "Whether it reflects the scholars' interests or that of the editors," he complained, "the literature on deterrence and related concepts has been mainly preoccupied with solving immediate problems rather than with a methodology for dealing with them."[129] And so when he had to choose, method trumped policy for him.

Finally, Schelling was nothing if not intellectually consistent. But in some instances his predilection for intellectual consistency led him to advocate some paradoxical and counterintuitive policy positions that policymakers found hard to accept. He maintained, for example, that the loss of control or a lack of freedom of choice could be a powerful tool of statecraft.[130] His famous argument about the "rationality of irrationality"—that "it does not always help to be, or to be believed to be, fully rational, cool-headed, and in control of oneself or of one's country"—makes sense in the context of his theory.[131] But few policymakers, even a proponent of the "madman" theory such as Richard Nixon, would actually be comfortable surrendering such control, and not many voters would elect a madman to put his finger on the nuclear button.

Concern about the survivability of America's nuclear deterrent followed logically from Schelling's arguments about the danger of surprise attack undermining strategic stability, but the implication that he drew from this— that the most important vulnerability in the post-Sputnik era was of weapons systems, rather than citizens—would be hard for most people to swallow.[132] Similarly, his nonchalance about the consequences for strategic stability of exotic new weapons such as space-based Fractional Orbital Bombardment Systems (FOBS) was likely not more generally reassuring.[133] And Schelling and other strategists had logically compelling and empirically well-grounded arguments against nuclear disarmament, and in favor of some sorts of arms races, but they were a hard sell not only to the man in the street but also the policymaker inside the beltway.[134]

Schelling's willingness to join not only the fictional Dr. Strangelove but also his real-life RAND colleague Herman Kahn in "thinking the unthinkable" about actually fighting a nuclear war moved his arguments beyond the pale for many policymakers. Like Stanley Kubrick's character General Buck Turgidson, Schelling never denied that we would get our hair mussed in a nuclear war. But his demand that "if we can talk about wars in which tens of millions could be killed thoughtlessly, we ought to be able to talk about wars in which hundreds of thousands might be killed thoughtfully," undoubtedly left many of them cold.[135] In comments on a draft of Schelling's manuscript for *Arms and Influence*, Brodie criticized his cold-bloodedness: "In general, I think you greatly understate the degree to which states, even hostile ones, accommodate to each other, so long as they have an unambiguous desire to avoid war. . . . Notice what you are saying—that both sides 'would choose to fight a major nuclear war' rather than sustain what seems to be mostly a loss of face."[136]

That Schelling was ultimately dissatisfied with MAD was clear as he explicitly staked out his own position in between it and nuclear war fighting.[137] The key assumption that separated him from proponents of MAD was his rejection of the notion that any use of even a handful of nuclear weapons would inevitably escalate to all-out general war. He cavalierly dismissed escalation on the grounds that "there is nothing 'natural' about it."[138] Indeed, his insouciance about the ability of policymakers to manipulate risk under the nuclear shadow was chilling: "Risky behavior is not risky, any more than a threat is risky, if it is credibly brought to the attention of the other side."[139]

In his view, the October 1962 Cuban Missile Crisis was a compelling illustration of his proposition that adroit statesmanship (guided by his theories of coercive bargaining) could advance America's national interests in nuclear crises. He concluded that "realistic negotiation requires an element of threat."[140] That was not, however, the lesson that most American policymakers drew from it. Even McNamara, an early believer in theories of limited and controlled nuclear war, eventually recoiled from it in practice.[141]

Thus, there were clear limits to the influence of civilian scientific strategists like Schelling, particularly when their increasingly arcane theories led them to blur the clear distinction between nuclear and other types of war. Bundy noted that

> there is an enormous gulf between what political leaders really think about nuclear weapons and what is assumed in complex calculations of relative "advantage" in simulated strategic warfare. Think Tank analysts can set levels of "acceptable" damage well up in the tens of millions of lives. They can assume that the loss of dozens of great cities is somehow a real choice for sane men. They are in an unreal world. In the real world of real political leaders . . . a decision that would bring even one hydrogen bomb on one city of one's own country would be recognized in advance as a catastrophic blunder.[142]

German Defense Minister Franz Josef Strauss similarly dismissed post-MAD American strategic thought as "conceptual aids for the precalculation of the inconceivable and incalculable nature of the specific."[143]

To be sure, Schelling, who won The Nobel Prize in economics in 2005, remains highly esteemed in scholarly circles these days. And he undoubtedly made "an original (and very important) contribution to the study of strategy," though it was by applying concepts from economics to the world of strategy.[144] But after reviewing Schelling's contributions to strategy, his intellectual biographer Robert Ayson concluded that he ultimately fell "victim to the sense of unreality which afflicts aspects of nuclear strategy."[145] When Deputy Secretary of Defense Roswell Gilpatric sent Kennedy's military adviser General Maxwell Taylor a 1959 Schelling RAND Paper, America's most intellectual general dismissed it to an aide as "too metaphysical for me."[146] As P.M.S. Blackett put it, Schelling's approach, and that of other game theorists like John von Neumann and Oskar Morgenstern, ultimately failed because it did not "clothe the skeleton conflicts of the theory of games with the complex flesh and blood attributes of real nations; hence the bizarre nature of some of their practical conclusions."[147] Ironically, Schelling's effort to rehabilitate what he dismissed as the "retarded science of international strategy" had the effect of making it autistic in its neglect of political reality.[148]

Schelling himself eventually acknowledged the limits of using domestic bargaining analogies to analyze international conflict between states in the nuclear age.[149] He also conceded that defense politics were not analogous to a market.[150] And as early as in 1963, he lamented that JSAC was losing steam on arms control issues and focusing increasingly on "strategy and foreign policy."[151] As he observed at another JSAC session: "He had himself lost interest in arms control somewhat, and felt that the seminar had been running out of interesting things to do."[152] And by 1964, well before the Vietnam War had begun to weaken the bridge between the Ivory Tower and the Beltway, he began to move away from strategic studies, perhaps a tacit admission that his economic approach to strategy had in fact reached a dead end.[153] In fact, increasingly most mainstream economists lost any interest in national security affairs and those few who did would become increasingly marginal to the discipline.[154]

The obvious question is why these internal disciplinary pathologies would manifest themselves in the early 1960s? Changes in the external security environment were a permissive factor. While it would be a stretch to characterize the early 1960s as a low threat environment, at least in terms of the nuclear balance, it was dawning on the leaders of both of the nuclear superpowers that mutual nuclear vulnerability at least made that part of their rivalry somewhat less intense.[155] The concern shifted, although never completely abandoned, from achieving nuclear advantage to ensuring strategic stability. As Soviet premier Nikita Khrushchev recounted: "When I was appointed First Secretary of the Central Committee and learned all the facts about nuclear power I couldn't sleep for several days. Then I became convinced that we could never possibly use these weapons and I was able to sleep again."[156] Even nuclear strategists such as Schelling agreed. "His view was that people were not scared and were getting less scared. If overkill was accumulating steadily, it was not a subject of concern for most people. Nor did people see the risk of war as a function of piling up overkill."[157]

The theory of the nuclear revolution predicts great power peace, fewer international crises, less intense bargaining, the bolstering of the status quo, and a growing disconnect between the military balance and international outcomes. The "long peace" of the Cold War seems to bear those predictions out, at least in the direct relations between nuclear powers.[158] The end of the Golden Age was not only brought about by real-world events like Vietnam; it was also a consequence of the effort to make strategy a "science" modeled on economics which led it to an intellectual dead end by privileging abstract models and abstruse methods over substance.[159]

A Theoretical Bridge Too Far: Schelling's Bargaining Model's Cameo Role in the Vietnam Tragedy

Once he hit a dead end in nuclear strategy, Schelling shifted his bargaining approach to the analysis of limited war and conventional coercion. In doing so, with catastrophic consequences, he put the last nail in the coffin of scientific strategy. In recent years, much attention has been paid to his role in the Vietnam War.[160] While these treatments vary in their judgment of the extent of his influence, they agree that there was some. Journalist Fred Kaplan provocatively concluded that "this dark side of Tom Schelling is also the dark side of social science—the brash assumption that neat theories not only reflect the real world but can change it as well, and in ways that can be precisely measured."[161] Elsewhere, he argued that America's "Vietnam strategy was essentially a conventional-war version of the counterforce/no cities theory—using force as an instrument of coercion, withholding a larger force that could kill the hostage of the enemy's cities if he didn't back down."[162]

It is easy to overstate Schelling's influence, but in two areas he helped draft the "mental map" that guided U.S. policymakers to deeper involvement in Vietnam. The first concerned the stakes involved in the triumph of communism in South Vietnam. Here, Schelling's influence was quite modest. It simply reinforced the widespread sense among policymakers that U.S. credibility—as both an ally and an adversary—was on the line. As Secretary of Defense Robert McNamara recalled, "We (particularly Dean Rusk) feared our NATO status would be weakened if we failed to honor what he interpreted as our SEATO obligations to South Vietnam."[163] This view was more widely shared among senior national security policymakers.[164] It was also ubiquitous at lower levels of the bureaucracy and the think tank world. As RAND analyst Charles Wolf explained apropos of Laos, its value "is related to contingencies involving countries other than Laos itself. It is in this sense that the 'stack of cards' or 'dominoes' analogy, which has sometimes been applied to the countries of Southeast Asia, makes a certain amount of sense. A 'loss' of Laos increases the vulnerability of environing countries; stated another way, such a loss requires that additional costs be incurred if the vulnerability of environing countries is to be held constant."[165] One of Wolf's RAND colleagues even fretted that if the region were lost to the non-Communist world, "atomic blackmail would then enter the picture."[166]

The fact that America's stake in Vietnam was primarily about credibility shaped how the United States fought the war there, particularly its unwillingness to expand it beyond certain levels of violence and across particular geographic boundaries.[167] Former national security advisor McGeorge Bundy explained the logic: "My own sense of the matter is that what was decided was to do the maximum amount that did not create a major international noise level and see what happened, and did not create a major domestic noise level and see what happened."[168] Kattenburg called this concern with credibility the "underlying yet insufficiently analyzed premise" of U.S. policy in Vietnam that was embraced by policymakers "without the benefit of very profound analysis."[169] But he was mistaken in suggesting that this issue was not the subject of deep analysis. Indeed, it was a major focus of Schelling's intellectual agenda.[170]

Schelling (along with other strategists like Kaufmann) explicitly linked the credibility of commitment problem that mutually assured destruction (MAD) caused for extended deterrence with events in other parts of the world.[171] As he explained in *Arms and Influence*, "Few parts of the world are intrinsically worth the risk of serious war by themselves, especially when taken slice by slice, but defending them or running risks to protect them may preserve one's commitments to action in other parts of the world and at later times."[172] And he characterized the Johnson administration's military response after the August 1964 Gulf of Tonkin incidents as successful: "With regard to the bombing of North Vietnam, he thought that it had been successful, since it has established throughout the world the idea that sanctuaries may not be respected in case of aggression. Implications for Malaysia, Israel, India, etc., are crucial here. Perhaps the effects on the Viet Cong are the least important in this case."[173] And he telegraphed his concern that U.S. policymakers might insufficiently appreciate the importance of maintaining its credibility: "Schelling also feared that the U.S., by failing to appreciate fully certain aspects of its own policy, might underestimate how much its conduct in Vietnam was communicating to others—both to those engaged in the war and those merely observing it. Tonkin, for example, had its effect on national attitudes to modes of reprisal as far away as Israel."[174] In other words, one could start out reading Schelling on nuclear strategy and end up fighting a guerilla war in Vietnam following the logic of his credibility argument.

Schelling and other civilian nuclear strategists also took ideas developed about nuclear deterrence and crisis bargaining and sought to make them applicable to military coercion more generally.[175] He found a textbook illustration of successful coercive bargaining in the early days of the Rolling Thunder bombing campaign against Hanoi.[176] Schelling supported Gulf of Tonkin retaliations and as late as 1966 he remained cautiously optimistic about the coercive air campaign's likely success.[177] As late as the early 1980s, he remained puzzled that the United States had lost the war given its military superiority.[178]

Both of these policies followed logically from various aspects of Schelling's bargaining model of strategic interaction. Already in his 1961 strategic magnum opus, we see him advocating Third World intervention as a means of manipulating risk in the Cold War rivalry with the Soviet Union: "In the author's opinion the dispatch of United States troops to Lebanon in 1958 was not only both risky and successful but successful precisely because of the risk—a risk that the Communists could lessen or aggravate according to their response."[179] And the template he derived from his theory about the requirements of a successful exercise in coercive bargaining very closely matched at least the initial U.S. strategy in the air war against the North: "The ideal compellent action would be one that, once initiated, causes minimal harm if compliance is forthcoming and great harm if compliance is not forthcoming, is consistent with the time schedule of feasible compliance, is beyond recall once initiated, and cannot be stopped by the party that started it but *automatically* stops upon compliance, with all of this fully understood by the adversary."[180] Other analysts of the bombing campaign have also heard echoes of Schelling in it.[181]

But in order to make the case that Schelling's models actually influenced Kennedy and Johnson administration policies toward Vietnam, we need to do more than show their consistency with administration policies; we also need to establish a direct causal chain. We can do this once again through

McNaughton. As assistant secretary of defense for International Security Affairs, McNaughton was responsible for formulating strategy for Vietnam in the McNamara Pentagon.[182] Despite harboring deep reservations about escalating American involvement in the war, he dutifully sought to find a way to extricate the United States from the war without losing it. His old friend and colleague Schelling's bargaining model offered a way to square that circle through an air campaign of gradually escalating pressure.[183]

To illustrate Schelling's limited but real influence here, it is useful to review the entire program of coercive activities the United States undertook against North Vietnam. They began in early 1964 with the bombing of Laos and the initiation of covert aerial and amphibious operations against North Vietnam under Oplan 34A. This continued with the reprisals after the Gulf of Tonkin Incidents in August 1964 and the attack on the American base at Pleiku in early 1965. But it was not until late 1964 that President Johnson authorized sustained air strikes against North Vietnam, which due to weather restrictions did not begin until early March 1965.[184] Once these strikes commenced under the code name Rolling Thunder, U.S. strategy would develop through three different phases. The first three weeks seem to follow most closely Schelling's strategy of coercion designed primarily to bring Hanoi to the bargaining table. The second phase, lasting roughly from late February through late March, seems more compatible with Walt Rostow's alternative coercive strategy aimed at holding at risk North Vietnam's incipient industrial base, which we will consider in depth in the next chapter. Finally, from then until the large-scale introduction of U.S. ground forces that summer, the objective seemed closer to the military's strategy of coercion through interdiction and attrition.[185] By November 1965, most of the designated targets had been hit and the possibility of successful coercion of North Vietnam seemed more remote.[186]

This quickly evolving coercive strategy was the result of two factors: First, various proponents actually had different rationales for supporting air strikes: some sought to punish North Vietnam for aiding the Viet Cong. Others wanted to use them to bolster flagging morale in South Vietnam. Still others saw them as a means to directly interdict supplies flowing down the Ho Chi Minh Trail.[187] This stimulated, in the words of an analyst in the *Pentagon Papers*, "considerable theorizing during this period about the best manner of persuading North Vietnam to cease aid to the NLF/VC by forceful but restrained pressures which would convey the threat of greater force if the North Vietnamese did not end their support of the insurgency in South Vietnam."[188] To be sure, Wallace Thies cautioned that U.S. strategy was not the result of one plan but rather "of several distinct planning efforts, the implementation of which happened to overlap."[189] Still, the terms of reference for this debate were set by the civilian strategists in the 1950s and early 1960s, including Schelling.[190] Support for coercive or compellent strategies was largely confined to civilians as most military officers chafed at restrictions on targets connected to the Viet Cong war effort.[191] Typical was the commander of the Military Assistance Command Vietnam (MACV) General William Westmoreland, who dismissed the strategy of "graduated response" as "one of the most lamentable mistakes of the war."[192]

The *Pentagon Papers* describe a concerted effort to formulate a coercive strategy through "graduated pressures" beginning in February 1964 with the establishment of a working group under State Department Policy Planning Council staffer Robert Johnson. On May 23, Assistant Secretary of State William Bundy briefed members of the Southeast Asia Executive Committee on a draft presidential memorandum outlining a concrete thirty-day program that combined graduated military and diplomatic actions to force North Vietnam to end its support of the Viet Cong.[193] While this proposal did not go anywhere, between August and October 1964, the State Department and McNaughton's office engaged in a joint effort to devise a "new scenario for graduated pressures against NVN" that provided the conceptual basis for the first stages of the air campaign against the North.[194] The ISA slow "squeeze" strategy seemed cribbed directly from a prepublication draft of Schelling's *Arms and Influence.*[195]

According to McNaughton's daily planner, he met regularly with Schelling during this period, often at key decision points. For example, prior to his formally taking office as ASD/ISA, and right around the time in December 1963 during which the MACV and the CIA Station in Saigon were formulating the covert Oplan 34A strikes against North Vietnam, Schelling and McNaughton met in the Office of the Secretary of Defense on the sixteenth. Coincident with the establishment of a committee at State under Policy Planning Council member Robert Johnson, there is a notation to "tell RSM re Schelling," which McNaughton apparently did during the week of February 9. When Secretary of Defense Robert McNamara returned from Vietnam in mid-March, after which President Johnson urged "immediate preparation of a capability to 'mount new and significant pressures against NVN,' to include a 72-hour capability for a full range of SVN 'border control' operations and 'retaliatory actions against NVN,' and a capability to initiate 'graduated overt military pressure within 30 days of notification,'" Schelling and McNaughton had lunch together at the Pentagon followed by a

2:00 p.m. briefing. Three days after the Joint Staff submitted its own proposal for gradually increasing pressures on the North, Schelling and McNaughton met with McNaughton's deputy Harry Rowen on April 16 in the latter's office. The two met again on June 17, right after McGeorge Bundy directed the secretaries of defense and state to consider various options for limited operations against the North. McNaughton and Schelling met again on August 12, just as the discussion about the "Next Courses of Action in Southeast Asia" kicked off within the Johnson administration. Three days after the third Gulf of Tonkin Incident on September 18, McNaughton reminded himself to "write Tom." Finally, during the week of October 4, McNaughton scheduled a lunch with Schelling and also listed him among the "personnel" matters with which he had to deal.[196]

There are also compelling substantive reasons for thinking that McNaughton was drawing on Schelling's bargaining model. As with Schelling's (and McNaughton's) dovish rationale for a "no cities" nuclear doctrine, which aimed to preserve American cities not through counterforce, damage-limiting strikes but rather by keeping the hostage Soviet cities alive while threatening them with destruction, McNaughton saw the coercive campaign against the North as the last exit from the road leading into the quagmire in South Vietnam.[197] As he later confided to his diary, "What we need is a theory that will limit our role."[198] McNamara agreed with this rationale for bombing: "I believed we should make every possible effort to spark negotiations leading to an end to the conflict. This remained my position until I left the Pentagon three years later."[199] Explicitly connecting Schelling with this rationale, Kattenburg observed that "like 'flexible response,' which came to replace 'massive retaliation' in strategic (nuclear) war doctrine, after Secretary McNamara endorsed it in the early 1960s, graduated escalation or pressure was a relatively crude national security policy distillation of complex academic thinking stimulated by economist Thomas Schelling's book *The Strategy of Conflict* (1959), later refined in Schelling's *Arms and Influence*."[200] Schelling's model of coercive bargaining could provide the last clear chance to swerve away from disaster in Vietnam.

That the air campaign was informed by a (series) of general theories of coercion is clear. How they led the country to grief is less so. NSC analyst James Thomson blamed game theory, which was all the rage among civilian strategists in the late 1950s and early 1960s.[201] Certainly, it was in the intellectual toolbox of some Kennedy national security policymakers. McNamara, for example, confessed that the only book he had read on nuclear strategy prior to taking office was pioneer game theorist Oskar Morgenstern's

The Question of National Defense.[202] The problem was that even very simple game theory like Schelling's utilized models of coercive bargaining assumed both sides share the same cost/benefit preferences. The author of an early military assessment of it conducted for the RAND Corporation explained "practical methods are not available for the solution of games in which the two opponents use differing concepts of worth."[203] The problem was that North Vietnam and the United States had very different concepts of what was at stake in the conflict. The former fought to liberate their homeland; the latter merely sought an opportunity to demonstrate its resolve to defend more important regions of the world.

Supposedly when McNaughton approached Schelling for concrete advice on the actual implementation in Vietnam, the latter was "stumped."[204] As Wohlstetter observed, "A man who has done good work on the protection of strategic forces is not inevitably an authority on civil defense, conventional war in Europe, and guerrilla warfare in South Vietnam."[205] Still, it is not at all difficult to connect Schelling's bargaining model to the subsequent quagmire in Southeast Asia.[206] It was, in part, the result of taking his theoretical road map for coercive bargaining and following it to its (il)logical conclusion. Thus, there is more to Schelling's role in the Vietnam debacle than his defenders would admit.[207]

Conclusions and Recommendations

Social science did have important effects on strategy. At times this was direct, as was the case with Wohlstetter's basing study or Kaufmann's critique of massive retaliation. More often it was indirect, working not through the formulation of doctrine or the drafting of operational plans, but rather by providing the intellectual frameworks and mental road maps that shaped senior policymakers' and presidents' thinking about the utility of nuclear weapons during confrontations with other nuclear states. In other words, civilian strategists like Brodie, Wohlstetter, Kaufmann, and Schelling limned the bounds of the nuclear revolution for both scholars and policymakers.[208]

In the final analysis, however, it was the theoretically and methodologically more eclectic Brodie, rather than the economist Schelling, whose ideas better captured the reality of the nuclear revolution.[209] Already in 1946, the former had set the "basic axioms of the nuclear age"—the absence of any meaningful defense against nuclear attack, the inevitable mutual vulnerability of each sides' population, and the need for secure second-strike capability—which were the enduring facts of the nuclear age that policymakers recognized they had to operate under.[210] At the height of the nuclear war-fighting/counterforce craze at RAND, Brodie rejected counterforce well before the Kennedy administration toyed with it.[211]

While Brodie never achieved the insider influence on U.S. nuclear strategy—particularly doctrine and war plans—that he craved, he nonetheless became a very influential public commentator on these issues.[212] Via that route, Brodie's views eventually influenced Secretary of Defense Robert McNamara's thinking on the subject.[213] The reason they did, in Lawrence Freedman's judgment, was that Brodie had a better feel for real world politics because he "was not a formal strategist in that he lacked confidence in conclusions derived from 'war gaming' or rigorous but abstracted analysis, isolated from the real world."[214] Appropriately, Schelling's eulogy of Brodie seemed to cede the field of nuclear strategy to "the dean of us all."[215]

The history of the Golden Age is thus a cautionary tale: intellectual dynamics among civilian social scientists in universities and even those working at places like RAND can under certain circumstances lead nuclear strategists into intellectual dead ends when internal disciplinary incentives encourage the privileging of sophisticated methods and elegant models over real world problems. This is not an across-the-board indictment of sophisticated social science methods, but it is an illustration of their limits. It does suggest, though, that the quest to completely remake strategy as a "science" modeled on economics is misguided.

7

Strategic Modernization Theory Bogs Down in the Vietnam Quagmire

This chapter continues the story of how the Wizards of Armageddon's efforts to create a policy science of strategy spilled over from the nuclear realm into other areas of national security such as political development and nation building, conventional coercion, and counterinsurgency, what I refer to here as strategic modernization theory. One of the key figures in bridging the worlds of nuclear strategy and political and economic development, not to mention academia and policy, was the economist Walt W. Rostow. He saw bridging these gaps as kindred efforts: "To formulate and execute policies which will link the more developed and less developed nations of the free world requires of us a marriage of ideas and action as challenging as that required to conduct a rational military policy in a world of nuclear weapons."[1]

What made the Cold War unique was that it was characterized by an effort to maintain this collaboration for a protracted period of peace, though one punctuated with intense international crises and small-scale wars. As Brigadier General Richard Stillwell conceded in his keynote for the army's 1962 Limited War Symposium, "I was equally struck by some nostalgic remark that in World War II we had a focus. There was nothing we could not do. We could coalesce our efforts. We had direction, we knew exactly what was needed, and we did it. That experience represents the apex of our respective careers. Now, the real problem I think, for all of us is to somehow find the symbol, the value. . . . we need—all of us, in uniform and out—the same dedication, the same coalescing of effort, the same reversal of trends toward fragmentation, the same uni-direction which we expect and get when that magic threshold is reached."[2] Given this complex security environment, it is hardly surprising that we would see oscillations in the relationship between policymakers and the academy during the Cold War on these issues.

Indeed, we see a familiar pattern once again in this case: early optimism about the compatibility of a "scientific" approach to economic and political development and its direct relevance to policy. But this optimism would eventually give way to disillusionment as the tensions between "rigor" and "relevance" resurfaced and it became clear that a choice might have to be made between them. This choice coincided with growing debate about the strategic stakes in the Third World rivalry with the Communist world. A handful of scholars believed that the Developing World was the central front of the Cold War but a growing number of academics and even policymakers increasingly manifested far less urgency about developments there.[3] Faced with these renewed tensions, the social sciences increasingly favored a narrow definition of rigor over relevance. In doing so, they left the field to a handful of scholar/practitioners like Rostow who tried to maintain a foot in each camp but ultimately failed to produce either sound scholarship or effective policies. In both cases, a complex threat environment and disciplinary dynamics played the leading role in the tragic story of the road to Vietnam being paved with the best of theoretical and policy intentions.

This chapter further qualifies the widespread view that the Vietnam War and the associated political controversies of the mid-1960s—particularly the exposure of Project Camelot—were the only factors that brought to a close cooperation between the Ivory Tower and the Beltway in the formulation of U.S. strategy for waging the Cold War in the Developing World.[4] To the extent that scholars concede that problems began earlier, they blame political controversies such as McCarthyism and the related debate about the loss of China as causes for the hemorrhage of critical Asia expertise that might have averted the Vietnam debacle.[5] There is, to be sure, an element of truth in the argument that Vietnam ended the "golden age" of civilian strategists. These political controversies certainly reinforced the estrangement between scholars and policymakers. But they were the last nails in the coffin of policy-relevant social science rather than the primary causes of the growing disconnect between academia and government, which had begun much earlier and also had disciplinary, rather than just political, roots.

While Vietnam accelerated this trend, it did so because some of the concrete policy recommendations of the scientific development strategists actually contributed to the debacle there. Indeed, we can directly indict their universal models in both providing a rationale for the U.S. commitment to an unwinnable war in Southeast Asia and also in shaping some of the failed tactics the United States employed in it.

To make the case that Rostow was the most important civilian academic strategist in the formulation and implementation of U.S. policy in the developing world during the Cold War, it is necessary first to outline the intellectual context in which he formulated his universal model of strategic modernization and development. Then we have to unpack his arguments and show how and why they provided U.S. policymakers with the mental map to interpret the Cold War in the Third World in a particularly threatening way and also to recommend strategies to respond to the challenge of underdevelopment there. Unique among civilian development strategists, Rostow was not only a scholar of these issues; he also held a series of high-level U.S. government positions, which made him a direct formulator and implementer of policy. So, finally, it explores his government career to see how he put his theoretical ideas in action. Rostow is both a positive example of how an academic theorist can be influential in the making of strategy but also a cautionary tale about how not to go about doing so.[6] I conclude by arguing that despite Rostow's failings, Vietnam did not discredit the notion that social scientists should be engaged with policy. The problem in Vietnam was not an excess of scholarly engagement but rather its surfeit.

Strategic Modernization Theory's Starring Role in the Vietnam Tragedy

Some scholars doubt that academic social science had much influence on government policy during the Vietnam era.[7] While this skepticism about the early influence of the antiwar movement might be justified, a broader dismissal of the role of social science in U.S. government debates about how to wage the Cold War in the Third World is not. Former White House and State Department Asia expert James Thomson, for example, recounted that "the increased commitment to Vietnam was also fueled by a new breed of military strategists and academic social scientists (some of whom had entered the new administration) who had developed theories of counterguerrilla warfare and were eager to see them put to the test."[8] Vietnam-era defense official Leslie Gelb similarly indicted "the outpouring of books and articles in popular and scholarly journals by academicians and think tank researchers extolling the virtues and necessity of fighting guerrilla wars."[9] Hilsman, another academic action intellectual who spent significant time in both worlds, came away from his experience in government convinced that academics "have power and they are as much a part of the government process as the traditional legislative, judicial, and executive branches of government."[10] Echoing this judgment, former State Department Vietnam desk officer Paul Kattenburg concluded that "events in history cannot be fully comprehended without some understanding of the intellectual baggage carried by those charged with decision making during the period under consideration. It is especially spurious to wave intellectuals and theorists away on the grounds that 'they don't really count.' Intellectuals and theorists always count, because they furnish the substantive theories of history which make up the usually meager conceptual baggage of the decision makers."[11] Indeed, it is not a stretch to say that if the Cold War was truly "the social scientists' war," their most important front was in the less-developed parts of the world.[12]

Scholars had influence because policymakers are dependent on nongovernmental experts for the substantive expertise on which they make decisions. Given that senior (and even mid-level) policymakers are not usually elected or appointed based on national security expertise, and their heavy workload once in office, it is unrealistic to expect them to have, or acquire, the deep expertise in various regions of the world or knowledge of the wide variety of issues about which they have to make decisions. The evidence that modernization concepts shaped policymakers' thinking was the close correspondence between what policymakers were discussing in the counsels of government and what modernization theorists were writing and saying in public.[13]

The Cold War high point of the effort to connect academic social science and national security policymaking was undoubtedly the Kennedy administration. Even before Massachusetts senator John F. Kennedy threw his hat in the ring for the presidency in 1960, he had already established a pattern of reaching out to Boston-area scholars for advice on various issues of domestic and foreign policy. He formalized this brain trust in January 1960 when he assembled thirty "action intellectuals" to advise him on his campaign.[14] So close was this relationship that campaign staffer Frederick Holborn remarked that "I actually found the gulf between academic work and the kind of work I was doing there, was not as wide as I had expected.... I was surprised that there were bridges across this gulf."[15] The list of the academic "best and brightest" whom Kennedy brought to Washington in

January 1961 to serve as bridges back to academia was a veritable who's who of academic luminaries, including historian Arthur Schlesinger Jr.; economists John Kenneth Galbraith, Carl Kaysen, and Charles Hitch; and political scientists Roger Hilsman and Richard Neustadt, to name just a few.[16]

Former Harvard dean and Kennedy national security advisor McGeorge Bundy was in many peoples' eyes "the Administration's premier academic." Historians have pondered the irony of the Kennedy administration's leading intellectual light pursuing such ill-conceived policies toward Vietnam. It is undoubtedly true, as many have suggested, that part of the problem lay in Bundy's personal flaws. When Bundy joined the Kennedy administration, his colleague David Riesman later reminisced that "I grieved for Harvard and grieved for the nation; for Harvard because he was the perfect dean, for the nation because I thought that the very same arrogance and hubris might be dangerous."[17] However, hubris is hardly a sufficient explanation for his mistakes.

Bundy was also fully in the thrall of many of the same ideas about modernization theory as other modernization strategists. To be sure, as Harvard dean, he had initially been a supporter of "area studies," seeing them as an important bridge between the academy and government, as they had been during the Second World War.[18] But Bundy also became enamored of the new policy science of "modernization theory" and shared its growing disdain for the atheoretical and methodologically primitive area studies approach, preferring instead to see the more up-to-date methods then fashionable in Cambridge classrooms applied in the policy world.[19] Once in power, he was institutionally and personally committed to the policies he helped formulate and implement in the Kennedy and Johnson administrations. This made it harder for him to view them dispassionately and walk away from them when they were clearly failing. Never much of a scholar, Bundy had little alternative; it was either academic administration or Washington for him. This is why, in my view, the title of leading intellectual policymaker in the Kennedy administration should be bestowed instead on Rostow, who not only matched Bundy's administrative seniority but whose scholarship also provided the Kennedy and Johnson administrations with the intellectual frameworks that connected the Cold War and Third World development and modernization.

Some people downplay Rostow's influence on Vietnam policymaking. His NSC boss McGeorge Bundy reminisced that "I've always thought that one of the reasons the President put Walt Rostow [Walt Whitman Rostow] in the Department of State was so he wouldn't have to read quite so many papers which he didn't have to decide on."[20] Rostow's Policy Planning Staff deputy Robert Johnson agreed that "Walt Rostow . . . just fired off memos here, there, and everywhere. That's one reason that he's taken more responsibility than he should in the public eye, I think, for the escalation of the war in Vietnam in 1964. In my view he had very little to do with that. But he was unquestionably sending memos and these got scooped up when they did the Pentagon Papers."[21] However, these skeptical views understate Rostow's influence. Given his role as a leading strategic modernization thinker, Rostow belongs in Camelot's intellectual firmament, for better or worse.[22]

HETERODOX, BUT STILL AN ECONOMIST

Born into a Russian-Jewish émigré family, Rostow was groomed for the lamp by his parents from an early age. After excelling in primary and secondary school, he matriculated to Yale in 1931 and gravitated toward economic history and Keynesianism, which he studied with James Harvey Rogers and an economics graduate student by the name of Richard Bissell. Continuing his bravura intellectual performance, Rostow earned a prestigious Rhodes scholarship to Oxford from 1936 to 1938 where he did much of the research on economic development in Britain that would subsequently earn him a Ph.D. from Yale. During the Second World War, Rostow joined the OSS and was assigned to its Economic Objectives Unit in the U.S. Embassy in London, which helped formulate Allied bombing strategy. Turning down a job offer from Harvard in 1946, he returned to England to take additional fellowships at Oxford and then Cambridge. While in Europe, he worked for Swedish economist Gunnar Myrdal at the Economic Commission for Europe and was credited by his colleague Charles Kindelberger with developing its foundational rationale.[23] Returning to Cambridge, Massachusetts, in 1950 to take up a faculty position at MIT, Rostow became one of the founding members of its new Center for International Studies. After Kennedy's inauguration in January 1961, he was named special assistant to the president under Bundy and then moved to the chairmanship of the State Department's Policy Planning Staff, before returning to the NSC to replace Bundy during the one full term of the Johnson administration.[24]

Economics very quickly had become his substantive focus at Yale but as he recalled he "emerged from [his tutorial with Bissell] not intent on becoming a mathematical economist, but with two other objectives: (a) to apply economic theory to economic history, then a rather descriptive, institutional field; and (b) to try [his] hand at relating the economic sectors of society to the cultural, social, and political sectors assuming, contrary to Marxism, that the various sectors interacted."[25] Rostow was swimming against the intellectual currents in economics, which ran increasingly in the direction of a deductive and mathematical science. He derided the "neo-Newtonians" like Simon Kuznets who thought that economic concepts could only be expressed mathematically.[26] Rather than physics, Rostow thought the discipline should emulate biology.[27] "I found mainstream economics, including the so-called neo-classical synthesis," he later reflected, "an incomplete framework for a serious economic historian or analyst of the current scene; and, as I learned more, I judged it increasingly necessary to introduce as systematically as I could political, social, cultural, and other non-economic forces as they bore on economic behavior."[28] Rostow's intellectual objection to mainstream economics' understanding of development was that "the neoclassical growth models which absorbed so much high-grade theoretical talent in the 1960s ran into the sand precisely because their method ruled out changes in most of the variables relevant to the process of economic growth."[29] In other words, they could tell us little about the actual determinants of development. Rostow, like another heterodox economist serving in the Kennedy administration—John Kenneth Galbraith—was undaunted. He conceded that while the study of short-term economic phenomena could safely neglect noneconomic factors, the study of long-term economic development required systematic attention to them. And to analyze long-term change that was shaped by many factors, both economic and noneconomic, only the approach of the traditional economic historian would do.[30]

This inability was not only an intellectual failing, in Rostow's view; it also meant that neoclassical macroeconomists were not very useful to policymakers.[31] As he later put it, "Mainstream economics is not now coming to grips with some such array of palpably urgent and relevant problems," and he went on to complain that "our graduate students are, by and large, taught to respect the primacy of method and technique, and problems are cut down to the size the chosen techniques can handle."[32] Still later he would reflect that the "tension between the model chosen and the disarray of reality is both our glory—as compared to the pure theorist or institutional historian—and it is our basic limitation."[33]

Even at the height of his scholarly career, and well before he had descended from the Ivory Tower to toil full-time within the corridors of power in Washington, Rostow was already becoming marginalized within the discipline of economics. He had three strikes against him among his academic colleagues. He was interested in development economics, a subset of macroeconomics and a field not readily amenable to the preferred methods of the ascendant microeconomists. He was a traditional economic historian, and his approach satisfied neither mainstream economists nor the new cliometricians who were working to make history a social science. Finally, he was a Keynesian proponent of government intervention in the economy in a field increasingly predisposed to favor the unfettered workings of the market. Rostow's faith in the role of the governments of developed countries in fostering development in the Third World flowed naturally from that latter orientation.[34]

Rostow's magnum opus—*The Stages of Economic Growth*—was not well received among mainstream economists. They dismissed it as a "combination of confident growthmanship and cold-war propaganda."[35] Typical was a notice by Kenneth Boulding: Its "contents are disappointing. The method might be best described as 'anecdotal' and whatever quantitative matter is introduced—and there is a fair amount of it—is introduced by way of illustration, rather than in terms of systematic analysis."[36] Another reviewer complained that Rostow's work was not "directly associated with the degree of technical sophistication, and relatively sharp focus of objective, which have been among the attributes of cliometric or econometric method."[37] Mancur Olson observed apropos of a later *festschrift* volume for Rostow that it had more critiques and dissents than essays that endorsed and expanded on *The Stages of Economic Growth*.[38] On the other hand, Rostow's ambitious effort to construct a universal framework of economic development did not win him many friends among historians either. A. K. Cairncross dismissed his grand theorizing on the grounds that it "made the Muse of History lie on the bed of Procrustes."[39]

While Rostow was a heterodox economist, he remained a man of his intellectual times in his desire to formulate a universal model of development and then use it to guide actual policymaking. While he was less enamored of quantification and formal modeling than other economists, he did fall victim to some of the other pathologies of his discipline. He was, in Mark Berger's words, like all economists "ahistorical and technocratic."[40] More importantly, Rostow was strikingly resistant to modifying universal frameworks in light of local circumstances.[41] Perhaps a harbinger of future trouble, some of his CENIS colleagues were less than enthusiastic about his moving closer to the seat of power. "'You know,'" his MIT colleague Lucian Pye reportedly "confessed to his students, 'you don't quite sleep so well any more when you know some of the people going to Washington.'"[42]

A UNIVERSAL MODEL OF DEVELOPMENT LEADS
ROSTOW TO VIETNAM

Rostow's universal model of economic development directly shaped his policy recommendations.[43] His "stages of economic development" consti-tuted, in Michael Latham's view, "a powerful ideology about the nature of American society and its ability to accelerate, shape, and direct the forces of change in an increasing post-colonial world."[44] Theory and practice came together disastrously in the Vietnam War, which many held him responsible for by establishing the original rationale for the U.S. commitment and then formulating counterproductive strategies for waging the war.[45] Rostow's policy engagement had two discrete phases. The first was as an engaged academic; the second as a scholar-in-exile inside the Beltway.

Rostow's early influence in Washington was undoubtedly magnified by the unique academic institutions he was associated with. The most important of these, both in terms of length of association and general scholarly ethos, were the Massachusetts Institute of Technology and its CENIS. The latter provided Rostow with a direct bridge between academia and the policy world in his field of development.[46] Political development quickly became its central focus of policy-relevant research.[47] While Rostow was by no means the only prominent scholar there, his *Stages of Economic Growth* was the intellectual "heart" of CENIS in the 1950s.[48] Just as important as substance, Rostow's ethos of linking policy and scholarship pervaded the center's in-stitutional culture. Asserting that his "theoretical prism is that of a social scientist," Rostow went on to note that "the intellectual problems to which the social scientist has addressed himself over the past twenty years have been shaped by America's emerging world role to a degree which matches the extent to which science and engineering have been drawn into the chal-lenges of weaponry and space."[49]

As he explained, "The process of linking ideas and action with respect to foreign aid in the 1950s occurred in a rather curious triangular way. The ideas were generated in universities and research institutions, of which CENIS was a significant example but by no means unique. These ideas flowed in two important directions: to sympathetic members of Congress and their staffs, and to like-minded members of the executive branch at both high and working levels. They flowed also to the World Bank and other international institutions, and, of course, to other academics and interested laypersons in the United States and abroad."[50] In other words, he conceived CENIS as a central node in a larger nexus of government and nongovernment institutions producing policy-relevant social science research.

Rostow epitomized the early Cold War "action intellectual." In his view, the academic and policy worlds ought to be convergent: "In the end . . . a rude pragmatism shapes the content of intellectual life; and in turn, the behavior of practical men is governed by the abstractions which men of ideas have created in an effort to give a degree of order to the world of human beings and the things about them."[51] That is why he was eager to use his scholarship to shape policy. The guiding principle of Rostow's intellectual agenda was to "apply theory to concrete circumstances."[52] Conversely, he also believed that important theory developed out of practical problems.[53] While Rostow's success and influence were hardly typical of his generation of academics, his desire to influence policy and his willingness to split his time between government service and the Ivory Tower was.[54]

Rostow struggled at first to translate his models into practice during the Eisenhower administration. Like many of the early Cold War action-intellectuals, he was critical of the former general's conservative, laisse-faire approach to national security issues, particularly in the area of development.[55] Nonetheless, former Eisenhower NSC official C. D. Jackson asked Rostow and his colleague Max Millikan to organize a meeting of scholars and policymakers at the Princeton Inn in the spring of 1954 to discuss the role of development aid in waging the Cold War.[56] Out of it came the widely circulated paper "A Proposal for a New United States Foreign Economic Policy," which landed in the in-box of many foreign policy and national security decision makers in Washington. Despite its wide circulation, this initial effort to put development aid on the policy agenda failed. Unfazed, Millikan and Rostow put together a series of follow-on panels in Quantico, Virginia, in the mid-1950s. These meetings were more successful in terms of putting aid on the Eisenhower agenda. In fact, Rostow would eventually be assigned to write a speech for the president in August 1958 on development as a means of keeping newly independent states out of the Soviet orbit.[57]

Rostow and Millikan subsequently expanded their paper into a small book, which caused a big splash in Washington, DC, by making strategic modernization theory accessible to the policy world.[58] It had its most important influence on the junior senator from Massachusetts who eagerly embraced it.[59] The Soviet Union's 1957 Sputnik launch added urgency to a major development push, and this spurred Senator John F. Kennedy's 1958 India initiative.[60] Rostow helped him draft the Kennedy-Cooper Resolution, which bestowed on the former crown jewel of the British Empire

$225 million in development assistance.[61] Texas senator and majority leader Lyndon Johnson supported this effort as well.[62] CENIS conducted a 1960 study for the Senate entitled "Economic, Social, and Political Change in the Underdeveloped Countries," which suggested that social science could produce universal models of development and modernization that could guide policy.[63] Through this and other research, Rostow eventually persuaded Kennedy to make the 1960s the "Development Decade."[64]

There was, in fact, broad agreement in the early 1960s that academia should provide information about the world and policy advice for how the United States should deal with it early in the Cold War.[65] As Rostow would later explain, the reason development started gaining traction on the policy agenda was "the sense of gathering crisis in the developing regions."[66] He attributed this success to the increasing sense of international threat: "The pathbreaking victories won in the form of [International Development Association] IDA, the [Interamerican Development Bank] IADB, the India and Pakistan consortia, the Alliance for Progress, and the Development Decade did not come about because, at last, we persuaded the opposition that our long-term arguments we were right. They came about because of a series of short-term crises emerged in the developing regions, which forced on responsible politicians an acute awareness of the political and strategic danger of not assisting the process of development in Latin America, Africa, the Middle East, and Asia."[67] Highlighting development's urgency, Kennedy would compare the "Economic Gap" with the "Missile Gap" as pressing national security issues in a 1959 speech advocating additional funding for development aid.[68]

Rostow would not remain content just to shape policy indirectly through scholarship and consulting, however. When the call came to ride down to Camelot he did not tarry in the Ivory Tower. His first opportunity to serve in the administration was as McGeorge Bundy's deputy on the NSC staff. The two former professors reportedly operated more like academic colleagues than government bureaucrats, establishing a division of labor in which, in former NSC and State Department official Robert Johnson's words, "Rostow handled the LDC [less developed countries outside of the Western Hemisphere] and Bundy handled Europe and East-West relations."[69] When he moved out of the White House and over to Foggy Bottom, some of his colleagues thought his policy star was setting. That was not the case. As chair of the Policy Planning Staff, he drafted Kennedy's "Basic National Security Policy" (BNSP), which John Lewis Gaddis characterizes as "the most comprehensive guide to what the [Kennedy administration] was trying to do in world affairs."[70] And the Policy Planning Staff under Rostow was in on the ground floor in shaping U.S. government debates about the coercive air campaign against North Vietnam before it actually began, conducting a major study on "Alternatives for Imposition of Measured Pressures Against North Vietnam" toward the end of 1963.[71] The most compelling evidence of his growing influence was his replacement of Bundy as Johnson's National Security Advisor in 1966, a post he won after Johnson confidante Jack Valenti persuaded the president that Rostow and other social scientists could provide useful advice to help make South Vietnam a functioning democracy.[72]

Policymakers suspected that development somehow affected U.S. national security. For example, in part four of his 1949 inaugural speech, Harry Truman committed his administration to promoting global development.[73] This concern with underdevelopment was reinforced by the Soviet Communist Party's Nineteenth Congress in 1952, which, among other things, intimated that the Cold War was shifting to peripheral areas.[74] But the tocsin sounded loudest when Soviet premier Nikita Khrushchev delivered his provocative "wars of national liberation" speech just days before Kennedy's inauguration in January 1961.[75] The Charles River group of modernization scholars (intellectually dominated by Rostow) offered an alternative development approach that sought to channel modernization in a Lockean, rather than Marxist, direction and was highly influential within the Kennedy administration.[76] Modernization theory was Janus-faced; it not only led scholars and policymakers to be sanguine about the spread of American-style democracy and free markets but also to view them as under siege around the world.[77] Academic modernization specialists provided policymakers a framework for understanding how the world worked, identified the threats to U.S. national security, and helped formulate policies in response to them.[78] In other words, modernization theory served policymakers as the script for America's part in the Cold War drama in the developing world.[79]

STRATEGIC MODERNIZATION THEORY'S THREAT ASSESSMENT

Rostow and other strategic modernization theorists provided the framework through which events in the developing world could be linked to other Cold War national security issues.[80] Impugning Communists as the "scavengers of the process of modernization," he worried that Third World instability provided the Communist world with an opening it could exploit.[81] As Millikan and Rostow explained,

The danger is that increasing numbers of people will become convinced that their new aspiration [for modernization] can be realized only through violent social change and the renunciation of democratic institutions. That danger has no single cause. It is inherent in the revolutionary process. But it is greatly increased by the existence of communism—not because of any authentic attractions in its ideology but because the Communists have recognized their opportunities to exploit the revolution of rising expectations by picturing communism as the road to social opportunity or economic improvement or individual dignity and achievement or national self-respect, whichever fitted a given situation.[82]

"It is therefore reasonable to assume," he argued once in government, "that if the United States and other advanced countries had not responded to, say, Indian and Latin American needs in the 1950s, the Soviet Union might well have done so with great vigor; and that Moscow's political and strategic influence and authority in the developing regions would probably have been considerably greater than it was when the Soviet Union came to an end."[83]

It is clear that Rostow the intellectual directly shaped Rostow the policymaker's view of the threat. Former State Department officer Paul Kattenburg hinted at his broader influence:

What in fact Soviet propaganda emphasis on these struggles in the late fifties and early sixties threatened most was not America's security or power, but America's *will* to develop the Third World along the lines of its own models and theories of what the New Frontier now called 'nation building.' The danger that men like Rostow, U.S. AID director David Bell, and a bevy of other intellectuals brought in by the New Frontier perceived most was the danger that if we did not proceed quickly and firmly with our own nation-building programs, these might be altogether preempted. We would, in effect, be put out of the development business; and with that they feared that the balance of forces in the world would change tremendously.[84]

In line with the widely held view among many strategists that America's primary Cold War vulnerability was psychological, Rostow explained how events in the Third World could call into question its resolve to stand up to the Communist challenge.[85] Speaking in the third person, he reported that "it was the believed vulnerability of the West to nuclear blackmail and the apparent vulnerability of the developing nations to communist intrusion that formed the foundation for Khrushchev's post-Sputnik offensives."[86]

Making clear that he personally shared this concern, Rostow admitted his fear that the free world would lose its "nerve and will" in the face of Soviet nuclear blackmail.[87] Indeed, he and other senior American leaders fretted that if the United States did not respond to Communist aggression in Vietnam it could eventually lead to a nuclear conflict between the superpowers.[88] In addition to this psychological argument about credibility, Rostow also endorsed the geographical argument for intervening in Third World conflicts, the so-called Domino Theory.[89] That these views played a significant role in American involvement in Vietnam is likely given that Rostow drafted one of the earliest memos arguing for greater U.S. involvement there in the fall of 1961.[90]

Did policymakers really need Rostow and other social scientists to convince them of this threat? Former CIA analyst Douglas Blaufarb did not think so, crediting President Kennedy with independently seeing the Communist threat from Third World Communist insurgency.[91] The first question he reportedly asked his aides after he was inaugurated was "what are we doing about guerrilla warfare?"[92] But that hardly diminishes the role that Rostow and other civilian strategists played not only in explaining the threat from Third World insurgencies but also devising means to deal with it for busy policymakers. Indeed, Blaufarb himself conceded that "the subject ... could only occupy a fraction of the time of the president and the attorney general and their immediate staffs."[93] As McNamara explained, "One reason the Kennedy and Johnson administrations failed to take an orderly, rational approach to the basic questions underlying Vietnam was the staggering variety and complexity of other issues we faced. Simply put, we faced a blizzard of problems, there were only twenty-four hours in a day, and we often did not have time to think straight."[94] In brief, most policymakers do not have the time to develop well-thought out views of the causes, consequences, or responses to various threats.[95] This is why the mental maps social scientists draw for them are so important. There are thus good reasons for crediting Rostow and strategic modernization theory for President Kennedy's infatuation with counterinsurgency.[96]

STRATEGIC MODERNIZATION THEORY'S POLICY MENU

In addition to limning the threat, strategic modernization thinkers like Rostow offered policy advice for how to deal with it based on their intellectual framework.[97] Indeed, this inchoate sense that development could affect U.S. national security needed substantial fleshing out, particularly in the nuclear age when others argued that Hiroshima and Nagasaki had unalterably changed warfare and largely relegated the developing world to strategic irrelevance.[98] The Eisenhower administration's early optimism that nuclear weapons could provide security on the cheap was dashed by a series of crises that flared up around the world despite U.S. nuclear superiority. Rostow himself recalled that "the Korean War convinced some of us that the struggle to deter and contain the thrust for expanded communist power would be long and that new concepts would be required to underpin U.S. foreign policy in the generation ahead."[99] The challenge for American policymakers was both intellectual—what were the prospects for other types of conflict in a nuclear world?—and practical: How could we avoid the escalation of lesser military conflicts to all-out nuclear war without surrendering to communism?[100]

The answer was provided by other scholars such as Schelling and Robert Osgood who were pioneering the new field of limited war.[101] While limited war had many facets, including conventional operations and limited nuclear war, it quickly became associated with counterinsurgency and nation building. The final report of a 1962 Limited War Symposium put it well: "Whether one is concerned with programs to alleviate political, social, or economic sources of discontent, with techniques of indirect influence, with the social environment in which actions occur, or with the social and political factors which are targets of action, the kind of underlying knowledge required is the *understanding and prediction of human behavior at the individual, political and social group, and society levels.*"[102] Limited war notions, supplemented by the modernization framework, led directly to U.S. intervention in the Vietnam War.[103] RAND analyst Bernard Brodie confirmed that "this miserable and obviously unfortunate intervention was largely stimulated by the ideas of a group that included some very enlightened and talented people."[104] Rostow was the major figure among them, with his model of the stages of development providing the conceptual foundation for determining U.S. interests in Southeast Asia and identifying threats to them.[105]

Once he went into government, Rostow could put his universal models directly into practice. He was, in fact, hired by Bundy as his deputy precisely because he was an expert on the interrelationship of underdevelopment and insurgency.[106] One of his earliest public speeches in that role was at Ft. Bragg in June 1961.[107] Former under secretary of state George Ball confessed that "the inclusion of Rostow [in Vietnam discussions] worried me. . . . [He was] an articulate amateur tactician . . . unduly fascinated by the then faddish theories about counterinsurgency and that intriguing new invention of the professors, nation-building."[108] Given all of this, it is hardly surprising that Rostow would provide one of the primary intellectual rationales for the war in Vietnam.[109]

MODERNIZATION AS A STRATEGIC IMPERATIVE

Rostow's and strategic modernization theory's most important contribution was to connect development with containing communism in the Third World.[110] As Millikan and Rostow maintained, "The nation's stake in the ideological and political balance in Eurasia is as legitimate as its interest in the military balance of power in Eurasia. Two national efforts, one military and the other political, interacting intimately, must go forward together as part of a total effort to protect the interests of American society."[111] Following the logic he laid out in *Stages of Economic Growth*, Rostow argued that the developing countries were acutely vulnerable to external meddling at the critical pre-takeoff stage of modernization. Anti-Western nationalism (a legacy of colonialism) and instability due to the collapse of old institutions of government provided the Soviets with opportunity to gain influence there.[112] Rostow warned that developing countries would need protection as they passed through this stage of modernization.[113] But he was confident that once through it, Third World nationalism would evolve in a liberal, democratic direction.[114]

Getting less-developed countries through this development window of vulnerability required active U.S. involvement in the transition because, in Rostow's view, "modern societies [there] must be built."[115] Indeed, the core argument of his and Millikan's coauthored book was "that a much-expanded long-term program of American participation in the economic development of the under-developed areas can and should be one of the most important means for furthering the purposes of American foreign policy."[116] Rostow's Kennedy administration colleague Roger Hilsman agreed that Rostow's "conclusion was that the task for the United States was not only to hasten the process of modernization, to get a country past the vulnerable period of transition, but also to protect its independence during that vulnerable period." He also pointed out that "it was the difficulty of this task of protection at the period of greatest vulnerability that led Rostow to the conclusion that it might be necessary to 'seek out and engage the ultimate source of aggression.'"[117] Hence, Rostow's universal model of the stages of economic growth provided the rationale for linking nation building in South Vietnam to coercive operations against North Vietnam.

THE "ROSTOW THESIS" AND COERCIVE
BOMBING OF NORTH VIETNAM

Given the depth and duration of his involvement in the planning and execution of attacks on the North, Rostow, rather than Schelling, certainly merits the dubious distinction of being the primary intellectual architect of the coercive air campaign.[118] As early as June 1961, Rostow had begun to argue that external support for the Viet Cong was the root of the problem in the South that had to be cut off before the Saigon regime could pacify the countryside.[119] In October, along with Kennedy's military advisor General Maxwell Taylor, he conducted a fact-finding trip to South Vietnam.[120] Upon his return, Rostow first broached the idea of bombing the North to accomplish that objective.[121] Chairing a November 1, 1962, White House after-action review on the successful resolution of the Cuban Missile Crisis, Rostow concluded that the United States had succeeded in coercing the Soviets to remove their nuclear missiles through implementing a "program of ascending political pressures against a background of military preparations with the aim not of conquest but of restoration of our vital interests intact."[122]

The "Rostow thesis" explaining how to coerce the North was widely discussed and debated throughout the U.S. government. Drawing on *The Stages of Economic Growth* for conceptual support, Rostow proposed using airpower to threaten North Vietnam's incipient industrial base in order to compel it to end support for the insurgency in the South.[123] In important respects, his thesis led directly to Rolling Thunder, the campaign of air strikes against the North.[124] While Rostow did not shape every aspect of the coercive campaign against the North, particularly its initial stages, he had the most intellectual influence on it overall. Further, he was the most ardent proponent of bombing within the Johnson administration, continuing to support it and bolstering the president's resolve to continue with it even as other aides lost faith in it. He was, in Secretary of Defense Robert McNamara's words, a "big bomber man."[125] Not surprisingly, Rostow was much more popular among many in uniform who thought he, unlike other civilian strategists, had a "real understanding of the applications of power."[126]

Rostow was not simply an amateur academic armchair strategist; during the Second World War, as we saw, he had served in the OSS with the Economic Objectives Unit in London helping to formulate bombing strategy in the European Theater.[127] Based on this wartime experience, Rostow would later boast that he had been a "real professional in the bombing business in my time."[128] Of course, not everyone was impressed by Rostow's wartime credentials. The EOU was made up largely of economists, and their track record in OSS/R&A analyses was decidedly mixed. Moreover, unlike many of the in-house critics of the "Rostow Thesis" such as George Ball and John Kenneth Galbraith, who thought that sustained bombing was unlikely to succeed in coercing a "fanatical enemy," Rostow had not participated in the post–World War II United States Strategic Bombing Survey. That may explain his overconfidence in the efficacy of coercive airpower.[129] W. Averell Harriman, another Rostow critic, served in London during the Blitz and concluded from that experience that bombing would not break popular morale in the North.[130]

Rostow, however, never lost faith in the potential of the coercive air campaign to persuade the North to cut off support for the insurgency in the South, even as analysts in the CIA and outside scientists associated with the Institute for Defense Analyses JASON Division concluded that the bombing was not working and proposed different approaches such as the construction of an electronic barrier to impede the flow of supplies down the Ho Chi Minh Trail.[131] Rostow dug in his heels, harkening back to EOU bombing "doctrine [which] insisted on the need to concentrate bombing attacks against the minimum number of targets whose destruction would achieve the specified military goal and on the need for *perseverance* and *thoroughness* when the attack on a target system had been launched."[132] This mind-set likely convinced Rostow that coercion using limited air power would work as long as we stuck to it. And this dogged adherence to the Rostow thesis was a function of his unbounded confidence in his general models and his imperviousness to any empirical evidence that did not accord with them.

ROSTOW AND COUNTERINSURGENCY DOCTRINE

Rostow maintained that "in the underdeveloped areas of Asia, the Middle East, Africa, and Latin America, Moscow sought to extend its power by orchestrating the instruments of guerrilla warfare, subversion, trade, and aid; by appealing to anticolonial and nationalist sentiments; and by projecting an image of communism as the most efficient method for modernizing the underdeveloped region and as a system closing rapidly on the sluggish American front runner."[133] Since the threat was not a traditional military one, U.S. responses had to reflect that difference. This is where some analysts see a direct connection between Rostow's *Stages of Economic Growth* and some elements of pacification programs in Vietnam such as the Civil Operations, Revolutionary Development Support (CORDS).[134] Indeed, the former provided the theoretical rationale for the latter by emphasizing the fragility of South Vietnam's institutions at its current stage of underdevelopment.[135]

The primary U.S. government forum for the development of counterinsurgency doctrine during the Kennedy administration was an interdepartmental committee nominally under the chairmanship of Rostow's old Yale tutor Richard Bissell, then a CIA official. In reality, Rostow was its driving force.[136] The Kennedy administration established a formal mechanism for disseminating this newly formulated doctrine in "United States Overseas Defense Policy" promulgated in National Security Action Memorandum (NSAM) 182; it was the Inter-Departmental Seminar on Counterinsurgency (IDS).[137] As Michael Shafer noted, this "seminar embodied the interpenetration of academic and official thinking on the issues of modernization and insurgency and the high hopes held for the collaboration."[138] Its intellectual content was mostly provided by CENIS-connected scholars.[139] Rostow's MIT colleagues Lucian Pye and James Eliot Cross had been working on insurgency in connection with CENIS policy-relevant development work for years.[140]

Given Rostow's major role in both aspects of insurgency strategy, White House advisor Arthur Schlesinger Jr. dubbed him "the high priest of counterinsurgency."[141] Recognizing that his outsized role in this issue might seem strange given his focus on economic development, Rostow later explained that "I have for many years been professionally interested in the problems of economic development; and there are those who may find it odd for an economist to be also concerned—as I have been—with the problems of countering Communist methods of guerilla warfare and subversion. But it is, in fact, quite natural for a student of modernization to interest himself in the economic, social, and political development of Vietnam and also in its protection against indirect invasion from the north."[142] And Rostow's interest in counterinsurgency grew as his dissatisfaction with Eisenhower's strategy of nuclear massive retaliation and his associated interest in limited war theory increased.[143]

THE REST OF ACADEMIA RETREATS FROM COUNTERINSURGENCY

Overall, CENIS proved to be quite unique in bridging the world of scholarship and policy in the area of insurgency. True, two major conferences on social science and counterinsurgency were held at American University and Princeton in 1961 and 1962.[144] And an Institute for Defense Analyses

(IDA) study on the topic tallied eighteen major reports sponsored by DoD alone.[145] The two most prominent examples were the Advanced Research Projects Agency's (ARPA) Project Agile and Special Operations Research Office's (SORO) infamous Project Camelot.[146] But as the IDA report also conceded, "an outstanding deficiency in the current DOD program is the absence of long-term support for the development of behavioral and social science methodology applicable to counterinsurgency. The DOD has not committed a single university to the long-term study of social change and economic growth of the underdeveloped countries, the basic conditions which give rise to insurgency. As a result, there is no community of scholars to lead to the growth of knowledge in and the training of investigators concerned with these problems."[147] CENIS director Max Millikan complained at a Joint Seminar on Arms Control that "in dealing with the foreign aid problem recently he realized that crucial intellectual problems which could not have been dealt with in Washington had been avoided by academics."[148]

This absence of engagement was not due to a lack of interest in social science frameworks in the Pentagon. As the IDA report recognized,

> there is an underlying need for a large variety of reliable information about many countries in Africa and Latin America; e.g., composition of masses and elite groups, channels of communication and influence, attitudes toward the local government and toward foreigners of various origins, levels of education, resources for economic growth, and so forth. Such information must be collected and evaluated, but it is even more important that we attempt to understand the nature of social changes that are going on in these countries and the underlying processes which govern them. In the long run, the development of appropriate theories will most enhance our ability to understand, predict and influence the social changes which confront us around the world.[149]

In response, the IDA study suggested the need to establish academic "centers of excellence" to foster the interdisciplinary "study of social conflict in the under-developed world."[150] But it was not overly optimistic that the Defense Department would find what it needed in the Ivory Tower. The report observed that "much of the work at universities is basic in nature, and not obviously relevant to counterinsurgency." This is why such a small percentage (8 percent) of "directly relevant" DoD funding went to support research there.[151] Therefore, most of the work it ended up supporting was by social scientists at nonacademic institutions such as the FFRDCs, including IDA and the RAND Corporation.[152]

Vietnam would ultimately prove to be behavioral social science's intellectual Waterloo. As a later IDA report concluded, "Vietnam has produced little evidence supporting a sanguine view of how well behavioral research has worked out."[153] The problem, according to that subsequent assessment, was the tension between the methodological canons of social science and the reality of conducting research in a war zone.[154] These tensions may explain why university-based social scientists were not major contributors to DoD social science counterinsurgency efforts. Even before the Vietnam War became controversial on university campuses, only 14 percent of attendees at a March 1962 symposium on "The Army's Limited War Mission and Social Science Research" were university affiliated.[155] And in 1964, only 9 percent of social science work on the topic was conducted by universities.[156] This led Seymour Deichtman, then DDR&E's key proponent for counterinsurgency, to complain that "serious deficiencies [in U.S. government research on the topic] are not offset by an adequate research effort on the part of universities or other civilian organizations."[157]

The problem with getting university-based social scientists engaged in this topic was that outside of government, there was not a widespread consensus that insurgency posed the same level of danger to the United States as did previous threats. Without such a consensus, it is hardly surprising that the social scientists' war would see large numbers of academics AWOL. There was, according to one U.S. government working paper, "a poverty of knowledge" among academic social scientists about the sources of insurgency.[158]

So Are We Just Better Off without Academic Influence on Policy?

Does the unfortunate role that Rostow and other economics-influenced scientific strategists played in Vietnam discredit the whole idea of having academic social scientists engage with policymakers?[159] Given that President Kennedy, supposedly following Harvard government professor Richard Neustadt's advice, wanted his staff to function like an academic faculty, does the decidedly mixed record of Camelot in national security affairs more generally justify skepticism?[160]

Boulding, for one, thought it did: "More, perhaps, than any other decade in American history, except that of Woodrow Wilson, the sixties mark the emergence of a small group of intellectuals, mostly from Cambridge, Mass., as a major force in American life. If this experience was a failure, as

I think on the whole it was, the reason . . . was an intellectual failure, that these men were bright, but just not bright enough, and that the image of the world which they held was derived from a garbled view of a partly irrelevant past."[161] McGeorge Bundy recalled telling President Kennedy before the Bay of Pigs "that this was bound to be all right because all of his advisors were professors," a reassurance the former Harvard dean subsequently regretted.[162] Others on the left also saw Vietnam as a cautionary tale about mixing ivy and policy. For some scholars, the whole notion of government drawing on academia inevitably "distorted" social science by undermining its objectivity and tying it to immoral policies.[163] Finally, like many on the political right, who saw Vietnam as emblematic of the failure of the whole enterprise of the academic civilian strategist, General Westmoreland lamented that "[top DoD officials like McNamara and McNaughton] and some White House and State Department advisers appeared to scorn professional military thinkers in a seeming belief that presumably superior Ivy League intellects could devise some hocus-pocus or legerdemain to bring the enemy to terms without using force to destroy his war-making capability."[164] If critics are correct, then deeper engagement by the Academy with policymakers would not have averted America's missteps in Vietnam.[165]

The problem during Vietnam was not too much, but rather too little, scholarly engagement with policy. To begin with, the U.S. government had shockingly little independent area expertise relevant to Vietnam, and it is likely that had area specialists had greater input into policymaking, the United States might have averted many mistakes in Vietnam.[166] Former State, Defense, and CIA official William P. Bundy subsequently asked, "Was there not far too much emphasis on doctrine and management, and far too little on the importance of a real grasp of the culture of the country involved?"[167] Schelling himself later conceded that "there was a poverty of knowledge about Vietnam, unlike the Soviet Union, which had been studied for some thirty years by professional Kremlinologists and historians. It would have been difficult to choose any place of comparable importance about which so little was known as about Vietnam. There was a quality of benightedness, not only among the populace, but even among those in foreign policy."[168]

Asia expert James Thomson explained that "the American government was sorely *lacking in real Vietnam or Indochina expertise*. Originally treated as an adjunct of Embassy Paris, our Saigon embassy and the Vietnam Desk at State were largely staffed from 1954 onward by French-speaking Foreign Service personnel of narrowly European experience."[169] Secretary of Defense McNamara admitted that "none of [his intellectual expertise or previous experience] made me anything close to an East Asian expert, however. I had never visited Indochina, nor did I understand or appreciate its history, language, culture, or values. The same must be said, to varying degrees, about President Kennedy, Secretary of State Dean Rusk, National Security Advisor McGeorge Bundy, military adviser Maxwell Taylor, and many others. When it came to Vietnam, we found ourselves setting policy for a region that was terra incognita. . . . Worse, our government lacked experts for us to consult to compensate for our ignorance."[170] Taylor similarly confessed that "we were inclined to assume . . . that [the North Vietnamese] would behave about like the North Koreans and the Red Chinese a decade before; that is, they would seek an accommodation with us when the cost of pursuing a losing course became excessive."[171] Former State Department director of Southeast Asian affairs Kenneth T. Young admitted that "we have never checked out or 'researched' what makes an effectual adviser in the context of Vietnamese psychology, behavior patterns and political institutions."[172]

Tellingly, the two places in the U.S. government where at least some residual Southeast Asia area expertise remained were in the CIA's Directorate of Intelligence and State's Bureau of Intelligence and Research. It is no coincidence that both produced some of the most prescient analyses of the course of the war and critiques of U.S. policy.[173] Moreover, unlike their policy science–oriented colleagues Nathan Leites and Charles Wolf, RAND area experts like Melvin Gurtov (China), Paul Langer (Japan), and Arnold Horelick (Soviet Union) advocated unilateral withdrawal from Vietnam starting as early as 1966, a policy that in retrospect looks more sensible than escalation, nation building, and counterinsurgency.[174]

Admittedly, policymakers were not totally bereft of area expertise about Vietnam. For example, McNamara and McNaughton occasionally consulted with London University School of Oriental Studies Asia expert Patrick Honey.[175] But the few consultations with Honey are the exceptions that prove the rule that area expertise was not widely available to policymakers. They gravitated toward Honey precisely because they knew that he supported their policies in Vietnam.[176] What Kennedy and Johnson administration officials really needed was not the opinion of one or two cherry-picked experts but rather the consensus of a broader swath of area expertise and opinion concerning Vietnam.

In his later reflections on Vietnam, five out of eleven of McNamara's lessons learned involved the need for greater area expertise. As he concluded, "Top government officials need specialists—experts—at their elbows when they make decisions on matters outside their own experience. If we had had more Asia experts around us, perhaps we would not have been so simple-minded about China and Vietnam."[177] Consulting a broader range of area specialists could have provided policymakers with a better understanding of the dynamics of the rebellion against the U.S.-backed government in South Vietnam.[178] Area experts might also have alerted policymakers to the limits of the United States' ability to shape developments in the Third World and provided them with reasons to think that a more assertive American presence was not necessary to contain communism there.[179] Also, independent assessments based on that expertise are more likely to come from outside the government. For both of these reasons, academia should have been the obvious place from which some of it would come.

Unfortunately, such academic expertise was in short supply. A group called the Council on Vietnamese Studies (CVS) conducted a survey of the "existing state of scholarly study of Vietnam in 1966–67." CVS was an outgrowth of the Southeast Asia Development Advisory Group of the U.S. Agency for International Development (USAID) which emerged from the Southeast Asia Development Advisory Group (SEADAG), a cooperative venture between USAID and the Asia Society.[180] It found a "widespread feeling among many university administrators and academics that Vietnam was a 'government problem' that independent scholars should avoid. In fact, well over ninety percent of the serious social science work on Vietnam is being conducted under the auspices of the United States Government."[181] As the study's author Harvard government professor Samuel Huntington noted, "It is a sad commentary on the state of Vietnamese studies that there were no scholars available in the academic community who could produce comparable analyses [to those produced within the U.S. government]."[182] In other words, even had senior administration officials wanted more area expertise about Vietnam, they would not have found much of it in the nation's universities. This was largely the result of the decline of area studies among increasingly behaviorally oriented social science disciplines.

Rostow's insensitivity to local context was not just a failing of policymakers. Kattenburg observed that "some of the sources for this sort of reasoning . . . are to be found in the globalistic methodologies introduced into the study of political science in the United States in the fifties. 'Comparativism' entered the field along with and as a generic ingredient of behaviorism."[183] The lack of robust area knowledge about Vietnam was a failure of the comparative politics subfield of political science, which under the influence of the Behavioral Revolution had increasingly marginalized area studies in its quest to become more scientific. The academy became less and less inclined to provide such expertise as the social science disciplines endeavored to become more scientific. So the problem of the lack of area expertise was not just on the demand side within the U.S. government; it was also a supply-side problem in the academy. The paucity of area expertise had less to do with political controversies such as McCarthyism and the purge of China experts after the fall of China than with the dominant tendencies among comparative politics scholars who increasingly substituted universal models for deep knowledge of the local context.[184]

And while some scholars blame containment specifically, and realpolitik in general, for Vietnam, it is striking how many leading academic realists were in the forefront of opposition to the growing U.S. role there.[185] The leading realist opponent of the war was University of Chicago political science professor Hans J. Morgenthau. According to his biographer, Morgenthau's objection to U.S. policy in Vietnam was its "crusading spirit," which he feared reflected "a permanent inclination to neglect sober calculations of power and self-interest in favor of abstract moral and ideological principles such as freedom, democracy, human-rights, or anti-communism."[186] President Johnson's White House staff regarded Morgenthau's critiques of their Vietnam policy as so telling that they regularly circulated copies of his articles among themselves to better rebut them.[187] Other academic realists such as Kenneth Waltz were also early skeptics of the war.[188] In addition to academic realists, realist-inclined journalists such as Walter Lippmann and practitioners such as former ambassador to Yugoslavia George Kennan, dissented from the Rostow line. Indeed, Kennan attacked Rostow's Basic National Security Policy root and branch.[189] Unfortunately, it was Rostow, the architect of strategic modernization theory, who carried the day in terms of Cold War U.S. grand strategy in the Third World.[190]

How would the realist approach have led to a more restrained U.S. foreign policy? First, realism embraced a narrower definition of "threat," which led adherents to conclude that by the mid-1960s the United States was actually quite secure as a result of European recovery, the growing Sino-Soviet split, and mutual nuclear deterrence between the Soviet Union and the United States.[191] In a widely discussed piece in the *New York Times* in 1965, Morgenthau argued that the United States had no interest in South Vietnam because what threat there was emanated from China, not the Soviet Union, and it was political, not military, as in Europe.[192] He made this same point in his famous television debate with McGeorge Bundy on June 21, 1965.[193] Indeed, realists were in the forefront of those who realized early that the threat from communism in Vietnam to U.S. national interests was minimal. The realist focus on material power both kept realists engaged in the developed world but led them to take a more relaxed view of developments in the developing world. They understood that the international Communist movement since the death of Stalin had ceased to be monolithic, they questioned both the domino theory and the related credibility of commitment arguments, and in general recognized that nationalism was the primary fuel for the antigovernment conflagration in South Vietnam.

Realists were also skeptical about the ability of even as powerful a state as the United States to remake the developing world in its image. "Our civilization assumes that the social world is susceptible to rational control conceived after the model of the natural sciences," Morgenthau wrote, but "the experiences, domestic and international of the age, contradict this assumption."[194] As Waltz remarked at a 1964 Harvard-MIT seminar, "If one wanted to succeed in Vietnam, the only way was to capture the spirit and natural imagination of the people." But in his view, "this was not something we could do."[195] Though critical of the tendency of some area specialists to eschew theory completely, Morgenthau was nonetheless a defender of their importance in the face of attack by the behaviorally oriented comparativists.[196]

Finally, realists led the opposition to Vietnam War because unlike the rest of the discipline, which was increasingly retreating from policy engagement in the name of becoming more scientific, leading members of that school like Morgenthau swam furiously against that current. Well before the war politicized academic involvement with government, Morgenthau was already complaining about political science's "retreat into the trivial, the formal, the methodological, the purely theoretical, the remotely historical—in short the politically irrelevant."[197] Moreover, he reminded his colleagues that "all the great contributions to political science, from Plato to Aristotle to *The Federalist* and Calhoun, have been responses to . . . challenges arising from political reality. They have not been self-sufficient theoretical developments pursuing theoretical concerns for their own sake."[198] Such an approach led him to strike a better balance between theory and methods, on the one hand, and policy engagement and distance, on the other. It also avoided the danger of policy capture, clearly evident in the cases of many administration officials who realized the war was not going well but could not openly dissent because they had been coopted through being part of the decision-making process. Their measured threat assessment prompted realists to remain engaged in national security relevant scholarship but also to advocate circumspection in how the United States waged the global Cold

War. The problem with realism is that its numbers were so few that it had little influence on larger political debates.

A third group of scholars who got things right in important respects were the growing number of critics of modernization theory, particularly Samuel Huntington. Again, this claim cuts against the conventional wisdom, which holds that Huntington's support for the war reflected his commitment to modernization theory.[199] There is no doubt that Huntington was a long-standing supporter of the war, and that support tarnishes his otherwise bright intellectual luster.[200] Still, we should not ignore the fact that he also delivered some of the most telling intellectual and policy blows against modernization theory and the Johnson administration's Vietnam policy.[201]

On the former, Huntington emerged as the leading conservative critic of modernization theory, calling into question whether the developed world could successfully social engineer the developing world and raising doubts about whether modernization was a wholly "progressive" process.[202] In his magnum opus *Political Order and Changing Societies* and related publications, Huntington famously argued that modernization and stable institutions were negatively correlated.[203] The book was widely regarded as the "most important" book on modernization theory by the 1970s.[204] And it led to modernization theory's intellectual eclipse.[205]

On the latter, Huntington spent two months in Vietnam assessing CORDS for the Department of State. Upon his return, he wrote a ninety-five-page report that was a "veiled critique" of Rostow and other strategic development theorists.[206] A closer look at Huntington's published version of this report in the journal *Foreign Affairs* reveals that it was quite moderate in its conclusions that the war would only be settled by compromise. As he telegraphed in his title, and expounded on in the text, "American objectives and American expectations of what can be achieved at the conference table and on the battlefield should, correspondingly, be based on the realities of power and the opportunities for accommodation."[207]

Finally, like Morgenthau and other realists, Huntington was skeptical about making strategy a science in the mold of the Behavioral Revolution's policy science movement, despite his early sympathy with some of its intellectual aspirations. His critique of the McNamara approach was also a critique of powerful intellectual trends in the Academy.[208] Indeed, Huntington's approach throughout his successful intellectual career was to identify pressing real-world problems and then use social science theory to try to make sense of them conceptually rather than starting with political science's preferred techniques and finding topics amenable to them.[209]

Conclusions: Lessons Learned? What Is to Be Done?

So what lessons does the rise and fall of strategic modernization theory teach? Rostow was a complex figure; both an engaged and influential action-intellectual of the sort that epitomized Kennedy's Camelot but also a scholarly Rasputin who set the intellectual stage for a darker version of that mythical kingdom. I have dwelled at length on the negative side of Rostow's influence but to that critical appraisal I would add some caveats: Rostow's penchant for universal models was a double-edged sword: his critics often dismissed his theories on the grounds that they were not sufficiently scholarly.[210] But University of Chicago historian and State Department Policy Planning Staff member William Polk explained that Rostow was influential among policymakers precisely because his notion of "takeoff" was one of those "vivid phrases or conceptual notions which bring order or, at least some light into the darkened lanes of international affairs."[211] While many academics of his era sought to bridge the theory/policy divide, Rostow was singularly successful in doing so, in part due to his policy-relevant theorizing.

In addition, Rostow engaged issues that policymakers, particularly in the Kennedy administration, cared about. As his fellow action-intellectual Hilsman recounted, the president "was interested in ideas and theories, but not for their own sake. His interest was aroused only when the ideas had some practical consequence, only if they could make it possible to shape the world, to accomplish something."[212] Rostow provided such a theory of economic growth. His preference for employing a qualitative, historical approach to theorizing about economic development was also much more accessible to policymakers than the increasingly abstruse formal modeling and complex econometrics that were coming to dominate the academic discipline of economics. Moreover, Rostow's generally Keynesian approach to economics, which granted government a significant role in fostering economic development, was more palatable to policymakers than the emerging neoclassical privileging of the independent workings of the hidden hand of the market, which tended to confine the policy space to removing impediments to its unfettered operation.[213]

Finally, atypical among callow academics, Rostow had an acute sense not only of what was politically feasible but also what dovetailed with larger ideological currents. Again, Hilsman emphasized that "the best way to improve policy . . . is probably to conduct it with an eye—but a highly discriminating eye—to the political realities of the process by which it is made."[214] Rostow's lofty aspiration to become the liberal answer to Karl Marx certainly fit the mood of the country in the early Cold War, which was at once both triumphalist in the wake of victory over Nazism and its allies but also uncertain in the face of the global Communist challenge.[215] In this respect, he presaged both the approach and the success in influencing policy of some the neoconservative action-intellectuals of the subsequent 9/11 generation.[216]

Still Rostow's experience teaches three cautionary lessons for scholars trying to influence national security policymaking. First, it demonstrates the downside of academics going directly into government. Rostow could have stayed at CENIS and MIT as he originally promised and conducted the sort of policy-relevant scholarship to which he originally felt called. Had he done so, he would have produced it unbiased by the vested interest in the particular policies he made once in government. Also, he would have remained engaged with the rest of the academic community, which would have been salutary for both him and his colleagues.

Second, Rostow's disdain for the messy reality of particular parts of the world to which he applied his elegant models was widely noted. The result of Rostow's penchant for universal theorizing was the devaluation of country-specific knowledge among policymakers. This lack of area expertise directly contributed to the failure of Kennedy and Johnson administration policies in Vietnam. In the long run, economics' preoccupation with universal models, combined with the decline of area studies among the other social sciences, meant that Rostow's application of them to policy faced little scrutiny from the rest of the academy, which increasingly eschewed engagement in policy affairs in favor of focusing on basic science.

A final lesson of this case, therefore, is the need to provide incentives to make academic research more relevant to the concerns of the policymaker, both to provide analysis and advice as well as to serve as a check on other sources of them.[217] Academics' failure to do so during the Vietnam era reflected the growing retreat from relevance within the social sciences. The best way to counter Rostow and the other scientific modernization strategists would have been for other scholars to engage, rather than ignore, the Vietnam policy debate in their own scholarship.

8

The "Renaissance of Security" Languished until the Owl of Minerva Flew after 9/11

The conventional wisdom remains that the Vietnam War constitutes one of the most serious challenges to the standing of policy-relevant security studies in the academy.[1] Attesting to the deteriorating intellectual climate for policy-relevant national security research, leading academic security scholars such as William Kaufmann and Thomas Schelling lamented that the unrest caused by the Vietnam War in Cambridge nearly put an end to the academic study and teaching of national security. As Schelling remarked apropos of his post-Vietnam intellectual reorientation away from security studies, "I lost the access, I lost the audience, and I lost the motivation."[2] Looking back, MIT political scientist Barry Posen blamed Vietnam for causing a "lost" second generation of security specialists in the 1970s; as a result of that war, "academia was not very hospitable" to them.[3]

But exactly how did Vietnam undermine academic security studies? Most analysts of the period explain it by virtue of ideology. The war itself became politically controversial, particularly on the left of the political spectrum, and as antiwar sentiment spread, so the argument goes, it discredited academic collaboration with the U.S. government and fanned the flames of antimilitarism.[4] As part of this general ideological reaction against the war, many scholars and academic administrators turned against the subfield of security studies, and its standing in the academy plummeted as the legitimacy of studying war and engaging in policy-relevant research was undermined by the ideological backlash against it.[5]

While there is no doubt that the Vietnam War nudged the political center of gravity on campus further to the left, this ideological shift was not the only factor in the decline of academic security studies in the 1970s. There are two problems with attributing the decline of academic national security studies exclusively to the Vietnam War. The first of these is timing: resistance within universities to close collaboration with government policymakers began well before the United States became directly involved in Vietnam.[6] The second problem with the Vietnam explanation is that its causal mechanism is flawed. The professoriate has long been to the left of the public politically so this has been a constant, rather than a variable, factor.[7] Such a constant factor (professors' political orientations) cannot explain a pattern of variation (changing attitudes about the appropriateness of policy-relevant scholarship among them). In fact, ideological skepticism about the military in general, and security studies as an academic field of thought in particular, is also a relatively constant element in American political culture.[8]

While there were both ideological and methodological attacks on the intellectual legitimacy of policy-relevant national security studies, the former were rarely successful while the latter gained the most traction in times of peace or reduced international threats.[9] Moreover, it was disciplinary professionalism, as much as ideology, which widened the gap between the academic and policy worlds after Vietnam. Thus, a complete explanation for the decline of policy-relevant national security studies must also include the dynamics of academic normal social science combined with the changing international security environment.[10]

This chapter begins by briefly tracing the development of political science after Vietnam, chronicling how the discipline continued to professionalize on the model of the natural sciences. The result was to privilege the refinement of method over practical relevance. It then looks at the standing of national security studies in political science—its natural home in the academy—highlighting how it waxed during times of greater threat and waned when the international environment seemed more benign, as table 8.1 suggests. It also traces the causal links between them, demonstrating that in peacetime scholars were more inclined to respond to the tensions between basic and applied research by embracing the former. It then considers how national security policymakers have sought to use social science and what

TABLE 8.1. The Pattern of the Waxing and Waning of Security Studies after Vietnam

Period	Threat environment	Status of security studies
Détente	↓	"Lost Generation"
Cold War II	↑	The Renaissance
Post–Cold War	↓	Efforts to "abolish" it
Post-9/11	↑↓	Minerva's mixed result

they discovered about when and how it was useful to them. It concludes by suggesting that political science is most useful to policymakers when it takes a problem-, rather than method-driven, approach to setting the scholarly agenda for academic security specialists.

The Relevance Question in Political Science since the Late 1960s

POLITICAL SCIENCE'S POST-VIETNAM METHODS OBSESSION . . .

One standard history of the discipline of political science posited a cycle in "which political scientists have become enamored of, and then disenchanted with, the idea of a scientific politics."[11] This pattern was evident in the recurrent efforts to craft a "science of politics," which included the interwar New Science of Politics movement; the post–World War II Behavioral Revolution; and most recently four other manifestations of this impulse during the post-Vietnam period: the Rational Choice wave during détente; the Empirical Implications of Theoretical Models (EITM) movement, which arose in response to Rational Choice; the renewed interest among quantitative political scientists in establishing "causation"; and the current emphasis on Multimethod Research.[12] Despite a rhetorical commitment to policy relevance, each in fact ultimately worked to the detriment of policy-relevant national security studies in the discipline, particularly in peacetime.

What unites the Rational Choice, EITM, experiments, and multimethod approaches of recent years is the same impulse: to privilege method as the defining feature of "scientific" work in political science. Gary King, Robert Keohane, and Sidney Verba, authors of the multimethods wave's ur-text *Designing Social Inquiry* illustrate the continuing methods preoccupation in political science. As they stipulated from the very first pages, "the content of 'science' is primarily the *methods* and rules, *not the subject matter*, since we can use these methods to study virtually anything."[13] In the face of the inevitable tensions between rigor and relevance, they ultimately side with the former: *"A proposed topic that cannot be refined into a specific research project permitting valid descriptive or casual inference should be modified along the way or abandoned."*[14] When faced with tensions between the demands of science and "mere relevance," adherents of this approach will bow before the demands of method rather than acceding to the importance of the question itself.[15] In other words, technique will trump relevance.

Many contemporary political scientists nonetheless remain confident that the correlational approach will prove satisfactory for the needs of policymakers. King, Keohane, and Verba, for instance, deny any tension between the importance of the question and its answer through "science."[16] Some scholars go further, asserting that only with the complete triumph of the effort to remake social science in the image of the natural sciences will it prove truly useful more broadly.[17] This optimism persists today.[18] At its root is the notion that the results of "basic research"—the pursuit of knowledge for its own sake—will eventually and effortlessly find direct policy application.[19] In other words, this trickle-down (or bubble-up from methodologically sophisticated staff) theory makes the relevance question moot in many people's minds.[20] However, this optimism assumes what needs to be demonstrated: that basic research automatically and without additional effort from scholars somehow translates itself into useful applied knowledge. Natural scientists have long recognized the tensions between basic and applied research, which is why engineering emerged as a separate discipline. The same is true of policymakers.[21] Even some methodologically sophisticated social scientists engaged in applied research projects are coming to recognize these tensions as well.[22]

The most important reason that disciplinary professionalization of political science has resulted in its decreasing relevance is that its most advanced techniques are, whatever their other virtues, weak on identifying and understanding the causal mechanisms of political behavior. Despite recent attention to improving "causal inference" using experiments in quantitative political science, it is not clear that this will help the discipline solve the relevance problem. Roughly speaking, social scientists have pursued one of two ways to establish causation. The first is to focus on observing and tracing the actual causal "process" through direct observation of its workings.[23] This mechanisms approach is mostly a qualitative, historical exercise of *observing* the casual mechanisms linking a potential cause with its effect.[24]

In contrast, other political scientists have worked to refine correlational approaches in order to *infer* causation by more precisely establishing associations between variables, most recently through the use of experiments that seek to impose the structure of the laboratory on the messy world of politics.[25] As statistician Paul Holland explained, this correlational statistical regularities approach seeks to measure "the impossible-to-observe causal effect of *t* on a specific unit with the possible-to-estimate *average* causal effect of *t* over a population of units."[26] In practice, this approach is almost exclusively quantitative.[27] It is fair to say that it now "prevails in quantitative research and its methodology."[28] There are grounds for skepticism, however, that this correlational approach is a more reliable way of establishing causation than process tracing and whether its results will prove as useful to policymakers as the alternative causal mechanisms' strategy.

Some political scientists deny there is any meaningful difference between the correlation and process tracing approaches.[29] But experiments remain at bottom a correlational approach to inferring causation. They differ from other large-N approaches only "in the degree of control an *experimenter* has over the phenomena under investigation compared with that which an *observer* has."[30] Moreover, controlled experiments remain limited in the applicability of their findings to larger populations.[31] Conversely, the mechanisms' approach focuses on identifying which factor actually has an effect on the outcome in the first place.[32] This difference explains why there is growing recognition among scholars that "causal-process observations offer a *different* approach to inference" from large-N statistical studies.[33]

It is, though, precisely this identifying and manipulating causal mechanisms in concrete cases that is central to policymaking. The problem is that the "explanatory" causal inference that large-N approaches provide often does not meet the "pragmatic" needs of practitioners.[34] Moreover, policymakers are more interested in the outcome in a specific case than in producing a general model of social behavior. Because qualitative case study approaches using process tracing identify precisely the things that policymakers seek to understand and manipulate, it is not surprising that they gravitate toward the results of this type of social science research. No wonder that the late Stanford political scientist Alexander George, a scholar deeply committed to bridging the gap between academia and the policy world throughout his career, devoted substantial intellectual effort to refining causal process-tracing as a tool of social science.[35]

SPARKS WIDESPREAD DISSATISFACTION INSIDE
AND OUTSIDE OF THE DISCIPLINE

Unhappiness about how developments in political science have affected its broader relevance has been evident within the discipline itself. Strikingly, one of the early leaders of the Behavioral Revolution—University of Chicago political scientist David Easton—would later confess to second thoughts, in large part on the grounds of the discipline's growing irrelevance.[36] In his 1969 American Political Science Association Presidential Address he sought "an answer as to how we as political scientists have proved so disappointingly ineffectual in anticipating the world of the 1960s."[37] He offered concrete evidence to back up this charge: "There can be little doubt that political science as an enterprise has failed to anticipate the crises that are upon us. One index of this is perhaps that in the decade from 1958 to 1968, [the discipline's flag-ship journal *American Political Science*] *Review* published only 3 articles on the urban crises; 4 on racial conflicts; 1 on poverty; 2 on civil disobedience; and 2 on violence in the United States." Easton explained that as the discipline increasingly focused on "basic research" it "shift[ed] the focus away from current concerns and . . . delay[ed] the application of knowledge until we are more secure about its reliability."[38] He predicted that this growing irrelevance of behavioral political science was setting the stage for a post–Behavioral Revolution.[39] As we will see, his hope that the discipline would recommit itself to balancing science and reform was overly optimistic. As two political scientists later concluded, "By the 1970s, social science triumphed, with the discipline becoming explicitly theoretical and empirical [meaning large-N] and its rewards going to those scholars who embraced a scientific approach."[40]

Easton was not alone in his disenchantment and the discipline's decreasing relevance has continued to trouble many political scientists.[41] For example, a report to the American Political Science Association Council of member responses to a survey showed that a high percentage of current (43 percent) and former (51 percent) members were dissatisfied with the *American Political Science Review* for being "too narrow, too specialized and methodological, and too removed from politics."[42] Despite this growing discontent, real changes in the discipline would not come until a few years later, perhaps not coincidentally after the attacks of September 11, 2001, and the beginning of the Global War on Terror.[43] In 2002, APSA president Theda Skocpol established a task force on Graduate Education in the discipline. Its final report to the APSA Council conceded the need for political science to better communicate internally across subfields and externally with the broader public. It also frankly acknowledged that recent disciplinary developments in political science had created various "tensions."[44] In addition, long-standing unhappiness with the *APSR* finally prompted the association to establish a new journal *Perspectives on Politics* to promote greater dialogue both within and outside the discipline.[45] This disciplinary ferment was somewhat more effective in the context of the post-9/11 world than had been the previous efforts of the late 1960s and early 1970s, but as we shall see did not finally settle political science's relevance question.

No Fighting in the Classroom: The Waxing and Waning of Academic Security Studies since Vietnam

While the history of the discipline of political science since the end of the Vietnam War has been one of continuing disciplinary professionalization modeled on the natural sciences and economics, the standing of the subfield of security studies has waxed and waned dramatically during this same period. Variation in its standing tracks most closely with changes in the nature of the international security environment. Security studies garnered at least grudging acceptance in the academy in times of intense external threat but found it difficult to maintain its precarious toehold in the Ivory Tower during peacetime. The reason for its periodic decline was the dominance of "scientific impulses" in the discipline.[46]

That security studies should find its academic footing unsteady after the end of the Vietnam War and the beginning of a period of détente between the United States and the Soviet Union is not surprising. It follows that such a relaxation in tensions would increase the relative importance of other policy concerns.[47] Moreover, this less pressing sense of threat reduced public interest in what academic national security experts had to say.[48] Even scholars deeply committed to the security studies enterprise conceded that détente mandated a radical reassessment in how we think about its place in the academy.[49] Such a reconceptualization undermined the previously close relations between the academy and government. This explains why Michigan political scientist Raymond Tanter and Princeton political scientist Richard Ullman reported during the early 1970s that their "search of the existing literature of international relations theory has rather forcibly impressed upon us that academic theorists and working practitioners have had, and appear to continue to have, relatively little to say to one another."[50]

By the early 1970s there was a marked change in the attitudes on campus about academics participating in national security policymaking. Many still did participate as individuals, but the bridge from the Ivory Tower to the Beltway increasingly became a one-way street, with most of those crossing over it to Washington such as Henry Kissinger and Zbigniew Brzezinski never really returning to academe.[51] To be sure, a handful of senior scholars in political science managed to go back and forth—people like Samuel Huntington, Joseph Nye, Robert Jervis—but as time went on they became more and more the exception rather than rule among leading scholars. Today, those academics with greatest visibility in the policy world are less likely to be among the leaders of the discipline.[52]

Nongovernmental organizations such as the New York Council on Foreign Relations have sought to bridge what they saw as a growing Ivory Tower/Beltway gap through innovative programs like their International Affairs Fellowships (IAF) intended to encourage scholars to take time off to spend a year in government.[53] But as the data in figure 8.1 makes clear, this effort has had only mixed success in getting scholars off campus. Their interest in doing so seems to wax and wane with periods of international threat, though the overall trend has been downward since the beginning of the program.

Conversely, the post-détente period coincided with renewed interest on campus in defense-related work more generally.[54] The ouster of the shah of Iran, a pillar of the U.S. security architecture in the Persian Gulf; the Soviet invasion of Afghanistan; increasing unrest in Central America following the Nicaraguan Revolution and a growing insurgency in El Salvador; and indications that the Soviet Union might not be content with nuclear parity all helped bring détente to an end and reinvigorate the Cold War rivalry.[55] As the late Ohio State political scientist and occasional national security official Joseph Kruzel explained, such a dangerous security environment is a "time when scholarly advice is most useful: when some catastrophic or unexpected event puts an end to bureaucratic politics as usual," which was surely what this period represented.[56]

After serving in the Carter administration, Harvard political scientist Joseph Nye returned to campus in 1979 with a newfound appreciation of the wide gap that had opened between scholarship and the world of affairs during the détente era and a commitment to bridging it. He also concluded that the social scientists' "trickle-down approach of diffusing ideas through one's students and academic articles is insufficient."[57] Foundation leaders such as former Kennedy and Johnson national security advisor McGeorge Bundy had also grown concerned that security studies was no longer well-ensconced in the universities of the 1970s.[58] Under his leadership, the

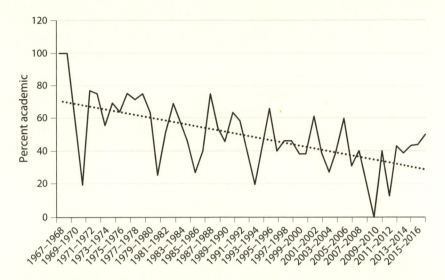

FIGURE 8.1. Percentage of academic IAF fellows. (Data at http://www3.nd.edu/~carnrank/.)

Ford Foundation made major investments in supporting national security programs at Harvard ($8 million), Stanford ($1.5 million), MIT ($1.5 million), and Cornell ($500,000) among other places.[59] Other foundations such as Carnegie, Hewlett, Sloan, and Olin would later follow suit, helping to construct a new academic infrastructure to support security studies at many of the nation's leading universities in the waning days of the détente era.[60]

What political scientist Stephen Walt characterized as the "Renaissance of Security" coincided with this second phase of the Cold War. Unlike the "Golden Age" generation of the 1950s—which was focused on nuclear strategy, counterinsurgency, and nation building—this new generation of academic strategists explored different issues such as the further refinement of rational deterrence theory, conventional deterrence and general purpose forces, and grand strategy. It did so explicitly in the context of the interface between security studies and international relations theory. Indeed, its members were more committed to the academic enterprise of theory creation, theory testing, and theory application. And while members of the previous generation had made their intellectual homes primarily in government, think tanks, and the new FFRDCs such as RAND and the IDA, this new wave of security scholars entrenched themselves deeply in academe.

The renaissance generation of academic strategists believed that they had finally found a stable balance of rigor with relevance that would consolidate the subfield's place in the academy and answer its relevance question once and for all.[61] Walt celebrated the 1980s-era "marriage between security studies and social science" that "improved [its] standing within the academic world."[62] His Harvard colleague Steven Miller, the editor of the subfield's leading scholarly journal *International Security*, likewise affirmed that "we have never felt any tension between our university base and our scholarly mode of operation, on the one hand, and our orientation to the current problems of security on the active policy agenda, on the other."[63] Columbia University political scientist Jack Snyder held up the then-current effort to make comparative case studies more rigorous as the basis for a happy marriage between social science and policy.[64] The subfield finally seemed to have achieved Schelling's objective of producing an "academic counterpart" to the military profession, his prescription for finally curing the subfield's "retarded" condition.[65]

This renewed Cold War optimism soon gave way to doubts that a balance between rigor and relevance was sustainable. Even as he was proclaiming a renaissance, Walt fretted that some social scientists studying war were confusing the "product" of science (laws and numbers) with its "process" (logical and systematic inquiry).[66] Further, some of the hallmarks of security studies' success contained the seeds of its eventual isolation. For example, the renaissance had seen the flourishing of the subfield's flagship journal *International Security* at Harvard. *IS* emerged from the late détente period, "a revival of intellectual ferment as well as intuitive uneasiness," seeking to bring an interdisciplinary perspective to security studies and "balance articles of assessment and opinion with those of analysis and research."[67] While this was a positive development in many respects, it had the unintended consequence of ghettoizing security studies within international relations and political science. Prior to *International Security*, the leading international relations journal, *World Politics*, had been the most prestigious venue for the publication of security studies scholarship.[68] Figure 8.2 shows that after *International Security* began publishing work on nuclear weapons, the topic largely disappeared from the pages of *World Politics*. Figure 8.3 shows that during this period, *International Security* became almost the sole venue for publication of policy relevant scholarship in international relations, perhaps taking pressure off other journals to publish such work.

A second worrisome trend was continuing ideological opposition to security studies even during the darkest days of the second phase of the Cold War. Some international relations scholars began to call for a redefinition of the subfield of security studies, focusing both on broadening its substantive focus and rethinking its previously close relationship with U.S. government policymakers.[69]

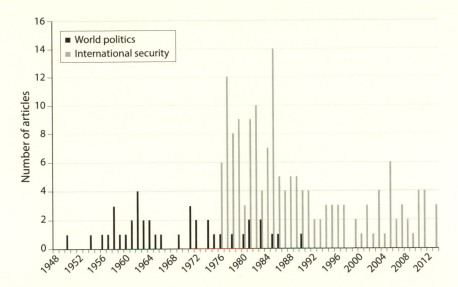

FIGURE 8.2. Articles on nuclear weapons in world politics and international security. (Source: TRIP.)

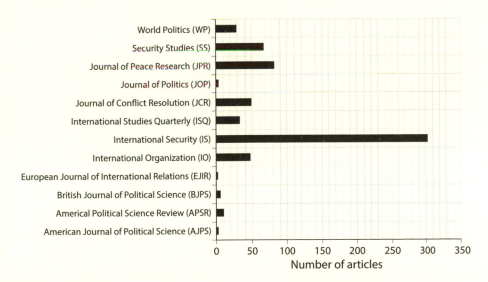

FIGURE 8.3. Numbers of articles with policy recommendations in international relations journals. (Source: TRIP.)

Underwriting this anti–security studies sentiment were the ample re-sources of one of America's largest philanthropic foundations, Chicago's John T. and Catherine M. MacArthur Foundation. Unlike the Ford Foundation, which sought to reform security studies from within, MacArthur tried to dra-matically change it from outside.[70] Establishing a joint International Peace and Security Program with the Social Science Research Council, MacArthur aimed to extinguish the rekindled Cold War by "broadening" security stud-ies.[71] The foundation's operating assumption was that the study of strategy was part of the problem because it was overly narrow and lacked intellec-tual perspectives from disciplines beyond political science.[72] Telegraphing MacArthur's philosophy, program staffer Robert Latham complained that security studies "before the 1980s had been [comprised of] a rather narrow set of foreign policy experts, strategic analysts, and scientists."[73] The main architect of MacArthur's efforts to broaden the definition of "security" was Ruth Adams, a former editor of the dovish *Bulletin of Atomic Scientists*, who found allies in academia among international relations scholars like Cornell political scientist Peter Katzenstein, a member of the SSRC's Committee on Peace and International Security during the 1990s.[74]

Preventing nuclear war was a priority for MacArthur during the second phase of the Cold War. In the foundation's view, the prospects for peace and nuclear disarmament could only be improved by bringing in broader perspectives and listening to new voices. To that end, Latham explained that "the program has endeavored to expand the diversity of researchers who might be counted as part of the security field, on the basis of nationality, gender, race, and ethnicity." This broadening was not just an effort to expand the pool of security scholars but was also a direct critique of mainstream security studies itself. As Latham noted, this broadening "has meant drawing young scholars to security-related research whose intellectual identity was *not* associated with the security field."[75]

Despite the foundation's ample resources, MacArthur's effort largely failed while the Cold War remained hot. Latham himself admitted that de-spite its efforts to bring in new voices and perspectives during the Cold War, almost 40 percent of MacArthur funding was spent on traditional security topics. It was only with the end of the Cold War that support for such work dropped to 3 percent of projects funded.[76] With an easing of the Cold War sense of international threat, complaints about the narrowness of the subfield finally began to resonate more broadly.[77] Nothing highlighted this change within the mainstream U.S. foreign policy community more clearly than the admission by a figure with impeccable establishment credentials like

Jessica Tuchman Mathews, writing in the most venerable of foreign policy journals *Foreign Affairs*, that "the 1990s will demand a redefinition of what constitutes national security."[78] In short, it was only as the Cold War ebbed for good in the early 1990s that the widespread and well-financed efforts to redefine "security" began to gain traction. This timing highlights the central role of the security environment in shaping scholarly attitudes about security studies. However, it was not the ideological argument for doing so that proved most telling. Rather, the critique from within academic social science that security studies was methodologically deficient ultimately carried the day, which demonstrates the importance of disciplinary professionalization.

The first hint that critics of security studies were out to do away with the subfield on these grounds involved a senior faculty appointment at Harvard. In the early 1980s, Samuel Huntington had raised funds to endow the Beaton Michael Kaneb Professorship of National Security and Military Affairs in the Government Department. After some years of searching, the Government Department voted overwhelmingly to offer the chair to Richard Betts, at that time at the Brookings Institution but weighing a faculty offer from Columbia University. Despite Betts's sterling credentials as a scholar, and the strong support from the department, the appointment was stopped by Harvard President Derek Bok in November 1989, ironically almost coincident with the fall of the Berlin Wall. Other security studies scholars were stunned by the decision. Confident that Betts's case could not have been denied on its merits, critics of Bok's decision suspected that it was the result of two other considerations: the view that the end of the Cold War made security studies irrelevant and doubts about the social scientific rigor of the subfield.[79] While the professorship was eventually filled after six more years of searching, the Kaneb chair incident marked the opening skirmish in the post–Cold War methods war over the fate of the subfield of policy-relevant post–Cold War security studies.[80]

The next indicator that academic security studies was under assault in the Ivory Tower came during another faculty search at the University of California, San Diego. For a number of years, the Political Science Department there had been unsuccessfully searching for a security scholar.[81] Broader controversy erupted in September 1993 when UCSD faculty member David Lake sent a letter to prominent figures in the subfield, including the University of Chicago's John Mearsheimer, soliciting suggestions for candidates for a security studies position at San Diego's School of International Relations and Pacific Affairs, noting specifically that "we are taking an expansive definition of the field."[82]

Mearsheimer responded in a letter circulated to many other security scholars charging that UCSD was not "serious about hiring in the security field." He attributed this lack of seriousness in part to hostility toward the qualitative social science approach of the Renaissance generation of security scholars on the part of the many adherents of Rational Choice in the UCSD department.[83] In effect, he was charging that they were repurposing the Cold War MacArthur Foundation ideological broadening argument, but using it to justify a narrow definition of the legitimate methods for social science research that excluded many scholars in security studies. Betts agreed that "the unmistakable implication of insisting on 'broader' or 'more comprehensive' conceptions is that the standard work in the field is inadequate."[84]

In response, search committee chair Stephen Haggard defended UCSD's broad definition of the subfield.[85] Peter Gourevitch, dean of IR/PS, weighed in, pointing out that a previous search had resulted in an offer to a mainstream security studies scholar and dismissing Mearsheimer's letter "as a broadside against many ills he sees in the profession, in political science, foundations, universities, somehow all bound up in UCSD behavior."[86] Even some of Mearsheimer's fellow security scholars initially thought that he had overstated the case against UCSD, though they agreed that there were grounds for Mearsheimer's concerns.

Typical of this view was Columbia political scientist Jack Snyder's complaint about

> a blind spot—even a double standard—in the way rational-choice people evaluate work that does not employ formal models. I have been in many conversations lately, where it seemed to me that preferences for a very specific methodology led people to misunderstand and underestimate the work of mainstream security scholars or to overestimate the novelty of the modelers' results. I have noticed rational-choice scholars reinventing the wheel in security studies, borrowing existing ideas, or exaggerating the extent to which formalization really adds a new concept—all the while criticizing the backwardness of traditional security studies. I have caught pro-rational-choice scholars praising formal models of security problems, but when pressed being unable to explain the ideas in the model. Evidently the thing to be praised was the attempt to make a formal model, irrespective of its content.[87]

But what really galvanized the security studies community behind Mearsheimer's jeremiad was the circulation of another letter from Haggard to Betts in December dismissing the whole controversy as merely "special pleading for a field in terminal decline" and lumping security studies with area studies, both of which he thought had "stagnated" intellectually.[88] Initially among those who thought Mearsheimer had overstated the case, Betts annotated a copy of Haggard's letter, which he sent to Mearsheimer with the handwritten note: "The smoking gun to prove your arguments."[89]

This controversy quickly spread to other instances of international relations scholars publically questioning the methodological rigor of the subfield. In response to a scolding letter from Stephen Walt, Harvard international political economy specialist Robert Keohane admitted that he had "been critical of the policy-oriented work on nuclear issues done during the 1980s . . . on the grounds that . . . it tended to be too closely oriented to contemporary policy issues, and sometimes to technical issues, without sufficient theoretical or historical content, or methodological sophistication."[90] This was apparently a view widely held among his colleagues.[91] Walt pointed out that this critique of security studies constituted a broader challenge to policy relevance.[92] Tellingly, both sides of the debate acknowledged that what had brought it to a head was the end of the Cold War and the changing international security environment.[93]

The UCSD contretemps anticipated a larger debate about whether Rational Choice constituted the best methodological approach for security studies in the post–Cold War world. Following the latest fashion in the discipline of political science, other international relations scholars increasingly advocated it adopt the tools of economics. Security studies, however, had long included economists in the subfield.[94] Many of them like Carl Kaysen and Charles Hitch would become critics of the methodological trends within their own discipline that were leading it to increasingly privilege rigor over relevance. As Hitch later recalled, "Simultaneously, I was repelled by the sterility of much of what I was teaching [at Oxford in 1935]. It was sterile in two senses—lacking in empirical content, and in relevance to the staggering economic policy problems of the decade of the Great Depression."[95] Not surprisingly, later calls that security studies should emulate economics fell on deaf ears among traditional security scholars.[96]

In an influential essay, Walt charged that Rational Choice privileged logical consistency over originality and empirical validity.[97] In doing so, it sacrificed policy relevance, which in his view constituted "a major liability of formal work in the field of security studies."[98] Proponents of Rational Choice in security studies dismissed his concerns on somewhat contradictory grounds. On the one hand, some argued that the role of scholars was to conduct basic research that "should not be driven by policy." But they also remained optimistic about such research eventually trickling down to policymakers in some fashion.[99] Others maintained that unless security studies became more scientific (by which they meant formal and mathematical) it would never constitute more than "mere journalism."[100] The battle lines over Rational Choice in post–Cold War security studies were clearly drawn over the proper balance between rigor and relevance.

These post–Cold War skirmishes over the future of academic security studies finally escalated to all out intellectual warfare in the mid-1990s in the pages of *World Politics* with the publication of Columbia international political economy scholar David Baldwin's call to "abolish" the subfield. Using the end of the Cold War as his springboard, Baldwin opined that "the field of security studies seems poorly equipped to deal with the post–cold war world, having emerged from the cold war with a narrow military conception of national security and a tendency to assert its primacy over other public policy goals." Taking aim at traditional security studies, he posited that "the question now is whether security studies so conceived is adequate for coping with post–Cold War security problems." His answer was a resounding "no." Security studies overlapped too much with the neighboring subfields of foreign policy and international relations. It was too focused on military threats and so it ignored pressing nonmilitary problems. Finally, and ironically, in Baldwin's view, the subfield's inability to deal with the new international challenges of the post–Cold War world made it less policy relevant. The time had come, in his estimation, "to abolish the subfield of security studies."[101] Other international relations scholars agreed that its members should at least contemplate significant reform.[102]

Despite such criticisms, enhancing relevance did not appear to be the main concern for most of the post–Cold War critics of security studies. Rather, the key issue was scientific rigor, or rather, security studies' lack thereof. Indeed, most critics blamed the subfield's pursuit of policy relevance for its supposed methodological defects. As University of Illinois political scientist Edward Kolodziej diagnosed it, the problem with renaissance-era security studies was that "in the name of relevance, [it] delegates too much of the agenda of security studies to policymakers."[103] "The desire to be 'policy relevant,'" Baldwin agreed, "had led some scholars into such close relationships with policymakers that they ceased to be perceived as autonomous intellectuals and came to be considered instead as part of the policy-making establishment."[104] The solution, then, was for security studies to be better "integrated into the professional concerns and canons of as inclusive a spectrum of disciplinary units as possible within the academy."[105]

To be sure, interest in pressing real-world security issues among some political scientists remained in the 1990s. Indeed, the explosion of civil wars and ethnic conflicts in the wake of the breakup of the Warsaw Pact and the Soviet Union attracted much scholarly attention. In addition to the clear national security implications of these conflicts, many of which were raging literally on Europe's borders, the fact that they were apparently amenable to the preferred tools of academic political science such as large-N statistical analysis and formal theory make them exceptions that prove the rule about the subfield's tenuous post–Cold War standing.[106] Still, Baldwin's attack and the other developments of the post–Cold War era fostered a sense of professional pessimism among security studies scholars.[107] Unfortunately, there was ample evidence to justify it. A survey conducted by the Smith Richardson Foundation found that by 2001, on the eve of the attacks of September 11, courses in security studies in American universities had declined by 30 percent since end of the Cold War.[108] This situation would only improve somewhat after 9/11 and the beginning of the Global War on Terror.

Government Efforts to Use Social Science during Peace and War

DÉTENTE AND THE EFFORT TO CRAFT A SCIENCE OF EARLY WARNING

There were a number of efforts by the U.S. government to use quantitative political science as a tool of national security policymaking in the post-Vietnam era. These experiments tended to be launched during periods of relaxation in the international threat environment. And they began with great optimism about the compatibility of cutting-edge social science models and approaches. Very quickly, however, the tensions between rigor and relevance reemerged and neither scholars nor policymakers were fully satisfied with the results.

The first such effort took place at the Central Intelligence Agency in 1973 when Director William Colby established the Methods and Forecasting Division of the Office of Regional and Political Analysis (ORPA) with the objective of bringing into the agency previously ignored methods from the behavioral sciences.[109] That unit's first major product was a 1976 Bayesian statistical study of the probability of major military attack. Other components of the intelligence community also experimented with these approaches. For example, in the early 1970s, the State Department's Bureau of Intelligence and Research inaugurated Project Quest, a series of demonstration studies of quantitative techniques of estimation and forecasting to see how useful they would be. The initial reaction from INR analysts was not favorable. As the authors of a summary analysis explained, "In contrast to the quantitative scholar, the INR analyst deals with a range of units of analysis which are more diverse; he deals with topics which are much more specific and detailed; he deals with the kinds of variables, and with the relationships among those variables, which are more demanding of complex analytical techniques."[110]

Parallel efforts also took place at the Department of Defense. Recall that DoD, or at least the more technical research offices such as the Defense Advanced Research Projects Agency (DARPA) and the Department of Defense, Research and Engineering (DDR&E) offices, were more sympathetic to quantitative approaches to social sciences, which seemed familiar to the natural scientists and engineers who dominated these agencies. DARPA provided $1 million from 1967 to 1973 for the World Event Interaction Survey at the Universities of Michigan and then Southern California. It also funded the Quantitative Indicators for Defense Analysis from 1970 to 1975 for $2 million. Initially, there were high expectations about the potential of these approaches to bring rigorous social science to bear on policy problems. Characteristic was an ARPA assessment: "No other research spawned in the quantitative IR movement has gone as far in contributing to the solution of real-world political problems."[111] A particular advantage proponents saw was that it would produce "cumulative" findings.

One longer-term project that emerged out of these early efforts was the Early Warning and Monitoring System (EWAMS). Project director Charles McClelland predicted that "during the next few years, it may be possible to mobilize a global warning system directed to the detection of every kind of seriously endangering situation. Most of the necessary conditions are now right for such a development. Computer technology for large-scale information management has advanced sufficiently during the past two decades to make feasible the storage and retrieval of data on a scale not even conceived of as possible in earlier times."[112] Like later efforts, EWAMS employed "retrodiction" (extrapolation) from past events to construct models that would predict future political instability. McClelland would subsequently claim 80 percent accuracy for them.[113]

McClelland's and his DoD patrons' early enthusiasm soon flagged and Event Data research never really took hold in the Department of Defense. One problem was that the EWAMS data came from media sources.[114] This raised doubts in the minds of potential U.S. government users that the findings of the model might reflect media coverage rather than real-world events.

More serious, in Stephen Andriole and Defense Intelligence College instructor Gerald W. Hopple's view was that "basic event data researchers never reached the point where they could confidently list and rank any causal variables; consequently, we should not have expected applied event data-based indicators to satisfy any explanatory needs."[115] They attributed the weakness of the EWAMS approach to the fact that quantitative international relations scholars like McClellend were more interested in establishing "covariation" (x seems to occur with y) than providing "explanation" (x causes y).[116] This inability to clearly identify causal relationships reduced EWAMS's usefulness to policymakers.

With the reinvigoration of the Cold War, interest in this effort to bring cutting-edge social science to bear on national security policymaking waned. Indeed, by that point, Andiole and Hopple candidly admitted that the natural science biases among their DARPA colleagues may have led them to have unrealistic expectations about the potential of these approaches to successfully balance rigor and relevance: "Too often, engineers and hard scientists, who dominate DOD (and quite a few other) research decision processes, impose standards from engineering and the natural sciences which are quite simply irrelevant to soft or social science research."[117]

MODELING STATE FAILURE IN THE POST-COLD WAR ERA

A second wave of enthusiasm for this effort to employ advanced quantitative techniques to make real-time predictions crested in the post–Cold War era.[118] The most important manifestation of this was the State Failure Task Force, which subsequently would be rechristened the Political Instability Task Force (PITF).[119] PITF was reportedly the brainchild of Vice President Al Gore who tasked the CIA in October 1994 to find a formula for understanding and predicting "the correlates of state failure." His concern was not surprising given the unanticipated, dramatic, and in some cases costly state failures in Somalia, Bosnia, Liberia, and Afghanistan, and also instances of mass political violence and genocide such as had occurred in Rwanda. It was launched with high expectations and ambitious claims, such as those evident in an article in *The Week* breathlessly entitled "The CIA has a Team of Clairvoyants."[120] What made the PITF distinctive was that the CIA mandated that "advanced analytic methods" be employed to help U.S. policymakers see into the future.[121]

Another distinctive element of the Task Force was that it would be primarily composed of civilian academics working under contract to Science

Applications International Corporation (SAIC). The original members of the team included Ted Robert Gurr, Maryland; William Dixon, University of Arizona; Barbara Harff, U.S. Naval Academy; Ronald Inglehart, University of Michigan; Charles Taylor, Virginia Tech; Jack Goldstone, UC Davis; Aristide Zolberg, New School for Social Research; Daniel Esty, Yale; Richard Cooper, Harvard; Thomas Homer-Dixon, Toronto; Mancur Olson, Maryland; Douglas Way, OSU; Pamela Surko, SAIC; Alan Unger, SAIC.[122] During subsequent years, the Task Force would include many other prominent political and social scientists. Their charge was to construct a framework "using open-source data . . . to develop statistical models that can accurately assess vulnerability to instability two years hence and can identify key risk factors of interest to policymakers."[123] Specifically, the Task Force looked at four sorts of events: (1) revolutionary wars, (2) ethnic wars, (3) genocides, and (4) "adverse or disruptive" regime changes. The Task Force adopted this broader definition of "state failure" because only twenty actual "central state authority collapses" occurred between 1958 and 1998, "too few for robust statistical analysis."[124] Political instability, it turns out, is a rare event in their data set, with only 114 episodes in 7,500 country years (<2 percent). Interestingly, the Task Force was not directed to examine nonviolent democratization such as that which occurred in the "color revolutions." According to one founding member, "The assumption was that such events would be welcome, and hence not constitute the kind of unexpected crisis that required advance warning or emergency intervention. Ironically, precisely such events, from the Orange and Maidan revolutions in Ukraine, to the Tunisian and Egyptian revolutions of 2010–11, later became of critical interest to U.S. policymakers."[125]

One part of the effort involved compiling "a truly unparalleled global data set" of various manifestations of state failure.[126] The Task Force's activity, however, was not limited to simply collecting data. Members analyzed it using logistic regression and neural networks to "retrodict" state failure in the hope of constructing models of state failure that could subsequently be used for prediction of future events. Eventually, the PITF would produce eight such models: (1) global, (2) sub-Saharan Africa, (3) predominantly Muslim countries, (4) autocracies, (5) ethnic war, (6) genocide/politicide, (7) Indian subnational political violence, and (8) terrorism.[127] Their primary criteria in constructing these models was to focus on "measureable characteristics."[128]

The Task Force's objective was to sift through a large number of potential causal variables and try to identify "covariates" of state failure. In essence, its approach was to scan the data set to see what factors best predicted various types of political instability. To do so, Task Force members disaggregated their database into "problem" and "control" sets and then proceeded to test 75 candidate variables.[129] This "case control comparison" involved taking failed states 2 years before failure and comparing them to conditions in stable countries.[130] Task Force members identified 113 cases of failed states involving 62 discrete events and 51 mixed ones.[131] Later they increased this number to 139.[132] In keeping with their goal of achieving greater precision, Task Force members reported increasing accuracy in each revision of their model climbing from 66 percent in Phase I to 80–90 percent by Phase IV.[133]

Initially, the Task Force identified three statistically significant variables: demographic and societal factors such as infant mortality; economic measures like liberalization; and political measures of regime type.[134] By 1999, the Task Force had zeroed in on "transitions to democracy and autocracy," identifying "anocracies"—partial democracies with factionalism—as the regime type most vulnerable to state failure.[135] By 2010, the Task Force had concluded that "regime type is by far the most influential risk factor," judging that "partial democracies" were "exceptionally vulnerable" to state failure.[136] Perhaps anticipating one obvious criticism of this finding, a boosterish article in *U.S. News & World Report* rationalized that "findings such as the success of democracies may seem obvious but the study nevertheless represents a unique attempt to empirically back such truisms."[137]

Indeed, various Task Force members have been candid in admitting these and other limitations of their forecasting enterprise. These include recognizing that their approach is largely inductive because it is based on retrodiction from the same historical data used to formulate the models rather than based on prediction of new events, that they lack measures for many potentially important variables (e.g., state capacity or dissent within the military), that most of the variables they have identified as significant change only slowly, and that in trying to construct models using the fewest variables possible they risk oversimplifying complex processes and perhaps comparing incommensurate manifestations of state failure.[138]

Potentially the most serious weakness of the PITF models is that they are weak establishing causation, a key component of policy relevance. As one Task Force report conceded, "This study identified factors associated with failure, rather than direct causes of failure. The task force believes that infant mortality and trade openness serve as indicators for more complex combinations of related conditions that affect the risks of state failure, rather than as direct causes of risk. The task force therefore fears that policies aimed at improving infant mortality or trade openness in isolation would have little impact on the risk of state failure."[139] Elsewhere, Task Force members seem to reject causal analysis itself.[140]

These sorts of concerns led former Task Force member Jack Goldstone to recommend that the PITF Global model should be employed only for first cut quantitative assessments, with more in depth qualitative assessments used for analyzing the dynamics of those countries in which the United States has important interests.[141] His reasoning was that even highly reliable models cannot predict which countries, and when, will face instability.[142] Moreover, by 2005 he and other analysts had also become concerned that PITF's model was declining in accuracy, with one independent assessment concluding it had dropped to 35 percent.[143]

Tellingly, Task Force members did not highlight the policy implications of their findings until 2003.[144] But once they did, the members of the Task Force were bullish about their prospects for influencing policymakers on the grounds that regime type is manipulatable, unlike per capita income, mountainous terrain, population, demography, and resources, which were core variables in competing models of political instability.[145] It is in fact not clear, though, that regime type, and the Task Force's other preferred variables such as economic development, regional instability, repression, and discrimination, are really subject to manipulation by U.S. national security policymakers.[146]

When asked to assess what impact PITF has had on policymakers, one Task Force member was unsure: "What the Agency did with the material was not communicated to the Task force except in the most general terms. They have claimed [it] became a popular, standard product distributed to all USG agencies, that it was used by the NSC in its forecasts, and was used in presidential briefings. *They have funded it for more than 20 years so they must consider it an important resource.*"[147] The Task Force remained active as of 2017, though by then under contract to new branch of SAIC called Leidos.[148] Given that, an assessment of its performance is of more than historical interest. In order to determine to what extent the Task Force found a successful means of balancing rigor and relevance, it is useful to consider what policymakers themselves concluded about the utility of the quantitative forecasting enterprise of which the PITF is only the most recent and sophisticated manifestation.

The reaction of the policy community outside of that part of CIA invested in the enterprise was not overwhelmingly positive. Some members of other parts of the intelligence community found the Task Force's models useful but they struck others as "very rigid and self-righteous" and regional experts "disputed its findings and did not think its output was credible."[149] An assessment of the policymakers' perspective on quantitative forecasting conducted by a prominent Washington, DC, think tank was similarly critical: "In interviews with decisionmakers in Washington, DC and other major capitals about the use of early warning models, [we] heard a similar refrain: such models have minimal value beyond confirming what is commonly known. One official referred to the National Intelligence Council (NIC) 'watch list' as 'conventional wisdom watch.' It was clear from these conversations that few U.S. decision makers rely on such lists when it actually matters—either to take politically risky decisions to shift resources or to take preventive action in advance of a crisis."[150]

Center for Strategic and International Studies analysts pointed to a number of problems that undermined these models: First, many of these models (including PITF) were based on underdeveloped theories of conflict. Second, they do not prioritize among conflicts. Third, analysts had doubts about the reliability of the evidence marshaled, complaining that "much of the data utilized in these models is not based on regularly updated field work, but rather on data entry by non-country experts, very far from the conflict zone." Fourth, the interpretation of the results was conducted by only a small pool of experts. Fifth, these models are not good at determining what are the key factors. Sixth, they often exclude important variables.[151] Finally, and most important, DARPA analyst Sean P. O'Brien cautioned that "many of the most interesting, policy-relevant theoretical questions are also the most complex, nonlinear, and highly context-dependent. They demand consideration of hundreds of massively interacting variables that are difficult to measure systematically and at a level of granularity consistent with the theory. In such cases it is at best impractical and at worst impossible to apply standard regression techniques within the context of a Large-N study, short of invoking unreasonable, oversimplifying assumptions."[152] In light of these concerns, other parts of government dabbled with alternative modeling efforts. These were often more complex and expensive than PITF's, and they did not result in more accurate predictive models.[153]

That the PITF would not in the final analysis live up to the optimists' early expectations should not be surprising given that the longer history of such efforts has provided scant grounds for such confidence. An analysis of the needs of U.S. government policymakers by a CIA analyst involved in initial efforts to bring cutting-edge social science tools into the policy process highlighted the challenges the effort faced. As he explained, there are five important differences between what policymakers want and social scientists can give them. First, policymakers want answers based on the requirements of policy, not availability of data. Second, policy problems often involve unquantifiable elements. Third, quantitative forecasting models have not facilitated causal analysis well. Fourth, policymakers need brief and clear answers that scholars are often not inclined to give. Finally, policy frequently deals with rare and unique events whereas social science gravitates toward general and universal explanations. No wonder, he concluded that futures research of the sort PITF was conducting would remain "only a very small part of the [intelligence community's] political research effort."[154] Another CIA analyst who advocated using formal models as a forecasting technique, similarly admitted that "despite the advantages of [such] models, which became known as 'factions' models within the CIA, the vast majority of analysts do not use them."[155]

What is striking is how consistent contemporary policymakers' assessments of the quantitative forecasting effort are with those of previous efforts. Writing in 2012 in the CIA's *Studies in Intelligence*, another government analyst concluded that quantitative forecasting models were only useful for general warning, not point prediction; could be misleading due to their approach of extrapolating from past events; tend to produce unsurprising results; and neglect critical case-specific details.[156] The data sets they rely on also get out of date quickly.[157] But their most critical weakness in terms of policy relevance is their continuing inability to guide policymaking by clearly identifying causal relationships among factors. As a senior army analyst subsequently observed, "Strategic forecasting models only provide general risk propensities for countries at the national level on an annual basis. As a result, they provide no insights into the specific timing, nature, and location of events that might trigger instability. They are based on correlations between broad conditions and instability. As a result, they cannot identify dynamic causal chains. Beyond vague generalizations, these models do not (and cannot) provide compelling, actionable, course of action analyses."[158]

Given these continuing problems with the quantitative forecasting enterprise, it is hardly surprising that they have not played a major role in policymaking.[159] Task Force members themselves caution that their "quantitative modeling and theoretical analysis of the dynamics of political crises is not designed to replace expert assessments."[160] But it is not clear that they have achieved even the more modest objective of supplementing traditional approaches to intelligence analysis. Indeed, as one senior academic who regularly consults with IC reported, "My lack of knowledge about [PITF] may tell you much of what you want to know. It has never come up in my conversations with IC folks & I don't see it cited much in academic work I read. I remember a spate of articles from people in the project a while ago, but didn't realize it had continued."[161]

Despite nearly a half-century of efforts to refine these models, their impact on policymakers remains modest, as even long-standing participants in the PITF came to conclude.[162] Policymakers continue to prefer qualitative models of political behavior, which seem more intuitive, more adaptable, and more compatible with the intelligence community's traditional strength in area studies.[163] This is why, despite the falling out of fashion of area studies among academic social scientists, policymakers continue to urge that universities "strengthen foreign language and area studies."[164] That the continuing disconnect between academic social science and the needs of policymakers is to some extent rooted in academic business-as-usual is widely recognized among analysts of the interface of academic social science and government policymakers.[165]

9/11 Brokers a Mixed Marriage of Mars and Minerva

The attacks of September 11, 2001, on the World Trade Centers in New York and the Pentagon in Washington, DC, ushered in the end of the post–Cold War era.[166] Once again, a "sense of urgency" affected the entire country, including academic social scientists. In response, many scholars not previously known for their engagement with national security policy answered the call of duty, taking on security-related topics of potential interest to policymakers.[167] Others who for much of their career had sought to bridge the gap between the two worlds found that their efforts were more successful after 9/11 and the associated wars in Afghanistan and Iraq.[168] Finally, efforts by the media to tap scholarly work in national security picked up again.[169] In one sense, the post-9/11 world was one in which sustained cooperation between scholars and national security policymakers once again seemed possible and mutually beneficial.[170]

The Global War on Terror, waged in various theaters around the world, was in one sense a return to a more threatening international environment. But in another sense it was, as a 2007 Defense Science Board summer study characterized it, "significantly different from the peer competitor nation-state of the Cold War era."[171] Despite the shock of 9/11 and the greater public awareness of the global threat of terrorism, the threat environment was in fact "mixed." Some scholars openly questioned "whether or not the handful of terrorists worldwide truly constitutes the kind of security threat that warrants this scale of research effort."[172] And the war in Iraq, initially quite popular among the public and even some academics, quickly became controversial as its rationales—Saddam Hussein's supposed links to the Al-Qaeda terror network and his alleged pursuit of nuclear weapons—proved false and the situation in newly liberated Iraq quickly deteriorated into civil war.[173] Even U.S. national security officials characterized the post-9/11 security environment as "complex" or "mixed."[174] Given that, its impact on the relationship between policymakers and scholars was likely to be somewhat different than during previous periods of total war.

When the George W. Bush administration came into office in January of 2001, it had initially intended to disband the Clinton-era Political Instability Task Force. As former member Jack Goldstone reports, "There were then, as there have been recurrently, arguments that 'state failure' was a meaningless or irrelevant category for U.S. policy."[175] In the immediate wake of the attacks on September 11, 2001, the administration changed its mind, believing that it should employ every possible resource in the Global War on Terror, including PITF. It was at this point that PITF started working on models of terrorism and state failure. However, as it became clear that U.S. efforts could not prevent state failures in Afghanistan and Iraq, PITF reverted to its original focus.

Military commanders in Iraq had been complaining about the lack of on-the-spot cultural expertise, sparking intellectual ferment in national security policy circles.[176] Initial U.S. government efforts to mobilize social science for the war on terror began with a November 2004 DARPA conference, Adversary Cultural Knowledge and National Security, reportedly the first such effort to mobilize social science for national security since the early 1960s.[177] In 2005 the Marine Corps established a Center for Advanced Operational Culture at its training base in Quantico, Virginia.[178] These efforts had to overcome the gap between the academic and policy communities that had existed for years.[179]

The social science discipline of most interest to DoD and the services was initially anthropology. In 2004 U.S. Army War College commandant General Robert Scales proposed to Vice Admiral Arthur Cebrowski, then director of the Pentagon's Office of Force Transformation, a social science program to ascertain how the enemy thought. This proposal led DARPA to reach out to anthropologists to provide the scholarly expertise that might assist in this effort, much as their predecessors had done during the Second World War. Montgomery McFate organized a joint DARPA/Office of Naval

Research conference on Adversary Cultural Knowledge and National Security in November of that year.[180] The Military Operations Research Society (MORS) also sponsored a workshop called The Global War on Terrorism: Analytical Support, Tools, and Metrics Assessment in late fall 2004 at the Naval War College.[181]

On the one hand, the demand for scholarship that could aid policymaking spiked in response.[182] The Defense Science Board (DSB), an advisory body to the Secretary of Defense, echoed this conclusion, observing that the lesson of Iraq and Afghanistan is that "social awareness" was as important as military capability for those missions.[183] To achieve this, the U.S. military and national security policy community would have to "gain deeper understanding of how individuals, groups, societies and nations behave and then use this information to (1) improve the performance of U.S. forces through continuous education and training and (2) shape behaviors of others in pre-, intra-, and post-conflict situations."[184] In 2009, the DSB Task Force on Understanding Human Dynamics pushed for the institutionalization of the "production, evaluation, circulation, and consumption of knowledge about human dynamics (economic, religious, political, and cultural influences on personal, interpersonal, and social behavior) to improve full-spectrum military operations."[185] The key challenge in the mind of many soldiers and policymakers was how to end the "disconnect" between academics who studied various countries in the developing world wracked by political violence and the soldiers the United States sent there to combat violence and build nations.[186]

In order to accomplish these objectives, the DSB concluded that "DOD needs to become more familiar with the theories, methods, and models from psychology, sociology, political science, economics, and cultural anthropology in order to identify those with potential to add value."[187] The DoD had consistently used social science for more mundane issues such as "personnel selection, training, leadership, and organization," but the board's recommendation went well beyond that to employ social science to help make policy in the war on terror.[188] This recommendation reflected the typical optimism early in a conflict about the compatibility between sophisticated, quantitative human, social, cultural, behavioral (HSCB) social science models and the needs of policymakers. Board members, dominated by natural scientists, not surprisingly saw great potential in "coupling [social science] to quantitative and computational modelling and simulation techniques from mathematics, physics, statistics, operations research, and computer science" to achieve breakthroughs in marketing research and election forecasting.[189]

In those heady days, leading academic political scientists even testified before Congress.[190]

On the other hand, given this mixed security environment, more akin to Vietnam than World War II, combined with continuing disciplinary professionalization, it should not be surprising that that the war on terrorism would not fully settle social science's relevance question. For both ideological and disciplinary reasons, this would not prove to be as desirable a partnership from the perspective of academics.[191] The DoD let a $40 million contract in 2006 to British Aerospace (BAE) to oversee the logistics for what it termed "Human Terrain Teams" (HTTs) in Iraq. The initial nineteen (it would later rise to twenty-six) teams of five members were comprised of social scientists embedded in military units to help them understand local cultural dynamics in their area of operation.[192] After getting over their initial skepticism, many military commanders became quite enthusiastic about the program.[193] Members of the HTTs wore uniforms and carried weapons when deployed with the troops, which was anathema to the majority of academic anthropologists. An even greater concern for them was that the cultural knowledge these teams would gather might be used for intelligence gathering and targeting, rather than just to save civilian lives.[194] An editorial in the distinguished journal *Nature* declared the program a failure in December 2008 and called for it to be terminated, with extreme intellectual prejudice.[195]

From the beginning, the DSB also recognized the practical limits of sophisticated HSCB models.[196] There were also concerns that related efforts lacked the deep regional expertise necessary for their tasks, but rather were "heavily weighted toward operators and [Operations Research and Systems Analysis] (ORSA) analysts from throughout DOD."[197] One analyst even suggested Project Camelot might provide a template for marshaling social science expertise for the Global War on Terror efforts despite the fact that only one person in attendance knew anything about it.[198] Given Camelot's unfortunate history, one wonders how much that individual really understood about that disastrous effort to apply social science to understanding how political stability in the Third World affected U.S. national security.

In the final analysis, national security policymakers were ultimately not persuaded that methodologically sophisticated social science was necessary for them to do their jobs. The MORS report noted that "the group agreed that the quality of the analyst is more important than the quality of the tools. A good analyst can produce good results from poor tools; but a poor analyst is unlikely to produce good results even with good tools." And its authors feared that the impulse to focus on technique over substance would be hard to resist because "the quality of the tools is easier to discuss."[199] The MORS group was also skeptical that applied results would automatically trickle down from even high-quality basic research.[200] Instead, they concluded that policymakers needed models that "include assessment of alternative policy options" to be of relevance to them.[201]

Secretary of Defense Robert Gates's 2008 Minerva Initiative testified to ongoing dissatisfaction among policymakers with purely in-house research and analysis and the lack of useful scholarly research on some of the most pressing post–Cold War security issues such as the consequences of cultural and religious change; the ideologies of terrorist groups; military transformation in China; the national security consequences of environmental change; new theories of deterrence; and the dynamics of failing states.[202] Minerva's mission was to:

- Leverage and focus the resources of the nation's top universities.
- Seek to define and develop foundational knowledge about sources of present and future conflict with an eye toward better understanding of the political trajectories of key regions of the world.
- Improve the ability of DoD to develop cutting-edge social science research, foreign area and interdisciplinary studies that is developed and vetted by the best scholars in these fields.[203]

Minerva signaled Gates's desire to rebuild the bridges between the Beltway and the Ivory Tower and change the status quo in the post–Cold War relationship between scholars and policymakers. The Minerva Initiative was the largest post-9/11 effort by DoD to engage with social scientists since the Vietnam War.[204] It also constituted the latest effort to square the circle between basic and applied social science research.

Deputy Assistant Secretary of Defense for Policy Thomas Mahnken, one of the architects of the Minerva Initiative, recounted that it was premised on the belief that "the US government has always turned to the nation's scholars and intellectuals for help in times of national crisis or emergency."[205] The original idea for the Minerva Initiative had been "bubbling up for some time" in the Department of Defense even before Gates was named secretary of defense. The initial plan was for Under Secretary of Defense for Policy Eric Edelman to propose establishing "a new FFRDC to focus on China, Islam, Anthropology, Demography and some other disciplines that seemed important to the department but where there seemed to be insufficient scholarly work that was useful for DoD."[206] Once he was confirmed, Gates embraced the general goal of developing greater scholarly expertise in these areas but opposed setting up a new organization like RAND on the grounds it was too expensive and Congress would not support it.[207]

Gates outlined a different approach in a speech to the American Association of Universities in April 2008 on the fiftieth anniversary of the National Defense Education Act (NDEA), which among other things had established the Title VI area studies programs that had previously constituted a major bridge between government and academia in the national security realm. He explicitly linked Minerva to the emergence of global terrorism, pointing out that "the country is again trying to come to terms with new threats to national security." Like Title VI, his initial conception of the type of social science expertise he sought seemed more akin to the area studies model.[208] This preference "for better knowledge of the culture and people" of the post-9/11 battlefields should not be surprising given that Gates's own training had been in Cold War–era Soviet studies.

The initial response to Minerva among academics, especially anthropologists, was tepid. Admittedly, some of the opposition was ideological, reflecting lingering antiwar sentiments from the Vietnam era. But disciplinary concerns were apparent as well. The president of the American Anthropological Association, Setha Low, argued that since "peer review . . . plays such a vital role in maintaining the integrity of research in social science disciplines," the Department of Defense should not manage these grants to scholars on its own.[209] AAU president Robert M. Berdahl also pushed Gates on this issue.[210] In response, the Department of Defense forged a compromise: University Research Grants were to be administered by both DoD and the National Science Foundation (NSF) while DoD would simultaneously issue a separate Broad Area Announcement (BAA) managed by the service research organizations, who would contract directly with scholars. Congress would later impose a third element, the "Minerva Chairs" (R-Def: Research for Defense Education Faculty) to fund the research of scholars teaching in the military's Professional Military Education (PME) system.[211]

NSF was receptive to participating in the Minerva Initiative. Mark L. Weiss, Division Director for Behavioral and Cognitive Sciences at NSF, testified on April 24, 2008, that "because warfare is a human activity, there are deep and compelling reasons for the military to be cognizant of research in the social and behavioral sciences."[212] The part of the Minerva involving NSF was entitled the Social and Behavioral Dimensions of National Security, Conflict, and Cooperation (NSCC).[213] In it, proposals were supposed to be judged on both intellectual merit and also "broader impact." Worryingly, this latter category was a catchall that included many other things like diversity and public education along with "what may be the benefits of the proposed activity to society?"[214]

The office of the Under Secretary of Defense for Policy (OSD(P)) embraced the two-track approach—NSF and the DoD BAA—as a means to get the program up and running as quickly as possible. Mahnken, however, preferred the DoD/BAA route, believing it would be quicker and more likely to produce research in line with Secretary Gates's original intent. And he feared that the NSF route would be slower, would result in research not as close to secretary's original vision, and would not enjoy as much support from Congress.[215] What the architects of Minerva sought was to promote "*engaged scholarship* in the social sciences."[216] Their concern, however, was that NSF's mission was to support "*basic* social and behavioral science research."[217] André Van Tilborg, deputy Under Secretary of defense, science and technology, recognized early on that tensions between basic and applied research would likely complicate DoD/NSF collaboration.[218] In fact, these tensions would be central to subsequent congressional reservations about the Minerva program.

While cooperating with NSF in some aspects of Minerva, the Office of the Under Secretary of Defense for Policy kept open the option to pursue "a number of other approaches for engaging the social science community."[219] These included different OSD programs such as the Human Social Culture Behavior Modelling Program (HSCBM) and the Strategic Multi-Layer Assessment (SMA) efforts. The former was another effort to understand "the human, social, cultural, behavioral and political forces that affect the strategic and operational security environment" while the latter was an organization tasked with tailoring such research for operational "customers."[220] HSCM actually predated Minerva.[221] Overall, Minerva emphasized basic research, HSCBM emphasized applied work, and SMA handled customer relations.

Despite these compromises, neither scholars nor national security policymakers and members of Congress have found the program fully satisfactory. The most vocal scholarly concerns tended to echo lingering ideological opposition to cooperation with government in the national security realm. Some critics lamented that, in contrast to the Cold War area studies programs like Sovietology, Minerva was not intended to build a broad academic community producing new knowledge about these issues and areas of the world, but was a rather narrow and highly directed effort to encourage some professors to meet the Department of Defense research needs.[222] Many others feared that insufficient attention has been paid to the danger cooperation with government poses to scholarly integrity.[223] Some rejected Minerva's core premise that scholars even need external incentives to do work that would inform policy.[224] Expressing a typical attitude, Stanford's Priya Satia suggested that "the most efficient way for the DoD to support social scientific research is to expand the funding, without strings, of existing agencies like NSF and the NEH. Academics do, after all, live in the real world; it is arguably what inspires much of their work. The DoD can trust them to turn to pressing practical questions of their own accord."[225] And a few worried that the quality of Minerva-sponsored academic research would suffer because the best academics will eschew taking government money, leaving only less-capable scholars willing to participate in the program.[226] There is reason for concern that its constituency in the academy is somewhat narrow.[227]

Skeptics within the U.S. government feared that this ideological opposition would doom the program.[228] But top-flight scholars did not refuse to participate in it on ideological grounds. Minerva attracted widespread interest among some leading social scientists. As of 2015, it had supported 99 projects (64 regular PI projects; 17 Minerva Chair projects; and 18 R-DEF projects), and produced 97 peer-reviewed articles, 237 presentations, 72 briefings, 62 Op/Eds, 24 books, 76 book chapters, and 29 workshops or conferences. Awardees have been multidisciplinary, representing economics (8), psychology (7), sociology (7), history (7), international relations (4), anthropology (3), geography (3), law (2), with one each in religion, geology, physics, environmental studies, computer science, engineering, applied psychology, war studies, health, middle eastern studies, and strategic studies. However, the largest number of PIs were political scientists (50).

The real danger was that the program, or at least important parts of it, would be captured by the disciplines and come to increasingly reflect academic interest in conducting basic research rather than meeting government needs for applied research relevant to the pressing issues of the Global War on Terror.[229] This skewing of the original program was the result of two factors. Once the NSF got involved, its mandate for supporting basic research projects meant that only direct DoD Minerva funding would provide much support for applied projects.[230] Tellingly, the NSF's Weiss admitted that only "10–15% [of research supported within NSF's SBE directorate] might be of clear and immediate interest to the military."[231] Moreover, academics sought to coopt the program to support their own agendas. Representatives of academic lobbying groups, like other special interests, even offered to draft reports and legislative language about the program for Congress.[232] The greater the involvement of academic organizations in the Minerva program, the larger the relevance question would loom.[233] To be fair, Minerva's relevance problem was also exacerbated by the research community within the services and DoD. Natural science–oriented officials sought to graft their methods on the social science projects Minerva was supporting. Mirroring many academic social scientists' emphasis on methodology over substance and manifesting a decided preference for basic as opposed to applied research, their voice in the process sometimes "has not been useful," at least in the estimation of one of the program's originators.[234]

Minerva also faced skepticism in Congress. As it was initiated "out of cycle" of the normal appropriations process, it raised some red flags on the Hill. But more importantly in light of the original NSF debate, sentiment on the Hill favored funding for applied rather than basic research.[235] Many members had an "allergy" toward the NSF and initially demanded that it provide half the funding for the NSCC grant program. Congress then opposed the separate, parallel NSF track after the first year.[236] A Senate Appropriations Committee Report for FY 11 explained that "the Committee remains *concerned about funding long-term academic research projects* and does not support transferring funds to non-Department of Defense agencies." In FY 2012 the committee supported expanding the Minerva Chairs but also noted "*the limited value of long-term studies for the war-fighter and recommends no funding to initiative new studies.*"[237] Some members also wondered why Minerva was not supporting research in the service professional military education (PME) system. This concern led to the establishment of the Minerva Chairs program.[238] Congress seemed much more committed to building "in-house" DoD and service research capability than to supporting external research.[239] Finally, there were questions about the extent to which Minerva duplicated other DoD funded social science research.[240]

Another open question is the impact of Minerva-sponsored research projects. Former OSD(P) Minerva program manager Anne Dreazen conceded that there has been no "scientific assessment of [Minerva's] impact."[241] Indeed, conducting such an assessment would be challenging.[242] Thus far, very few Minerva projects have been cited in congressional testimony and those that have been tend not to be the academic ones funded through NSF. Just 9 of the 102 (less than 9 percent) Minerva grantees during this period either testified, or had their Minerva-sponsored research cited by others testifying, before Congress.[243] Mahnken, for example, effusively praised a project at UCSD on Chinese military modernization that was led by a Chinese military analyst who was only recently appointed there as a regular faculty member.[244] SOCOM combatant commander admiral Eric Olson cited two

Minerva projects in testimony—"Finding Allies for the War of Words: Mapping the Diffusion and Influence of Counter Radical Muslim Discourse," and "Terrorism, Governance, and Development"—both of which were funded directly by DoD rather than NSF.[245] Since Minerva is funding basic research, the results of which will be clear only over time, it may be unfair to expect immediate practical impact.[246]

Still, given congressional concerns on precisely this score, proponents will have to be prepared to answer Minerva's relevance question sooner rather than later. Only a quarter of the peer-reviewed articles produced by Minerva grantees as of 2015 have offered explicit policy recommendations, which will do little to assuage these concerns.[247] Moreover, Minerva has not escaped the inherent tensions between rigor and relevance that have kept social science's relevance question open for years. As Eli Berman and Lawrence Freedman conceded in a 2013 report on NSF/Minerva, "Tension between topics that are important and topics that lend themselves to precise inference must be recognized."[248] This may explain why recently, Minerva has begun working with think tanks such as the United States Institute of Peace (USIP) to support policy-relevant research.[249]

In the final analysis, focusing purely on basic social science research was unlikely to be either politically or operationally useful. On the former, as the 1976 Report of the Defense Science Board Summer Study Group on Fundamental Research in Universities noted, the "Mansfield syndrome" continued to tax congressional patience with DoD support for basic research in universities.[250] This has been, as chapter 5 shows, a recurrent concern. In fact, these post-9/11 efforts to balance social science scholarship and policy in national security research constituted evidence of lingering doubts about the National Science Foundation notion that by supporting basic research, useful policy information would also trickle down.[251] In sum, given both the strengths and weaknesses of the various Minerva programs to date, a fair assessment of its efforts to answer the relevance question is likely to be mixed. That should not be surprising given the complex nature of the international security environment in which it emerged and the continuing preoccupation of academic social science with disciplinary concerns over practical relevance.[252]

Conclusions

This history of the post-Vietnam period is not a brief for any particular methodological approach to strategy. Indeed, figure 8.4 tells a cautionary tale in this regard inasmuch as almost all of the leading methods used in

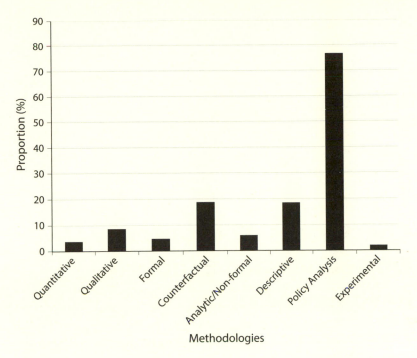

FIGURE 8.4. Methods that offer policy prescriptions in IR journals. (Source: TRIP.)

political science today are not very policy relevant. Instead, it is a call for a problem-, rather than method-driven, approach to scholarship in the field. Important problems—defined in terms not just of internal disciplinary agendas but also the priorities of policymakers and the general public—ought to be the primary focus. Scholars should choose their methods based on their judgment of which is most appropriate to illuminating and perhaps resolving them. In order to truly realize another "renaissance" in policy relevant academic strategy, the current generation of scholars should embrace the sort of problem-driven approach to their work that characterized the early years of the subfield. Only that can ensure that today's academic strategists do not wait until the Owl of Minerva flies at dusk to realize that policy-relevant work does not flow effortlessly from the wellspring of normal social science basic research.

9

Conclusions, Responses to Objections, and Scholarly Recommendations

I want to reiterate that I am not arguing that scholarship that is formal or quantitative is by definition irrelevant. Indeed, one can point to examples of both that are. When applied to economic issues, the discipline of economics has managed to be both highly "scientific" and, at times, quite relevant, though for both good and ill. Likewise, there are examples of highly quantitative political science that policymakers have found useful.[1] Finally, there is much nonquantitative scholarship, particularly but not exclusively in the humanities that, is jargon laden and otherwise inaccessible to a wider audience, including government policymakers.[2] This is by no means an anti–social science methods screed, just a reminder of the tensions between rigor and relevance that need to managed rather than assumed away.

Nor is this in any way a brief against theory. Former State Department official Roger Hilsman reminded us that everyone, including policymakers, uses theory. Paraphrasing John Maynard Keynes, he concluded that "it seems obvious that all thinking involves notions of how and why things happen. Even the 'practical' man who despises theory has a number of assumptions and expectations which lead him to believe that when certain things are done, certain results follow. . . . It is this 'theory' that helps a problem solver select from the mass of facts surrounding him those which he hopes are relevant."[3] Given that, I fully associate myself with Hans Morgenthau's balanced view that "theory without verification is metaphysics, but empiricism without theory is aimless."[4] Since policymakers implicitly use theory in analyzing situations and assessing their alternatives, such theories should be stated explicitly and analyzed systematically, which is a comparative advantage of the scholars.

Instead, what I offer is simply a critique of the increasing tendency of many social scientists to embrace methods and models for their own sake rather than because they can help us answer substantively important questions. This inclination is in part the result of the otherwise normal and productive workings of science, but is also reinforced by less positive factors such as organizational self-interest and intellectual culture. As a result of the latter, many political scientists have committed themselves to particular social science methods not so much because they believe they will illuminate real-world policy problems but because they serve a vested interest in disciplinary autonomy and dovetail with a particular image (mathematized and model-based) of what a "science" of politics should look like. In other words, the professionalization of social science is the root of the enduring relevance question.

This tendency to equate rigor with technique imposes costs on the rest of society as well as the discipline, especially when it excludes a more balanced approach to rigor and relevance of the sort that characterized the subfield of security studies in the past. On the former, as diplomat George Kennan rightly observed, policymakers need academic expertise because they have to make decisions about issues and areas of the world "about which they cannot be expert and learned."[5] They depend on the academy for the raw data—whether quantitative or historical—that they use in decision making. They also rely on the social sciences for the theories they use to analyze and make sense of this data. The problem with relying exclusively on in-house government research to make up for the lack of policy-relevant academic research is that it is often of low quality.

The role of the "independent policy analyst" is essential for three reasons:[6] He or she can challenge basic policy assumptions. As RAND's Hans Spier put it, they can undertake "research which does not necessarily take the mission of the military for granted and admits the possibility U.S. may be wrong."[7] And academic social scientists are particularly well suited to this role by virtue of the fact that they both conduct research and also teach future policymakers.[8]

Academics have some other advantages over policymakers. They have the time to develop greater depth of knowledge on issues and regions than most policymakers can. The institution of tenure also gives them, at least in theory, the freedom to explore controversial issues and take unpopular stands. And while peer review can homogenize and narrow scholarship, it also plays an indisputably positive role in advancing it. Finally, university-based scholars have less of a vested interest in certain policies and programs than do policymakers, though of course that is not to deny that they have their own institutional interests and biases.[9]

I am not suggesting, of course, that scholars would make better policy than bureaucrats and elected officials. They lack inside knowledge, have little actual power, and are often politically out of step with the rest of American society.[10] They also come to policy issues with a markedly different intellectual orientation than policymakers.[11] Rather, my point is simply that our democratic political system depends on the successful functioning of the marketplace of ideas and checks and balances in which individuals and groups with various strengths and weaknesses and offsetting biases participate in the larger policy debate, thereby compensating for each other's limitations.[12]

We run into trouble when we lack one of these perspectives in policy debates. Indeed, there are instances—the war in Vietnam and the recent Iraq War—in which had the majority consensus of scholars in academia influenced policy, the country's national interest would have been better served. As the flawed Iraq War debate demonstrates, our nation's marketplace of ideas is bankrupt, particularly in national security affairs.[13] Of course, our political problems run much deeper than just the Beltway/Ivory Tower gap, but closing it would represent an important step in the country's intellectual recapitalization. This nation's universities need to reclaim their place as one of society's main sources of independent ideas about the problems that it faces.[14]

Less widely recognized, and perhaps more controversial given the prevailing sentiments in the Academy for a sharp distinction between "science" and "policy," is my contention that the growing gap is ultimately bad for the generation of new knowledge. There are at least two reasons why greater attention to policy relevance produces better scholarship. First, it leads to more realistic theorizing. As John Kenneth Galbraith warned his economics colleagues nearly forty years ago, "No arrangement for the perpetuation of thought is secure if that thought does not make contact with the problems that it is presumed to solve."[15] Second, a focus on manipulatable variables makes it more likely that they are testable because the analyst can ensure variation on them. Also, the hyperspecialization of knowledge today makes it difficult for even scholars in related disciplines to understand each other, much less the general public. Such intellectual fragmentation makes the application of scholarly knowledge to policymaking extremely difficult. Therefore, a deeper and more regular engagement between the Ivory Tower and the Beltway will be mutually beneficial for both sides.[16]

Ultimately, even the most sophisticated social science will be judged by what it tells us about things that affect the lives of large numbers of people and which policymakers therefore seek to influence and control.[17] The recurrent congressional debates about National Science Foundation funding for political science highlight the direct costs to the discipline of not being able to justify itself in terms of broader impact on the rest of society. Harkening back to the debate about the Mansfield Amendment, an article in *Science* cautioned that "to the extent that the research community disdains work on major national missions or behaves self-servingly in mission-oriented work, anti-intellectualism will increase its influence on the fate of American science."[18] Also, public and philanthropic community support for investment in academia generally reflects the belief that it will produce work that will speak to problems of broader importance. When the academy fails on that score, it can undermine that support.[19] Political science's subfield of international security studies can plausibly claim to save large amounts of money and even lives and so its increasing marginalization is a self-inflicted wound on the discipline.

Response to Objections

There are at least eight reasonable, though ultimately unpersuasive, objections to my argument that we should consider.

First, some point to the influence of the Democratic Peace Theory (DPT) on the Clinton, George W. Bush, and Obama administrations as evidence that one of the most scientific of social science theories in international relations was both useful and influential among policymakers.[20] The argument that democracies are unlikely to go to war with each other gained currency among social scientists based on statistical analysis of every major interstate war since 1815. In the words of Rutgers political scientist Jack Levy, the Democratic Peace Theory is "as close as anything we have to an empirical law in international relations."[21] Two scholars argued that the theory became relevant outside of the academy precisely "because of the law-like status of a particular empirical finding."[22] Others hold it up as a model of how basic research in political science can contribute to policymakers.[23]

It is not clear, though, that the influence of the DPT on recent U.S. foreign policy was due to its unassailable social scientific standing. While former Defense Department official and Ohio State political scientist Joseph Kruzel conceded that DPT "had substantial impact on public policy," he attributed its attractiveness to policymakers to its simplicity rather than its social scientific rigor.[24] It clearly identifies America's enemies (nondemocratic states) and prescribed a simple response to them (make them democratic). It is also likely that the much less methodologically sophisticated articulation of the theory in the work of Michael Doyle was far more influential.[25] And the process by which DPT entered the Clinton White House did not involve sophisticated social science. Rather, the key administration proponent of the democratic peace was National Security Advisor (and former college professor) Anthony Lake.[26] It is clear, however, that to the extent that Lake was drawing support for the democratic peace from academic sources, it was not from statistically based research, but rather from the qualitative work of scholars like Harvard's Samuel Huntington.[27] The results of a survey of senior national security policymakers found that more than half of those familiar with the methodologically sophisticated democratic peace theory reported *not* being influenced by it in their government work.[28] Finally, one could argue that U.S. policymakers have embraced the democratic peace because of its compatibility with our political culture rather than its scientific standing.[29]

A second, and in some ways, flip side of the first critique, is that the relevance problem with contemporary security studies is the result of the subfield's domination by realism, and particularly its most abstruse and theoretical manifestation, neorealism.[30] Critics point particularly to neorealist arguments that tout the virtues of nuclear proliferation as examples of theoretically elegant but politically unacceptable social science.[31] Despite its respectability among scholars, neorealist proliferation optimism has reportedly had little influence on actual policy.[32] While that particular policy issue may not have been influenced by realist thinking, as this book has shown realists have remained committed to policy relevance at times when the rest of the discipline has eschewed it. And they have more often been on the right side of policy debates as well.[33]

A third potential challenge to my argument is that many social scientists believe that they should avoid offering policy recommendations in favoring of focusing on basic research tasks such as identifying empirical regularities and offering generalizations to explain them.[34] As Dartmouth political scientist Kalman Silvert warned, "It is not the legitimate role of the social scientist as scholar to advocate specific courses of governmental action or to act as implementer of government decisions."[35] Another rationale is that doing so is unnecessary given that the applied implications of basic research tend to trickle down by themselves.[36] Policy engagement—particularly offering explicit policy recommendations—is both unwise and unnecessary in the view of many social scientists.

Neither of these views, however, are shared by policymakers. Most believe that in addition to providing basic research findings, "scientists must explicitly define the linkage, whether immediate or remote, of the knowledge acquired or being acquired, to specific operational problems and continually assess the import of such knowledge to solution of the problems."[37] Nor are current and former policymakers sanguine about the trickle-down (or bubble-up in which senior policymakers get the results of scholarly work through their methodologically savvy staffs) process. As John K. Plank of the Brookings Institution, a former DoD official, recollected, "There is presumably a process whereby the research product is filtered up to [senior policymakers], but in point of fact very little of operational usefulness is transmitted."[38]

Fourth, some political scientists believe that there are now so many new outlets for scholars to engage in the policy debate, it is both easier for them to do so and also unnecessary for them to concern themselves with doing so in their scholarship.[39] Academics can now publish basic research in scholarly venues and then disseminate its applied implications through the new media. George Washington political scientist and blogger Marc Lynch effused that with the rise of the new media "this is in most ways a golden age for policy-relevant public spheres."[40] Indeed, many see the proliferation of new media outlets as the answer to political science's perennial problem: its diminished public profile.[41] The assumption here is that political scientists are simply not communicating their results effectively.

There are three problems with these arguments: Until recently, we had no idea whether blogs and other new media reached policymakers. As one optimist conceded, we have "no solid statistics" on our impact.[42] But we do now and it suggests that blogs and other new media are in fact not an important source of information for policymakers and therefore are unlikely to effectively convey the implications of basic research to policymakers, the media, or the general public. [43] Moreover, even if a few blogs get some attention, many others do not, simply making more noise in an already cacophonous marketplace of ideas.[44] And suggesting that the failure of communication argument misses the mark, Social Science Research Council president Craig Calhoun noted that scholarly "engagement with public constituencies must move beyond a dissemination model" that assumes that "pure research" will naturally trickle down, even with better communication.[45] In other words, it is not the medium that matters as much as the message. And the message must be made more intelligible and useful to policymakers and the general public. Finally, there is systematic evidence that academic bloggers and scholars who utilize other new media venues receive little professional credit for them in the critical areas of promotion and tenure.[46] In short, despite the explosive growth of new media outlets, professional incentives still do not encourage scholars to use them.

A fifth conceivable objection is that advanced social science techniques and basic research will eventually become more useful to policymakers as they (or at least their staffs) become more sophisticated in their understanding of them. One optimist, for example, noted that most graduate public policy schools now include one or two required courses in economics and social science methods in their curricula. As these increasingly methodologically savvy young bureaucrats become senior policymakers, so this argument goes, they will be more adept at using them and more appreciative of their policy relevance.[47]

However, this argument assumes that training in advanced research techniques is a recent development. Policy schools, however, have long had methods courses as part of their required curriculum. Even prior to this, many national security policymakers came out of academic Ph.D. programs in which they were exposed to the latest innovations in social science methodology. It also ignores that the security studies subfield played a leading role in developing many of these sophisticated social science techniques, particularly at RAND in the 1950s.[48] An example of the reverse flow of ideas from the policy world to the Academy was the "unquestionably" leading role that RAND mathematicians and other social scientists played in the development of game theory, a mathematical framework for strategizing under uncertainty.[49] Despite early enthusiasm, many at RAND concluded that game theory had an Achilles Heel in its application to national security policy: how to assign the numerical values that were to be plugged into its formulas. That was not a trivial limitation, which led Hitch to confess that "for our purposes, Game Theory has been quite disappointing."[50]

It also assumes that today's aspiring policymakers come away from these methods courses with an unqualified appreciation of their usefulness. My experience after ten years in teaching in such schools, and familiarity with the evaluations students give these courses, leaves me skeptical. They often do not see the usefulness of such courses and suspect they are being forced to take them for academic, not professional, reasons.[51] Other colleagues at professional schools share this impression.[52] Finally, an earlier survey of current and former national security policymakers reveals that the more highly educated the policymaker, the greater the skepticism about their utility.[53] This is consistent with the argument that familiarity with advanced techniques instills greater appreciation not only for their promise but also their limits. Even proponents of modern social science methods in international relations concede that "the emerging science of international relations has a long way to go before it can be of direct use to policy makers."[54] It is hard to find much evidence that the most sophisticated approaches to international relations are of much direct use to policymakers, and there are ample reasons for caution about how much of the discipline's "basic" research is really trickling down to indirectly influence policymakers.

Sixth, some point to the post-9/11 resurgence of interest among younger social scientists as a harbinger of another renaissance of interest in policy relevance. Others suggest that changes in the nature of the "new paradigm of knowledge production," which is "socially distributed, application-oriented, trans-disciplinary, and subject to multiple accountabilities" constitute grounds for optimism about a broader return to relevance among the social sciences.[55] To be sure, there are reasons for optimism on this score but also for continuing caution. As we have seen, previous periods of optimism about answering the relevance question have given way to disappointment. Moreover, many scholars have claimed to be policy relevant even though policymakers did not find them so.[56] As one CIA analyst warned, "Social scientists commonly define policy-relevant research far more broadly than the foreign policy community does."[57]

A seventh potential criticism of my argument is there are other forms of "relevance" beyond just influencing government policymakers by offering policy recommendations to which scholars should aspire.[58] Especially in a democratic political system, a scholar's vocation for politics can also involve educating students and informing the wider public about pressing issues of policy. Moreover, an engaged scholar could serve with nongovernmental and private organizations rather than just through government service. While there is no doubt that policy influence is broader than just affecting government policy, that is ultimately the goal of the enterprise, either directly through policymakers or indirectly through the media or the public. Moreover, it is the clearest and most demanding standard of relevance available. So if we want to understand when and how social science matters to policymakers that is the most important, if not the only, aspect of it to consider.[59]

Finally, many political scientists share Daniel Drezner's view that economics has solved the relevance question in being both rigorous and relevant.[60] The logical implication of such a belief is that the rest of social sciences should follow that discipline's lead in terms of its approach and methodology. This economics envy is based on a misapprehension that academic trends in economics have not also created a relevance problem. For example, a recent review of research at the World Bank by leading academic economists raised questions about how much of the scholarship of bank analysts that was written for publication in academic journals was of any use to the bank.[61] Their answer was not much. They blamed intellectual trends in the discipline because it encouraged research that was "*too* academic, too focused toward the previously existing *academic* agenda, and too directed towards technical rather than pressing policy issues."[62]

Behind this economics envy lies an even deeper inferiority complex vis-à-vis the natural sciences. Many social scientists believe that the physical sciences have two advantages over the "softer" social sciences: more reliable data and a consensus on how to analyze it. Quantifiable data, in this view, is more persuasive, because it is clearer and less subject to dispute.[63] This view of the superiority of the physical over the social sciences is widespread, with many of the former reveling in their preeminence and some of the latter manifesting two classic symptoms of an inferiority complex: resentment or reflexive emulation. Neither of these responses is healthy.

It is simply not true that expressing propositions mathematically ensures that they are clearer and more transparent than conveying them in English. Economist Paul Romer admitted that "with enough math, an author can be confident that most readers will never figure out where FWUTV [facts with unknown truth values] is buried. A discussant or referee cannot say that an identification assumption is not credible if they cannot figure out what it is and are too embarrassed to ask."[64] On the latter, one would think that the 2008 Great Recession, in which the misguided belief that quantitative models of the economy could be used to guide investment decisions on the grounds they could reveal "the truth" about what drives the market, would temper confidence that such scientific approaches could ensure effective policy.[65] In a much discussed essay in the *New York Times Magazine*, Princeton economist Paul Krugman concluded that "the economics profession went astray because economists, as a group, mistook beauty, clad in impressive-looking mathematics, for truth. . . . The central cause of the profession's failure was the desire for an all-encompassing, intellectually elegant approach that also gave economists a chance to show off their mathematical prowess."[66]

It is not even clear that natural scientists have been most influential when they have employed their most rigorous and mathematically sophisticated approaches, at least in the national security realm. Indeed, there is more evidence that they have been most influential when they have offered practical solutions to real-world problems. These solutions have often come from scientifically uncertain and incomplete data.[67] These are the hallmarks of much of the best of qualitative social science.

Social scientists also ought to take heart that they not only can make an important contribution using their own distinct approaches, but also that in some instances they might even be superior to those of the physical scientists. For example, many of the nuclear scientists involved in the Manhattan Project soon came to regret their role in the escalating nuclear arms race of the Cold War. Reflecting a collective sense of guilt, chemist and peace activist Linus Pauling got almost nine thousand scientists to sign a January 1958 petition to end nuclear testing as first step toward universal disarmament.[68] Taking an equally impractical tack, Hungarian physicist Leo Szilard wrote to Franklin Delano Roosevelt's science adviser Vannevar Bush in January 1944, "This weapon is so powerful that there can be no peace if it is simultaneously in the possession of any two powers unless these two powers are bound by an indissoluble political union."[69] While not all of the atomic scientists harbored doubts—recall the famous debates between Robert Oppenheimer and Edward Teller—the majority became advocates of international control of nuclear weapons, a policy that in retrospect was politically unrealistic. In comparing the assessments and policy recommendations of the physical scientists in the Golden Age, with those of social scientists like Jacob Viner, Bernard Brodie, and William T. R Fox, it is hard to avoid the conclusion that the latter's views of the nuclear problem (that the genie of nuclear weapons could not be stuffed back in the bottle), and their recommendations for dealing with that situation (nuclear deterrence), were far more "realistic" than those of the nuclear "one world" physical scientists.

What Is to Be Done?

There are, of course, some nuts-and-bolts issues that scholars should be mindful of if they want to participate in the broader policy debate. Since policymakers have short attention spans given the number and breadth of issues they have to deal with, scholarly efforts to engage them need to be brief in conveying their ideas.[70] This explains why Op/Eds are particularly influential and why so many are optimistic that blogs could play a similar role. Moreover, policymakers find much current scholarly work—from across the methodological spectrum—inaccessible. The common sentiment animating their views is that scholars should cut the jargon. Policymakers don't want scholars to write in Greek or French, but rather just plain English.[71]

There are also some much bigger issues undergirding the relevance question.[72] To begin with, political science needs to rethink how it balances scholarly rigor with practical application. There is a middle ground between policy analysis and journalism, on one side, and scholastic irrelevance on the other.[73] The best approach to balancing scholarly rigor with continuing policy relevance is methodological pluralism, which includes a commitment to using not any particular method (or all of them) but rather just the approach most appropriate for the question at hand. But methodological pluralism, by itself, is not sufficient. The latest trend in political science requiring the simultaneous use of multiple methods could, ironically, prove to be even more limiting of policy relevance. Indeed, given the need to employ all of these methods simultaneously, it is potentially even more constraining in terms of the problems it can address because it has to be limited to those which can be quantified, modeled, and studied in depth at the same time.[74] Therefore, reinforcing methodological pluralism must also be a commitment to problem-, rather than method-, driven research agendas. It is only the combination of these two principles that will ensure that policy-relevant security studies can not only survive, but thrive, in political science.[75]

Scholars also need to think carefully about the role of theory in policy-relevant security studies scholarship. While there is no doubt that theory is important to policymakers, scholars need to be aware that as with many other things, too much of it can be a bad thing. In particular, the effort to cram the rich complexity of the social world into universal models can do intellectual violence to the phenomenon under study as well as produce suboptimal policy. Paul Nitze, then the director of the Secretary of State's Policy Planning Staff, readily conceded policymakers' need for theory but also noted that "there is the opposing consideration . . . that [theoretical] oversimplification presents great dangers."[76] Albert Wohlstetter advocated a balanced approach to theory, noting that the key to his success throughout his career "was the practical experience I had in working with engineers. I worked with them from two sides, so to speak, as someone who had been concerned with very abstract theory more basic than that familiar to design engineers, but on the other hand, I was also concerned with production, and therefore generally trying to get them to do things more practical than they wanted to do."[77] Theory is a powerful tool of statecraft, but when scholars embrace universal models they also risk irrelevance or worse.

Likewise, the transmission belts conveying scholarly findings to the policy world must be repaired. Kennan envisioned the State Department's Policy Planning Staff in the late 1940s serving this function, and in some respects it continues to do so to this day.[78] However, there are limits to how effectively a part of the bureaucracy can serve as an honest research broker. A plethora of think tanks in Washington are also supposed to translate knowledge into action, though the trend in recent years has been toward the establishment of overtly political and advocacy organizations, rather than nonpartisan, translational research centers.[79] Reinventing the role of think tanks as bridges between the Ivory Tower and the beltway is long overdue.

While nonacademic transmission belts can mediate between the Ivory Tower and the Beltway, they are no substitute for the scholars who produce knowledge to themselves serve as their own translators of it into policy. To be sure, scholars should not stop writing scholarly books and monographs utilizing the most sophisticated techniques of their discipline, if appropriate. In addition to doing these things, scholars should address pressing real world problems, not just chase after disciplinary fads. No one is in a better position to highlight the policy implications of a given piece of research than the individual who conducted it. Academic social scientists, if they want to be heard by senior policymakers, and heard correctly, need to be their own policy "transmission belts."[80]

The role of the Democratic Peace Theory in the recent Iraq war demonstrates the problems with scholars not specifying the concrete policy implications of their research.[81] Drawing on DPT, some officials in the George W. Bush administration justified the invasion of Iraq as part of a larger strategy to bring peace to the region by spreading democracy.[82] Democratic Peace proponent Bruce Russett objected to this conclusion after the fact though his voice had been largely mute in the run up to the war.[83] Had he and other democracy scholars participated more actively in the prewar debate, this rationale may have been less credible.

Academics also need to develop a more nuanced appreciation of the various influences on policy. Many, even in democratic political systems, tend to have an unrealistically "technocratic" attitude toward policymaking.[84] They often underestimate the role of politics in government decision making. Scholars must therefore understand that the policymaking process is inherently political and that without such an appreciation of the political considerations associated with any policy choice, even a good one may not be implemented.[85]

Those interested in affecting policy also need to set modest expectations for the sort of influence they can exercise on policy and not oversell what they can contribute. Doing so is a recipe both for discrediting academic participation in the policy process and also for making scholars overly pessimistic when their unrealistic expectations are not met. Paraphrasing Max Weber, scholars need to regard doing policy-relevant work as like "a slow, powerful drilling through hard boards, with a mixture of passion and a sense of proportion." A true vocation for this effort means the scholar's "spirit will not be broken if the world, when looked at from his point of view, proves too stupid or base to accept what he wishes to offer it, and who when faced with all that obduracy, can still say 'Nevertheless!' despite everything."[86] Scholars should take comfort that the challenges they face in getting the attention of policymakers are not dissimilar to those of government bureaucrats. United States' intelligence analysts, for example, also routinely complain about their inability to get policymakers to focus on complex issues and engage them on a sustained basis.[87] They also should time their interventions to open windows of opportunity because periods of crisis often constitute the best chance to successfully intervene in the policy process.[88] Finally, academics are more likely to have influence if they focus less on criticism of policies than on offering a positive policy agenda that provides a better solution within the general political and bureaucratic parameters in Washington and our political system.[89]

In light of the disciplinary pressures pushing toward irrelevance, scholars need to broaden their definition of excellence. There are two issues here: First, many social scientists have confused the forms of the natural sciences (mathematics and universal models) with the definition of science. This is, however, a category mistake for security studies, as Thomas Schelling warned long ago.[90] Second, in addition to precision and generalizability, research also has to address "important" questions. Importance cannot only be based on what scholars themselves regard as such; it also has to reflect the broader concerns of government officials and the rest of society. When it does not, scholarship proliferates which ignores many important issues because they are not "methodologically tractable" or employs methodological overkill on relatively trivial topics. To foster this, we need to honor the requirement by the National Science Foundation that potential grant recipients demonstrate the "broader impact" of their proposed projects by actually observing it.

To get such perspectives scholars will need to think outside of the Ivory Tower about including appropriate nonacademics as peer-reviewers, members of visiting committees, and even tenure letter writers. Imagine how the dynamics of academic promotion discussions would change if one or two of the evaluation letters came from practitioners in the candidate's field of study. Such outside perspectives are crucial because, as former Harvard president Bok cautioned, "We cannot assume that academic scientists will divide their efforts appropriately between basic and applied research."[91] Scholars need to break out of their disciplinary silos not only by engaging in interdisciplinary scholarship but also through cultivating a sense of "extradisciplinarity."

Like most people, academics respond to incentives. Therefore, in order to modify academic behavior, scholars will have to change the current incentive structure that rewards only a narrow disciplinary criterion of excellence. To change the current academic incentives that discourage relevance, reformers will also have to look outside their disciplinary guilds for allies; to higher-level university administrators and members of boards of trustees who tend to have broader visions than faculty in the disciplines; to government officials who need and can support policy relevant scholarship; and to the philanthropic community, the media, and the general public who presumably have an interest in the academy contributing more directly and consistently to the commonweal. In this effort, they should take a page out of economist John Kenneth Galbraith's book in which he recounted that "I made up my mind that I would never again place myself at the mercy of the technical economists who had enormous power to ignore what I had written. I set out to involve the larger community. I would involve economists by having the larger public say to them: 'Where do you stand on Galbraith's idea of price control?'"[92] Today, those outside actors should demand answers as to where scholars stand on the relevance question.

Another complicated issue is determining when and how scholars ought to directly participate in policymaking. On the one hand, doing so can enrich a scholar's understanding of a topic and the policymaking process, thereby providing him or her with a better sense of how to bring to bear their work more effectively on policy issues. On the other hand, once a scholar crosses the bridge to the policy world (as opposed to just sending his or her ideas across), the danger grows that he or she will become, like Walt Rostow, simply a well-credentialed bureaucrat whose critical faculties are crippled by a vested interest in particular policies. This is why, maintaining space in the academy for policy-relevant scholarship is so essential to bridging the scholar/policymaker gap.

Why Scholars Should Do It

Finally, no answer to the relevance question can sidestep a discussion of the ethical obligations of scholars to the rest of society. To be sure, ethical discussion is by no means unheard of in the Academy. Scholars spend a lot of time thinking about their obligations to the norms of their disciplines and also their relations with students and colleagues. Unfortunately, what little discussion there is about the proper relationship between science and policy overwhelmingly tends to favor the distancing of scholars and the Academy from it.[93] Some scholars are comfortable with service to society but not the state because they fear it corrupts their intellectual mission and threatens society.[94] But the most common argument against scholarly engagement with policymaking is that it presents insuperable moral and ethical problems to the integrity of the scientific process and also makes the academy complicit in the immoral policies that governments often undertake.[95]

Political theorist Anne Norton cited the authority of one of the founding fathers of modern social science, Max Weber, on behalf of maintaining this distance.[96] In doing so, she was following the lead of other distinguished political scientists.[97] Weber was, to be sure, an opponent of preaching from "the academic chair" and maintained that "the professor should not demand the right as a professor to carry the marshal's baton of the statesman or reformer in his knapsack."[98] Norton and others, however, misread Weber as repudiating policy relevance. Weber himself was personally deeply engaged with policy issues throughout his career, from his very first study of the East Elbian land question to the end of his career when he sought to help the Weimar Republic establish a constitutional system. His argument on behalf of scholarly objectivity was simply a salutary warning that the methods of science cannot adjudicate among competing ethical claims.[99] Today we need to formulate an "ethics" of scholarship that combines the important insights that Weber offered separately in his two important essays "Science as a Vocation" and "Politics as a Vocation" to ensure that obligations as scholars mesh with their obligations to the rest of society.[100] In other words, we need a third essay entitled "Science *and* Politics as a Vocation."[101]

Tellingly, the ethical obligation of political science to society has been a recurrent theme in American Political Science Association presidential addresses: in 1988 Harvard's Samuel Huntington proposed that "works in the social sciences should be judged not only on their intellectual merit but also by the contributions they make to achieving moral purposes."[102] Fifteen years later his colleague Robert Putnam concurred: "I believe that attending to the concerns of our fellow citizens is not just an optional add-on for the profession of political science, but an obligation as fundamental as our pursuit of scientific truth."[103] Given that political scientists at the pinnacle of their careers have come to this conclusion, it is well past time for the rest of the discipline to follow their leads in recognizing its moral obligation to answer its enduring relevance question.[104]

NOTES

Chapter 1. The Relevance Question

1. Full text is available at http://archive.defense.gov/Speeches/Speech.aspx?SpeechID=1228.

2. Thomas Schelling, "Academics, Decision Makers, and Security Policy During the Cold War: A Comment on Jervis," in Edward D. Mansfield and Richard Sisson, eds., *The Evolution of Political Knowledge: Democracy, Autonomy and Conflict in Comparative and International Politics* (Columbus: Ohio State University Press, 2004), 101, 137. Also see Fred Kaplan, *The Wizards of Armageddon* (Palo Alto: Stanford University Press, 1983), 336.

3. David D. Newsom, "Foreign Policy and Academia," *Foreign Policy* 101 (Winter 1995–96): 52.

4. Ithiel de Sola Pool, "The Necessity for Social Scientists Doing Research for Governments," *Background* 10, no. 2 (August 1966): 111–22; also in Irving Louis Horowitz ed., *The Rise and Fall of Project Camelot* (Cambridge, MA: MIT University Press, 1967), 267–68.

5. Advisory Committee on the Management of Behavioral Science Research in the Department of Defense, *Behavioral and Social Research in the Department of Defense: A Framework for Management* (Washington, DC: National Academy of Sciences, 1971), 2.

6. Daniel Maliniak, Amy Oakes, Susan Peterson, and Michael J. Tierney, "International Relations in the US Academy," *International Studies Quarterly* 55, no. 2 (June 2011): 439, 450–54.

7. Paul C. Avey and Michael C. Desch, "What Do Policymakers Want From Us? Results of a Survey of Current and Former Senior National Security Decision-makers," *International Studies Quarterly* 58, no. 2 (June 2014): 227–46.

8. Joseph S. Nye, Jr., "Scholars on the Sidelines," *Washington Post*, April 13, 2009, A15.

9. Alexander L. George, *Bridging the Gap: Theory and Practice in Foreign* Policy (Washington, DC: U.S. Institute of Peace, 1993); Philip Zelikow, "Foreign Policy Engineering: From Theory to Practice and Back Again," *International Security* 18, no. 4 (Spring 1994): 143–71; Joseph Kruzel, "Review: More a Chasm Than a Gap, But Do Scholars Want to Bridge It?" *Mershon International Studies Review* 38, no. 1 (April 1994): 179–81; Joseph Lepgold, "Is Anyone Listening? International Relations Theory and the Problem of Policy Relevance," *Political Science Quarterly* 113, no. 1 (Spring 1998): 43–62; Peter D. Feaver, "The Theory-Policy Debate in Political Science and Nuclear Proliferation," *National Security Studies Quarterly* 5, no. 3 (Summer 1999): 69–82; Joseph Lepgold and Miroslav Nincic, *Beyond the Ivory Tower: International Relations Theory and the Issue of Policy Relevance* (New York: Columbia University Press, 2001); Bruce W. Jentleson, "The Need for Praxis: Bringing Policy Relevance Back In," *International Security* 26, no. 4 (Spring 2002): 169–83; Stephen M. Walt, "The Relationship Between Theory and Policy in International Relations," *Annual Review of Political* Science 8 (June 2008): 23–48; Kenneth Lieberthal, "Initiatives to Bridge the Gap," *Asia Policy* 1, no. 1 (2006): 7–15; Joseph S. Nye, Jr., "International Relations: The Relevance of Theory to Practice," *Oxford Handbook of International Relations* (New York: Oxford University Press, 2008), 648–60; and Bruce W. Jentleson

and Ely Ratner, "Bridging the Beltway-Ivory Tower Gap," *International Studies Review* 13, no. 1 (March 2011): 6–11.

10. The teaching and research in international politics journal coding project is described in Daniel Maliniak, Amy Oakes, Susan Peterson, and Michael J. Tierney, "International Relations in the Academy," *International Studies Quarterly* 55, no. 2 (2011): 437–64. (Hereafter, TRIP) The data from which I generated these figures is available at http://www3.nd.edu/~carnrank/.

11. See, for example, Gene M. Lyons and Louis Morton, *Schools for Strategy: Education and Research in National Security Affairs* (New York: Praeger, 1965), 4, 69; and Ellen Herman, "The Career of Cold War Psychology," *Radical History Review* 63, no. 3 (Fall 1995): 62.

12. Barry D. Karl, *Charles E. Merriam and the Study of Politics* (Chicago: University of Chicago Press, 1974), x.

13. For an example see Raymond Tanter, "The Policy Relevance of Models in World Politics," *World Politics* 16, no. 4 (December 1972): 555–83.

14. Karl W. Deutsch, John Platt, and Dieter Senghass, "Conditions Favoring Major Advances in Social Science," *Science* 171, no. 3970 (February 5, 1971): 458–59. Also see David Glenn, "Calculus of the Battlefield," *Chronicle of Higher Education*, November 8, 2002, A14–16.

15. Joseph Lepgold, "Scholars and Statesmen: Framework for a Productive Dialogue," in Miroslav Nincic and Lepgold, eds., *Being Useful: Policy Relevance of International Relations Theory* (Ann Arbor: University of Michigan Press, 2000), 89.

16. Dorothy Ross, *The Origins of American Social Science* (New York: Cambridge University Press, 1991), 393. Also see the classic treatment of this tension in Mary O. Furner, *Advocacy and Objectivity: A Crisis in the Professionalization of American Social Science, 1865–1905* (New Brunswick, NJ: Transaction Publishers, 2011), xxiii.

17. Robert N. Proctor, *Value-Free Science? Purity and Power in Modern Knowledge* (Cambridge, MA: Harvard University Press, 1991), 3–5.

18. Joy Rohde, "Gray Matters: Social Scientists, Military Patronage, and Democracy in the Cold War," *Journal of American History* 96, no. 1 (June 2009): 101, 117.

19. For example, see Harold D. Lasswell cited in Bernard Crick, *The American Science of Politics: Its Origins and Conditions* (Berkeley: University of California Press, 1959), 181. Also see Furner, *Advocacy and Objectivity*, xxiv; and Warner R. Schilling, "Scientists, Foreign Policy, and Politics," *American Political Science Review* 56, no. 2 (June 1962): 295.

20. Walt, "The Relationship between Theory and Policy in International Relations," 25. For an example of optimism that this will happen, see Andrew Bennett and G. John Ikenberry, "The *Reviews'* Evolving Relevance for U.S. Foreign Policy, 1906–2006," *American Political Science Review* 100, no. 4 (November 2006): 651.

21. Quoted in The Earl of Birkenhead, *The Professor and the Prime Minister: The Official Life of Professor F. A. Lindemann, Viscount Cherwell* (Boston: Houghton Mifflin, 1962), 82.

22. Schilling, "Scientists, Foreign Policy, and Politics," 294.

23. Kenneth N. Waltz, *Man, the State, and War: A Theoretical Analysis* (New York: Columbia University Press, 1959), 76.

24. On the differences, see Ian Shapiro, "Problems, Methods, and Theories in the Study of Politics: Or, What's Wrong with Political Science and What to Do About It," in Kristen Renwick Monroe, ed., *Perestroika: The Raucous Rebellion in Political Science* (New Haven, CT: Yale University Press, 2005), 66–67, 71–73.

25. Michael E. Latham, "Ideology, Social Science, and Destiny: Modernization and the Kennedy-Era Alliance for Progress," *Diplomatic History* 22, no. 2 (Spring 1998): 205–6.

26. Quoted in Nicolas Guilhot, ed., *The Invention of International Relations Theory: Realism, the Rockefeller Foundation, and the 1954 Conference on Theory* (New York: Columbia University Press, 2011), 241.

27. Miroslav Nincic, "Introduction," in Nincic and Lepgold, *Being Useful*, 10.

28. Also using this metaphor are Hans J. Morgenthau, "The Theoretical and Practical Importance of a Theory of International Relations," in Guilhot, *The Invention of International Relations Theory*, 266; and Ernest J. Wilson, "How Social Science Can Help Policymakers: The Relevance of Theory," in Nincic and Lepgold, *Being Useful*, 122.

29. Bruce L.R. Smith, *The RAND Corporation: Case Study of a Nonprofit Advisory Corporation* (Cambridge, MA: Harvard University Press, 1966), 230.

30. Hamilton Cravens, "Part III: Have the Social Sciences Mattered in Washington?" in Cravens, ed., *The Social Sciences Go to Washington*, 129. Also see Philip Hauser, "Social Science and Social Engineering," *Philosophy of Science* 16, no. 3 (July 1949): 214; and Robert K. Merton, "The Role of Applied Social Science Research in the Formation of Policy: A Research Memorandum," *Philosophy of Science* 16, no. 3 (July 1949): 161.

31. John W. Kingdon, *Agendas, Alternatives, and Public Policies*, 2nd ed. (New York: Longman, 2003), 199.

32. Howard Furnas Memorandum for Mr. James S. Lay, Jr., Executive Secretary, National Security Council, "Utilization of Non-governmental Studies Bearing on National Security Problems," July 21, 1959, FOR OFFICIAL USE ONLY, National Archives and Record Administration [NARA], Record Group [RG] 273, Box 11, 1, Freedom of Informational Act [FOIA] copy in author's possession, 2.

33. Peter A. Hall, "Introduction," in Hall, ed., *The Political Power of Economic Ideas: Keynesianism Across Nations* (Princeton, NJ: Princeton University Press, 1989), 3–4. Also see Jeffrey W. Legro, "The Transformation of Policy Ideas," *American Journal of Political Science* 44, no. 3 (July 2000): 419–32.

34. The phrase is Thomas Schelling's. See his "Bernard Brodie (1910–1978)," *International Security* 3, no. 3 (Winter 1978–1979): 2.

35. Robert Jervis, "Security Studies: Ideas, Policy, and Politics," in Edward D. Mansfield and Richard Sisson, eds., *The Evolution of Political Knowledge* (Columbus: Ohio State University Press, 2004), 101. Also see Kaplan, *Wizards of Armageddon*, 336.

36. Skeptics include Paul Nitze, "The Role of the Learned Man in Government," *Review of Politics* 20, no. 3 (July 1958): 275–88; Ezra F. Vogel, "Some Reflections on Policy and Academics," *Asia Policy* 1 (2006): 31–34; Allen S. Whiting, "The Scholar and the Policymaker," *World Politics* 24 [Supplement: Theory and Policy in International Relations] (Spring 1972): 229–47; Marc Trachtenberg, "Social Scientists and National Security Policymaking," Unpublished paper for Notre Dame International security Program Conference, April 23, 2010; Stephen Krasner, "Garbage Cans and Policy Streams: How Academic Research Might Affect Foreign Policy," *Power, the State, and Sovereignty: Essays on International Relations* (London: Taylor and Francis, 2009), 254–74; Ernest J. Wilson III, "Is There Really a Scholar-Practitioner Gap? An Institutional Analysis," *PS: Political Science and Politics* 40, no. 1 (January 2007): 147–51; and Andrew R. Hom, et al., "Forum: 'A Bridge Too Far'? On the Impact of Worldly Relevance on International Relations," *International Studies Review* 19, no. 4 (December 2017): 692–721. The most comprehensive scholarly statement is Bruce Kuklick, *Blind Oracles: Intellectuals and War from Kennan to Kissinger* (Princeton, NJ: Princeton University Press, 2006).

37. Alexander H. Leighton, *Human Relations in a Changing World: Observations on the Use of the Social Sciences* (New York: E. P. Dutton, 1949), 128. Copyright © 1949, renewed 1977 by A. H. Leighton. Reprinted by permission of Russell & Volkening as agents for the author.

38. Kuklick, *Blind Oracles*, 6, 15–16, 143–44, 150, 223–30. Also see Francis J. Gavin, *Nuclear Statecraft: History and Strategy in America's Atomic Age* (Ithaca, NY: Cornell University Press, 2012), 4; and Christina Boswell, *The Political Uses of Expert Knowledge: Immigration Policy and Social Research* (New York: Cambridge University Press, 2009), 12.

39. William R. Allen, "Economics, Economists, and Economic Policy: Modern American Experiences," *History of Political Economy* 9, no. 1 (1977): 51.

40. Krasner, "Garbage Cans and Policy Streams," 255, 274. For a similar argument about domestic social policy, see Henry Aaron, *Politics and the Professors: The Great Society in Perspective* (Washington, DC: Brookings, 1978), 9–10.

41. Robert Gilpin, *American Scientists and Nuclear Weapons Policy* (Princeton, NJ: Princeton University Press, 1962), 300; also see 7.

42. Gabriel A. Almond, "Separate Tables: Schools and Sects in Political Science," *PS: Political Science and Politics* 21, no. 4 (Fall 1988): 836, 838.

43. Peter Novick, *That Noble Dream: "The Objectivity Question" and the American Historical Profession* (New York: Cambridge University Press, 1988). Readers will also hear theoretical echoes of another University of Chicago book, sociologist Andrew Abbott's *The Chaos of Disciplines* (Chicago: University of Chicago Press, 2001).

44. *Behavioral and Social Science Research in the Department of Defense*, xii; and P. Kecskemeti, "Utilization of Social Research in Shaping Policy Decisions," *RAND Paper* [P-2289] (Santa Monica: RAND, April 24, 1961), 11. Also see Aaron Wildavsky, "Practical Consequences of the Theoretical Study of Defense Policy," *Public Administration Review* 25, no. 1 (March 1965): 93; Robert A. Packenham, "Social Science and Public Policy," in Sidney Verba and Lucian W. Pye, eds., *The Citizen and Politics: A Comparative Perspective* (Stamford, CT: Greylock, 1978), 237–57; and Philip Hauser, "Social Science and Social Engineering," *Philosophy of Science* 16, no. 3 (July 1949): 214.

45. Elizabeth T. Crawford, "The Social Sciences in International and Military Policy: An Analytic Bibliography," [Prepared under Contract AF 49(638)1344 with the Air Force Office of Scientific Research] (Washington, DC: Bureau of Social Science Research, October 1965), vii.

46. Steven Brint, "Rethinking Policy Influence of Experts: From General Characterizations to Analysis of Variation," *Sociological Forum* 5, no. 3 (September 1990): 361–85; and Boswell, *The Political Uses of Expert Knowledge*, 13–14.

47. On this see Tom Nichols, *The Death of Expertise: The Campaign against Established Knowledge and Why It Matters* (New York: Oxford University Press, 2017); and Daniel W. Drezner, *The Ideas Industry: How Pessimists, Partisan, and Plutocrats Are Transforming the Marketplace of Ideas* (New York: Oxford University Press, 2017), 11–12. This is a long-standing concern: Robert Nisbet, "Knowledge Dethroned," *New York Times*, September 28, 1975, at https://mobile.nytimes.com/1975/09/28/archives/knowledge-dethroned-only-a-few-years-ago-scientists-scholars-and.html; and James S. Coleman, Morris Janowitz, Harry G. Johnson, Robert Lekachman, Martin Mayer, Daniel P. Moynihan, Harold Orlans, Thomas Sowell, and James Q. Wilson, "Social Science: The Public Disenchantment: A Symposium," *American Scholar* 45, no. 3 (Summer 1976): 335–59.

48. For similar concerns, see Stephen Van Evera, "Director's Statement: Trends in Political Science and the Future of Security Studies," *MIT Security Studies Program Annual Report, 2009–2010* (Cambridge, MA: MIT Press, 2010), 4–9; Lawrence M. Mead, "Scholasticism in Political Science," *Perspectives on Politics* 8, no. 2 (June 2010): 453–64, 212; and John Mearsheimer, "A Self-Enclosed World?" in Ian Shapiro, Rogers M. Smith, and Tarek E. Masoud, eds., *Problems and Methods in the Study of Politics* (New York: Cambridge University Press), 388–94.

49. Robert Lynd, *Knowledge for What? The Place of Social Science in American Culture* (Princeton, NJ: Princeton University Press, 1939); and Ian Shapiro, *The Flight From Reality in the Human Sciences* (Princeton, NJ: Princeton University Press, 2005).

50. Furner, *Advocacy and Objectivity*, 7–8; and Rogers M. Smith, "Still Blowing in the Wind: The American Quest for a Democratic, Scientific Political Science," *Daedelus* 126, no. 1 (Winter 1997): 253.

51. James Farr, Jacob S. Hacker, and Nicole Kazee, "The Policy Scientist of Democracy: The Discipline of Harold D. Lasswell," *American Political Science Review* 100, no. 4 (November 2006): 582; and Furner, *Advocacy and Objectivity*, 113.

52. Miroslav Nincic, "Policy Relevance and Theoretical Development: The Terms of the Trade-off," in Nincic and Lepgold, *Being Useful*, 36–44.

53. Thomas F. Gieryn, "Boundary-Work and the Demarcation of Science from Non-Science: Strains and Interests in Professional Ideologies of Scientists," *American Sociological Review* 48, no. 6 (December 1983): 787. Also see Mark C. Smith, *Social Science in the Crucible: The American Debate Over Objectivity and Purpose, 1918–1941* (Durham, NC: Duke University Press, 1994), 13, 157–61; and Furner, *Advocacy and Objectivity*, 31.

54. Jürgen Habermas, *Theory and Practice* (Boston, MA: Beacon, 1974), 79.

55. Richard K. Betts, "Should Strategic Studies Survive?" *World Politics* 50, no. 1 (October 1997): 10–11.

56. In general, war sparks government interest in mobilizing science and other intellectual resources that can aid the war effort. On this, see *Science in War* (Harmondsworth, UK: Penguin, 1940); and Roger L. Geiger, *Research and Relevant Knowledge: American Research Universities Since World War II* (New York: Oxford University Press, 1993), 48, 332. The effect of war is greatest on those parts of the social sciences such as security studies with a plausible connection to military affairs. This fact explains both why the place of that subfield in the discipline has varied over the years and also its ability to periodically swim against the tide of irrelevance that is swelling in other social science disciplines. To be sure, external developments in other areas have also fostered disciplinary engagement with policy. Two examples are the academics who joined Roosevelt's "Brain Trust" during the Great Depression and Johnson's "Great Society" in the 1960s. On the former, see R. G. Tugwell, *The Brains Trust* (New York: Viking, 1968); on the latter, Henry J. Aaron, *Politics and the Professors: The Great Society in Perspective* (Washington, DC: Brookings, 1978).

57. Geiger, *Research and Relevant Knowledge*, 7. The logic of the dynamics of the two sets of factors interacting is similar to the argument Barry R. Posen makes about the role of threats and bureaucratic politics in shaping military doctrine. See his *The Sources of Military Doctrine: France, Britain, and Germany Between the World Wars* (Ithaca, NY: Cornell University Press, 1984), 37, 80.

58. The classic statement of the dependence of political order on war and military mobilization is Otto Hintze, "Military Organization and the Organization of the State," in Felix Gilbert, ed., *The Historical Essays of Otto Hintze* (New York: Oxford University Press, 1975), 178–215. My own view is laid out in "War and Strong States, Peace and Weak States?" *International Organization* 50, no. 2 (Spring 1996): 237–68. See also, inter alia, Bruce D. Porter, *War and the Rise of the State: The Military Foundations of Modern Politics* (New York: The Free Press, 1994); Geoffrey Perret, *A Country Made by War: From the Revolution to Vietnam—the Story of America's Rise to Power* (New York: Vintage, 1989); and Michael S. Sherry, *In the Shadow of War: The United States Since the 1930s* (New Haven: Yale University Press, 1995).

59. Carol S. Gruber, *Mars and Minerva: World War I and the Uses of Higher Learning in America* (Baton Rogue: Louisiana State University Press, 1975), 5.

60. Gene M. Lyons, *The Uneasy Partnership: Social Science and the Federal Government in the Twentieth Century* (New York: Russell Sage Foundation, 1969), 27.

61. Philip H. Melanson, "The Political Science Profession, Political Knowledge, and Public Policy," *Politics and Society* 2, no. 4 (September 1972): 491.

62. On the mobilizing effect of wartime nationalism, see Barry R. Posen, "Nationalism, the Mass Army, and Military Power," *International Security* 18, no. 2 (Fall 1993): 80–124; and Jeffrey Herbst, "War and the State in Africa," *International Security* 14, no. 4 (Spring 1990): 122.

63. For a similar dynamic, see Robert Art, "Bureaucratic Politics and American Foreign Policy: A Critique," *Policy Sciences* 4, no. 4 (1973): 467–90.

64. Smith, *Social Science in the Crucible*, 71.

65. Edward Shils, "Social Science and Social Policy," *Philosophy of Science* 16 (1949): 219–221.

66. The Humanities have experienced a similar trend as well. See Shapiro, *The Flight From Reality in the Human Sciences*, 2. The source of this impulse is the largely the same: institutional vested interest. The particular direction it has taken, however, is different, reflecting different ideas about the appropriate scholarly approach in those disciplines. For discussion of intellectual trends within the Humanities, see David Lehman, *Signs of the Times: Deconstruction and the Fall of Paul de Man* (New York: Poseidon, 1991).

67. Emile Durkheim, *The Division of Labor in Society*, Intro. Lewis Coser (New York: Free Press, 1984), 2, 23, 79, 293–94, and 306.

68. G.H. Theodor Eimer, "Specialization in Science," *Popular Science Monthly* 32, no. 11 (November 1887): 1, at http://en.wikisource.org/wiki/Popular_Science_Monthly/Volume_32 /November_1887/Specialization_in_Science.

69. Thomas S. Kuhn, *The Structure of Scientific Revolutions*, 2nd ed. (Chicago: University of Chicago Press, 1970), 21, 24.

70. Kuhn, *Structure of Scientific Revolutions*, 96.

71. Friedrich Nietzsche, "On the Future of Our Educational Institutions" (Edinburgh, UK: Foulis, 1872), at http://www.gutenberg.org/files/28146/28146-h/28146-h.htm, 17.

72. F. A. Hayek, "The Dilemma of Specialization," in Leonard D. White, ed., *The State of the Social Sciences* (Chicago: University of Chicago Press, 1956), 462.

73. Burton R. Clark, "Organizational Adaptation to Professionals," in Howard M. Vollmer and Donald L. Mills, eds., *Professionalization* (Englewood Cliffs, NJ: Prentice Hall, 1966), 285; and Thomas Bender, *Intellect and Public Life: Essays on the Social History of Academic Intellectuals in the United States* (Baltimore: The Johns Hopkins University Press, 1993), 46.

74. Max Weber, *The Protestant Ethic and the Spirit of Capitalism* (New York: Charles Scribner's Sons, 1958), 181–83. For discussion of Weber's application of this dynamic to universities, see Wolfgang J. Mommsen, *Max Weber and German Politics: 1890–1920* (Chicago: University of Chicago Press, 1984), 444.

75. Abbott, *Chaos of Disciplines*, 22.

76. Robert Multhauf, "The Scientist and the 'Improver' of Technology," *Technology and Culture* 1, no. 1 (Winter 1959): 43.

77. Samuel P. Huntington, *The Soldier and the State: The Theory and Politics of Civil-Military Relations* (Cambridge, MA: The Belknap Press of Harvard University Press, 1957), 8, 10.

78. Andrew Abbott, "Status and Status Strain in the Professions," *American Journal of Sociology* 86, no. 4 (January 1981): 819; 823–24, 830.

79. For evidence that universities behave in typical bureaucratic fashion, see Clark, "Organizational Adaptation to Professionals," 283–91. Also see Louis Menand, *The Marketplace of Ideas: Reform and Resistance in the American University* (New York: Norton, 2010), 15, on the inherently organizationally conservative nature of universities.

80. Clark, "Organizational Adaptation to Professionals," 285–86. For a similar sentiment, see Noam Chomsky, "The Responsibility of Intellectuals," in Theodore Roszak, ed., *The Dissenting Academy* (New York: Pantheon, 1968), 271.

81. John Kenneth Galbraith, "Power and the Useful Economist," *American Economic Review* 63, no. 1 (March 1973): 6.

82. For compelling arguments about how the process of academic disciplinary professionalization was spurred by concerns about ensuring the autonomy of the university faculty see

Talcott Parsons, "The Academic System: A Sociologist's View," *Public Interest* 13 (Fall 1968): 173–97; Bender, *Intellect and Public Life*, 60–61; and Furner, *Advocacy and Objectivity*, 144.

83. Quoted in Michael A. Bernstein, *A Perilous Progress: Economists and Public Purpose in Twentieth-Century America* (Princeton, NJ: Princeton University Press, 2001), 7. A compelling logical argument for this sort of group behavior is presented in Mancur Olson, *The Rise and Decline of Nations: Economic Growth, Stagflation, and Social Rigidities* (New Haven, CT: Yale University Press, 1982), 41–47.

84. Donald E. Stokes, *Pasteur's Quadrant: Basic Science and Technological Innovation* (Washington, DC: Brookings, Institution Press, 1997), 171n31.

85. Dorothy Ross, "Changing Contours of The Social Science Disciplines," in Theodore M. Porter and Dorothy Ross, eds., *Cambridge History of Science*, vol. 7, *The Modern Social Sciences* (New York: Cambridge University Press, 2003), 209, 219. Also see Ross, *The Origins of American Social Science*, 399–400.

86. Harold L. Wilensky, "The Professionalization of Everyone?" *American Journal of Sociology* 70, no. 2 (September 1964): 138. Also see Lionel Trilling, *The Liberal Imagination*, Intro. Louis Menand (New York: New York Review of Books, 1990), 182.

87. Leslie A. White, "Sociology, Physics and Mathematics," *American Sociological Review* 8, no. 4 (August 1943): 375.

88. Rogers Smith, "Public Sphere Forum: Political Science and the Public Sphere in the 21st Century" at http://publicsphere.ssrc.org/smith-political-science-and-the-public sphere/.

89. James J. Blascovich and Christine R. Hartel, eds., *Human Behavior in Military Contexts* (Washington, DC: The National Academies Press, 2008), 10.

90. Proctor, *Value-Free Science?* 4–5.

91. Geiger, *Research and Relevant Knowledge*, 16, 168.

92. Stokes, *Pasteur's Quadrant*, 135.

93. Proctor, *Value-Free Science?* 4–5.

94. Quoted in Richard Hofstadter, *Anti-Intellectualism in American Life* (New York: Vintage, 1962), 31.

95. Abraham Flexner, *The Usefulness of Useless Knowledge* (Princeton, NJ: Princeton University Press, 2017), 57.

96. Joseph A. Schumpeter, "Science and Ideology," *American Economic Review* 39, no. 2 (March 1949): 346; and Bender, *Intellect and Public Life*, 5–6, 131.

97. John G. Gunnell, "The Founding of the American Political Science Association: Discipline, Profession, Political Theory, and Politics," *American Political Science Review* 100, no. 4 (November 2006): 479.

98. Jon R. Bond, "The Scientification of the Study of Politics: Some Observations on the Behavioral Evolution in Political Science," *Journal of Politics* 69, no. 4 (November 2007): 897.

99. Sheldon S. Wolin, "Political Theory as a Vocation," *American Political Science Review* 63, no. 4 (December 1969): 1063. Also see Gary King, Robert O. Keohane, and Sidney Verba, *Designing Social Inquiry: Scientific Inference in Qualitative Research* (Princeton, NJ: Princeton University Press, 1994), 9.

100. David Collier, Henry Brady, and Jason Seawright, "Sources of Leverage in Causal Inference: Toward An Alternative View of Methodology," in Henry E. Brady and David Collier, eds., *Rethinking Social Inquiry: Diverse Tools, Shared Standards* (Lanham, MD: Rowman & Littlefield, 2004), 266.

101. For evidence that the discipline of political science is finally acknowledging that it has a problem, see Bruce E. Cain and Lynn Vavreck, "Keeping It Contemporary: Report to the American Political Science Association of the Ad Hoc Committee on Public Understanding

of Political Science" (Washington, DC, APSA, circa 2012), at http://www.aei.org/publication /the-irrelevance-of-modern-political-science/. The gestalt of this disciplinary response is that contemporary political science has much to contribute to public debates but political scientists have failed to effectively communicate this. Other analysts argue that the problem is more fundamental to how the discipline sees itself. See, for example, Steven F. Hayward, "The Irrelevance of Modern Political Science," *The American*, September 14, 2010, at http://www.american.com /archive/2010/september/the-irrelevance-of-modern-political-science; and Michael P. McDonald, "'Paracademics': Mixing an Academic Career with Practical Politics," *PS: Political Science and Politics* 44, no. 2 (April 2011): 251.

102. Paul J. DiMaggio and Walter W. Powell, "The Iron Cage Revisited: Institutional Isomorphism and Collective Rationality in Organization Fields," *American Sociological Review* 48, no. 2 (April 1983): 147–60. For a related argument, see John W. Meyer and Brian Rowan, "Institutionalized Organizations: Formal Structure as Myth and Ceremony," *American Journal of Sociology* 83, no. 2 (September 1977): 340–63.

103. Abbott, *Chaos of Disciplines*, 126–27.

104. Bernstein, *A Perilous Progress*, 122.

105. Samuel C. Patterson, Brian D. Ripley, and Barbara Trish, "The American Political Science Review: A Retrospective of Last Year and the Last Eight Decades," *PS: Political Science and Politics* 21, no. 4 (Autumn 1988): 920; and Lee Sigelman, "The Coevolution of American Political Science and the *American Political Science Review*," *The American Political Science Review* 100, no. 4 (November 2006): 463n3.

106. Sigelman, "The Coevolution of American Political Science and the *American Political Science Review*," 475.

107. Russell Jacoby, *The Last Intellectuals: American Academic Culture in the Age of Academe* (New York: Farrar, Strauss and Giroux, 1987), 6.

108. Theda Skocpol, "Doubly Engaged Social Science: The Promise of Comparative Historical Analysis," in James Mahoney and Dietrich Rueschemeyer, eds., *Comparative Historical Analysis in the Social Sciences* (New York: Cambridge University Press, 2003), 410. Also see Gieryn, "Boundary Work and the Demarcation of Science from Non-Science," 781.

109. Sigelman, "The Coevolution of American Political Science and the *American Political Science Review*," 466, Table 1, Column 2+3. These judgments of whether an article offers a "policy prescription" are Sigelman's. Also see Bennett and Ikenberry, "*The Review*'s Evolving Relevance for U.S. Foreign Policy 1906–2006," 652, table 2, which shows a drop from a high of about 25 percent of articles aspiring to near-term relevance in the early 1950s to less than 5 percent in the mid-1960s.

110. Sigelman, "The Coevolution of American Political Science and the *American Political Science Review*," 467.

111. Boswell, *The Political Uses of Expert Knowledge*, 7; "Report Says Social Sciences Can Help Avoid Policy Goofs," *Science* 165, no. 3893 (August 8, 1969): 574; and Cornelia Dean, "Groups Call for Scientists to Engage the Body Politic," *New York Times*, August 8, 2011, at https://mobile .nytimes.com/2011/08/09/science/09emily.html.

112. Stokes, *Pasteur's Quadrant*. Also see Proctor, *Value-Free Science*, 224.

113. C. P. Snow, *The Two Cultures: And a Second Look* (Cambridge: Cambridge University Press, 1965), 2, 11.

114. Ido Oren, *Our Enemies and Us: America's Rivalries and the Making of Political Science* (Ithaca, NY: Cornell University Press, 2003), 126–27.

115. Harold Guetzkow, "Conversion Barriers in Using the Social Sciences," *Administrative Science Quarterly* 4, no. 1 (June 1959): 71; and Bernstein, *A Perilous Progress*, 88. Also see Cain and Vavreck, "Keeping It Contemporary," 10; and Drezner, *The Ideas Industry*, 102–22.

116. Lisa L. Martin, "The Contributions of Rational Choice: A Defense of Pluralism," *International Security* 24, no. 2 (Fall 1999): 76.

117. Arguing for a longer perspective is Elizabeth T. Crawford, "The Social Sciences in International and Military Policy: An Analytic Bibliography," [Prepared under Contract AF 49(638)1344 with the Air Force Office of Scientific Research] (Washington, DC: Bureau of Social Science Research, Inc., October 1965), vii.

118. John Mearsheimer and Stephen Walt, "Leaving Theory Behind: Why Simplistic Hypothesis Testing Is Bad for International Relations," *European Journal of International Relations* 19, no. 3 (2013): 427–57.

119. Lyons and Morton, *Schools for Strategy*, 51, 302; and Betts, "Should Strategic Studies Survive?" 8.

120. Gary King, Robert O. Keohane, and Sidney Verba, *Designing Social Inquiry: Scientific Inference in Qualitative Research* (Princeton, NJ: Princeton University Press, 1994), 140–46.

Chapter 2. How War Opened the Door to the Ivory Tower during the First World War and Peace Closed It Again

1. In fact, one can argue that this process actually began much earlier during previous wars from the very beginning of the United States. On this, see, Appendix II, "Statement of Hon. John S. Foster, Jr., Director of Defense Research and Engineering; Accompanied By Col. James M. Brower; Donald M. MacArthur; Rodney W. Nichols; and Morton H. Halperin," "Department of Defense Sponsored Foreign Affairs Research," Committee on Foreign Relations, U.S. Senate, 90th Cong., 2nd sess., May 9, 1968, 86; and Warner R. Schilling, "Scientists, Foreign Policy, and Politics," *American Political Science Review* 56, no. 2 (June 1962): 287.

2. Phillip E. Mosely, "Research on Foreign Policy," in Daniel Lerner, ed., *The Human Meaning of the Social Sciences* (New York: Meridian, 1960), 48.

3. James G. Hershberg, *James B. Conant: Harvard to Hiroshima and the Making of the Nuclear Age* (Palo Alto: Stanford University Press, 1993), 41; Barry M. Katz, *Foreign Intelligence: Research and Analysis in the Office of Strategic Services, 1942–1945* (Cambridge, MA: Harvard University Press, 1989), xi; and Bruce L. R. Smith, *The RAND Corporation: Case Study of a Nonprofit Advisory Corporation* (Cambridge, MA: Harvard University Press, 1966), 12.

4. Dorothy Ross, "Changing Contours of the Social Science Disciplines," in Theodore M. Porter and Dorothy Ross, eds., *Cambridge History of Science*, vol. 7, *The Modern Social Sciences* (New York: Cambridge University Press, 2003), 219.

5. Peter Novick, *That Noble Dream: The "Objectivity Question" and the American Historical Profession* (New York: Cambridge University Press, 1988), 577.

6. Robert S. Lynd, *Knowledge for What? The Place of Social Science in American Culture* (Princeton, NJ: Princeton University Press, 1939), 118; also see 128–29. Emphasis in original.

7. Michael A. Bernstein, *A Perilous Progress: Economists and Public Purpose in Twentieth-Century America* (Princeton, NJ: Princeton University Press, 2001), 17; and Dorothy Ross, *The Origins of American Social Science* (New York: Cambridge University Press, 1991), 37.

8. Ross, *The Origins of American Social Science*, xiv.

9. Mary O. Furner, *Advocacy and Objectivity: A Crisis in the Professionalization of American Social Science, 1865–1905* (New Brunswick, NJ: Transaction, 2011); and Carol Gruber, *Mars and Minerva: World War I and the Uses of Higher Learning in America* (Baton Rogue: Louisiana State University Press, 1975), 13–21.

10. James Farr, "Political Science," in Theodore M. Porter and Dorothy Ross, eds., *Cambridge History of Science*, vol. 7, *The Modern Social Sciences* (New York: Cambridge University Press, 2003), 308. Also see Mark Solovey, "Riding the Natural Scientists' Coat-tails on to the Endless Frontier: The SSRC and the Quest for Scientific Legitimacy," *Journal of the History of the Behavioral Sciences* 40, no. 4 (Fall 2004): 400; and Gruber, *Mars and Minerva*, 21.

11. Robert N. Proctor, *Value-free Science? Purity and Power in Modern Knowledge* (Cambridge, MA: Harvard University Press, 1991), 99.

12. Ross, "Changing Contours of the Social Science Disciplines," 209.

13. Furner, *Advocacy and Objectivity*, 257–58.

14. David M. Ricci, *The Tragedy of Political Science: Politics, Scholarship, and Democracy* (New Haven, CT: Yale University Press, 1984), 13.

15. Gruber, *Mars and Minerva*, 29–30. Also see Barry D. Karl, *Charles E. Merriam and the Study of Politics* (Chicago: University of Chicago Press, 1974), 11.

16. Barry D. Karl and Stanley N. Katz, "The American Private Philanthropic Foundation and the Public Sphere, 1890–1930," *Minerva* 19, no. 2 (June 1981): 256.

17. Albert Somit and Joseph Tanenhaus, *The Development of American Political Science: From Burgess to Behavioralism* (Boston: Allyn and Bacon, 1967), 8, 18.

18. John G. Gunnell, "The Founding of the American Political Science Association: Discipline, Profession, Political Theory, and Politics," *American Political Science Review* 100, no. 4 (November 2006): 481–83; and Furner, *Advocacy and Objectivity*, 262.

19. Bernard Crick, *The American Science of Politics: Its Origins and Conditions* (Berkeley: University of California Press, 1959), 101.

20. Ross, *The Origins of American Social Science*, 279. Also see Somit and Tanenhaus, *The Development of Political Science*, 43; and Furner, *Advocacy and Objectivity*, 278 and 286.

21. Somit and Tanenhaus, *The Development of Political Science*, 55.

22. Mark C. Smith, *Social Science in the Crucible: The American Debate Over Objectivity and Purpose, 1918–1941* (Durham, NC: Duke University Press, 1994), 21–24.

23. Sidney Kaplan, "Social Engineers as Saviors: Effects of World War I on Some American Liberals," *Journal of the History of Ideas* 17, no. 3 (June 1956): 347.

24. Smith, *Social Science in the Crucible*, 85. Also see Somit and Tanenhaus, *The Development of Political Science*, 111.

25. Karl, *Charles E. Merriam and the Study of Politics*, viii.

26. Proctor, *Value-free Science?* 68.

27. Quoted in Ross, *The Origins of American Social Science*, 393.

28. Alexander H. Leighton, *Human Relations in a Changing World: Observations on the Use of the Social Sciences* (New York: E. P. Dutton, 1949), 40.

29. Ross, *The Origins of American Social Science*, 390; and Ross, "Changing Contours of the Social Science Disciplines," 214. Also see Ricci, *The Tragedy of Political Science*, 39, for evidence that this view is common in political science.

30. Leslie A. White, "Sociology, Physics, and Mathematics," *American Sociological Review* 8, no. 4 (August 1943): 375. Also see Smith, *Social Science in the Crucible*, 40, 69.

31. Smith, *Social Science in the Crucible*, 28. Also see Joseph W. Ryan, *Samuel Stouffer and the GI Survey: Sociologists and Soldiers during the Second World War* (Knoxville: University of Tennessee Press, 2013), 159.

32. A Statement by the Research Committee of the American Political Science Association, "Instruction and Research: War-time Priorities," *American Political Science Review* 37, no. 3 (June 1943): 513.

33. Lynd, *Knowledge for What?* 17; also see 35.

34. Charles Beard, "Time, Technology, and the Creative Spirit in Political Science," *American Political Science Review* 21, no. 1 (February 1927): 9.

35. Proctor, *Value-free Science?* 77. Also see Lynd, *Knowledge for What?* 12.

36. Beard, "Time, Technology, and the Creative Spirit in Political Science," 6; also see 10.

37. Lynd, *Knowledge for What?* 167–68.

38. Tang Tsou, "Fact and Value in Charles E. Merriam," *Southwestern Social Science Quarterly* 36, no. 1 (June 1955): 11.

39. Ross, *The Origins of American Social Science*, 63.

40. Smith, *Social Science in the Crucible*, 13.

41. Quoted in Lynd, *Knowledge for What?* 242.

42. Proctor, *Value-free Science?* 86. Also see Ross, *The Origins of American Social Science*, 158.

43. Crick, *The American Science of Politics*, 20.

44. Gene M. Lyons, *The Uneasy Partnership: Social Science and the Federal Government in the Twentieth Century* (New York: Russell Sage Foundation, 1969), 26. Also see Gruber, *Mars and Minerva*, 32.

45. Ricci, *The Tragedy of Political Science*, 23.

46. Crick, *The American Science of Politics*, 100.

47. Novick, *That Noble Dream*, 2, 21, and 47–60.

48. Ibid., 205.

49. APSA Research Committee, "Instruction and Research: War-time Priorities," 505–6.

50. Lynd, *Knowledge for What?* 170–74.

51. Ross, "Changing Contours of the Social Science Disciplines," 219.

52. The Committee on War-time Services of the American Political Science Association, "The Political Scientist and National Service in War-time," *American Political Science Review* 35, no. 5 (October 1942): 944.

53. Peter Mandler, *Return from the Natives: How Margaret Mead Won the Second World War and Lost the Cold War* (New Haven: Yale University Press, 2013), 50–51.

54. Novick, *That Noble Dream*, 111–32.

55. The Committee on War-time Services of the American Political Science Association, "The Political Scientist and National Service in War-time," 931.

56. Lynd, *Knowledge for What?* 177.

57. The Committee on War-time Services of the American Political Science Association, "The Political Scientist and National service in War-time," 940. Also see APSA Research Committee, "Instruction and Research: War-time Priorities," 505.

58. Lynd, *Knowledge for What?* 114–15. Emphasis in original.

59. Karl, *Charles E. Merriam and the Study of Politics*, 40–41.

60. E. A. Shils, "Social Science and Social Policy," *Philosophy of Science* 16, no. 3 (July 1949): 222. Also see Richard Hofstadter, "A Note on Intellect and Power: Review of *The Servants of Power* by Loren Baritz," *American Scholar* 30, no. 4 (Fall 1961): 588; and Theda Skocpol, *Protecting Soldiers and Mothers: The Political Origins of Social Policy in the United States* (Cambridge, MA: The Belknap Press of Harvard University Press, 1992).

61. Karl, *Charles E. Merriam and the Study of Politics*, 84. Also see the discussions in Crick, *The American Science of Politics*, 19–20; and William E. Leuchtenburg, "The New Deal and the Analogue of War," in John Braeman, Robert H. Bremner, and Everett Walters, eds., *Change and Continuity in Twentieth-Century America* (Columbus: Ohio State University Press, 1964), 85.

62. Gruber, *Mars and Minerva*, 44. Also see 46, 82, and 172.

63. Bernstein, *A Perilous Progress*, 36–37.

64. Gruber, *Mars and Minerva*, 95.

65. Ross, *The Origins of American Social Science*, 17.

66. Crick, *The American Science of Politics*, 73–94.

67. Ross, *The Origins of American Social Science*, 320.

68. David M. Kennedy, *Over Here: The First World War and American Society* (New York: Oxford University Press, 1980), 50.

69. Crick, *The American Science of Politics*, 110.

70. Leuchtenburg, "The New Deal and the Analogue of War," 87. For further discussion, see John A. Thompson, *Reformers and War: American Progressive Publicists and the First World War* (Cambridge: Cambridge University Press, 1987), 91–92.

71. Randolph S. Bourne, "Twilight of Idols," in Carl Resek, ed., *War and the Intellectuals: Collected Essays 1915–1919* (1964; reprint Indianapolis, IN: Hackett, 1999), 59.

72. Richard Hofstadter, *Anti-Intellectualism in American Life* (New York: Vintage, 1963), 211.

73. Lyons, *The Uneasy Partnership*, 28. Also see Hershberg, *James B. Conant*, 43.

74. Hershberg, *James B. Conant*, 45.

75. Harvey M. Sapolsky, *Science and the Navy: The History of the Office of Naval Research* (Princeton, NJ: Princeton University Press, 1990), 13.

76. Jonathan M. Nielson, "The Scholar as Diplomat: American Historians at the Paris Peace Conference of 1919," *International History Review* 14, no. 2 (May 1992): 230–31.

77. Lawrence E. Gelfand, *The Inquiry: American Preparations for Peace, 1917–1919* (New Haven, CT: Yale University Press, 1963), x.

78. James T. Shotwell, *The Autobiography of James T. Shotwell* (Indianapolis, IN: Bobbs-Merrill, 1961), 77.

79. For a complete list of the participants see Gelfand, *The Inquiry*, 53–67.

80. For discussion of this and other aspects of the Inquiry's activities, see Ronald Steel, *Walter Lippmann and the American Century* (New York: Vintage, 1980), 129–40.

81. Gelfand, *The Inquiry*, 124. Also see 134–53, 225, and 323; and Nielson, "The Scholar as Diplomat," 233.

82. Gelfand, *The Inquiry*, 314–15, 330.

83. Shotwell, *The Autobiography of James T. Shotwell*, 106, note.

84. Nielson, "The Scholar as Diplomat," 250.

85. Gruber, *Mars and Minerva*, 243. Also see 98, 213, and 238.

86. James R. Mock and Cedric Larson, *Words that Won the War: The Story of the Committee on Public Information, 1917–19* (Princeton, NJ: Princeton University Press, 1939), 159.

87. Ibid., 183 and 185.

88. Gruber, *Mars and Minerva*, 109.

89. Robert Lynd, "The Science of Inhuman Relations: Review of *The American Soldier* by Samuel A. Stouffer," *New Republic* (August 29, 1949), 22.

90. Deborah Shapley, *Promise and Power: The Life and Times of Robert McNamara* (Boston: Little, Brown, 1993), 13. Also see the discussion of the influence of pragmatism among intellectuals in Bruce Kuklick, *Blind Oracles: Intellectuals and War from Kennan to Kissinger* (Princeton, NJ: Princeton University Press, 2006), 8–14; and Samuel Beer, "Liberalism and the National Idea," *Public Interest* 5 (1966): 70–82.

91. Kaplan, "Social Engineers as Saviors," 360.

92. Smith, *Social Science in the Crucible*, 63.

93. Ross, *The Origins of American Social Science*, 397.

94. Lyons, *The Uneasy Partnership*, 29–30.

95. Hofstadter, *Anti-Intellectualism in American Life*, 213.

96. Lyons, *The Uneasy Partnership*, 31.

97. Barry D. Karl, "Presidential Planning and Social Science Research: Mr. Hoover's Experts," *Perspectives in American History* 3 (1969): 347. Karl suggests that it was in fact the U.S. Civil War that first sparked interest in mobilizing "national knowledge," though he concedes (350) that the First World War was really catalytic in this regard. For excerpts from "Research Committee on Social Trends" report, see Lyons, *The Uneasy Partnership*, appendix I.

98. On this, see Peter A. Hall, "Conclusion: The Politics of Keynesian Ideas," in Peter A. Hall, ed., *The Political Power of Economic Ideas: Keynesianism Across Nations* (Princeton, NJ: Princeton University Press, 1989), 386–89.

99. Roger L. Geiger, *Research and Relevant Knowledge: American Research Universities since World War II* (New York: Oxford University Press, 1993), viii and 4.

100. Geiger, *Research and Relevant Knowledge* 4.

101. Lyons, *The Uneasy Partnership*, xiii–xiv.

102. Karl and Katz, "The American Private Philanthropic Foundation and the Public Sphere," 238.

103. Lyons, *The Uneasy Partnership*, 42.

104. Ibid., 277–79.

105. Kennedy, *Over Here*, 90.

106. Ross, "Changing Contours of the Social Science Disciplines," 215–16.

107. Hamilton Cravens, "Part II: Social Sciences as Process and Procedure," in Cravens, ed., *The Social Sciences Go to Washington*, 62.

108. Ross, *The Origins of American Social Science*, 462. Also see 157–59 and 311.

109. Smith, *Social Science in the Crucible*, 70.

110. Ross, *The Origins of American Social Science*, 295, 321, 399, and 499. Also see Crick, *The American Science of Politics*, 134, 140.

111. Ross, *The Origins of American Social Science*, 400.

112. David C. Engerman, "Social Science in the Cold War," *Isis* 101, no. 2 (June 2010): 395.

113. Lyons, *The Uneasy Partnership*, 8. Also see 6–7.

114. Somit and Tanenhaus, *The Development of Political Science*, 134

115. Ibid., 63, 87.

116. Karl, *Charles E. Merriam and the Study of Politics*, 106. Also see Ross, *The Origins of American Social Science*, 449.

117. Somit and Tanenhaus, *The Development of Political Science*, 87.

118. Smith, *Social Science in the Crucible*, 90 and 98–99.

119. Ibid., 92 and 100. Also see Ross, *The Origins of American Social Science*, 454.

120. Karl, *Charles E. Merriam and the Study of Politics*, 121.

121. Crick, *The American Science of Politics*, 144.

122. Thomas H. Reed, "Report of the Committee on Policy of the American Political Science Association for the Year 1935," *American Political Science Review* 30, no. 1 (February 1936): 142.

123. Tsou, "Fact and Value in Charles E. Merriam," 22. Also see Karl, *Charles E. Merriam and the Study of Politics*, x.

124. Somit and Tanenhaus, *The Development of Political Science*, 87–100.

125. The Committee on War-time Services of the American Political Science Association, "The Political Scientist and National Service in War-time," 932.

126. Crick, *The American Science of Politics*, 157.

127. Frederick M. Davenport and Lewis B. Sims, "Public Administration: Political Science and Federal Employment," *American Political Science Review* 35, no. 2 (April 1941): 304.

128. Davenport and Sims, "Public Administration," 307n7, which says that Civil Service Commission recommended only one class in statistics or accounting.

129. Ido Oren, *Our Enemies and Us: America's Rivalries and the Making of Political Science* (Ithaca, NY: Cornell University Press, 2003), 88.

130. Irving Louis Horowitz, "Social Science and Public Policy: Implications of Modern Research," in Irving Louis Horowitz, ed., *The Rise and Fall of Project Camelot: Studies in the Relationship between Social Science and Practical Politics* (Cambridge, MA: MIT Press, 1967), 370–71. Also see Panagiotis Hatzis, "The Academic Origins of John F. Kennedy's New Frontier," Unpublished Master's Thesis, Concordia University, Montreal, CA, November 1996, vi; and Hofstadter, *Anti-Intellectualism in American Life*, 217.

131. Jeremi Suri, *Henry Kissinger and the American Century* (Cambridge, MA: The Belknap Press of Harvard University Press, 2007), 100–101.

132. Smith, *Social Science in the Crucible*, 76.

133. Bernstein, *A Perilous Progress*, 60.

134. Smith, *Social Science in the Crucible*, 83.

135. Hershberg, *James B. Conant*, 83. This analogy began with Herbert Hoover. See Leuchtenburg, "The New Deal and the Analogue of War," 82.

136. Lyons, *The Uneasy Partnership*, 77, 125; appendix II, 332–33, 342–43, and 345–46. Also see Ross, "Changing Contours of the Social Science Disciplines," 225.

137. William T. R. Fox, "Interwar International Relations Research: The American Experience," *World Politics* 2, no. 1 (October 1949): 68–69, 75.

138. For a discussion of these efforts and how they segued into the subsequent wartime mobilization of the social sciences, see David Ekbladh, "Present at the Creation: Edward Meade Earle and the Depression Era Origins of Security Studies," *International Security* 36, no. 3 (Winter 2011/12): 107–41. Also see the briefer discussion in David A. Baldwin, "Security Studies and The End of the Cold War," *World Politics* 48, no. 1 (October 1995): 119–20.

139. For discussion of IIS and *World Politics* see William T. R. Fox, "Frederick Sherwood Dunn and the American Study of International Relations," *World Politics* 15, no. 1 (October 1962): 12–19. Also see Michael Klare, compiler, *The University-Military-Police Complex: A Directory and Related Documents* (New York: North American Congress on Latin America, 1970), 44.

140. Hans J. Morgenthau, *Scientific Man versus Power Politics* (Chicago: Phoenix, 1946), 94, 101.

141. Dartmouth College, Faculty Biographical Data for Bernard Brodie, June 14, 1941, in Brodie Personnel File, Department of Political Science, Dartmouth College Records Management [BPF] and Quincy Wright to Dean E. Gordon Bill, June 16, 1941 in BPF.

142. Bill to Edward M. Earle, March 8, 1943 and Earle to Bill, March 12, 1943 in BPF.

143. Memorandum from Bill to President, Dartmouth College, June 12, 1941 in BPF.

144. Brodie to Bill, June 5, 1942 in BPF.

145. Hanson W. Baldwin, "How Modern Navies Developed," *New York Times Sunday Book Review*, June 11, 1942, no page number; and Brodie to Bill, January 26, 1942 in BPF.

146. Brodie to Bill, February 13, 1942 in BPF.

147. Brodie Telegram to Bill, Between August 11 and 13, 1942 in BPF.

148. Brodie to Bill, August 25, 1942; Brodie to Bill, February 19, 1943; and Brodie to Bill, June 26, 1944 in BPF.

149. Bill to Brodie, March 8, 1943 in BPF. Also see Bill to Earle, March 8, 1943; Bill to Brodie, March 18, 1943; and Bill to Brodie, September 20, 1943, in BPF, which emphasize this last issue.

150. Earle to Bill, November 5, 1943 in BPF. Lippmann's piece was entitled "Today and Tomorrow: The Serious Study of War" and a copy is in BPF.

151. Brodie to Bill, March 15, 1943 in BPF.

152. Brodie to Bill, January 17, 1945 in BPF.

153. For details of the IIS ethos, particularly under its second director, see Fox, "Frederick Sherwood Dunn and the American Study of International Relations," 14.

154. William T. R. Fox, "A Middle Western Isolationist-Internationalist's Journey toward Relevance," in Joseph Kruzel and James N. Rosenau, eds., *Journeys through World Politics: Autobiographical Reflections of Thirty-four Academic Travelers* (Lexington. MA: Lexington Books, 1989), 233–42.

155. A good history of the institute is provided by Frederick Sherwood Dunn, "The Growth of the Yale Institute of International Studies," *100 Years: The Rockefeller Foundation*, November 7, 1950, https://rockfound.rockarch.org/digital-library-listing/-/asset_publisher /yYxpQfeI4W8N/content/the-growth-of-the-yale-institute-of-international-studies.

156. The proposed program is described in "Research in International Law and International Relations at Yale University," May 1931, at https://rockfound.rockarch.org/digital -library-listing/-/asset_publisher/yYxpQfeI4W8N/content/research-in-international-law -and-international-relations-at-yale-university.

157. Charles Edward Clark, "Letter from Charles E. Clark to Edmund E. Day, 1931 December 11," *100 Years: The Rockefeller Foundation*, December 11, 1931, https://rockfound .rockarch.org/digital-library-listing/-/asset_publisher/yYxpQfeI4W8N/content/letter -from-charles-e-clark-to-edmund-e-day-1931-december-11.

158. Edmund Ezra Day, "Letter from Edmund E. Day to Charles E. Clark, 1931 December 15," *100 Years: The Rockefeller Foundation*, December 15, 1931, https://rockfound. rockarch.org/documents/20181/35639/Letter+from+Edmund+E.+Day+to+Charles+E.+- Clark%2C+1931+December+15.pdf/afeca112-a94b-4262-bfd0-3e7cfd9eee91 and Edmund Ezra Day, "Letter from Edmund E. Day to Charles E. Clark, 1932 January 23," 100 Years: The Rockefeller Foundation, accessed December 27, 2017, https://rockfound.rockarch.org /digital-library-listing/-/asset_publisher/yYxpQfeI4W8N/content/day-edmund-ezra-letter -from-edmund-e-day-to-charles-e-clark-1931-december-24-.

159. Dunn, "The Growth of the Yale Institute of International Studies."

160. Rockefeller Foundation, "Minutes of the Rockefeller Foundation Regarding the Study of International Relations at Yale University," 5/17/35 at https://rockfound.rockarch.org /digital-library-listing/-/asset_publisher/yYxpQfeI4W8N/content/minutes-of-the-rockefeller -foundation-regarding-yale-university-s-research-into-international-relations.

161. Nicholas J. Spykman, "Letter from Nicholas J. Spykman to Sydnor Walker, 1938 April 14," *100 Years: The Rockefeller Foundation*, April 14, 1938, https://rockfound.rockarch .org/digital-library-listing/-/asset_publisher/yYxpQfeI4W8N/content/letter-from-nicholas -j-spykman-to-sydnor-walker-1938-april-14; and Sydnor H. Walker, "Report on Research in International Relations at Yale University," *100 Years: The Rockefeller Foundation*, 1941, https:// rockfound.rockarch.org/digital-library-listing/-/asset_publisher/yYxpQfeI4W8N/content /report-on-research-in-international-relations-at-yale-university.

162. Sydnor H. Walker, "Memorandum Regarding Yale's Work on International Relations," *100 Years: The Rockefeller Foundation*, April 6, 1940, https://rockfound.rockarch .org/digital-library-listing/-/asset_publisher/yYxpQfeI4W8N/content/memorandum -regarding-yale-s-work-on-international-relatio-1.

163. Rockefeller Foundation, "Minutes of the Rockefeller Foundation Regarding the Study of International Relations at Yale University," *100 Years: The Rockefeller Foundation*, May 16, 1941, https://rockfound.rockarch.org/digital-library-listing/-/asset_publisher/yYxpQfeI4W8N /content/minutes-of-the-rockefeller-foundation-regarding-the-study-of-international -relations-at-yale-universi-2.

164. Rockefeller Foundation, "The United States and the Balance of Power," *100 Years: The Rockefeller Foundation*, May 1942, https://rockfound.rockarch.org/digital-library-listing /-/asset_publisher/yYxpQfeI4W8N/content/the-united-states-and-the-balance-of-power.

165. Frederick Sherwood Dunn, "The Place of University Research Agencies in International Relations," *100 Years: The Rockefeller Foundation*, December 23, 1943, https://rockfound

.rockarch.org/digital-library-listing/-/asset_publisher/yYxpQfeI4W8N/content/
the-place-of-university-research-agencies-in-international-relations.

166. Frederick Sherwood Dunn, "The Position of a Creative Research Organization within a University," *100 Years: The Rockefeller Foundation*, January 8, 1944, https://rockfound
.rockarch.org/digital-library-listing/-/asset_publisher/yYxpQfeI4W8N/content/the
-position-of-a-creative-research-organization-within-a-university.

167. Joseph H. Willits, "Memorandum regarding Yale's Institute of International Studies," *100 Years: The Rockefeller Foundation*, January 18, 1944, https://rockfound
.rockarch.org/digital-library-listing/-/asset_publisher/yYxpQfeI4W8N/content
/memorandum-regarding-yale-s-institute-of-international-studies.

168. L. M. Hanks, Jr., "Summary and Epilogue," in "Social Research in Political Decision," A Special Issue of *The Journal of Social Issues* 3, no. 4 (Fall 1947): 57–59.

Chapter 3. World War II

1. Bernard Brodie, "The American Scientific Strategists," *RAND Paper* [P-2979] (Santa Monica: RAND Corporation, October 1964), 11–12.

2. James G. Hershberg, *James B. Conant: Harvard to Hiroshima and the Making of the Nuclear Age* (Palo Alto: Stanford University Press, 1993), 127.

3. Gene M. Lyons, *The Uneasy Partnership: Social Science and the Federal Government in the Twentieth Century* (New York: Russell Sage Foundation, 1969), 97; and U.S. Congress, Office of Technology Assessment, *A History of Department of Defense Federally Funded Research and Development Centers* (Washington, DC: Government Publishing Office, June 1995), 14.

4. David C. Engerman, "Rethinking the Cold War Universities: Some Recent Histories," *Journal of Cold War Studies* 5, no. 3 (Summer 2003): 81.

5. *Subcommittee Report on Research Activities in the Department of Defense and Defense Related Agencies* (Washington, DC: Commission on Organization of the Executive Branch of the Government, April 1955), 5. The same was true of Britain. See, *Science in War* (Harmondsworth, UK: Penguin, 1940).

6. Phillip E. Mosely, "Research on Foreign Policy," in Daniel Lerner, ed., *The Human Meaning of the Social Sciences* (New York: Meridian, 1960), 49.

7. The Earl of Birkenhead, *The Professor and the Prime Minister: The Official Life of Professor F.A. Lindeman, Viscount Cherwell* (Boston: Houghton Mifflin, 1962); C. P. Snow, *Science and Government* (New York: Mentor, 1962); and Stephen Budiansky, *Blackett's War: The Men Who Defeated the Nazi U-Boats and Brought Science to the Art of Warfare* (New York: Knopf, 2013).

8. Warner R. Schilling, "Scientists, Foreign Policy, and Politics," *American Political Science Review* 56, no. 2 (June 1962): 288.

9. Hershberg, *James B. Conant*, 128.

10. Harvey M. Sapolsky, *Science and the Navy: The History of the Office of Naval Research* (Princeton, NJ: Princeton University Press, 1990), 14–15.

11. Barry M. Katz, *Foreign Intelligence: Research and Analysis in the Office of Strategic Services, 1942–1945* (Cambridge, MA: Harvard University Press, 1989), xi.

12. Alexander H. Leighton, *Human Relations In A Changing World: Observations on the Use of the Social Sciences* (New York: E. P. Dutton, 1949), 43.

13. Quoted in ibid., 128. Also see the discussion of Leighton's service in Peter Mandler, *Return from the Natives: How Margaret Mead Won the Second World War and Lost the Cold War* (New Haven: Yale University Press, 2013), 162–69.

14. Mandler, *Return from the Natives*, 161.

15. *Effective Use of Social Science Research in the Federal Services* (New York: Russell Sage Foundation, 1950), 29–47, quote from 42.

16. Ibid., 14–20; Robert Lynd, "The Science of Inhuman Relations: Review of *The American Soldier* by Samuel A. Stouffer," *New Republic* (August 29, 1949): 22–23; Leighton, *Human Relations in a Changing World*, 43; Talcott Parsons, "Social Science—A Basic National Resource," in Samuel Z. Klausner and Victor M. Lidz, eds., *The Nationalization of the Social Sciences* (Philadelphia: University of Pennsylvania Press, 1986), 79–101; and Roy F. Nichols, "War and Research in Social Science," *Proceedings of the American Philosophical Society* 87, no. 4 (Jan. 1943): 361–62.

17. John McDiarmid, "The Mobilization of Social Scientists," in Leonard D. White, ed., *Civil Service in Wartime* (Chicago: University of Chicago Press. 1945), 85.

18. Estimated from data in McDiarmid, "The Mobilization of Social Scientists," 73–75. Basically, I assumed that the same percentage as held in 1938 would obtain in 1943. This surely produces a conservative estimate.

19. Terence Ball, "The Politics of Social Science in Postwar America," in Lary May, ed., *Recasting America: Culture and Politics in the Age of Cold War* (Chicago: University of Chicago Press, 1989), 81.

20. Mark C. Smith, *Social Science in the Crucible: The American Debate over Objectivity and Purpose, 1918–194* (Durham, NC: Duke University Press, 1994), 253. Also see Dorwin Cartwright, "Social Psychology in the United States During the Second World War," *Human Relations* 1, no. 3 (June 1948): 334.

21. Smith, *Social Science in the Crucible*, 255.

22. Robert S. Lynd, *Knowledge for What? The Place of Social Science in American Culture* (Princeton, NJ: Princeton University Press, 1939), 1.

23. Mandler, *Return from the Natives*, xi.

24. Michael A. Bernstein, *A Perilous Progress: Economists and Public Purpose in Twentieth Century America* (Princeton, NJ: Princeton University Press, 2001), 82.

25. Katz, *Foreign Intelligence*, 190.

26. Uta Gerhardt, *Talcott Parsons: An Intellectual Biography* (New York: Cambridge University Press, 2002), 75.

27. Julian L. Woodward, "Making Government Opinion Research Bear Upon Operations," *American Sociological Review* 9, no. 6 (December 1944): 670.

28. Lynd, "The Science of Inhuman Relations," 22–23. For a detailed discussion of psychology's contributions, see Charles W. Bray, *Psychology and Military Proficiency: A History of the Applied Psychology Panel of the National Defense Research Committee* (Princeton, NJ: Princeton University Press, 1948).

29. Samuel A. Stouffer, "Social Science and the Soldier," in William Fielding Ogburn, ed., *American Society in Wartime* (Chicago: University of Chicago Press, 1953), 105–17.

30. For discussion of this period in McNamara's life, see Deborah Shapley, *Promise and Power: The Life and Times of Robert McNamara* (Boston: Little, Brown, 1993), chapter 2. On Operations Research see, Bruce Kuklick, *Blind Oracles: Intellectuals and War from Kennan to Kissinger* (Princeton, NJ: Princeton University Press, 2006), 19–22; Bernstein, *A Perilous Progress*, 94; and Bruce L.R. Smith, *The RAND Corporation: Case Study of a Nonprofit Advisory Corporation* (Cambridge, MA: Harvard University Press, 1966), 6–9.

31. Charles Hitch, "Economics and Military Operations Research," *Review of Economics and Statistics* 40, no. 3 (August 1958): 199–200; Gene M. Lyons and Louis Morton, *Schools for Strategy: Education and Research in National Security Affairs* (New York: Frederick A. Praeger, 1965), 236–40; and Stephen P. Waring, "Cold Calculus: The Cold War and Operations Research," *Radical History Review* 63, no. 3 (Fall 1995): 28–51.

32. Smith, *The RAND Corporation*, 35–38. Also see Budiansky, *Blackett's War*, 87.

33. Walt W. Rostow, "The London Operation: Recollections of an Economist," in George C. Chalou, ed., *The Secrets War: The Office of Strategic Services in World War II* (Washington, DC: National Archives and Records Administration, 1992), 49.

34. Snow argues that Churchill's scientific adviser F. A. Lindemann was enamored of strategic bombing theory and given his personal relationship with the prime minister he was able to marginalize other scientists like Henry Tizard, the chair of the British government's Aeronautical Research Committee, who did not endorse it. This is discussed in Snow, *Science and Government*, 53; and Budiansky, *Blackett's War*, 198–200.

35. W. W. Rostow, *Concept and Controversy: Sixty Years of Taking Ideas to Market* (Austin, TX: University of Texas Press, 2009), 33–34.

36. Rostow, "The London Operation," 49. Also see W. W. Rostow, *Pre-Invasion Bombing Strategy: General Eisenhower's Decision of March 25, 1944* (Austin, TX: University of Texas Press, 1981), 22–23.

37. Katz, *Foreign Intelligence*, 112–24. Also see Michael A. Bernstein, "American Economics and the National Security State, 1941–43," *Radical History Review* 63, no. 3 (Fall 1995): 11–12.

38. Rostow, "The London Operation," 50–54; and Rostow, *Pre-Invasion Bombing Strategy*, 43.

39. Rostow, *Pre-Invasion Bombing Strategy*, 79–80.

40. From an EOU report reproduced in Rostow, *Pre-Invasion Bombing Strategy*, 110–12.

41. Gregg Herken, *Counsels of War: The Revealing Story of the Experts and Advisers—Scientist, Academics, Think Tank Strategists—Who Have Influenced and Helped Determine American Nuclear Arms Policy since Hiroshima* (New York: Knopf, 1985), 77; and David Halberstam, *The Best and the Brightest* (New York: Ballentine Books, 1992), 461–62, 495.

42. Their results were published after the war as "Cohesion and Disintegration in the *Wehrmacht* in World War II," *Public Opinion Quarterly* 12, no. 2 (Summer 1948): 280–315.

43. Gerhardt, *Talcott Parsons*, 121.

44. Parsons, "Social Science—A Basic National Resource," 94–97. Also see Ryan, *Samuel Stouffer and the GI Survey*, 85.

45. Compare Arnold M. Rose, "Army Policies Toward Negro Soldiers—A Report on a Success and a Failure" with Roy K. Davenport, "The Negro in the Army—A Subject of Research" both in "Social Research in Political Decision," a special issue of *The Journal of Social Issues* 3 (no. 4 (Fall 1947): 26–39.

46. For discussion, see Charles C. Moskos and John Sibley Butler, *All That We Can Be: Black Leadership and Racial Integration the Army Way* (New York: Basic Books, 1996).

47. Joseph W. Ryan, *Samuel Stouffer and the GI Survey: Sociologists and Soldiers during the Second World War* (Knoxville, TN: University of Tennessee Press, 2013), 5, 28, and 48.

48. Ibid., 11 and 27.

49. Quoted in ibid., 62.

50. Samuel A. Stouffer, "Studying the Attitudes of Soldiers," *Proceedings of the American Philosophical Society* 92, no. 5 (November 1948): 337.

51. Carleton Mabee, "Margaret Mead and Behavioral Scientists in World War II: Problems in Responsibility, Truth, and Effectiveness," *Journal of the History of the Behavioral Sciences* 23, no. 1 (January 1987): 8–9. See Benedict's *The Chrysanthemum and the Sword: Patterns of Japanese Culture* (New York: Houghton Mifflin, 1946).

52. Lyons, *The Uneasy Partnership*, 118–19.

53. On this see Franz Boas, "Correspondence: Scientist as Spies," *The Nation*, December 20, 1919, 797; and G. W. Stocking's discussion of it in "The Scientific Reaction against Cultural Anthropology," in G. W. Stocking, ed., *Race, Culture and Evolution* (Chicago: University of Chicago, 1982), 270–307.

54. David H. Price, "Lessons from Second World War Anthropology: Peripheral, Persuasive, and Ignored Contributions," *Anthropology Today* 18, no. 3 (June 2002): 14–15.

55. Mandler, *Return from the Natives*, 36.

56. David H. Price, "Gregory Bateson and the OSS: World War II and Bateson's Assessment of Applied Anthropology," *Human Organization* 57, no. 4 (Winter 1998): 379. Also see Mandler, *Return from the Natives*, 65.

57. Mandler, *Return from the Natives*, 21.

58. Ibid., 161–62.

59. On OWI and its Japan activities, see Allan M. Winkler, *The Politics of Propaganda: The Office of War Information, 1942–1945* (New Haven, CT: Yale University Press, 1978), 136–48.

60. Mandler, *Return from the Natives*, 78.

61. Leighton, *Human Relations In A Changing World*, 298–301.

62. John Dower, *War Without Mercy: Race and Power in the Pacific War* (New York: Pantheon, 1987).

63. Leighton, *Human Relations in a Changing World*, 46–75.

64. Parsons, "Social Science—A Basic National Resource," 92.

65. Mandler, *Return from the Natives*, 174.

66. Mabee, "Margaret Mead and Behavioral Scientists in World War II," 3–4.

67. Mandler, *Return from the Natives*, 87–121.

68. Margaret Mead, "Anthropological Contributions to National Policies During and Immediately After World War II," in Walter Goldschmidt, ed., *The Uses of Anthropology* (Washington, DC: The American Anthropological Association, 1970), 149.

69. Price, "Gregory Bateson and the OSS," 380.

70. Mead, "Anthropological Contributions to National Policies During and Immediately After World War II," 150–51.

71. Mandler, *Return from the Natives*, 173.

72. Albert Somit and Joseph Tanenhaus, *The Development of Political Science: From Burgess to Behavioralism* (Boston: Allyn and Bacon, 1967), 138.

73. Bernard Crick, *The American Science of Politics: Its Origins and Conditions* (Berkeley: University of California Press, 1960), 147; also see 152–54.

74. John H. Herz, "An Internationalist's Journey through the Century," in Joseph Kruzel and James N. Rosenau, eds., *Journeys through World Politics: Autobiographical Reflections of Thirty-four Academic Travelers* (Lexington, MA: Lexington Books, 1989), 251–52.

75. Carl J. Friedrich, "Instruction and Research: Political Science in the United States in Wartime," *American Political Science Review* 41, no. 5 (October 1947): 988–89. Also see John W. Gardner, "Are We Doing Our Homework in Foreign Affairs?" *Yale Review* 37, no. 3 (Spring 1948): 406.

76. Gerhardt, *Talcott Parsons*, 147.

77. Friedrich, "Instruction and Research," 985.

78. David C. Engerman, "Social Science in the Cold War," *Isis* 101, no. 2 (June 2010): 396.

79. The Committee on War-time Services of the American Political Science Association, "The Political Scientist and National Service in War-time," *The American Political Science Review* 35, no. 5 (October 1942): 932.

80. The Committee on War-time Services of the American Political Science Association, "The Political Scientist and National Service in War-time," 941. Also see 932 and 933–35.

81. Mabee, "Margaret Mead and Behavioral Scientists in World War II," 9, 11.

82. Leighton, *Human Relations In A Changing World*, 120–21.

83. Detail in Joseph C. Grew, *Turbulent Era: A Diplomatic Record of Forty Years, 1904–1945* (Boston, MA: Houghton Mifflin, 1952), 1377–86.

84. See his Memorandum to Brigadier General William J. Donovan, June 26, 1944, Office of Strategic Services, in Grew, *Turbulent Era*, 1400.

85. The Advisor on Liberated Areas for the Far East (Moffat) to the Director of Civil Affairs Division, War, War Department (Hilldring), Washington, December 14, 1943, *Foreign Relations of the United States [FRUS] 1944*, vol. 5, *The Near East, South Asia, and Africa, The Far East* (Washington, DC: Government Printing Office, 1965), 1187–88.

86. Memorandum Prepared in the War and Navy Departments, Washington, 18 February 1944 in FRUS, 1192.

87. Memorandum by the Director of the Office for Far Eastern Affairs (Ballantine) to the Under Secretary of State (Grew) [Washington] August 6, 1945 in https://history.state.gov/historicaldocuments/frus1945v06/dd370. Also see Grew, *Turbulent Era*, 1411. This U.S. public opinion data almost certainly came from OWI.

88. Grew, *Turbulent Era*, 1424–27, fn. 12 and 1437.

89. Ibid., 1406.

90. Memorandum Prepared by the Inter-Divisional Area Committee on the Far East, [Washington], March 21, 1944, and Memorandum Prepared by the Inter-Divisional Area Committee on the Far East, [Washington], May 9, 1944 both in *FRUS*, 1210 and 55.

91. Memorandum by the Under Secretary of State (Grew) to the Secretary of State, [Washington], January 3, 1944 [1945] in https://history.state.gov/historicaldocuments/frus1945v06/d370.

92. Memorandum of Conversation, by the Acting Secretary of State, [Washington] May 28, 1945, in https://history.state.gov/historicaldocuments/frus1945v06/d379.

93. Grew, *Turbulent Era*, 1428.

94. Memorandum of Conversation, by the Acting Secretary of State, [Washington] May 29, 1945, in https://history.state.gov/historicaldocuments/frus1945v06/d380.

95. Memorandum of Telephone Conversation, by the Acting Secretary [Washington] August 4, 1945, in https://history.state.gov/historicaldocuments/frus1945v06/d390.

96. John F. Kreis et al., *Piercing the Fog: Intelligence in Army Air Forces Operations in World War II* (Washington, DC: Air Force History and Museums Program, 1996), 367; and Sherman Kent, "The First Year of the Office of National Estimates," [no date] in https://www.cia.gov/library/center-for-the-study-of-intelligence/csi-publications/books-and-monographs/sherman-kent-and-the-board-of-national-estimates-collected-essays/7year.html.

97. Katz, *Foreign Intelligence*, chart 3.

98. Grew, *Turbulent Era*, 1414, 1421, and 1422–23, fn. 9.

99. Price, "Lessons from Second World War Anthropology," 19.

100. Leighton, *Human Relations In A Changing World*, 11 and 45. Also see 117–18 and 126.

101. Quoted in Mandler, *Return from the Natives*, 13.

102. Mabee, "Margaret Mead and Behavioral Scientists in World War II," 3.

103. William L. Langer, *In and Out of the Ivory Tower: The Autobiography of William L. Langer* (New York: Neale Watson Academic Publications, 1977), 181. Also see Katz, *Foreign Intelligence*, 3.

104. William L. Langer, "Scholarship and the Intelligence Problem," *Proceedings of the American Philosophical Society* 92, no. 1 (March 8, 1948), 43–44. Also see Roger Hilsman Jr., "Intelligence and Policy-Making in Foreign Affairs," *World Politics* 5, no. 1 (October 1952): 1 and 35; Robert Jervis, "Intelligence and Policy," *International Security* 11, no. 3 (Winter 1986–1987): 143; and Klaus Knorr, "Failures in National Intelligence Estimates: The Case of the Cuban Missiles," *World Politics* 16, no. 3 (April 1964): 455, on the similarities between academic research and intelligence analysis.

105. Katz, *Foreign Intelligence*, 84.

106. Rostow, *Concept and Controversy*, 29.

107. Langer, "Scholarship and the Intelligence Problem," 45. Robin W. Winks, *Cloak and Gown: Scholars in the Secret War, 1939–1961*, 2nd ed. (New Haven, CT: Yale University Press, 1996), 112, is more circumspect on the question of R&A's contribution to policy.

108. Rostow, "The London Operation," 56.

109. Winks, *Cloak and Gown*, 29.

110. See the list in ibid., 495–97.

111. Langer, *In and Out of the Ivory Tower*, 191.

112. Raffaele Laudani, "Introduction" in Laudani, ed., *Secret Reports on Nazi Germany: The Frankfurt School Contribution to the War Effort* (Princeton, NJ: Princeton University Press, 2013), 2. Also see Katz, *Foreign Intelligence*, 28. Also see 93–94.

113. Katz, *Foreign Intelligence*, 29. Also see 168.

114. Laudani, "Introduction," 1.

115. Ibid., 12–21.

116. Winks, *Cloak and Gown*, 23.

117. Ibid., 62–63 and 475; Langer, "Scholarship and the Intelligence Problem," 43; Robert D. Steele, "Open Source Intelligence," Loch K. Johnson and James Wirtz, eds., *Intelligence and National Security: The Secret World of Spies, An Anthology*, 2nd ed. (New York: Oxford University Press, 2008), 138.

118. Langer, *In and Out of the Ivory Tower*, 186–87. Also see Katz, *Foreign Intelligence*, 1, 17; and Bernard Brodie, "Scientific Progress and Political Science," *Scientific Monthly* 85, no. 6 (December 1957): 318.

119. Katz, *Foreign Intelligence*, 15; also see 18 and 20.

120. Ibid., 29–96 and 101.

121. Ibid., 102–3.

122. Ibid., 131; also see 125.

123. Ibid., 129.

124. David C. Engerman, *Know Your Enemy: The Rise and Fall of America's Soviet Experts* (New York: Oxford University Press, 2009), 100–101.

125. Katz, *Foreign Intelligence*, 17.

126. "Testimony of Pendelton Herring, President, Social Science Research Council, New York, NY," "Federal Support of International Social Science and Behavioral Research," Subcommittee on Government Research, Committee on Government Operations, U.S. Senate, 89th Cong., 2nd sess., June 27, 28; July 19, 20, 1966, 199.

127. Langer, *In and Out of the Ivory Tower*, 230–31.

128. Richard Lambert, "Blurring the Disciplinary Boundaries: Area Studies in the United States," *American Behavioral Scientist* 33, no. 6 (July 1990): 714.

129. William Nelson Fenton, *Area Studies In American Universities* (Washington, DC: American Council on Education, 1947), v–vi.

130. Katz, *Foreign Intelligence*, 22; and Williams, "Some Observations on Sociological Research in Government During World War II," 573–74.

131. Engerman, *Know Your Enemy*, 26.

132. Lyons, *The Uneasy Partnership*, 123.

133. Katz, *Foreign Intelligence*, 16.

134. Ibid., 198. Also see Andrew Abbott, *The Chaos of Disciplines* (Chicago: University of Chicago Press, 2001), 132.

135. Nichols, "War and Research in Social Science," 362.

136. Julian L. Woodward, "Making Government Opinion Research Bear Upon Operations," *American Sociological Review* 9, no. 6 (December 1944): 670.

137. Williams, "Some Observations on Sociological Research in Government During World War II," 576.

138. Stouffer, "Studying the Attitudes of Soldiers," 339–40.

139. Leighton, *Human Relations In A Changing World*, 142–43.

140. Ibid., 101–2 and 132–34.

141. Ibid., 146. Emphasis added.

142. Katz, *Foreign Intelligence*, xi and xiii.

143. Lyons, *The Uneasy Partnership*, 81–96. Also see Engerman, *Know Your Enemy*, 2–3; Lyons and Morton, *Schools for Strategy*, 231.

144. Leighton, *Human Relations In A Changing World*, 307n.

145. For a critical appraisal which nonetheless acknowledges Shils and Janowitz major influence, see Omer Bartov, "Daily Life and Motivation in War: The *Wehrmacht* in the Soviet Union," *Journal of Strategic Studies* 12, no. (1989): 200–14. For evidence of the long shadow Shils and Janowitz still cast, see Ron Robin, *The Making of the Cold War Enemy: Culture and Politics in the Military Industrial Complex* (Princeton, NJ: Princeton University Press, 2001), 99.

146. Quoted in Michael Klare, compiler, *The University-Military-Police Complex: A Directory and Related Documents* (New York: North American Congress on Latin America, 1970), 45. Also see Lyons, *The Uneasy Partnership*, 100–4; and Lynd, "The Science of Inhuman Relations," 22–23.

147. Gerhardt, *Talcott Parsons*, 103n197.

148. "They Also Served: How Statisticians Changed the War, and the War Changed Statistics," *The Economist*, December 20, 2014, 97–99.

Chapter 4. Social Science's Cold War

1. Dorothy Ross, "Changing Contours of the Social Science Disciplines," in Theodore M. Porter, ed., *Cambridge History of Science*, vol. 7, *The Modern Social Sciences* (New York: Cambridge University Press, 2003), 229.

2. David C. Engerman, "Social Science in the Cold War," *Isis* 101, no. 2 (June 2010): 395. For a parallel discussion of the natural sciences' similar hopes for the peacetime applicability of the wartime experience, see Stephen Budiansky, *Blackett's War: The Men Who Defeated the Nazi U-Boats and Brought Science to the Art of Warfare* (New York: Knopf, 2013), 254.

3. Robin M. Williams Jr., "Some Observations on Sociological Research in Government during World War II," *American Sociological Review* 11, no. 5 (October 1946): 573–74.

4. Talcott Parsons, "Social Science—A Basic National Resource," in Samuel Z. Klausner and Victor M. Lidz, eds., *The Nationalization of the Social Sciences* (Philadelphia: University of Pennsylvania Press, 1986), 47.

5. John Lewis Gaddis, *Strategies of Containment: A Critical Appraisal of Postwar American National Security Policy* (Oxford: Oxford University Press, 1982), 6, 22–23, and 90. For evidence that this was the view within the academic community, see Roger L. Geiger, *Research and Relevant Knowledge: American Research Universities since World War II* (New York: Oxford University Press, 1993), 33.

6. Geiger, *Research and Relevant Knowledge*, 161 and 173.

7. Charles W. Bray, "Toward a Technology of Human Behavior for Defense Use," *American Psychologist* 17, no. 8 (August 1962): 540.

8. Jacob Viner, "The Implications of the Atomic Bomb for International Relations," in *International Economics* (Glencoe, IL: The Free Press, 1946), 300–309.

9. Exchange following "Testimony of Dr. Gabriel Almond, President of the American Political Science Association, Stanford University," "Federal Support of International Social Science

and Behavioral Research," Subcommittee on Government Research, Committee on Government Operations, U.S. Senate, 89th Cong., 2nd sess., June 27, 28; July 19, 20, 1966, 114.

10. Albert Somit and Joseph Tanenhaus, *The Development of Political Science: From Burgess to Behavioralism* (Boston, MA: Allyn and Bacon, 1967), 122.

11. David C. Engerman, *Know Your Enemy: The Rise and Fall of America's Soviet Experts* (New York: Oxford University Press, 2009), 127.

12. Mark Solovey, *Shaky Foundations: The Politics-Patronage-Social Science Nexus in Cold War America* (New Brunswick, NJ: Rutgers University Press, 2013), 87 and 100. This is also a major theme in Ido Oren, *Our Enemies and Us: America's Rivalries and the Making of Political Science* (Ithaca: Cornell University Press, 2003).

13. Harvey M. Sapolsky, *Science and the Navy: The History of the Office of Naval Research* (Princeton, NJ: Princeton University Press, 1990), 4. Also see Richard V. Damms, "James Killian, the Technological Capabilities Panel, and the Emergence of President Eisenhower's 'Scientific-Technological Elite,'" *Diplomatic History* 24, no. 1 (Winter 2000): 58.

14. Donald E. Stokes, *Pasteur's Quadrant: Basic Science and Technological Innovation* (Washington, DC: Brookings, 1997), 45–46.

15. Daniel J. Kevles, "The National Science Foundation and the Debate Over Postwar Research Policy, 1942–1945: A Political Interpretation of *Science—The Endless Frontier*," *Isis* 68, no. 1 (March 1977): 11–12; and Geiger, *Research and Relevant Knowledge*, 15.

16. Vannevar Bush, "Science—The Endless Frontier," *Transactions: Kansas Academy of Science* 48, no. 3 (December 1945): 231–64.

17. Stokes, *Pasteur's Quadrant*, 3, 4–5, and 49. Also see Damms, "James Killian, the Technological Capabilities Panel, and the Emergence of President Eisenhower's 'Scientific-Technological Elite,'" 66; Daniel Lee Kleinman and Mark Solovey, "Hot Science/Cold War: The National Science Foundation After World War II," *Radical History Review* 63, no. 3 (Fall 1995): 113.

18. For a helpful history of the convoluted process of establishing the NSF, see Talcott Parson, "National Science Legislation: Part 1: An Historical Review," *Bulletin of Atomic Scientists* 2, nos. 7–8 (November 6, 1946): 7–9.

19. Geiger, *Research and Relevant Knowledge*, 15; and Kevles, "The National Science Foundation and the Debate Over Postwar Research Policy," 26. On early congressional interest in government support for scientific research, see Robert Franklin Maddox, "The Politics of World War II: Science, Senator Harley M. Kilgore, and the Legislative Origins of the National Science Foundation," *West Virginia History* 41, no. 1 (Fall 1979): 20–39.

20. Stokes, *Pasteur's Quadrant*, 95. Also see Damms, "James Killian, the Technological Capabilities Panel, and the Emergence of President Eisenhower's 'Scientific-Technological Elite,'" 65.

21. Kevles, "The National Science Foundation and the Debate Over Postwar Research Policy," 18.

22. Geiger, *Research and Relevant Knowledge*, 179.

23. Mark Solovey, "Riding the Natural Scientists' Coattails on to the Endless Frontier: The SSRC and the Quest for Scientific Legitimacy," *Journal of the History of the Behavioral Sciences* 40, no. 4 (Fall 2004): 395. Also see Kleinman and Solovey, "Hot Science/Cold War," 110–11.

24. Kevles, "The National Science Foundation and the Debate Over Postwar Research Policy," 19.

25. Thomas F. Gieryn, "Boundary Work and the Demarcation of Science from Non-Science: Strains and Interests in Professional Ideologies of Scientists," *American Sociological Review* 48, no. 6 (December 1983): 791.

26. James G. Hershberg, *James B. Conant: Harvard to Hiroshima and the Making of the Nuclear Age* (Palo Alto: Stanford University Press, 1993), 558–59.

27. *Effective Use of Social Science Research in the Federal Services* (New York: Russell Sage Foundation, 1950), 13.

28. Kevles, "The National Science Foundation and the Debate Over Postwar Research Policy," 26; Solovey, "Riding the Natural Scientists' Coattails Onto the Endless Frontier," 402.

29. Sapolsky, *Science and the Navy*, 37.

30. Hershberg, *James B. Conant*, 396.

31. Gene M. Lyons, *The Uneasy Partnership: Social Science and the Federal Government in the Twentieth Century* (New York: Russell Sage Foundation, 1969), 131–32.

32. Kevles, "The National Science Foundation and the Debate Over Postwar Research Policy," 24; Solovey, "Riding the Natural Scientists' Coattails Onto the Endless Frontier," 396–97.

33. Mark Solovey, *Shaky Foundations: The Politics-Patronage-Social Science Nexus in Cold War America* (New Brunswick, NJ: Rutgers University Press, 2013), 24–25.

34. Solovey, "Riding the Natural Scientists' Coattails Onto the Endless Frontier," 404. Also see Kleinman and Mark Solovey, "Hot Science/Cold War," 118.

35. Howard P. Segal, "Progress and Its Discontents: Postwar Science and Technology Policy," in Hamilton Cravens, ed., *The Social Sciences Go to Washington: The Politics of Knowledge in the Postmodern Age* (New Brunswick, NJ: Rutgers University Press, 2004), 110–11.

36. Lyons, *The Uneasy Partnership*, 199–200.

37. Quoted in Solovey, "Riding the Natural Scientists' Coattails Onto the Endless Frontier," 409.

38. Lyons, *The Uneasy Partnership*, 126.

39. Ibid., 134.

40. Harry Alpert, "Congressmen, Social Scientists, and Attitudes Toward Federal Support of Social Science Research," *American Sociological Review* 23, no.6 (December 1958): 685.

41. Lyons, *The Uneasy Partnership*, 272. Also see Solovey, *Shaky Foundation*, 148–63.

42. Lyons, *The Uneasy Partnership*, 137 and 271. Also see Kleinman and Mark Solovey, "Hot Science/Cold War," 124; and Solovey, *Shaky Foundations*, 163–69.

43. Solovey, *Shaky Foundation*, 146–47.

44. "Henry W. Riecken, "National Resources in the Social Sciences," in William A. Lybrand, ed., *Symposium Proceedings: The U.S. Army's Limited-War Mission and Social Science Research* (Washington, DC: SORO, March 26–28, 1962), 304.

45. Solovey, "Riding the Natural Scientists' Coattails Onto the Endless Frontier," 404–6; also see 399.

46. Segal, "Progress and Its Discontents: Post-war Science and Technology Policy," 111.

47. Fred R. Harris, "Political Science and the Proposal for a National Social Science Foundation," *American Political Science Review* 61, no. 4 (December 1967): 1093–94, and his question following "Testimony of Donald R. Young, Chairman, The Advisory Committee on Government Programs in the Behavioral Sciences of the National Academy of Sciences—National Research Council," "Federal Support of International Social Science and Behavioral Research," Subcommittee on Government Research, Committee on Government Operations, U.S. Senate, 89th Cong., 2nd sess., June 27, 28; July 19, 20, 1966, 134. Also see Thomas Gieryn, *The Cultural Boundaries of Science* (Chicago: The University of Chicago Press, 1999), 65–114; and Dennis W. Brezina, "The Congressional Debate on the Social Sciences in 1968," [PB 192 556] (Washington, DC: George Washington University, December 1968), 19.

48. Joy Elizabeth Rohde, "'The Social Scientists' War': Expertise in a Cold War Nation," (Unpublished doctoral dissertation, University of Pennsylvania, 2007), 224.

49. Solovey, "Riding the Natural Scientists' Coattails Onto the Endless Frontier," 410–11, quoting a study that University of Chicago Sociologist Louis Wirth conducted for the SSRC.

50. Solovey, *Shaky Foundations*, 175.

51. Hershberg, *James B. Conant*, 556–57.

52. David C. Engerman, "Rethinking the Cold War Universities: Some Recent Histories," *Journal of Cold War Studies* 5, no. 3 (Summer 2003): 91.

53. Solovey, "Riding the Natural Scientists' Coattails Onto the Endless Frontier," 413.

54. *Effective Use of Social Science Research in the Federal Services*, 10. Also see the 1962 President's Science Advisory Committee report *Strengthening the Behavioral Sciences* in Lyons, *The Uneasy Partnership*, appendix 3, 350–51; Ron Robin, *The Making of the Cold War Enemy: Culture and Politics in the Military Industrial Complex* (Princeton, NJ: Princeton University Press, 2001), 26.

55. Solovey, "Riding the Natural Scientists' Coattails Onto the Endless Frontier," 416.

56. Ibid., 395–96; and Solovey, *Shaky Foundations*, 189.

57. Uta Gerhardt, *Talcott Parsons: An Intellectual Biography* (New York: Cambridge University Press, 2002), 150–51.

58. Ibid., 155.

59. Parsons, "Social Science—A Basic National Resource," 42–3, 45, 46 and 78.

60. Ibid., 47, 51, 53, 104, and 105.

61. Ibid., 104.

62. Quoted in Ellen Herman, "The Career of Cold War Psychology," *Radical History Review* 63, no. 3 (1995): 57.

63. Parsons, "Social Science—A Basic National Resource," 109.

64. Gerhardt, *Talcott Parsons*, 163–64.

65. In addition to Behaviorism, other major early Cold War paradigms included modernization theory, systems theory, and rational choice. On this, see Joel Isaac, "Tangled Loops: Theory, History, and the Human Sciences in Modern America," *Modern Intellectual History* 6, no. 2 (2009): 410.

66. Somit and Tanenhaus, *The Development of Political Science*, 27n16.

67. Engerman, "Rethinking the Cold War Universities," 89.

68. "Testimony of Dr. Carl Pfaffmann, Vice President of the Rockefeller University and Former Chairman of the Division of Behavioral Sciences of the National Academy of Science," "Federal Support of International Social Science and Behavioral Research," Subcommittee on Government Research, Committee on Government Operations, U.S. Senate, 89th Cong., 2nd sess., June 27, 28; July 19, 20, 1966, 120. Also see Robert Adcock, "Interpreting Behavioralism," in Adcock, Robert, Mark Bevir, and Shannon Stimson, eds., *Modern Political Science: Anglo-American Exchanges Since 1880* (Princeton, NJ: Princeton University Press, 2007), 191.

69. Lyons, *The Uneasy Partnership*, 285–86.

70. Gabriel Almond, "The New Intelligence Requirements," *Background* 9, no. 3 (November 1965): 173.

71. Ross, *The Origins of American Social Science*, xiv.

72. Nils Gilman, *Mandarins of the Future: Modernization Theory in Cold War America* (Baltimore, MD: Johns Hopkins University Press, 2003), 115.

73. Mark Solovey, "Project Camelot and the 1960s Epistemological Revolution: Rethinking the Politics-Patronage-Social Science Nexus," *Social Studies of Science* 31, no. 2 (April 2001): 178. Also see Solovey, *Shaky Foundations*, 133; Robert N. Proctor, *Value-free Science? Purity and Power in Modern Knowledge* (Cambridge, MA: Harvard University Press, 1991), 175, 226.

74. Mark C. Smith, *Social Science in the Crucible: The American Debate over Objectivity and Purpose, 1918–1941* (Durham, NC: Duke University Press, 1994), 69. Adcock, "Interpreting Behavioralism," 202.

75. Robin, *The Making of the Cold War Enemy*, 69.

76. "Strengthening the Behavioral Sciences," *Science* 136, no. 3512 (20 April 1962): 234.

77. Dorothy Ross, *The Origins of American Social Science* (New York: Cambridge University Press, 1991), 157. Also see Ross, "Changing Contours of the Social Science Disciplines," 206.

78. Emily Hauptman, "The Ford Foundation and the Rise of Behavioralism in Political Science," *Journal of the History of the Behavioral Sciences* 48, no. 2 (Spring 2012): 154. Also see Somit and Tanenhaus, *The Development of Political Science*, 178–79.

79. Lyons, *The Uneasy Partnership*, 279.

80. Bernard Crick, *The American Science of Politics: Its Origins and Conditions* (Berkeley: University of California Press, 1960), xiv. Also see Somit and Tanenhaus, *The Development of Political Science*, 113 and 133; Barry D. Karl, *Charles E. Merriam and the Study of Politics* (Chicago: University of Chicago Press, 1974), viii; and Ross, *The Origins of American Social Science*, 17.

81. John G. Gunnell, "The Reconstitution of Political Theory: David Easton, Behaviorism, and the Long Road to System," *Journal of the History of the Behavioral Sciences* 49, no. 2 (Spring 2013): 190. Also see Hauptman, "The Ford Foundation and the Rise of Behavioralism in Political Science," 156.

82. Philip H. Melanson, "The Political Science Profession: Political Knowledge and Public Policy," *Politics and Society* 2, no. 4 (Summer 1972): 492.

83. Lyons, *The Uneasy Partnership*, 279; Gunnell, "The Reconstitution of Political Theory," 191; and Hauptman, "The Ford Foundation and the Rise of Behavioralism in Political Science," 160, 165.

84. Solovey, "Project Camelot and the 1960s Epistemological Revolution," 173–77.

85. Hunter Crowther-Heyck, "Patrons of the Revolution: Ideals and Institutions in Postwar Behavioral Science," *Isis* 97, no. 3 (September 2006): 430; and Peter Mandler, *Return from the Natives: How Margaret Mead Won the Second World War and Lost the Cold War* (New Haven, CT: Yale University Press, 2013), 192–93.

86. Crowther-Heyck, "Patrons of the Revolution," 421–22.

87. Somit and Tanenhaus, *The Development of Political Science*, 185.

88. Crowther-Heyck, "Patrons of the Revolution," 434.

89. Samuel J. Eldersveld, Alexander Heard, Samuel P. Huntington, Morris Janowitz, Avery Leiserson, Dayton McKean, and David B. Truman, "Research in Political Behavior," *American Political Science Review* 46, no. 4 (December 1952): 1003–45.

90. Hans J. Morgenthau, *Scientific Man versus Power Politics* (Chicago: Phoenix Books, 1946), 165.

91. David M. Ricci, *The Tragedy of Political Science: Politics, Scholarship, and Democracy* (New Haven, CT: Yale University Press, 1984), 67.

92. James Farr, Jacob S. Hacker, and Nicole Kazee, "The Policy Scientist of Democracy: The Discipline of Harold D. Lasswell," *American Political Science Review* 100, no. 4 (November 2006): 582.

93. Terence Ball, "The Politics of Social Science in Postwar America," in Lary May, ed., *Recasting America: Culture and Politics in the Age of Cold War* (Chicago: University of Chicago Press, 1989), 76–77.

94. Solovey, *Shaky Foundations*, 105.

95. Somit and Tanenhaus, *The Development of Political Science*, 139; and Crick, *The American Science of Politics*, 191.

96. Ira Katznelson, "The Subtle Politics of Developing Emergency: Political Science as Liberal Guardianship," in David Montgomery, ed., *The Cold War and The University: Toward an Intellectual History of the Postwar Years* (New York: New Press, 1997), 238.

97. Farr, Hacker, and Kazee, "The Policy Scientist of Democracy," 580. Lasswell's University of Chicago Ph.D. dissertation was eventually published as *Propaganda Technique in the World War* (1938; reprint Mansfield Centre, CT: Martino, 2013).

98. David Easton, "Harold Lasswell: Policy Scientist for a Democratic Society," *Journal of Politics* 12, no. 3 (August 1950): 459.

99. Ross, "Changing Contours of the Social Science Disciplines," 209.

100. Harold Lasswell, "The Policy Orientation," in Daniel Lerner and Harold Dwight Lasswell, eds., *The Policy Sciences: Recent Developments in Scope and Method* (Palo Alto, CA: Stanford University Press, 1951), 7.

101. Gunnell, "The Reconstitution of Political Theory," 207. Also see Kenneth N. Waltz, *Man, the State, and War: A Theoretical Analysis* (New York: Columbia University Press, 1954), 44.

102. George A. Lundberg, "The Senate Ponders Social Science," *Scientific Monthly* 64, no. 5 (May 1947): 409–10.

103. Gunnell, "The Reconstitution of Political Theory," 201.

104. James Farr, "Political Science," in Theodore M. Porter and Dorothy Ross, eds., *Cambridge History of Science*, vol. 7, *The Modern Social Sciences* (New York: Cambridge University Press, 2003), 318.

105. Farr, Hacker, and Kazee, "The Policy Scientist of Democracy," 582–85. Also see Paul Kecskemeti, "Review: The 'Policy Sciences:' Aspiration and Outlook," *World Politics* 4, no. 4 (July 1952): 535.

106. Geiger, *Research and Relevant Knowledge*, 99–105 and Crowther-Heyck, "Patrons of the Revolution," 435.

107. Easton, "Harold Lasswell," 468, 475.

108. Quoted in Solovey, *Shaky Foundations*, 104.

109. Emily Hauptman, "From Opposition to Accommodation: How Rockefeller Foundation Grants Redefined Relations Between Political Theory and Social Science in the 1950s," *American Political Science Review* 100, no. 4 (November 2006): 644.

110. Tim B. Mueller, "The Rockefeller Foundation, the Social Science, and the Humanities in the Cold War," *Journal of Cold War Studies* 15, no. 3 (Summer 2013): 114, 134.

111. Geiger, *Research and Relevant Knowledge*, 105.

112. Adcock, "Interpreting Behavioralism," 208.

113. Irving Louis Horowitz, "Social Science and Public Policy: Implications of Modern Research," in Irving Louis Horowitz, ed., *The Rise and Fall of Project Camelot: Studies in the Relationship Between Social Science and Practical Politics* (Cambridge, MA: MIT Press, 1967), 356.

114. Solovey, *Shaky Foundations*, 119.

115. Kimber Charles Pearce, *Rostow, Kennedy, and the Rhetoric of Foreign Aid* (East Lansing: Michigan State University Press, 2001), 120.

116. Mandler, *Return from the* Natives, 216. Also see 177–81, 213–16, and 282–86.

117. Charles E. Lindblom, "Political Science in the 1940s and 1950s," *Daedalus* 126, no. 1 (Winter 1997): 231. Emphasis in the original.

118. Somit and Tanenhaus, *The Development of Political Science*, 45. Also see "Testimony of Irving L. Horowitz, Department of Sociology, Washington University, St. Louis, MO.; In Association With Herbert Blumer, University of California," "Federal Support of International Social Science and Behavioral Research," Subcommittee on Government Research, Committee on Government Operations, U.S. Senate, 89th Cong., 2nd sess., June 27, 28; July 19, 20, 1966, 248–49.

119. Proctor, *Value-free Science?* 231.

120. Ricci, *The Tragedy of Political Science*, 139.

121. Barrington Moore Jr., "The New Scholasticism and the Study of Politics," *World Politics* 6, no. 1 (October 1953): 137.

122. Lasswell, "The Policy Orientation," 5.

123. Gabriel A. Almond, "Political Theory and Political Science," *American Political Science Review* 60, no. 4 (December 1966): 879.

124. Crick, *The American Science of Politics*, 237.

125. Wesley W. Posvar, "The Impact of Strategy Expertise on the National Security Policy of the United States," *Public Policy* 13 (1964): 46.

126. Nicolas Guilhot, "The Realist Gambit: Postwar American Political Science and the Birth of IR Theory," *International Political Sociology* 2, no. 4 (December 2008): 300.

127. Parsons, "Social Science—A Basic National Resource," 56.

128. Almond, "Political Theory and Political Science," 870.

129. Ricci, *The Tragedy of Political Science*, 171.

130. Somit and Tanenhaus, *The Development of Political Science*, 175. Also see Eldersveld, Heard, Huntington, Janowitz, Leiserson, McKean, and Truman, "Research in Political Behavior," 1003–4; and "Testimony of Dr. Carl Pfaffmann, Vice President of the Rockefeller University and Former Chairman of the Division of Behavioral Sciences of the National Academy of Science," "Federal Support of International Social Science and Behavioral Research," Subcommittee on Government Research, Committee on Government Operations, U.S. Senate, 89th Cong., 2nd sess., June 27, 28; July 19, 20, 1966, 120.

131. Adcock, "Interpreting Behavioralism," 183.

132. Oren, *Our Enemies and Us*, 88.

133. Gunnell, "The Reconstitution of Political Theory," 191.

134. Adcock, "Interpreting Behavioralism," 189.

135. Somit and Tanenhaus, *The Development of Political Science*, 172, 192. Also see Gilman, *Mandarins of the Future*, 115; Karl W. Deutsch, "A Path Among the Social Sciences," in Joseph Kruzel and James N. Rosenau, eds., *Journeys through World Politics: Autobiographical Reflections of Thirty-four Academic Travelers* (Lexington, MA: D.C. Heath, 1988), 18.

136. Peter J. Seybold, "The Ford Foundation and the Triumph of Behaviorism in American Political Science," in Robert F. Arnove, ed., *Philanthropy and Cultural Imperialism* (Boston, MA: G. K. Hall, 1980), 285. Also see Solovey, *Shaky Foundations*, 129.

137. Gunnell, "The Reconstitution of Political Theory," 198. Also see Leo Strauss, "Epilogue," in Herbert J. Storing, ed., *Essays on the Scientific Study of Politics* (New York: Holt, Rinehart and Winston, 1962), 305–27; and Morgenthau, *Scientific Man Versus Power Politics*.

138. Eldersveld, Heard, Huntington, Janowitz, Leiserson, McKean, and Truman, "Research in Political Behavior," 1006.

139. Karl, *Charles E. Merriam and the Study of Politics*, x.

140. Ibid., 108–15; and Ross, *The Origins of American Social Science*, 449.

141. Gunnell, "The Reconstitution of Political Theory," 208–9.

142. Guilhot, "The Realist Gambit," 297.

143. Crowther-Heyck, "Patrons of the Revolution," 438.

144. Karl W. Deutsch, "Quincy Wright's Contribution to the Study of War: A Preface to the Second Edition," *Journal of Conflict Resolution* 14, no. 4 (December 1970): 473–78.

145. Seybold, "The Ford Foundation and the Triumph of Behaviorism in American Political Science," 273.

146. Ibid., 269–303.

147. Dinna A. Zinnes, "The Study of Conflict Processes: An Intellectual Autobiography," in Joseph Kruzel and James N. Rosenau, eds., *Journeys through World Politics*, 84.

148. J. David Singer, "The Making of a Peace Researcher," in Joseph Kruzel and James N. Rosenau, eds., *Journeys Through World Politics*, 225.

149. Ibid., 227–28. Also see Harold Guetzkow, "Conversion Barriers in Using the Social Sciences," *Administrative Science Quarterly* 4, no. 1 (June 1959): 69.

150. Bruce Russett, "Confession From the Normative Closet," in Joseph Kruzel and James N. Rosenau, eds., *Journeys Through World Politics*, 334.

151. Guilhot, "The Realist Gambit," 281–304.

152. Joseph Kruzel, "Reflections on the Journeys," in Joseph Kruzel and James N. Rosenau, eds., *Journeys Through World Politics*, 501–13.

153. Morton A. Kaplan, "A Poor Boy's Journey," in Kruzel and Rosenau, eds., *Journeys Through World Politics*, 47.

154. Morgenthau, *Scientific Man Versus Power Politics*, 1.

155. For the classic critique of atheoretical, "purist induction" in the Behavioralist approach to international relations, see Oran Young, "Professor Russett: Industrious Tailor to a Naked Emperor," *World Politics* 21, no. 3 (April 1969): 493.

156. Albert O. Hirschman, "The Search for Paradigms as a Hindrance to Understanding," *World Politics* 22, no. 3 (April 1970): 329. Emphasis in original.

157. Guilhot, "The Realist Gambit," 281–82, 284, 289–92, 285–86, and 300–301.

158. Engerman, *Know Your Enemy*, 236. Also see 248–49.

159. See *Annual Report of the Social Science Research Council* (New York: SSRC, various years) for 1944–1945 and 1945–1946, 33 and 41. The topics and dates come from the SSRC annual reports for the years 1944 through 1964.

160. *Annual Report of the Social Science Research Council* (New York: SSRC, 1954), 39. The article was Carl Kaysen, "The Vulnerability of the United States to Enemy Attack," *World Politics* 6, no. 2 (January 1954): 190–208.

161. *Annual Report of the Social Science Research Council* (New York: SSRC, 1964), 17, 36, 37, 40, 44, 49; and *Annual Report of the Social Science Research Council* (New York: SSRC, 1963), 46.

162. Solovey, "Project Camelot and the 1960s Epistemological Revolution," 179.

163. Aaron I. Friedberg, "Science, Cold War, and the American State," *Diplomatic History* 20, no. 1 (Winter 1996): 111. Also see Posvar, "The Impact of Strategy Expertise on the National Security Policy of the United States," 37.

164. For discussion of this see Gene M. Lyons and Louis Morton, *Schools for Strategy: Education and Research in National Security Affairs* (New York: Frederick A. Praeger, 1965), 58.

165. Robin, *The Making of the Cold War Enemy*, 7; also see 5.

166. Kecskemeti, "Review: The 'Policy Sciences,'" 527.

167. Advisory Committee on the Management of Behavioral Science Research in the Department of Defense, Division of Behavioral Sciences, National Research Council, *Behavioral and Social Science Research in the Department of Defense: A Framework for Management* (Washington, DC: National Academy of Sciences, 1971), xii. Emphasis added.

168. "Testimony of Dr. Henry Reining, Dean of the School of Public Administration, University of Southern California; American Society of Public Administration," "Federal Support of International Social Science and Behavioral Research," Subcommittee on Government Research, Committee on Government Operations, U.S. Senate, 89th Cong., 2nd sess., June 27, 28; July 19, 20, 1966, 102.

169. Exchange following "Testimony of Dr. Gabriel Almond, President of the American Political Science Association, Stanford University," "Federal Support of International Social Science and Behavioral Research," Subcommittee on Government Research, Committee on Government Operations, U.S. Senate, 89th Cong., 2nd sess., June 27, 28; July 19, 20, 1966, 111. Also see 108–9 and 114.

170. Jeremi Suri, *Henry Kissinger and the American Century* (Cambridge, MA: The Belknap Press of Harvard University Press, 2007), 95; also see 92–93.

171. Ibid., 112 and 116.

172. Walter Isaacson, *Kissinger: A Biography* (New York: Simon and Schuster, 2005), 83.

173. Ibid., 70.

174. Ibid., 97–8. The book was *Nuclear Weapons and Foreign Policy* (New York: Harper Brothers, 1957).

175. Isaacson, *Kissinger*, 98.

176. Suri, *Henry Kissinger and the American Century*, 132.

177. Quoted in Isaacson, *Kissinger*, 694. Also see 708.

178. Henry A. Kissinger, *The Necessity for Choice: Prospects of American Foreign Policy* (New York: Harper & Brothers, 1960), 353.

179. Suri, *Henry Kissinger and the American Century*, 95.

180. Ibid., 137.

181. Zbigniew Brzezinski, *Power and Principle: Memoirs of the National Security Adviser, 1977–1981* (New York: Farrar, Strauss, Giroux, 1985), 49. Also see Stephen F. Szabo, "The Professor," in Charles Gati, ed., *Zbig: The Strategy and Statecraft of Zbigniew Brzezinski* (Baltimore, MD: The Johns Hopkins University Press, 2013), 207–8; and Justin Vaïsse, *Zbigniew Brzezinski: America's Grand Strategist* (Cambridge: Harvard University Press, 2018), 67.

182. Quoted in Szabo, "The Professor," 208.

183. Brzezinski, *Power and Principle*, 545.

184. Quoted in Szabo, "The Professor," 210.

185. Bernard Brodie, "Scientific Progress and Political Science," *RAND Paper* [P-968] (Santa Monica: RAND, Revised November 30, 1956), 3 and 5. For similarly jaundiced views from a sociologist, see Morris Janowitz, "Sociological Research on Arms Control," *American Sociologist* 6, Supplementary Issue (June 1971): 24.

186. Kecskemeti, "Review: The Policy Sciences: Aspiration and Outlook," 527.

187. Ibid., 527.

188. "Testimony of Dr. Carl Pfaffmann, Vice President of the Rockefeller University and Former Chairman of the Division of Behavioral Sciences of the National Academy of Science," "Federal Support of International Social Science and Behavioral Research," Subcommittee on Government Research, Committee on Government Operations, U.S. Senate, 89th Cong., 2nd sess., June 27, 28; July 19, 20, 1966, 122.

189. Kecskemeti, "Review: The Policy Sciences: Aspiration and Outlook," 523.

Chapter 5. Summer Studies, Centers, and a Governmentwide Clearinghouse

1. See Seymour J. Deitchman, *The Best-Laid Schemes: A Tale of Social Research and Bureaucracy* (Quantico, VA: Marine Corps University Press, 2014), 30.

2. F. R. Collbohm and Warren Weaver, "Opening Plenary," in *Conference of Social Scientists, September 14 to 19, 1947* [R-106] (Santa Monica: RAND, June 9, 1948), 5.

3. Hamilton Cravens, "Part I: The Social Sciences Come to Washington," in Hamilton Cravens, ed., *The Social Sciences Go to Washington: The Politics of Knowledge in the Postmodern Age* (New Brunswick, NJ: Rutgers University Press, 2004), 6.

4. Bruce L.R. Smith, *The RAND Corporation: Case Study of a Nonprofit Advisory Corporation* (Cambridge, MA: Harvard University Press, 1966), 30. Also see Gene M. Lyons and Louis Morton, *Schools for Strategy: Education and Research in National Security Affairs* (New York: Frederick A. Praeger, 1965), 16.

5. J. A. Stratton, Provost, "Memorandum to Dr. Max F. Millikan," March 30, 1951, SECRET, April 23, 1951, Department of State, Bureau of Intelligence and Research Subject file (1945–60), "Project Troy," National Archives and Records Administration [NARA], Record Group [RG 59], MLR 1561, I, 1951, 3.

6. Collbohm and Weaver, "Opening Plenary," 5.

7. *Effective Use of Social Science Research in the Federal Services* (New York: Russell Sage Foundation, 1950), 5.

8. Bayes to Herring, February 26, 1965, Department of State, Bureau of Intelligence and Research Subject file (1945–60), "Social Science Research File," NARA, RG 59, MLR 1561, I, 1951.

9. Doherty to Evans, "Social Science Conference on *Point Four*," March 6, 1951, Department of State, Bureau of Intelligence and Research Subject file (1945–60), "Social Science Research File," NARA, RG 59, MLR 1561, I, 1951, 1–2.

10. Roger L. Geiger, *Research and Relevant Knowledge: American Research Universities Since World War II* (New York: Oxford University Press, 1993), 190.

11. Advisory Committee on the Management of Behavioral Science Research in the Department of Defense, Division of Behavioral Sciences, National Research Council, *Behavioral and Social Science Research in the Department of Defense: A Framework for Management* (Washington, DC: National Academy of Sciences, 1971), 13.

12. Herbert Goldhamer, "Fashion and Social Science," *World Politics* 6, no. 3 (April 1954): 394, 396.

13. F. R. Collbohm, "Scientific Aids to Decisionmaking—A Perspective," *RAND Paper* [P-1032] (Santa Monica: RAND Corp., 31 January 1957), 3.

14. *Behavioral and Social Science Research in the Department of Defense*, 1.

15. Ibid., 2–3.

16. Harvey Sapolsky, "The Science and Politics of Defense Analysis," in Cravens, ed., *The Social Sciences Go to Washington*, 74.

17. *Subcommittee Report on Research Activities in the Department of Defense and Defense Related Agencies* (Washington, DC: U.S. Government Printing Office, 1955), 5–7. Also see Steven L. Rearden, *History of the Office of the Secretary of Defense*, vol. 1, *The Formative Years, 1947–1950* (Washington, DC: Historical Office, Office of the Secretary of Defense, 1984), 96–97.

18. *Subcommittee Report on Research Activities in the Department of Defense and Defense Related Agencies*, 31.

19. Vannevar Bush, "Science—The Endless Frontier," *Transactions, Kansas Academy of Science* 48, no. 3 (December 1945): 231–64. For a helpful discussion of the origins of postwar government support for science, see Harvey M. Sapolsky, *Science and the Navy: The History of the Office of Naval Research* (Princeton, NJ: Princeton University Press, 1990).

20. *Behavioral and Social Science Research in the Department of Defense*, 17. Also see Richard V. Damms, "James Killian, the Technological Capabilities Panel, and the Emergence of President Eisenhower's 'Scientific-Technological Elite,'" *Diplomatic History* 24, no. 1 (Winter 2000): 59.

21. Gene M. Lyons, *The Uneasy Partnership: Social Science and the Federal Government in the Twentieth Century* (New York: Russell Sage Foundation, 1969), 198. Also see Lyons and Morton, *Schools for Strategy*, 204–5.

22. Sapolsky, *Science and the Navy*, 4.

23. Lyons, *The Uneasy Partnership*, 136–37,

24. Sapolsky, *Science and the Navy*, 57.

25. Geiger, *Research and Relevant Knowledge*, 24.

26. Quoted in James G. Hershberg, *James B. Conant: Harvard to Hiroshima and the Making of the Nuclear Age* (Palo Alto: Stanford University Press, 1993), 576. Also see Sapolsky, *Science and the Navy*, 5–6.

27. Quoted in Ellen Herman, "The Career of Cold War Psychology," *Radical History Review* 63, no. 3 (Fall 1995): 60.

28. "Strengthening the Behavioral Sciences," *Science* 136, no. 3512 (20 April 1962): 240.

29. Also see Chalmers W. Sherwin and Raymond Isenson, "Project Hindsight," *Science* n.s. 156, no. 3782 (June 23, 1967): 1572. Also see Sapolsky, *Science and the Navy*, 79; and Donald E. Stokes, *Pasteur's Quadrant: Basic Science and Technological Innovation* (Washington, DC: Brookings, Institution Press, 1997), 55.

30. Sherwin and Isenson, "Project Hindsight," 1575.

31. Geiger, *Research and Relevant Knowledge*, 190–92.

32. See Vincent P. Rock, "Science in National Policy: A Preliminary Inquiry," *Program of Policy Studies in Science and Technology*, Paper no. 1 (Washington, DC: George Washington University, November 1964), 16.

33. *Subcommittee Report on Research Activities in the Department of Defense and Defense Related Agencies*, 6.

34. Sapolsky, *Science and the Navy*, 31–33.

35. Lyons, *The Uneasy Partnership*, 137–40.

36. David C. Engerman, *Know Your Enemy: The Rise and Fall of America's Soviet Experts* (New York: Oxford University Press, 2009), 45.

37. Charles W. Bray, "Toward a Technology of Human Behavior for Defense Use," *American Psychologist* 17, no. 8 (August 1962): 527–28.

38. "Testimony of Pendleton Herring, President, Social Science Research Council, New York, NY," "Federal Support of International Social Science and Behavioral Research," Subcommittee on Government Research, Committee on Government Operations, U.S. Senate, 89th Cong., 2nd sess., June 27, 28; July 19, 20, 1966, 225.

39. *Behavioral and Social Science Research in the Department of Defense*, 9–11. For a slightly different list, see Lyons, *The Uneasy Partnership*, 137.

40. The efforts are summarized in Carroll L. Shartle, "Selected Department of Defense Programs in Social Science Research," and E. K. Karcher Jr., "Army Social Science Programs and Plans," both in Lybrand, *Symposium Proceedings*, 322–43, 344–60.

41. Louis D. Higgs, "Project Michelson: Status Report, I" (China Lake, CA: Naval Test Station, 1 February 1964), 16.

42. Robert C. North, "International Relations: Putting the Pieces Together," *Background* 7, no. 3 (November 1963): 123. Also see Seymour J. Deitchman, *The Best-Laid Schemes: A Tale of Social Research and Bureaucracy* (Quantico, VA: Marine Corps University Press, 2014), 126.

43. Higgs, "Project Michelson: Status Report, I," 3.

44. Ibid., 4.

45. Ibid., 16.

46. Ibid., 15.

47. Emails to author from Harvey Sapolsky, October 3, 2017, and Charles Hermann, May 16, 2017.

48. U.S. Congress, Office of Technology Assessment, *A History of the Department of Defense Federally Funded Research and Development Centers* [OTA-BP-ISS-157] (Washington, DC: Government Publishing Office, June 1995), 15–16. Also see Joy Elizabeth Rohde, "'The Social Scientists' War': Expertise in a Cold War Nation," (Unpublished doctoral dissertation, University of Pennsylvania, 2007), 57–58.

49. Lyons and Morton, *Schools for Strategy*, 244.

50. Lyons, *The Uneasy Partnership*, 141–42.

51. *A History of the Department of Defense Federally Funded Research and Development Centers*, 17 and 21. Also see Michael Klare, compiler, *The University-Military-Police Complex: A Directory and Related Documents* (New York: North American Congress on Latin America, 1970), 29; and Lyons, *The Uneasy Partnership*, 161.

52. Rohde, "'The Social Scientists' War,'" 57; Klare, *The University-Military-Police Complex*, 16–17.

53. Robin, *The Making of the Cold War Enemy*, 53.

54. Ibid., 147.

55. Hershberg, *James B. Conant*, 413.

56. Robin, *The Making of the Cold War Enemy*, 50.

57. Shartle, "Selected Department of Defense Programs in Social Science Research," 342.

58. Ithiel de Sola Pool et al., "Social Science Research and National Security" A Report prepared by the Research Group in Psychology and the Social Sciences (Washington, DC: Smithsonian Institution, March 5, 1963).

59. "Remarks of Dr. Morris Janowitz," in William A. Lybrand, ed., *Symposium Proceedings*, 148. Also see Lucien Pye, "The Role of the Military in Political Development," in Lybrand, *Symposium Proceedings*, 160–61.

60. Harry Alpert, "Congressmen, Social Scientists, and Attitudes toward Federal Support of Social Science Research," *American Sociological Review* 23, no. 6 (December 1958): 683.

61. Lyons, *The Uneasy Partnership*, 147–51, 194.

62. Annie Jacobsen, *The Pentagon's Brain: An Uncensored History of DARPA, America's Top Secret Military Research Agency* (New York: Back Bay Books, 2015), 151.

63. Deitchman, *The Best-Laid Schemes*, 43, 48, 5161–62, and 194.

64. Lyons, *The Uneasy Partnership*, 179–80.

65. Ron Robin, *The Making of the Cold War Enemy: Culture and Politics in the Military-Intellectual Complex* (Princeton, NJ: Princeton University Press, 2001), 41–44.

66. Charles E. Hutchinson, "An Institute for National Security Affairs," *American Behavioral Scientist* 4, no. 1 (September 1, 1960): 32.

67. Alfred de Grazia, "The Government in Behavioral Science: Some Critical Notes," *American Behavioral Scientist* 7, no. 9 (May 1, 1964): 29; and Ellis, "The Federal Government In Behavioral Science," 5, table 2.

68. William W. Ellis, "The Federal Government In Behavioral Science: Fields, Methods, and Funds," *American Behavioral Scientist* 7, no. 9 (May 1, 1964): 7.

69. Charles E. Hutchinson, "The Meaning of Military Sociology," *Sociology and Social Research* 41, no. 4 (July–August 1957): 431.

70. Engerman, *Know Your Enemy*, 6.

71. *Subcommittee Report on Research Activities in the Department of Defense and Defense Related Agencies*, 22.

72. Wayne Morse, "Dangers in Government Sponsorship of Research on Foreign Policy and Foreign Areas," *Background* 10, no. 2 (August 1966): 123.

73. Deitchman, *The Best-Laid Schemes*, 133–43. Also see "Testimony of Donald R. Young, Chairman, The Advisory Committee on Government Programs in the Behavioral Sciences of the National Academy of Sciences—National Research Council," "Federal Support of International Social Science and Behavioral Research," Subcommittee on Government Research, Committee on Government Operations, U.S. Senate, 89th Cong., 2nd sess., June 27, 28; July 19, 20, 1966, 127.

74. Robert H. Johnson and George Weber, "Memorandum for Mr. Anderson," February 17, 1956, SECRET, Records of the National Security Council, "P" Papers 2–46, NARA, RG 273, Box 1, "P" Paper #44.

75. "Record of Actions by the National Security Council at its Three Hundred and Seventy-Second Meeting," July 14, 1958, NSC Records, Official Meeting Minutes, NARA, RG 273, Box 22, Folder #372, 1–2.

76. Biographical information about Rock, who devoted much of his career in government and academia to these issues, is available in Robert H. Johnson and Albert H. Cantril, "Vincent P. Rock," *PS: Political Science and Politics* 34, no. 1 (March 2001): 167–69.

77. Gordon Gray to Karl G. Harr, January 7, 1960, Box 4, Subject Subseries, OCB Series of the White House Office: Office of the Special Assistant for National Security Affairs: Records, 1952–61, Folder, "Miscellaneous (9) [November 1959–February 1960], Dwight David Eisenhower Library [DDEL].

78. For a complete list of recipients, see "NSC Distribution Authorization Sheets," January 7, 1960, UNCLASSIFIED, NARA, RG 273, Box 11, 1, Freedom of Information Act [FOIA] copy in author's possession.

79. "Research Relating to National Security Policy," Attachment to Memorandum for Mr. Karl G. Harr, Jr., January 7, 1960, Box 4, Subject Subseries, OCB Series of the White House Office: Office of the Special Assistant for National Security Affairs: Records, 1952–61, folder, "Miscellaneous (9) [November 1959–February 1960], DDEL.

80. Memorandum for Mr. Rock, Subject: Research Relating to National Security Policy, January 29, 1960, Box 4, Subject Subseries, OCB Series of the White House Office: Office of the Special Assistant for National Security Affairs: Records, 1952–61, folder, "Miscellaneous (9) [November 1959–February 1960], DDEL.

81. See Vincent P. Rock, "Memorandum for Mr. Gordon Gray, Special Assistant to the President for National Security Affairs, Report on Research and National Security Policy," March 3, 1960, SECRET, NARA, RG 273, Box 11, 1–7, FOIA copy in author's possession. Excerpts also quoted in RHJ [Robert H. Johnson], "Briefing Note for the President: Establishment of a Research Clearing House Within the NSC Staff," April 18, 1960, Box 4, Special Assistant Series, Presidential subseries—Meetings With President—Volume 1(4), DDEL.

82. Rock, "Memorandum for Mr. Gordon Gray, Special Assistant to the President for National Security Affairs, Report on Research and National Security Policy," 15–18, 26, 30, 31, 34, 35, 38, and 43.

83. G.G. to Lay, March 12, 1960, NARA, RG 273, Box 11, FOIA copy in author's possession.

84. Memorandum for MAJ. General Wilton B. Persons, Subject: "Weekly Report of Gordon Gray," April 11, 1960, Box 3, Folder "Gordon Gray Vol. II (6) [March-April 1960] from the White House Office: Office of the Staff Secretary, Records: 1952–61—Subject Series—White House Subseries, DDEL.

85. *Terms of Reference for a Research Clearing House Within the NSC Staff*, April 13, 1960, Box 4, Special Assistant Series, Presidential subseries—Meetings With President—Volume 1(4), DDEL.

86. For background on Johnson, see Patricia Sullivan, "Security Official Robert H. Johnson Dies," *Washington Post* May 28, 2005, at http://www.washingtonpost.com/wp-dyn/content/article/2005/05/27/AR2005052701439_pf.html. Also see the discussion of Johnson's role in the restructuring of the NSC under Kennedy in Andrew Preston, *The War Council: McGeorge Bundy, The NSC, and Vietnam* (Cambridge, MA: Harvard University Press, 2006), 40.

87. "Minutes of the 443rd Meeting of the National Security Council," May 5, 1960, TOP SECRET, National Security Council records, Official Meeting Minutes, #443, NARA, Box 25, Tab F, 3.

88. "Briefing Note for the President: Establishment of a Research Clearing House Within the NSC Staff," 2.

89. See NSC PB Distribution Authorization Log for "Memorandum for the NSC Planning Board—Research and National Security Policy," March 29, 1960, NARA, RG 273, Box 11, FOIA copy in author's possession.

90. Memorandum for Mr. Rostow, Subject: External Research and National Security Policy Problems, March 29, 1961, Box 326, Staff Memoranda, Walt W. Rostow, Non-Government Research, 1961, John F. Kennedy Library [JFKL], 1.

91. Robert H. Johnson, "External Research and National Security Policy Problems," Box 326, Staff Memoranda, Walt W. Rostow, Non-Government Research, 1961, JFKL, 1–3.

92. Johnson, "External Research and National Security Policy Problems," 4 [emphasis in original], 5, 7, 12–13, 14–15, 16, 17–18, 18–19, 20–21, 21 [table], 21–23, 25–26, 26–27, and 30.

93. Howard Furnas Memorandum for Mr. James S. Lay, Jr., Executive Secretary, National Security Council, "Utilization of Non-governmental Studies Bearing on National Security Problems," July 21, 1959, FOR OFFICIAL USE ONLY, NARA, RG 273, Box 11, 1, FOIA copy in author's possession.

94. "Documentation Subcommittee Report to the Foreign Area Research Coordination Group," December 2, 1964, NARA, Bureau of Intelligence and Research, Department of State, Subject Files of the Dep. Dir, 1962–65, Box 1, "External Research 1964 -," 2.

95. Ibid., 2–3.

96. "The External Research Program," no date [5/18/64 written in pen], NARA, Bureau of Intelligence and Research, Department of State, Subject Files of the Dep. Dir, 1962–65, Box 1, "External Research 1964 -," 1.

97. Wm. J. Nagle, INR/XR to Mr. Hughes, INR, "Federal Agency Support of Social Science Research Related to Foreign Areas and International Affairs . . . ," August 12, 1963, NARA, Bureau of Intelligence and Research, Department of State, Subject Files of the Dep. Dir, 1962–65, Box 1, "External Research 1964 -,"1.

98. Quoted in Engerman, *Know Your Enemy*, 2.

99. Lyons, *The Uneasy Partnership*, 186–88.

100. "Documentation Subcommittee Report to the Foreign Area Research Coordination Group," 1.

101. Lyons, *The Uneasy Partnership*, 182.

102. Rohde, "'The Social Scientists' War,'" 174; and Lyons, *The Uneasy Partnership*, 200–201, 209.

103. R. W. Komer Memorandum for Robert Johnson, "Utilization of Non-Governmental Studies Bearing on National Security Problems," 22 July 1959, SECRET, NARA, RG 273, Box 11, 1, FOIA copy in author's possession.

104. "Federal Agency Support of Social Science Research Related to Foreign Areas and International Affairs . . . ," attachment. Total U.S. government social science spending in FY 63 was $95,210,000. Of this, anthropology got $7,669,00; economics received $39,586,000; sociology was allocated $11,227,000, and the other social sciences, including political science, divided $36,728,000.

105. "Interagency Agreement," no date, circa June 10, 1966, in Foreign Area Research Coordination Group [I], Files of Charles E. Johnson, Box 2, National Security File [NSF], Lyndon Baines Johnson Library [LBJL], 1.

106. "The External Research Program," 2.

107. "FAR Program Planning Proposals," no date circa July 11, 1967, Foreign Area Research Coordination Group [II], Files of Charles E. Johnson, Box 2, NSF, LBJL, 1.

108. George C. Denney, Jr., "State Department Procedures for Reviewing Government Sponsored Foreign Area Research," *Background* 10, no. 2 (August 1966): 96–97.

109. "Interagency Agreement," 3.

110. Charles E. Johnson, "Note for Mr. Smith, July 24, 1967," Foreign Area Research Coordination Group [II], Files of Charles E. Johnson, Box 2, NSF, LBJL.

111. "National Security Decision Memorandum 98," February 9, 1971, National Security Council, NARA, RG 273, NDSM 98, Box 1.

112. Smith, *The RAND Corporation*, 30.

113. For a fuller description of Troy, see "Memorandum from Robert J. Hooker of the Policy Planning Staff to the Director of the Policy Planning Staff (Nitze)," March 26, 1951, Document 59 in *Foreign Relations of the United States, 1950–1955: The Intelligence Community, 1950–1955*, at https://history.state.gov/historicaldocuments/frus1950–55Intel/d59.

114. Robin, *The Making of the Cold War Enemy*, 45.

115. Engerman, *Know Your Enemy*, 50.

116. Ibid., 52.

117. Hershberg, *James B. Conant*, 592.

118. Ibid., 591–92.

119. Lawrence Freedman, *The Evolution of Nuclear Strategy* (New York: St. Martins, 1983), 68.

120. Sapolsky, *Science and the Navy*, 111.

121. Robin, *The Making of the Cold War Enemy*, 100–101.

122. Klare, *The University-Military-Police Complex*, 22.

123. "Defense Department Initiates Project to Spur Academic Science," *Army Research and Development* 8, no. 2 (February 1967): 1, 4–5. Also see Klare, *The University-Military-Police Complex*, 8.

124. J. R. Marvin and F. J. Weyl, "The Summer Study," *Naval Research Reviews* 19, no. 8 (August 1966): 27–28.

125. Robin W. Winks, *Cloak and Gown: Scholars in the Secret War, 1939–1961*, 2nd ed. (New Haven, CT: Yale University Press, 1996), 40–41.

126. John W. Gardner, "Are We Doing Our Homework in Foreign Affairs?" *Yale Review* 37, no. 3 (Spring 1948): 402. Also see 404.

127. Winks, *Cloak and Gown*, 114–15, 384. Also see McGeorge Bundy, "The Battlefields of Power and the Searchlights of the Academy," in E. A. J. Johnson, ed., *The Dimensions of Diplomacy* (Baltimore, MD: Johns Hopkins University Press, 1964), 2–3; Edward Shils, "Social Science and Social Policy," *Philosophy of Science* 16 (1949): 230; and Lyons, *The Uneasy Partnership*, 112.

128. Peter Mandler, *Return from the Natives: How Margaret Mead Won the Second World War and Lost the Cold War* (New Haven: Yale University Press, 2013), 183. Also see Joy Rohde, *Armed With Expertise: The Militarization of American Social Research during the Cold War* (Ithaca, NY: Cornell University Press, 2013), 15–18.

129. Lyons, *The Uneasy Partnership*, 174

130. Rohde, *Armed With Expertise*, 21.

131. Engerman, *Know Your Enemy*, 14.

132. William L. Langer, *In and Out of the Ivory Tower: The Autobiography of William L. Langer* (New York: Neale Watson Academic Publications, 1977), 230–31.

133. Engerman, *Know Your Enemy*, 18–19.

134. Tim B. Mueller, "The Rockefeller Foundation, the Social Sciences, and the Humanities in the Cold War," *Journal of Cold War Studies* 15, no. 3 (Summer 2013): 115.

135. Lyons, *The Uneasy Partnership*, 176.

136. Engerman, *Know Your Enemy*, 93; also see 70, 76, and 339.

137. Joseph H. Willits, "A Security Policy for Postwar America," 100 Years: The Rockefeller Foundation, March 8, 1945, https://rockfound.rockarch.org/digital-library-listing/-/asset_publisher/yYxpQfeI4W8N/content/a-security-policy-for-postwar-america.

138. Joseph H. Willits, "Interview with Arnold Wolfers Regarding the Growth of the Yale Institute of International Studies," March 15, 1951, at http://rockefeller100.org/archive/files/464514a0e9fb3d64ddf7ae10c9b59789.pdf [copy in author's possession].

139. Joseph H. Willits, "Interview with A. Whitney Griswold Regarding Research at Yale University,"100 Years: The Rockefeller Foundation, March 12, 1951, https://rockfound.rockarch.org/digital-library-listing/-/asset_publisher/yYxpQfeI4W8N/content/interview-with-a-whitney-griswold-regarding-research-at-yale-university.

140. Frederick S. Dunn, "The Growth of the Yale Institute of International Studies," 100 Years: The Rockefeller Foundation, November 7, 1950, 8, https://rockfound.rockarch.org/digital-library-listing/-/asset_publisher/yYxpQfeI4W8N/content/the-growth-of-the-yale-institute-of-international-studies.

141. Geiger, *Research and Relevant Knowledge*, 88; also see 251.

142. Roger F. Evans, "Interview with David N. Rowe Regarding International Relations vs. Political Science," 100 Years: The Rockefeller Foundation, October 2, 1951, 1, https:// rockfound.rockarch.org/digital-library-listing/-/asset_publisher/yYxpQfeI4W8N/content /interview-with-david-n-rowe-regarding-international-relations-vs-political-science.

143. Geiger, *Research and Relevant Knowledge*, 99; and Richard Betts, Michael Doyle, and G. John Ikenberry, "An Intellectual Remembrance of Klaus Knorr," in Henry Bienen, ed., *Power, Economics, and Security* (Boulder, CO: Westview Press, 1992), 10–11.

144. Arnold Wolfers, "Letter from Arnold Wolfers to Joseph H. Willits, 1954 April 02," 100 Years: The Rockefeller Foundation, April 2, 1952, 2, https://rockfound.rockarch.org /digital-library-listing/-/asset_publisher/yYxpQfeI4W8N/content/letter-from-arnold -wolfers-to-joseph-h-willits-1954-april-02.

145. Fred Kaplan, *The Wizards of Armageddon* (Palo Alto: Stanford University Press, 1983), 49–50; and Bruce Kuklick, *Blind Oracles: Intellectuals and War from Kennan to Kissinger* (Princeton, NJ: Princeton University Press, 2006), 87.

146. Lyons and Morton, *Schools for Strategy*, 130–34.

147. Smith, *The RAND Corporation*, 143; and Klare, *The University-Military-Police Complex*, 48, fn. 1.

148. Deborah Welch Larson, "Deterrence Theory and the Cold War" *Radical History Review* 63, no. 3 (Fall 1995): 91–92.

149. Lyons and Morton, *Schools for Strategy*, 127–44.

150. Barry D. Karl and Stanley N. Katz, "The American Private Philanthropic Foundation and the Public Sphere, 1890–1930," *Minerva* 19, no. 2 (June 1981): 268.

151. Lyons and Morton, *Schools for Strategy*, 156–62.

152. Donald L.M. Blackmer, *The MIT Center for International Studies: The Founding Years 1951–1969* (Cambridge, MA: MIT Center for International Affairs, 2002), xv.

153. Nils Gilman, *Mandarins of the Future: Modernization Theory in Cold War America* (Baltimore, MD: Johns Hopkins University Press, 2003), 156–60. Also see W. W. Rostow, *Concept and Controversy: Sixty Years of Taking Ideas to Market* (Austin, TX: University of Texas Press, 2003), 113.

154. Walt Rostow, "Development: The Political Economy of the Marshallian Long Period," in G. M. Meier and D. Seers, eds., *Pioneers in Development* (New York: Oxford University Press, 1984), 240.

155. Rostow, *Concept and Controversy*, 97.

156. Klare, *The University-Military-Police Complex*, 5.

157. Allan Evans, OIR to Mr. W. Park Armstrong, Jr., "Meeting on Troy," SECRET, May 1, 1951, Department of State, Bureau of Intelligence and Research Subject file (1945–60), "Project Troy," NARA, RG 59, MLR 1561, I, 1951, 1.

158. Allan Evans, OIR, to Mr. W. Park Armstrong, Jr., "Continuation of TROY," SECRET, April 23, 1951, Department of State, Bureau of Intelligence and Research Subject file (1945–60), "Project Troy," NARA, RG 59, MLR 1561, I, 1951.

159. Blackmer, *The MIT Center for International Studies*, 2, 16. Also see Dorothy Nelkin, *The University and Military Research: Moral Politics at M.I.T.* (Ithaca, NY: Cornell University Press, 1972), 16, 50; and Geiger, *Research and Relevant Knowledge*, 9.

160. "Memorandum to Dr. Max F. Millikan," no date circa April 23, 1951, SECRET, April 23, 1951, Department of State, Bureau of Intelligence and Research Subject file (1945–60), "Project Troy," NARA, RG 59, MLR 1561, I, 1951, 2, 2–4, and 7–9.

161. Blackmer, *The MIT Center for International Studies*, 206–7. Also see Nelkin, *The University and Military Research*, 10.

162. Blackmer, *The MIT Center for International Studies*, 159–72 and 199.

163. Ibid., 148.

164. Nelkin, *The University and Military Research*, 23.

165. Blackmer, *The MIT Center for International Studies*, 205.

166. Sapolsky, *Science and the Navy*, 112. On summer studies, see, Damms, "James Killian, the Technological Capabilities Panel, and the Emergence of President Eisenhower's 'Scientific-Technological Elite,'" 66.

167. U.S. Congress, Office of Technology Assessment, *A History of the Department of Defense Federally Funded Research and Development Centers* (Washington, DC: Government Publishing Office, June 1995), 2.

168. Robin, *The Making of the Cold War Enemy*, 38–39.

169. *A History of the Department of Defense Federally Funded Research and Development Centers*, 5; and Collbohm and Weaver, "Opening Plenary," 6–7.

170. *A History of the Department of Defense Federally Funded Research and Development Centers*, iii.

171. Ibid., 20.

172. Lyons, *The Uneasy Partnership*, 148.

173. Rohde, "The Social Scientists' War," 211.

174. *A History of the Department of Defense Federally Funded Research and Development Centers*, 3.

175. Quoted in R. D. Specht, "RAND: A Personal View of Its History," *RAND Paper* [P-1601] (Santa Monica: RAND Corporation, October 23, 1958), 2.

176. Sharon Ghamari-Tabrizi, *The Worlds of Herman Kahn: The Intuitive Science of Thermonuclear War* (Cambridge, MA: Harvard University Press, 2005), 56.

177. Smith, *The RAND Corporation*, 39–40.

178. Lyons and Morton, *Schools for Strategy*, 247.

179. Smith, *The RAND Corporation*, 316. Also see Engerman, *Know Your Enemy*, 53.

180. Smith, *The RAND Corporation*, 41.

181. Alex Abella, *Soldiers of Reason: The RAND Corporation and the Rise of the American Empire* (Orland, FL: Harcourt, 2008), 10.

182. Kaplan, *Wizards of Armageddon*, 52–59. Also see Kuklick, *Blind Oracles*, 22–23.

183. Smith, *The RAND Corporation*, 57, 68.

184. J. R. Goldstein, "RAND: The History, Operations, and Goals of a Nonprofit Corporation," *RAND Paper* [P-2236-1] (Santa Monica: RAND Corporation, 23 February 1961), 1–2.

185. Quoted in Klare, *The University-Military-Police Complex*, 46.

186. Smith, *The RAND Corporation*, 59n32.

187. Gregg Herken, *Counsels of War* (New York: Knopf, 1985), 75.

188. Goldstein, "RAND," 12.

189. Specht, "RAND," 18.

190. Goldstein, "RAND," 8.

191. Ibid., 6–7.

192. Smith, *The RAND Corporation*, 46 and 61.

193. Ibid., 63–64.

194. Mandler, *Return from the Natives*, 243.

195. Kaplan, *Wizards of Armageddon*, 70.

196. Mandler, *Return from the Natives*, 238.

197. "Summary," in *Conference of Social Scientists, September 14 to 19, 1947*, vii. Also see Goldstein, "RAND," 9.

198. David Hounshell, "The Cold War, RAND, and the Generation of Knowledge, 1946–1962," *RAND History Project* [RP-729] (Santa Monica: RAND, 1998), 240.

199. Smith, *The RAND Corporation*, 108–11.

200. Wesley W. Posvar, "The Impact of Strategy Expertise on the National Security Policy of the United States," *Public Policy* no. 13 (1964): 58.

201. Smith, *The RAND Corporation*, 44–45.

202. Daniel Bessner, "Organizing Complexity: The Hopeful Dreams and Harsh Realities of Interdisciplinary Collaboration at the RAND Corporation in the Early Cold War," *Journal of the History of the Behavioral Sciences* 51, no. 1 (Winter 2015): 49.

203. Robin, *The Making of the Cold War Enemy*, 48–49.

204. T. C. Schelling, "Comment," *The Review of Economics and Statistics* 40, no. 3 (August 1958): 221.

205. Charles Hitch, "Economics and Military Operations Research," *Review of Economics and Statistics* 40, no. 3 (August 1958): 202.

206. Hitch, "Economics and Military Operations Research," 200.

207. Schelling, "Comment," 223.

208. James R. Schlesinger, "Quantitative Analysis and National Security," *World Politics* 15, no. 2 (January 1963): 298.

209. Ibid., 304. On Schlesinger's skepticism of Systems Analysis, see Freedman, *The Evolution of Nuclear Strategy*, 377.

210. Schlesinger, "Quantitative Analysis and National Security," 302.

211. Quoted in Ghamari-Tabrizi, *The Worlds of Herman Kahn*, 124–25.

212. Abella, *Soldiers of Reason*, 21.

213. Specht, "RAND," 22.

214. Mark Solovey, *Shaky Foundations: The Politics-Patronage-Social Science Nexus in Cold War America* (New Brunswick, NJ: Rutgers University Press, 2013), 112–19. Also see Hounshell, "The Cold War, RAND, and the Generation of Knowledge, 1946–1962," 265.

215. Bernard Brodie, "The American Scientific Strategists," *RAND Paper* [P-2979] (Santa Monica: RAND Corporation, October 1964), 20.

216. Ibid., 3 and 5.

217. Barry H. Steiner, *Bernard Brodie and the Foundations of American Nuclear Strategy* (Lawrence: The University Press of Kansas, 1991), 10.

218. Brodie, "The American Scientific Strategists," 29. Also see 22.

219. Ibid., 24. Also see Steiner, *Bernard Brodie and the Foundations of American Nuclear Strategy*, 196.

220. Brodie, "The American Scientific Strategists," 32. Also see 22.

221. Steiner, *Bernard Brodie and the Foundations of American Nuclear Strategy*, 210–20.

222. Collbohm and Weaver, "Opening Plenary," 6.

223. Specht, "RAND," 22.

224. Ibid., 23–24.

225. Smith, *The RAND Corporation*, 65, 104–5.

226. Lloyd S. Etheridge, "Introduction" to Ithiel de Sola Pool, in Etheridge, ed., *Politics in Wired Nations: Selected Writings of Ithiel de Sola Pool* (Abingdon, UK: Routledge, 1998), 2. Also see Joy Rohde, "The Last Stand of the Psychocultural Cold Warriors: Military Contract Research in Vietnam," *Journal of the History of the Behavioral Sciences* 47, no. 3 (Summer 2011): 234.

227. Deitchman, *The Best-Laid Schemes*, 31.

228. Ibid., 34.

229. *A History of the Department of Defense Federally Funded Research and Development Centers*, 21. For an extensive history of SORO/CRESS see Rohde, "'The Social Scientists' War'"; and Robin, *The Making of the Cold War Enemy*, 52–53.

230. Rohde, "'The Social Scientists' War,'" 69–71. Also see Lyons, *The Uneasy Partnership*, 193–94.

231. Lyons, *The Uneasy Partnership*, 167–68. Also see Rohde, "'The Social Scientists' War,'" 29.

232. Lyons, *The Uneasy Partnership*, 194.

233. Quoted in Irving Louis Horowitz, "The Rise and Fall of Project Camelot," in Irving Louis Horowitz, ed., *The Rise and Fall of Project Camelot: Studies in the Relationship Between Social Science and Practical Politics* (Cambridge, MA: MIT Press, 1967), 4–5.

234. Theodore R. Vallance, "Project Camelot: An Interim Postlude," in Horowitz, *The Rise and Fall of Project Camelot*, 204.

235. Ibid., 205.

236. See "Document Number 4," in Horowitz, *The Rise and Fall of Project Camelot*, 60–67.

237. Boguslaw, "Ethics and the Social Scientist," and Jesse Bernard, "Conflict as Research and Research as Conflict," in Horowitz, *The Rise and Fall of Project Camelot*, 115 and 128.

238. Robin, *The Making of the Cold War Enemy*, 207.

239. Rohde, "'The Social Scientists' War,'" 155.

240. Vallance, "Project Camelot: An Interim Postlude," in Horowitz, *The Rise and Fall of Project Camelot*, 203.

241. Klare, *The University-Military-Police Complex*, 13; Rohde, "'The Social Scientists' War,'" vi and 203; and Lyons, *The Uneasy Partnership*, 196.

242. Rohde, "'The Social Scientists' War,'" 226.

243. Rohde, *Armed With Expertise*, 127, 133, 136, and 147.

244. Bryce Nelson, "Political Scientists: More Concern About Political Involvement, Ethics," *Science* 161, no. 3846 (September 13, 1968): 1117–18; and John Walsh, "Cancellation of Camelot After Row in Chile Brings Research Under Scrutiny," *Science* 149, no. 3689 (September 10, 1965): 1211–13. Also see Kalman H. Silvert, "American Academic Ethics and Social Science Research Abroad: The Lesson of Project Camelot and Dante B. Fascell, 'Behavioral Sciences and the National Security,'" in Horowitz, *The Rise and Fall of Project Camelot*, 80–106 and 177–95; and Deitchman, *The Best-Laid Schemes*, 117.

245. Deitchman, *The Best-Laid Schemes*, 173.

246. Ibid., 148.

247. "Testimony of Thomas L. Hughes, Director of Intelligence and Research, Department of State, Washington, DC," "Federal Support of International Social Science and Behavioral Research," Subcommittee on Government Research, Committee on Government Operations, U.S. Senate, 89th Cong., 2nd sess., June 27, 28; July 19, 20, 1966, 12.

248. Alfred Blumstein and Jesse Orlansky, *Behavioral, Political, and Operational Research Programs on Counterinsurgency Supported by the Department of Defense* [Study S-190] (Arlington, VA: Institute for Dense Analysis, 1965), 28.

249. Horowitz, "The Rise and Fall of Project Camelot," and William R. Polk, "Problems of Government Utilization of Scholarly Research in International Affairs," in Horowitz, *The Rise and Fall of Project Camelot*, 32 and 240; and Herbert Blumer, "Threats from Agency-Determined Research: The Case of Camelot," in Horowitz, *The Rise and Fall of Project Camelot*, 153–74.

250. Vallance, "Project Camelot: An Interim Postlude," in Horowitz, *The Rise and Fall of Project Camelot*, 209.

251. Horowitz, "Social Science and Public Policy: Implications of Modern Research," 369.

252. Rohde, "'The Social Scientists' War,'" 4. Also see 28 and 33 and Rohde, *Armed With Expertise*, 40.

253. Rohde, "'The Social Scientists' War,'" 81–86.

254. Polk, "Problems of Government Utilization of Scholarly Research in International Affairs," in Horowitz, *The Rise and Fall of Project Camelot*, 254.

255. Deitchman, *The Best-Laid Schemes*, 180.

256. Robert Boguslaw, "Ethics and the Social Scientist," in Horowitz, *The Rise and Fall of Project Camelot*, 111–13.

257. Rohde, "'The Social Scientists' War,'" 92–92.

258. Mark Solovey, "Project Camelot and the 1960s Epistemological Revolution: Rethinking the Politics-Patronage-Social Science Nexus," *Social Studies of Science* 31, no. 2 (April 2001):181–82.

259. Robin, *The Making of the Cold War Enemy*, 212–14.

260. Blumstein and Orlansky, *Behavioral, Political, and Operational Research Programs on Counterinsurgency Supported by the Department of Defense*, 27–28. Also see Rohde, "'The Social Scientists' War,'" 36–37.

261. *A History of the Department of Defense Federally Funded Research and Development Centers*, 28.

262. Richard K. Betts, "Should Strategic Studies Survive?" *World Politics* 50, no. 1 (October 1997): 32.

263. Kolkowicz, "The Strange Career of the Defense Intellectuals," 190.

264. Freedman, *The Evolution of Nuclear Strategy*, 190.

265. Colin S. Gray, "What Rand Hath Wrought," *Foreign Policy* 4 (Autumn 1971): 124. Also see Freedman, *The Evolution of Nuclear Strategy*, 181.

266. On the USAF HRRI/RRC controversy, see Rohde, "'The Social Scientists' War,'" 48–50. On the debate about RAND analyst Paul Kecskemeti's book *Strategic Surrender*, see James E. King, Jr., "Strategic Surrender: The Senate Debate and the Book," *World Politics* 11, no. 3 (April 1959): 418–29.

267. Deitchman, *The Best-Laid Schemes*, 168.

268. "Department of Defense Research and Development," *Congressional Record—Senate*, November 6, 1969, 33403. Emphasis added.

269. Deitchman, *The Best-Laid Schemes*, 59 and 272.

270. Bryce Nelson, "Military Funds: Senate Whets Ax for ABM, Research, 'Think Tanks,'" *Science* 160, no. 3830 (May 24, 1968): 861.

271. Rodney W. Nichols, "Mission-Oriented R&D," *Science* 172 (2 April 1971): 30.

272. Herbert A. Laitinen, "Reverberations From the Mansfield Amendment," *Analytical Chemistry* 42, no. 7 (June 1970): 689.

273. Thomas N. Cooley and Deh-I Hsuing, *Report on Funding Trends and Balance of Activities, National Science Foundation, 1951–1988* (Washington, DC: NSF, December 1987), 1, 5.

274. Nichols, "Mission-Oriented R&D," 32.

275. Exchange following "Statement of Hon. John S. Foster, Jr., Director of Defense Research and Engineering; Accompanied By Col. James M. Brower; Donald M. MacArthur; Rodney W. Nichols; and Morton H. Halperin," "Department of Defense Sponsored Foreign affairs Research," Committee on Foreign Relations, U.S. Senate, 90th Cong., 2nd sess., May 9, 1968, 36.

276. Quoted in Deitchman, *The Best-Laid Schemes*, 171.

277. Quoted in ibid.,159–60.

278. Exchange following "Statement of Lt. Gen. W.W. Dick, Jr.," 48.

279. "Testimony of John K. Plank, Director of Political Development Studies, Brookings Institution, Washington, DC," "Federal Support of International Social Science and Behavioral Research," Subcommittee on Government Research, Committee on Government Operations, U.S. Senate, 89th Cong., 2nd sess., June 27, 28; July 19, 20, 1966, 259–60.

280. Roger Hilsman, "Recent Trends in Department of State Research," in Lybrand, *Symposium Proceedings*, 309.

281. Mosely, "Research on Foreign Policy," 68.

282. Irwin Altman, "Mainstreams of Research," in Lybrand, ed., *Symposium Proceedings*, 121–22.

283. Max F. Millikan, "Inquiry and Policy: The Relation of Knowledge to Action," in Daniel Lerner, ed., *The Human Meaning of the Social Sciences* (New York: Meridian, 1960), 169.

284. Phillip E. Mosely, "Research on Foreign Policy," in Daniel Lerner, ed., *The Human Meaning of the Social Sciences* (New York: Meridian, 1960), 45. Also see Adam Yarmolinsky, "Confessions of a Non-User," *Public Opinion Quarterly* 27, no. 4 (Winter 1963): 543–48.

285. Grazia, "The Government in Behavioral Science," 25.

286. Elizabeth T. Crawford, "The Social Sciences in International and Military Policy: An Analytic Bibliography," [Prepared under Contract AF 49(638)1344 with the Air Force Office of Scientific Research] (Washington, DC: Bureau of Social Science Research, Inc., October 1965), xx.

287. Rohde, "The Last Stand of the Psychocultural Cold Warriors," 236.

288. Karcher, "Army Social Science Programs and Plans," 352.

289. Millikan, "Inquiry and Policy," 158.

290. "Remarks of Dr. William C. Johnstone," in Lybrand, *Symposium Proceedings*, 191.

291. Millikan, "Inquiry and Policy," 168.

292. Polk, "Problems of Government Utilization of Scholarly Research in International Affairs," in Horowitz, *The Rise and Fall of Project Camelot*, 244.

293. George W. Croker, "Some Principles Regarding the Utilization of Social Science Research Within the Military," in Charles Y. Glock et al., eds., *Case Studies in Bringing Behavioral Science Into Use* (Stanford: Institute for Communication Research, 1961), 120–21.

294. Millikan, "Inquiry and Policy," 160. Emphasis added.

295. Ibid., 161.

296. Lyons, *The Uneasy Partnership*, 172.

297. *Behavioral and Social Science Research in the Department of Defense*, 12, 31–32.

298. Ibid., 13.

299. Robin M. Williams Jr., "Some Observations on Sociological Research in Government During World War II," *American Sociological Review* 11, no. 5 (October 1946): 576.

300. Smith, *The RAND Corporation*, 9, 13.

301. *Behavioral and Social Science Research in the Department of Defense*, 31.

302. Specht, "RAND," 11 and Williams, "Some Observations on Sociological Research in Government During World War II," 577.

303. "An Inventory of Federal Research in the Behavioral Sciences," *American Behavioral Scientist* 7, no. 9 (May 1, 1964): 32–47.

Chapter 6. The Scientific Strategists Follow the Economists to an Intellectual Dead End

1. The first is Joseph Kraft's phrase in "The War Thinkers," *Esquire* 58, no. 3 (1962): 103. Also see Thomas Schelling, "Bernard Brodie (1910–1978)," *International Security* 3, no. 3 (Winter 1978–1979): 2.

2. Bernard Brodie, "The American Scientific Strategists," *RAND Paper* [P-2979] (Santa Monica: RAND Corporation, October 1964), 2.

3. Roman Kolkowicz, "The Strange Career of the Defense Intellectuals," *Orbis* 31, no. 2 (Summer 1987): 187.

4. Kraft, "The War Thinkers," 103.

5. Robert Jervis, "Security Studies: Ideas, Policy, and Politics," in Edward D. Mansfield and Richard Sisson, eds., *The Evolution of Political Knowledge* (Columbus: Ohio State University

Press, 2004), 109. Also see Fred Kaplan, *Wizards of Armageddon* (Palo Alto: Stanford University Press, 1983), 11.

6. Wesley W. Posvar, "The Impact of Strategy Expertise on the National Security Policy of the United States," *Public Policy* 13, no. 13 (1964): 51.

7. P.M.S. Blackett, "Critique of Some Contemporary Defence Thinking," *Encounter* 16, no. 4 (April 1961): 14.

8. Edward Kaplan, *To Kill Nations: American Strategy in the Air-Atomic Age and the Rise of Mutually Assured Destruction* (Ithaca, NY: Cornell University Press, 2015), 19, notes that it was Paul Nitze who first drew this distinction.

9. Bruce Kuklick, *Blind Oracles: Intellectuals and War from Kennan to Kissinger* (Princeton, NJ: Princeton University Press, 2006), 6, 15–16, 143–44, 150, 223–30. Also see Francis J. Gavin, *Nuclear Statecraft: History and Strategy in America's Atomic Age* (Ithaca, NY: Cornell University Press, 2012), 4; Arthur Stein, "Counselors, Kings, and International Relations: From Revelation to Reason, and Still No Policy-Relevant Theory," in Miroslav Nincic and Joseph Lepgold, eds., *Being Useful: Policy Relevance and International Relations* (Ann Arbor: University of Michigan Press, 2000), 71n28; Deborah Welch Larson, "Deterrence Theory and the Cold War," *Radical History Review* 63 (1995): 88–89: and, ironically, Fred Kaplan, "Strategic Thinkers," *Bulletin of Atomic Scientists* 38, no. 10 (December 1982): 51–56.

10. Robert Jervis, "Commentary," *H-Diplo Roundtable—Blind Oracles*, 9, at https://issforum .org/roundtables/PDF/Jervis-KuklickRoundtable.pdf.

11. The first argument is correlation; the second involves process tracing. On that, see Stephen Van Evera, *Guide to Methods for Students of Political Science* (Ithaca, NY: Cornell University Press, 1997), 64–67; and Alexander L. George and Andrew Bennett, *Case Studies and Theory Development in the Social Sciences* (Cambridge, MA: MIT Press, 2005), 205–32.

12. Marc Trachtenberg, *History and Strategy* (Princeton, NJ: Princeton University Press, 1991), 44.

13. This theme is developed at length and applied to contemporary nuclear scholarship in Paul Avey and Michael Desch, "Why the Wizards of Armageddon Hit An Intellectual Dead-end: And What That Tells Us about the Relevance of Academic Nuclear Strategy Today," in Daniel Maliniak, Susan Peterson, Ryan Powers, and Michael J. Tierney, eds., *The Theory-Practice Divide in International Relations: An Empirical Assessment* (forthcoming).

14. Robin W. Winks, *Cloak and Gown: Scholars in the Secret War, 1939–1961*, 2nd ed. (New Haven, CT: Yale University Press, 1996); and Frederick Sherwood Dunn, "The Growth of the Yale Institute of International Studies," 100 Years: The Rockefeller Foundation, November 7, 1950, https://rockfound.rockarch.org/digital-library-listing/-/asset_publisher/yYxpQfeI4W8N /content/the-growth-of-the-yale-institute-of-international-studies.

15. Frederick S. Dunn, Bernard Brodie, Arnold Wolfers, Percy E. Corbett, and William T. R. Fox, *The Absolute Weapon: Atomic Power and World Order* (New York: Harcourt, Brace, 1946), 76.

16. Barry H. Steiner, *Bernard Brodie and the Foundations of American Nuclear Strategy* (Lawrence: The University Press of Kansas, 1991), 134.

17. The essay was Jacob Viner, "The Implications of the Atomic Bomb for International Relations," in *International Economics* (Glencoe, IL: The Free Press, 1946), 300–309. Also see Kaplan, *Wizards of Armageddon*, 27; and Albert Wohlstetter, Letter to Michael Howard, "On the Genesis of Nuclear Strategy," 1968, in Robert Zarate and Henry Sokolski, eds., *Nuclear Heuristics: Selected Writings of Albert and Roberta Wohlstetter* (Carlisle, PA: U.S. Army War College, January 2009), 227, at http://www.strategicstudiesinstitute.army.mil/pdffiles/PUB893.pdf.

18. Trachtenberg, *History and Strategy*, 11.

19. Robert Gilpin, *American Scientists and Nuclear Weapons Policy* (Princeton, NJ: Princeton University Press, 1962), 112–21. Also see the discussion of the effort to institutionalize such

efforts through the JASON Division of the Institute for Defense Analysis in Ann Finkbeiner, *The JASONS: The Secret History of Science's Postwar Elite* (New York: Penguin, 2006).

20. Kaplan, *Wizards of Armageddon*, 254. Also see Kraft, "The War Thinkers," 103.

21. Brodie, "The American Scientific Strategists," 13.

22. David Alan Rosenberg, "'Smoking Radiating Ruin at the End of Two Hours': Documents on American Plans for Nuclear War With the Soviet Union, 1954–55," *International Security* 6, no. 3 (Winter 1981–1982): 31.

23. Steiner, *Bernard Brodie and the Foundations of American Nuclear Strategy*, 20, 107, and 111.

24. Gregg Herken, *Counsels of War* (New York: Knopf, 1985), 75.

25. Kaplan, *Wizards of Armageddon*, 49, note, lays out the compelling circumstantial case. Also see Herken, *Counsels of War*, 32.

26. Gene M. Lyons and Louis Morton, *Schools for Strategy: Education and Research in National Security Affairs* (New York: Frederick A. Praeger, 1965), 130–34.

27. Kuklick, *Blind Oracles*, 63. For a recent book on Wohlstetter that attributes greater influence to his wife Roberta, see Ron Robin, *The Cold World They Made: The Strategic Legacy of Roberta and Albert Wohlstetter* (Cambridge, MA: Harvard University Press, 2016).

28. Kaplan, *Wizards of Armageddon*, 108, 110. Also see Trachtenberg, *History and Strategy*, 19, who concludes that Wohlstetter's conclusions "were . . . enormously influential"; and Morton H. Halperin, "The Gaither Committee and the Policy Process," *World Politics* 13, no. 3 (April 1961): 366n21, which argues that the "Committee's proposals on strategic vulnerability were heavily influenced by a classified RAND report prepared under the direction of Albert Wohlstetter."

29. Smith, *The RAND Corporation*, 233.

30. Albert Wohlstetter, "The Delicate Balance of Terror," *Foreign Affairs* 37, no. 2 (1959): 211–234. Also see Kaplan, *Wizards of Armageddon*, 108–10.

31. Herken, *Counsels of War*, 156.

32. Kaplan, *Wizards of Armageddon*, 171–73; Herken, *Counsels of War*, 124.

33. E. S. Quade, "The Selection and Use of Strategic Air Bases: A Case History," in Quade, ed., *Analysis for Military Decisions* [R-387-PR] (Santa Monica: RAND, November 1964), 63.

34. Lawrence Freedman, *The Evolution of Nuclear Strategy* (New York: St. Martins, 1983), 100–102.

35. Kaplan, *Wizards of Armageddon*, 186–89.

36. Herken, *Counsels of War*, 99.

37. Kaplan, *Wizards of Armageddon*, 201–19; Kuklick, *Blind Oracles*, 107–8.

38. Kaplan, *Wizards of Armageddon*, 245.

39. Ibid., 283–85; Herken, *Counsels of War*, 79 and 151; Deborah Shapley, *Promise and Power: The Life and Times of Robert McNamara* (Boston: Little, Brown, 1993), 139–40, 193.

40. For the former, see Henry S. Rowen, "The Evolution of Strategic Nuclear Doctrine," in Laurance Martin, ed., *Strategic Thought in the Nuclear Age* (Baltimore, MD: Johns Hopkins University Press, 1979), 133. For the latter, see Scott Douglas Sagan, *Moving Targets: Nuclear Strategy and National Security* (Princeton, NJ: Princeton University Press, 1989), 12–13.

41. Desmond Ball, "U.S. Strategic Forces: How Would They Be Used?" *International Security* 7, no. 3 (Winter 1982–1983): 47, 50.

42. Smith, *The RAND Corporation*, 230.

43. Robert Jervis, *The Meaning of the Nuclear Revolution: Statecraft and the Prospect of Armageddon* (Ithaca, NY: Cornell University Press, 1989), 8–9, 49–50, and 98.

44. Quoted in Sharon Ghamari-Tabrizi, *The Worlds of Herman Kahn: The Intuitive Science of Thermonuclear War* (Cambridge, MA: Harvard University Press, 2005), 192.

45. Kaplan, *To Kill Nations*, 1–3.

46. Marc Trachtenberg, "Preventive War and U.S. Foreign Policy," *Security Studies* 16, no. 1 (January–March 2007), 1–31.

47. Kaplan, *To Kill Nations*, 172–83.

48. See Robert S. McNamara, "The Military Role of Nuclear Weapons: Perceptions and Misperceptions," *Foreign Affairs* 62, no. 1 (Fall 1981): 59–80. For internal assessments about whether the Soviets could withstand a counterforce strike, see, for example, "Summary Record of the 517ᵗʰ Meeting of the National Security Council," September 12, 1963, in *Foreign Relations of the United States, 1961–1963*, vol. 8, *National Security Policy* (Washington, DC: United States Government Printing Office, 1996), at https://history.state.gov/historicaldocuments/frus1961 -63v08/d141. For evidence that future administrations followed a similar pattern, see Kaplan, *To Kill Nations*, 216.

49. Memorandum of Conference with President Kennedy, Washington, DC, February 6, 1961, in *Foreign Relations of the United States, 1961–1963*, vol. 8, *National Security Policy,* Document 11 at https://history.state.gov/historical documents/frus1961–63v08/d11. I thank Paul Avey for alerting me to this and the previous *FRUS* document.

50. Joseph E. O'Connor, "First Oral History Interview with Carl Kaysen," John F. Kennedy Library, July 11, 1966, 14.

51. McNamara, "The Military Role of Nuclear Weapons: Perceptions and Misperceptions," 79. Emphasis in original.

52. Quoted in Francis J. Gavin, *Nuclear Statecraft: History and Strategy in America's Atomic Age* (Ithaca, NY: Cornell University Press, 2012), 35–36.

53. Marcus G. Raskin, "The Megadeath Intellectuals," *New York Review of Books* November 14, 1963, at http://www.nybooks.com/articles/archives/1963/nov/14/the-megadeath-intellectuals/.

54. Kaplan, *To Kill Nations*, 108.

55. Ball, "U.S. Strategic Forces," 41–42.

56. Ibid., 44.

57. Kaplan, *To Kill Nations*, 163.

58. Aaron Wildavsky, "Practical Consequences of the Theoretical Study of Defense Policy," *Public Administration Review* 25, no. 1 (March 1965): 102.

59. Making this same point in a different context is Douglas S. Blaufarb, *The Counterinsurgency Era: U.S. Doctrine and Performance, 1950 to the Present* (New York: The Free Press, 1977), 88.

60. McNaughton comments recorded in Joint Seminar on Arms Control, Abstract of Discussion [JSAC/AD], November 19, 1962, UAV 462.1142.3, Harvard University Archives, 3.

61. Henry Kissinger, *The White House Years* (Boston: Little, Brown, 1979), 54.

62. Rosenberg, "A Smoking Radiating Ruin at the End of Two Hours," 13. Also see Rosenberg, "American Atomic Strategy and the Hydrogen Bomb Decision," *Journal of American History* 66, no. 1 (June 1979): 63.

63. Marc Trachtenberg, "An Interview With Carl Kaysen," 11, at http://www.sscnet.ucla. edu/polisci/faculty/trachtenberg/cv/Kaysen.pdf. On the famous SIOP-62 briefing, see Scott Sagan, "SIOP-62: The Nuclear War Plan Briefing to President Kennedy," *International Security* 12, no. 1 (Summer 1987): 22–51.

64. For a wide-ranging treatment of Schelling, see S. M. Amadae, *Prisoners of Reason: Game Theory and Neoliberal Political Economy* (New York: Cambridge University Press, 2016), 84–93.

65. "Thomas Schelling," in Richard Swedberg, ed., *Economics and Sociology: Redefining Their Boundaries: Conversations with Economists and Sociologists* (Princeton, NJ: Princeton University Press, 1990), 188–89.

66. As Schelling put it, arms control "assumes deterrence as the keystone of our security policy, and tries to improve it." T. C. Schelling, "Reciprocal Measures for Arms Stabilization," *Daedalus* 89, no. 4 (Fall 1960): 892.

67. See Thomas Schelling, "Bargaining, Communication, and Limited War," *Journal of Conflict Resolution* 1, no. 1 (March 1957): 19, where he frames his bargaining approach as the middle ground between MAD and surrender.

68. Schelling, "Reciprocal Measures for Arms Stabilization," 912.

69. Schelling comments recorded in Joint Seminar on Arms Control, Abstract of Discussion [JSAC/AD], October 18, 1965, UAV 462.1142.3, Harvard University Archives, 5; and Schelling comments recorded in JSAC/AD, November 20, 1961, UAV 462.1142.3, Harvard University Archives, 3. Emphasis in original.

70. Schelling comments recorded in JSAC/AD, March 19, 1962, UAV 462.1142.3, Harvard University Archives, 1–2.

71. Ayson, *Thomas Schelling and the Nuclear Age*, 114, 142–46.

72. Thomas C. Schelling, "An Essay on Bargaining," *American Economic Review* 46, no. 3 (June 1956): 282–86. He explicitly applies these two assumptions to national security issues in Schelling, "Bargaining, Communication, and Limited War," 23, 29.

73. Ayson, *Thomas Schelling and the Nuclear Age*, 152–54.

74. Thomas C. Schelling, *The Strategy of Conflict* (Cambridge, Mass.: Harvard University Press, 1960; reprint New York: Oxford University Press, 1963), 5. Copyright © 1960, 1980 by the President and Fellows of Harvard College. Copyright renewed 1988 by Thomas C. Schelling. Also see Thomas C. Schelling, *Arms and Influence* (New Haven, CT: Yale University Press, 1966), 181.

75. Schelling, *Arms and Influence*, 35.

76. Quoted in "Thomas Schelling," in Swedberg, ed., 190.

77. Schelling comments recorded in JSAC/AD, 6 February 1961, UAV 462.1142.3, Harvard University Archives, 2.

78. Schelling, "An Essay on Bargaining," 288.

79. Ibid., 294.

80. Schelling, *The Strategy of Conflict*, 193. Emphasis in the original.

81. Ibid., 189. Emphasis in the original.

82. Schelling comments recorded in JSAC/AD, October 22, 1962, UAV 462.1142.3, Harvard University Archives, 5.

83. Schelling, *Arms and Influence*, 51.

84. Ibid., 55. Also see 124 concerning the importance of saving "face."

85. Schelling, "An Essay on Bargaining," 297–98.

86. Schelling, *The Strategy of Conflict*, 232. Emphasis in the original.

87. Ibid., 252.

88. Schelling, "Bargaining, Communication, and Limited War," 32 and 36. Emphasis in the original.

89. Deborah Shapely, *Promise and Power: The Life and Times of Robert McNamara* (Boston, MA: Little, Brown, 1993), 139.

90. See William Kaufmann, "The Requirements of Deterrence," [Memorandum Number Seven] (Center for International Studies, Princeton University, November 15, 1954), 12–23, at http://findit.library.yale.edu/catalog/digcoll:560733.

91. Campbell Craig, *Destroying the Village: Eisenhower and Thermonuclear War* (New York: Columbia University Press, 1998), 159.

92. Thomas Schelling, "Nuclear Strategy in the Berlin Crisis," Washington, July 5, 1961, in *Foreign Relations of the United States, 1961–63*, vol. 14, *Berlin Crisis, 1961–62* (Washington, DC:

United States Government Printing Office, 1993) at https://history.state.gov/historicaldocuments /frus1961–63v14/d56.

93. McNaughton's role as a bridge is highlighted in his friend and colleague Adam Yarmolinsky's "Eulogy" delivered on July 25, 1967, at McNaughton's funeral at the Cathedral Church of St. Peter and St. Paul in Washington, DC. I thank his son Alexander McNaughton for a copy of it.

94. See John T. McNaughton, "Diary," 1949 and part of 1950.

95. Robert R. Bowie and Max Millikan, "Joint Seminar on Arms Control, First Annual Report, 1960–61," (Cambridge, MA, June 1961), UAV 462.1142.5, Harvard University Archives, 2.

96. Bowie and Millikan, "Joint Seminar on Arms Control," 4.

97. "Joint Seminar on Arms Control, Report (1960–63)," (Cambridge, no date [circa 1963]), UAV 462.1142.5 HUA, 3.

98. Interview with Dr. Morton Halperin, Washington, DC, November 3, 2015.

99. See the McNaughton Calendars from 1962 through 1966.

100. For the full report see Schelling Memorandum to Assistant Secretary of Defense (International Security Affairs) and Counselor and Chairman, Policy Planning Council, Department of State, October 12, 1962 and attached report at https://www.jfklibrary.org/Asset-Viewer /Archives/JFKNSF-303-012.aspx. For discussion of the Camp David meeting, see W.W. Rostow, to Carl Kaysen, October 2, 1962 at http://galenet.galegroup.com.proxy.library.nd.edu/servlet /DDRS?vrsn=1.0&slb=KE&locID=nd_ref&srchtp=basic&c=3&ste=4&txb=schelling&sortType =RevChron&docNum=CK2349272601.

101. See the discussion of the difference in Schelling, *Arms and Influence*, 162–63 and 190–94.

102. See Thomas C. Schelling, "Meteors, Mischief, and War," *Bulletin of the Atomic Scientists* 16, no. 7 (September 1960): 292–96 and 300. Also see Ayson, *Thomas Schelling and the Nuclear Age*, 34–35.

103. Schelling, *Arms and Influence*, 195n3 and 154n15.

104. The transcript of a speech McNaughton gave at the University of Michigan in December 18, 1962 was subsequently published as "Arms Restraint in Military Decisions," *Journal of Conflict Resolution* 7, no. 3 (September 1963): 228–34.

105. This figure is calculated from McNaughton's personal calendar for that year.

106. On his early role, see C. P. Kindleberger, "Review: Scientific International Politics," *World Politics* 11, no. 1 (October 1958): 84.

107. "Thomas Schelling," in Swedberg, ed., 189.

108. "Excerpt from Thomas C. Schelling's Interview: 2. Why Were You Initially Drawn to Game Theory," at http://www.gametheorists.com/Interviews/schelling.html.

109. Schelling, *The Strategy of Conflict*, 10n4.

110. Thomas Schelling, "The Role of Theory in the Study of Conflict," *Project RAND Research Memorandum* [RM-2515] (Santa Monica: RAND Corporation, January 13, 1960), 48.

111. Schelling, *Strategy of Conflict*, vi.

112. Schelling, "The Role of Theory in the Study of Conflict," 12.

113. Trachtenberg, *History and Strategy*, 3.

114. Ibid., 15, 13; and Herken, *Counsels of War*, 75–76.

115. Eliot Cohen, "Guessing Game: A Reappraisal of Systems Analysis," in Samuel Huntington, ed., *The Strategic Imperative: New Policies for American Security* (Cambridge, MA: Ballenger, 1982), 166.

116. Quoted in Steiner, *Bernard Brodie and the Foundations of American Nuclear Strategy*, 42.

117. Bernard Brodie, "Review: The McNamara Phenomenon," *World Politics* 17, no. 4 (July 1965): 674. Emphasis added.

118. Steiner, *Bernard Brodie and the Foundations of American Nuclear Strategy*, 133.

119. Brodie to Holland, July 13, 1966, Brodie Papers, Box 5, folder "Army War College," UCLA Library Manuscripts Room. I thank Marc Trachtenberg for this source.

120. Bernard Brodie, "Why Were We So (Strategically) Wrong?" *Foreign Policy*, no. 5 (Winter, 1971–1972): 156. Emphasis added.

121. Kindleberger, "Scientific International Politics," 84.

122. Richard K. Betts, *Nuclear Blackmail and Nuclear Balance* (Washington, DC: Brookings, 1987), 195.

123. McGeorge Bundy, "The Battlefields of Power and the Searchlights of the Academy," in *The Dimensions of Diplomacy*, ed. E.A.J. Johnson (Baltimore: Johns Hopkins University Press, 1964), 9.

124. Schelling, *The Strategy of Conflict*, 7.

125. Schelling, "The Role of Theory in the Study of Conflict," 2. Milton Friedman made this argument famous in his "The Methodology of Positive Economics," in his *Essays In Positive Economics* (Chicago: University of Chicago Press, 1966), 3–16 and 30–43.

126. Compare Schelling, "An Essay on Bargaining," 290 with his introduction on 281–82.

127. Schelling, *The Strategy of Conflict*, v. Text from the new introduction to the Oxford University Press edition.

128. Schelling, "The Role of Theory in the Study of Conflict," 13.

129. Schelling, *The Strategy of Conflict*, 7. Also see Schelling comments recorded in Joint Seminar on Arms Control, Abstract of Discussion [JSAC/AD], 21 November, 1960, UAV 462.1142.3, Harvard University Archives, 2.

130. Schelling, *Arms and Influence*, 150.

131. Ibid., 37.

132. Schelling, *The Strategy of Conflict*, 236. Also see *Arms and Influence*, 232 in which he maintains that the U.S. vulnerability problem was not its "women and children" but its bomber force!

133. Schelling comments recorded in JSAC/AD, December 19, 1960, UAV 462.1142.3, Harvard University Archives, 2–3.

134. Schelling, *The Strategy of Conflict*, 237. Also see Samuel P. Huntington, "Arms Races: Prerequisites and Results," in Carl J. Friedrich and Seymour E. Harris, eds., *Public Policy* (Cambridge, MA: Harvard University Press, 1958), 41–83.

135. Schelling, *Arms and Influence*, 178. Also see T. C. Schelling, "Nuclear Weapons and Limited War," *RAND Memorandum* [RM-2510] (Santa Monica: RAND Corporation, December 29, 1959), 9ff, where he suggests that the nuclear/conventional weapon distinction is manipulatable based on how we talk about it.

136. Brodie to Schelling, 18 December 1964, RAND Letter [L-25542]. I thank Marc Trachtenberg for this document.

137. T. C. Schelling, "Comment," in Klaus Knorr and Thornton Read, eds., *Limited Strategic War* (New York: Praeger, 1962), 246.

138. Schelling, *Arms and Influence*, 202. Also see 206 where he seems less sanguine but still has faith in rationality leading to the dampening down of escalatory pressure.

139. Schelling, "The Role of Theory in the Study of Conflict," 31.

140. Schelling comments recorded in JSAC/AD, April 22, 1963, UAV 462.1142.3, Harvard University Archives, 4.

141. Craig, *Destroying the Village*, 161.

142. Quoted in Freedman, *The Evolution of Nuclear Strategy*, 361. Bundy made a similar statement while in office, see Editorial Note, "Memorandum for the Record of the White House Daily Staff Meeting on February 4, 1963," *FRUS 1961–1963* 8, at https://history.state.gov/historical-documents/frus1961–63v08/d127. I thank Paul Avey for this source.

143. Quoted in Freedman, *The Evolution of Nuclear Strategy*, 325.

144. Ayson, *Thomas Schelling and the Nuclear Age*, 113.

145. Ibid., 200.

146. W[illiam]. Y. S[mith]. to General Taylor, 1 June 1962. I thank Marc Trachtenberg for this document.

147. Blackett, "Critique of Some Contemporary Defence Thinking," 16.

148. This was the title of the first chapter of his *The Strategy of Conflict*.

149. Ayson, *Thomas Schelling and the Nuclear Age*, 152–53.

150. Charles Hitch, "Economics and Military Operations Research," *Review of Economics and Statistics* 40, no. 3 (August 1958): 200, 203.

151. Schelling comments recorded in JSAC/AD, April 22, 1963, UAV 462.1142.3, Harvard University Archives, 1.

152. Schelling comments recorded in JSAC/AD, October 19, 1964 UAV 462.1142.3, Harvard University Archives, 6.

153. Ayson, *Thomas Schelling and the Nuclear Age*, 35.

154. John Lodewijks, "Rostow, Developing Economies, and National Security Policy," in Crawford D. Goodwin, ed., *Economics and National Security* (Durham, NC: Duke University Press. 1991), 285.

155. Sharing this view is John Lewis Gaddis, *Strategies of Containment: A Critical Appraisal of Postwar American National Security Policy* (Oxford: Oxford University Press, 1982), 208.

156. Quoted in Jervis, *The Meaning of the Nuclear Revolution*, 20.

157. Schelling comments recorded in JSAC/AD, 27 April 1963[65?], UAV 462.1142.3, Harvard University Archives, 5.

158. Jervis, *The Meaning of the Nuclear Revolution*, 20 and 182.

159. Bernard Brodie, "Scientific Progress and Political Science," *Scientific Monthly* 85, no. 6 (December 1957): 315–19. Also see Allen S. Whiting, "The Scholar and the Policy-maker," *World Politics* 24, Supplement: Theory and Policy in International Relations (Spring 1972): 237.

160. Lawrence Freedman, "Vietnam and the Disillusioned Strategist," *International Affairs* 72, no. 1 (1996): 133–51; Michael Nacht, "The War in Vietnam: The Influence of Concepts on Policy," *ACIS Working Paper No. 26* (Los Angeles: Center for International and Strategic Affairs, UCLA, July 1980), 12nn15 and 16; Robert A. Pape, *Bombing to Win: Air Power and Coercion in War* (Ithaca, NY: Cornell University Press, 1996), 177–81; Bruce M. Russett, "The Apolitics of Strategy: A Review," *Journal of Conflict Resolution* 10, no. 1 (March 1966): 122–27; Fred Kaplan, "All Pain, No Gain: Nobel Laureate Thomas Schelling's Little-Known Role in the Vietnam War," *Slate*, October 11, 2005, at http://www.slate.com/articles/news_and_politics/war_stories/2005/10/all_pain_no_gain.html.

161. Kaplan, "All Pain, No Gain," 1.

162. Kaplan, *Wizards of Armageddon*, 329.

163. Robert S. McNamara with Brian VanDeMark, *In Retrospect: The Tragedy and Lessons of Vietnam* (New York: Random House, 1995), 62. Also see Rusk quote on 195.

164. Gordon M. Goldstein, *Lessons in Disaster: McGeorge Bundy and the Path to War in Vietnam* (New York: Times Books, 2008), 168.

165. Charles Wolf Jr., "Some Aspects of the 'Value' of Less-Developed Countries to the United States," *World Politics* 15, no. 4 (July 1963): 626–27.

166. Guy J. Pauker, "Southeast Asia as a Problem Area in the Next Decade," *World Politics* 11, no. 3 (April 1959): 337–38.

167. Leslie Gelb, "Vietnam: The System Worked," *Foreign Policy* no. 3 (Summer 1971): 141. Also see Leslie H. Gelb with Richard K. Betts, *The Irony of Vietnam: The System Worked* (Washington, DC: Brookings, 1979); and Daniel Ellsberg, "The Quagmire Myth and the Stalemate Machine," *Public Policy* 19, no. 2 (Spring 1971): 217–74.

168. McGeorge Bundy, recorded interview by Richard Neustadt, March 1964, John F. Kennedy Library Oral History Program, 137.

169. Paul M. Kattenburg, *The Vietnam Trauma in American Foreign Policy, 1945–75* (New Brunswick, NJ: Transaction Books, 1982), 91, 96. Reproduced with permission of Transaction Publishers in the format Book via Copyright Clearance Center.

170. Lawrence Freedman, *The Evolution of Nuclear Strategy* (New York: St. Martins, 1983), 362. Also see Freedman, "Vietnam and the Disillusioned Strategist," 133.

171. Kaufmann, "The Requirements of Deterrence," 17–18.

172. Schelling, *Arms and Influence*, 124.

173. Schelling comments recorded in JSAC/AD, October 4, 1965, UAV 462.1142.3, Harvard University Archives, 7.

174. Schelling comments recorded in JSAC/AD, October 18, 1965, UAV 462.1142.3, Harvard University Archives, 2.

175. Wallace J. Thies, *When Governments Collide: Coercion and Diplomacy in the Vietnam Conflict, 1964–1968* (Berkeley: University of California Press, 1980), 7. Also see COL A.P. Sights, Jr. USAF (ret.), "Graduated Pressure in Theory and Practice," *U.S. Naval Institute Proceedings* 96, no. 7 (July 1970): 42.

176. Schelling, *Arms and Influence*, 171. Also see Freedman, "Vietnam and the Disillusioned Strategist," 140–41.

177. Schelling, *Arms and Influence*, 188. Also see "Statement of Dr. Thomas Schelling, Professor of economics at Harvard University," "United States Policy Toward Asia," Subcommittee on the Far East and the Pacific, Committee on Foreign Relations, 89th Cong., 2nd sess., January 25, 26, 27; February 1, 2, 3, 1966 (Washington, DC: U.S. G.P.O., 1966), 87.

178. Schelling in Stanley Hoffmann, Samuel P. Huntington, Ernest R. May, Richard Neustadt, and Thomas C. Schelling, "Vietnam Reappraised," *International Security* 6, no. 1 (Summer 1981): 9.

179. Thomas C. Schelling, *The Strategy of Conflict* (Cambridge, Mass.: Harvard University Press, 1960; reprint New York: Oxford University Press, 1963), 199n5.

180. Schelling, *Arms and Influence*, 89.

181. Thies, *When Governments Collide*, 15n46. Also see Richard Schultz, "Breaking the Will of the Enemy During the Vietnam War: The Operationalization of the Cost-Benefit Model of Counterinsurgency Warfare," *Journal of Peace Research* 15, no. 2 (1978): 124n15.

182. According to George C. Herring, *America's Longest War: The United States and Vietnam, 1950–1975*, 4th ed. (Boston, MA: McGraw, Hill, 2002), 147, this placed him in office during the crucial decisions of the war.

183. David Halberstam's anguished portrait of McNaughton the "secret dove" in *The Best and the Brightest* (New York: Ballentine Books, 1992), 362–69, finds even greater support in Benjamin T. Harrison and Christopher L. Mosher, "The Secret Diary of McNamara's Dove: The Long-lost Story of John T. McNaughton's Opposition to the Vietnam War," *Diplomatic History* 35, no. 3 (June 2011): 505–34. Schelling himself shared McNaughton's view that he wished we had never gotten involved but once we were, "cutting and going just doesn't look good." Schelling, "Vietnam Reappraised," 17. On Schelling and McNaughton's relationship, also see Andrew Preston, *The War Council: McGeorge Bundy, The NSC, and Vietnam* (Cambridge, MA; Harvard University Press, 2006), 174; and Tom Wells, *Wild Man: The Life and Times of Daniel Ellsberg* (New York: Palgrave, 2001), 195.

184. Herring, *America's Longest War*, 138–47.

185. William E. Simons, "The Vietnam Intervention, 1964–65," in Alexander L. George, David K. Hall, and William E. Simons, eds., *The Limits of Coercive Diplomacy: Laos, Cuba and Vietnam* (Boston: Little, Brown, 1971), 158 and 195–200.

186. Thies, *When Governments Collide*, 112 and 128n139. Also see Frederik Logevall, *Choosing War: The Lost Chance for Peace and the Escalation of War in Vietnam* (Berkeley: University of California Press, 1999), 147.

187. Hilsman, *To Move a Nation*, 531n. Also see A. L. George, "Some Thoughts on Graduated Escalation," *RAND Memorandum* [RM-4844-PR] (Santa Monica: RAND Corp., December 1965); Simons, "The Vietnam Intervention, 1964–65," 144–210.

188. Quoted in Thies, *When Governments Collide*, 1–2.

189. Ibid., 21.

190. Ibid., 5 and 15n46. Also see Michael Nacht, "The War in Vietnam," 12; and Kaplan, "All Pain, No Gain."

191. Thies, *When Governments Collide*, 60.

192. William C. Westmoreland, *A Soldier Reports* (Garden City, NY: Doubleday, 1976), 112.

193. Kaplan, "All Pain, No Gain," 2–3, wrongly puts the date at May 22.

194. The Senator Gravel Edition, *The Pentagon Papers: The Defense Department History of United States Decisionmaking on Vietnam*, vol. 3 (Boston: Beacon Press, 1971), 141, 143, and 146.

195. Richard Betts's observation on early draft of this chapter. Echoes of Schelling are very clear in McNaughton, ISA, "Plan of Action for South Vietnam," [2nd Draft] 9/3/64, Document 188, in *The Pentagon Papers*, vol. 3, 556–59.

196. The major events come from the "Chronology," in *The Pentagon Papers*, vol. 3, 117–46. The meetings with Schelling during this period are noted in McNaughton's calendars for 1963 and 1964.

197. Freedman, "Vietnam and the Disillusioned Strategist," 139–40. Also see Preston, *The War Council*, 144–47.

198. Asheley Smith, transcriber, "Unclassified Personal Diary of John T. McNaughton," January 1, 1966—April 22, 1967, 12.

199. McNamara with VanDeMark, *In Retrospect*, 181.

200. Kattenburg, *The Vietnam Trauma in American Foreign Policy*, 123. Also see 322–23; Simons, "The Vietnam Intervention," 148.

201. Thomson, "How Could Vietnam Happen?" 51.

202. Kaplan, *To Kill Nations*, 169–70.

203. Colonel Oliver G. Haywood, Jr., "Military Doctrine of Decision and the Von Neumann Theory of Games," *RAND Research Memorandum* [RM-528] (Santa Monica: RAND Corp., February 2, 1951), 9.

204. Kaplan, "All Pain, No Gain," 3. Also see Freedman, "Vietnam and the Disillusioned Strategist," 143.

205. Albert Wohlstetter, "Strategy and the Natural Scientist," in Robert Gilpin and Christopher Wright, eds., *Scientists and National Policy-making* (New York: Columbia University Press, 1964), 215.

206. Preston, *The War Council*, 81; also see 88.

207. For a representative example, see Daniel Drezner, "Thomas Schelling Gets His Due from Sweden—But Not from Slate," *Daniel Drezner.com*, October 12, 2005, at http://www.danieldrezner.com/archives/002356.html.

208. This by no means provides evidence for the whole defensive realist argument that nuclear states should not prefer nuclear superiority if they can get it, acquiesce willy-nilly in nuclear proliferation, or eschew damage limitation capabilities as a hedge in case the unthinkable happens. For a critique of that view, see Francis Gavin, "Strategies of Inhibition: U.S. Grand Strategy, the Nuclear Revolution, and Nonproliferation," *International Security* 40, no. 1 (Summer 2015): 9–46.

209. Jervis, *The Meaning of the Nuclear Revolution*, 49. Of course, other theorists made important contributions as well, such as Wohlstetter's distinction between first versus second strike capability; Glenn Snyder's examination of the challenges of extended deterrence; and Schelling's discussion of the "threat that leaves something to chance."

210. Freedman, *The Evolution of Nuclear Strategy*, 44.

211. Bernard Brodie, "The Anatomy of Deterrence," *World Politics* 11, no. 2 (January 1959): 173–91.

212. Steiner, *Bernard Brodie and the Foundations of American Nuclear Strategy*, 12. Also see Kaplan, *To Kill Nations*, 149.

213. Steiner, *Bernard Brodie and the Foundations of American Nuclear Strategy*, 21–22.

214. Freedman, *The Evolution of Nuclear Strategy*, 300.

215. Quoted in Ayson, *Thomas Schelling and the Nuclear Age*, 114.

Chapter 7. Strategic Modernization Theory Bogs Down in the Vietnam Quagmire

1. W. W. Rostow, *View from the Seventh Floor* (New York: Harper and Row, 1964), 51.

2. Brigadier General Richard Stillwell, "Invited Address," in William A. Lybrand, ed., *Symposium Proceedings: The U.S. Army's Limited-War Mission and Social Science Research* (Washington, DC: SORO, March 26–28, 1962), 113.

3. Townshend Hoopes, *The Limits of Intervention* (New York: W. W. Norton, 1987), 12, 58.

4. Mark Solovey, "Project Camelot and the 1960s Epistemological Revolution: Rethinking the Politics-Patronage-Social Science Nexus," *Social Studies of Science* 31, no. 2 (April 2001): 172–73; Ron Robin, *The Making of the Cold War Enemy: Culture and Politics in the Military Industrial Complex* (Princeton, NJ: Princeton University Press, 2001), 9; and Nils Gilman, *Mandarins of the Future: Modernization Theory in Cold War America* (Baltimore, MD: Johns Hopkins University Press, 2003), 23. For a more measured assessment of the role of the war in Vietnam, see David Ekbladh, *The Great American Mission: Modernization and the Construction of an American World Order* (Princeton, NJ: Princeton University Press, 2010), 255.

5. Mark Selden, "Introduction: Asia, Asian Studies, and the National Security State: A Symposium," *Bulletin of Concerned Asian Scholars* 29, no. 1 (January–March 1997): 4. Also see Robert S. McNamara with Brian VanDeMark, *In Retrospect: The Tragedy and Lessons of Vietnam* (New York: Random House, 1995), 32–33; James C. Thomson, Jr., "How Could Vietnam Happen? An Autopsy," *Atlantic Monthly*, April 1968, 47; and Paul M. Kattenburg, *The Vietnam Trauma in American Foreign Policy, 1945–75* (New Brunswick, NJ: Transaction Books, 1980), 39.

6. David C. Engerman, "Social Science in the Cold War," *Isis* 101, no. 2 (June 2010): 400.

7. Ido Oren, "The Enduring Relationship Between the American (National Security) State and the State of the Discipline," *PS: Political Science and Politics* 37, no. 1 (January 2004): 53; and Frederik Logevall, *Choosing War: The Lost Chance for Peace and the Escalation of War in Vietnam* (Berkeley: University of California Press, 1999), 168. D. Michael Shafer, *Deadly Paradigms: The Failure of U.S. Counterinsurgency Policy* (Princeton, NJ: Princeton University Press, 1988), 12–13, makes a slightly different argument: that academics and policymakers both shared the same cultural assumptions and this explains the similarities of their approaches during this period.

8. Thomson, "How Could Vietnam Happen?" 48.

9. Leslie H. Gelb with Richard K. Betts, *The Irony of Vietnam: The System Worked* (Washington, DC: Brookings Institution, 1979), 210–11.

10. Roger Hilsman, *To Move a Nation: The Politics of Foreign Policy in the Administration of John F. Kennedy* (New York: Doubleday, 1967), 10.

11. Kattenburg, *The Vietnam Trauma in American Foreign Policy*, 89.

12. Shafer, *Deadly Paradigms*, 111n25. Also see John Lewis Gaddis, "Foreword" to Michael E. Latham, *Modernization as Ideology: American Social Science and "Nation Building" in the Ken-*

nedy Era (Chapel Hill, NC: The University of North Carolina Press, 2000), ix; Andrew Preston, *The War Council: McGeorge Bundy, the NSC, and Vietnam* (Cambridge, MA: Harvard University Press, 2010), 76–77; Gordon M. Goldstein, *Lessons in Disaster: McGeorge Bundy and the Path to War in Vietnam* (New York: Holt, 2009), 38; Ekbladh, *The Great American Mission*, 201; and Michael E. Latham, "Ideology, Social Science, and Destiny: Modernization and the Kennedy-Era Alliance for Progress," *Diplomatic History* 22, no. 2 (Spring 1998): 209.

13. Latham, *Modernization as Ideology*, 209.

14. Kimber Charles Pearce, *Rostow, Kennedy, and the Rhetoric of Foreign Aid* (East Lansing: Michigan State University Press, 2001), 20–21.

15. Frederick L. Holborn, recorded interview with John F. Stewart, February 20, 1967, John F. Kennedy Library Oral History Program, 14.

16. Latham, *Modernization as Ideology*, 179; Hilsman, *To Move a Nation*; Robert H. Johnson, recorded interview with William W. Moss, August 29, 1974, John F. Kennedy Library Oral History Program, 34; Preston, *The War Council*, 38; and Ekbladh, *The Great American Mission*, 111–13.

17. Goldstein, *Lessons in Disaster*, 28, 35, and 218.

18. Preston, *The War Council*, 33.

19. Ibid., 29. Also see Goldstein, *Lessons in Disaster*, 156–57.

20. McGeorge Bundy, recorded interview by Richard Neustadt, March 1964, John F. Kennedy Library Oral History Program, 3.

21. Johnson, "Oral History," 57–58.

22. Preston, *The War Council*, 75.

23. David Milne, *America's Rasputin: Walt Rostow and the Vietnam War* (New York: Hill and Wang, 2008), 36–37.

24. M. M. Postan, "Walt Rostow: A Personal Appreciation," in Charles P. Kindelberger and Guido di Tella, eds., *Economics in the Long View: Essays in Honor of W. W. Rostow*, vol. 1, *Models and Methodology* (New York: New York University Press, 1982), 1–8; and John Lodewijks, "Rostow, Developing Economies, and National Security Policy," in Crawford D. Goodwin, ed., *Economics and National Security* (Durham, NC: Duke University Press, 1991), 299.

25. W. W. Rostow, *Concept and Controversy: Sixty Years of Taking Ideas to Market* (Austin: University of Texas Press, 2003), 15. Also see Pearce, *Rostow, Kennedy, and the Rhetoric of Foreign Aid*, 2.

26. Pearce, *Rostow, Kennedy, and the Rhetoric of Foreign Aid*, 31–32.

27. W. W. Rostow, "Reflections on Political Economy: Past, Present, and Future," in Michael Szenberg, ed., *Eminent Economists: Their Life Philosophies* (New York: Cambridge University Press, 1993), 224.

28. Rostow, "Reflections on Political Economy," 226.

29. Walt Rostow, "Development: The Political Economy of the Marshallian Long Period," in G. M. Meier and D. Seers, eds., *Pioneers in Development* (New York: Oxford University Press, 1984), 237.

30. Postan, "Walt Rostow," 11–12.

31. Pearce, *Rostow, Kennedy, and the Rhetoric of Foreign Aid*, 34.

32. Rostow, "Reflections on Political Economy," 233.

33. W. W. Rostow, "The Strategic Role of Theory: A Commentary," *Journal of Economic History* 31, no. 1 (March 1971): 76, also see 85.

34. Lodewijks, "Rostow, Developing Economies, and National Security Policy," 302, 304.

35. Anthony Brewer, "Review of *Economics in the Long View*," *Economic Journal* 93, no. 371 (September 1983): 650.

36. Kenneth E. Boulding, "The Intellectual Framework of Bad Policy Advice," *Virginia Quarterly Review* 47, no. 4 (Fall 1971): 604–5.

37. Barry Supple, "Revisiting Rostow," *Economic History Review* 37, no. 1 (February 1984): 113.

38. Mancur Olson, "Review of *Economics in the Long View*," *Journal of Economic Literature* 23, no. 2 (June 1985): 623.

39. A. K. Cairncross, "The Stages of Economic Growth," *Economic History Review* 13, no. 3 (1951): 458.

40. Mark Berger, "Decolonization, Modernization, and Nation-Building: Political Development Theory and the Appeal of Communism in Southeast Asia, 1945–1975," *Journal of Southeastern Asian Studies* 34, no. 2 (2003): 438.

41. Milne, *America's Rasputin*, 254–58. Richard Schultz, "Breaking the Will of the Enemy During the Vietnam War: The Operationalization of the Cost-Benefit Model of Counterinsurgency Warfare," *Journal of Peace Research* 15, no. 2 (1978): 122–23.

42. Quoted in Milne, *America's Rasputin*, 72.

43. Lodewijks, "Rostow, Developing Economies, and National Security Policy," 307.

44. Latham, "Ideology, Social Science, and Destiny," 199. Also see Ekbladh, *The Great American Mission*, 150.

45. Nils Gilman, "Modernization Theory, the Highest Stage of American Intellectual History," in David C. Engerman, ed., *Staging Growth: Modernization, Development, and the Global Cold War* (Amherst: University of Massachusetts Press, 2003), 66–67.

46. Pearce, *Rostow, Kennedy, and the Rhetoric of Foreign Aid*, 13.

47. Donald L.M. Blackmer, *The MIT Center for International Studies: The Founding Years 1951–1969* (Cambridge, MA: MIT Center for International Affairs, 2002), 95.

48. Gilman, *Mandarins of the Future*, 160–64.

49. Rostow, *View from the Seventh Floor*, 45.

50. Rostow, *Concept and Controversy*, 245.

51. Rostow, *View from the Seventh Floor*, 46.

52. Rostow, *Concept and Controversy*, ix.

53. Walt W. Rostow, "The Irrelevance of the Relevant," *Addendum* 1, no. 1 (March 1970): 7.

54. Rostow, *View from the Seventh Floor*, 45.

55. Pearce, *Rostow, Kennedy, and the Rhetoric of Foreign Aid*, 49.

56. Max Millikan and Walt W. Rostow, *A Proposal: Key to an Effective Foreign Policy* (New York: Harper Brothers, 1957), ix. Also see Blackmer, *The MIT Center for International Studies*, 96–97.

57. Rostow, *Concept and Controversy*, 156, 213, and 235.

58. Gilman, *Mandarins of the Future*, 179.

59. Blackmer, *The MIT Center for International Studies*, 104.

60. Rostow, *Concept and Controversy*, 196.

61. David C. Engerman, "The Romance of Economic Development and New Histories of the Cold War," *Diplomatic History* 28, no. 1 (January 2004): 39. Also see Pearce, *Rostow, Kennedy, and the Rhetoric of Foreign Aid*, 17; Milne, *America's Rasputin*, 58.

62. Transcript, Walt W. Rostow Oral History Interview I, 3/21/69 by Paige E. Mulhollan, Internet Copy, LBJ Library, 3.

63. Gilman, *Mandarins of the Future*, 180–81.

64. Pearce, *Rostow, Kennedy, and the Rhetoric of Foreign Aid*, 87.

65. Latham, "Ideology, Social Science, and Destiny," 207.

66. Rostow, *Concept and Controversy*, 230.

67. Ibid., 245–46. Also see Pearce, *Rostow, Kennedy, and the Rhetoric of Foreign Aid*, 73.

68. Rostow, *Concept and Controversy*, 238.

69. Johnson, "Oral History,"13. Also see Preston, *The War Council*, 54.

70. Gaddis quoted in Milne, *America's Rasputin*, 110.

71. Robert H. Johnson, "Escalation Then and Now," *Foreign Policy* no. 60 (Autumn 1985): 130.

72. Milne, *America's Rasputin*, 162.

73. Gilman, *Mandarins of the Future*, 70–71.

74. Pearce, *Rostow, Kennedy, and the Rhetoric of Foreign Aid*, 30.

75. Gilman, "Modernization Theory, the Highest Stage of American Intellectual History," 48, 92. Also see Gilman, *Mandarins of the Future*, 42–43; and Douglas S. Blaufarb, *The Counterinsurgency Era: 1950 to the Present* (New York: The Free Press, 1977), 52.

76. Robert A. Packenham, *Liberal America and the Third World: Political Development Ideas in Foreign Aid and Social Science* (Princeton, NJ: Princeton University Press, 1973), 62–63. Also see Gilman, *Mandarins of the Future*, 10.

77. Gilman, *Mandarins of the Future*, x.

78. Ekbladh, *The Great American Mission*, 2.

79. Latham, *Modernization as Ideology*, 17, 210.

80. Millikan and Rostow, *A Proposal*, 135–37.

81. Rostow, *View from the Seventh Floor*, 162.

82. Millikan and Rostow, *A Proposal*, 5–6. Also see Rostow, *View from the Seventh Floor*, 21–22.

83. Rostow, *Concept and Controversy*, 250.

84. Kattenburg, *The Vietnam Trauma in American Foreign Policy*, 86–87. Emphasis in original.

85. Charles Wolf, Jr., "Some Aspects of the 'Value' of Less-Developed Countries to the United States," *World Politics* 15, no. 4 (July 1963): 633–34.

86. Rostow, *View from the Seventh Floor*, 165. Also see Rostow Oral History II, 7.

87. Rostow, *View from the Seventh Floor*, 13, 157, and 160.

88. William C. Westmoreland, *A Soldier Reports* (Garden City, NY: Doubleday, 1976), 38–39.

89. Rostow Oral History II, 14. Also see Logevall, *Choosing War*, 31; Hugh M. Arnold, "Official Justifications for America's Role in Indochina, 1949–67," *Asian Affairs* 3, no. 1 (September-October 1975): 33.

90. Walt W. Rostow, "Guerrilla and Unconventional War," 20 November 1961, National Security Files, Meetings and Memoranda, Folder: 10/61–11/61, Box 326, Staff Memoranda, John F. Kennedy Library. I thank Peter Campbell for this document. Also see McGeorge Bundy, recorded interview by William W. Moss, February 22, 1971, John F. Kennedy Library Oral History Program, 47.

91. Blaufarb, *The Counterinsurgency Era*, 52–57.

92. Quoted in Hilsman, *To Move a Nation*, 413.

93. Blaufarb, *The Counterinsurgency Era*, 88.

94. McNamara with VanDeMark, *In Retrospect*, xvii; also see 277.

95. Wallace J. Thies, *When Governments Collide: Coercion and Diplomacy in the Vietnam Conflict, 1964–1968* (Berkeley: University of California Press, 1980), 384.

96. Latham, *Modernization as Ideology*, 167. Also see Shafer, *Deadly Paradigms*, 21

97. Jefferson P. Marquis, "The Other Warriors: American Social Science and Nation Building in Vietnam," *Diplomatic History* 24, no. 1 (Winter 2000): 79–80.

98. See Kennan's testimony before U.S. Congress, Senate committee on Foreign Relations, *To Amend Further the Foreign Assistance Act of 1961: Hearings on S. 2793*, 2 pts., 89th Cong., 2nd sess., February 10, 1966, 332–33.

99. Rostow, "Development: The Political Economy of the Marshallian Long Period," 240. Also see Hilsman, *To Move a Nation*, 53.

100. Rostow, *Concept and Controversy*, 302. Also see William W. Kaufmann, *The McNamara Strategy* (New York: Harper and Row, 1964), 130.

101. Seymour J. Deitchman, *The Best-Laid Schemes: A Tale of Social Research and Bureaucracy* (Quantico, VA: Marine Corps University Press, 2014), 23, 97.

102. William A. Lybrand, ed., *Symposium Proceedings: The U.S. Army's Limited-War Mission and Social Science Research* (Washington, DC: SORO, March 26–28, 1962), x. Emphasis in original.

103. George Herring, *LBJ and Vietnam: A Different Kind of War* (Austin: University of Texas Press, 1994), 3–6. Also see Stephen Peter Rosen, "Vietnam and the American Theory of Limited War," *International Security* 7, no. 2 (Fall 1982): 83, 88.

104. Bernard Brodie, "Learning to Fight a Limited War," in William P. Gerberding, ed., *The Political Dimension in National Strategy: Five Papers* (Los Angeles: UCLA, 1968), 28.

105. Lawrence E. Grinter, "How They Lost: Doctrines, Strategies, and Outcomes of the Vietnam War," *Asian Survey* 15, no. 12 (December 1975): 1123.

106. Michael W. Cannon, "Raising the Stakes: The Taylor-Rostow Mission," *Journal of Strategic Studies* 12, no. 2 (June 1989): 128.

107. Cannon, "Raising the Stakes," 132.

108. Ball quoted in Preston, *The War Council*, 93–94.

109. Gilman, *Mandarins of the Future*, 249.

110. Dean C. Tripps, "Modernization Theory and the Comparative Study of Societies: A Critical Perspective," *Comparative Studies in Society and History* 15, no. 2 (March 1973): 210.

111. Millikan and Rostow, *A Proposal*, 133.

112. Rostow, *View from the Seventh Floor*, 151.

113. Lodewijks, "Rostow, Developing Economies, and National Security Policy," 289.

114. Pearce, *Rostow, Kennedy, and the Rhetoric of Foreign Aid*, 68.

115. Rostow, *View from the Seventh Floor*, 117.

116. Millikan and Rostow, *A Proposal*, 1.

117. Hilsman, *To Move a Nation*, 425.

118. Ibid., 527. Also see Schultz, "Breaking the Will of the Enemy During the Vietnam War," 116.

119. William E. Simons, "The Vietnam Intervention, 1964–65," in Alexander L. George, David K. Hall, and William E. Simons, eds., *The Limits of Coercive Diplomacy: Laos, Cuba and Vietnam* (Boston: Little, Brown, 1971), 149.

120. Cannon, "Raising the Stakes," 125.

121. Rostow Oral History Interview I, 10.

122. Quoted in Lawrence Freedman, *Kennedy's Wars: Berlin, Cuba, Laos, and Vietnam* (New York: Oxford University Press, 2000), 280. Also making this connection are Kaufmann, *The McNamara Strategy*, 261, 274, and 294–95; and John McNaughton, Oral History, John F. Kennedy Memorial Library, November 14, 1964, 11.

123. Ekbladh, *The Great American Mission*, 208. Also see Milne, *America's Rasputin*, 10–11, 134.

124. Milne, *America's Rasputin*, 149.

125. Quoted in Asheley Smith, transcriber, "Unclassified Personal Diary of John T. McNaughton," January 1, 1966—April 22, 1967, 38.

126. Westmoreland, *A Soldier Reports*, 120.

127. Rostow, *Concept and Controversy*, 28–29.

128. Rostow Oral History II, 27.

129. George Ball quoted in Milne, *America's Rasputin*, 33.

130. Milne, *America's Rasputin*, 158.

131. "The Effect of U.S. Bombing on North Vietnam's Ability to Support Military Operations in South Vietnam and Laos: Retrospect and Prospect," JASON Summer Study, TOP SECRET—NORFORN, 29 August 1966, National Security Files, Country file, Vietnam, Box 192; and Special Subpanel of President's Science Advisory Committee, "The Effect of Air Strikes in

North Vietnam and Laos," TOP SECRET, April 26, 1968, National Security Files, Country Files, Vietnam, Box 83, Document 58b, Lyndon Baines Johnson Library. Also see Milne, *America's Rasputin*, 170–75; Schultz, "Breaking the Will of the Enemy During the Vietnam War," 118; Ann Finkbeiner, *The JASONS: The Secret History of Science's Postwar Elite* (New York: Penguin Books, 2006), 65–70; and Shapley, *Promise and Power*, 362–63; and McNamara with VanDeMark, *In Retrospect*, 246; and Christopher P. Twomey, "The McNamara Line and the Turning Point for Civilian Scientist-Adviser in American Defence Policy, 1966–1968," *Minerva* 37, no. 3 (1999): 235–58, which discuss the electronic barrier/McNarama Line alternative.

132. W. W. Rostow, *Pre-Invasion Bombing Strategy: General Eisenhower's Decision of March 25, 1944* (Austin: University of Texas Press, 1981), 23. Emphasis added.

133. Rostow, *View from the Seventh Floor*, 7.

134. Christopher T. Fisher, "The Illusion of Progress," *Pacific Historical Review* 75, no. 1 (February 2006): 42.

135. Milne, *America's Rasputin*, 104. Also see Lodewijks, "Rostow, Developing Economies, and National Security Policy," 293.

136. Blaufarb, *The Counterinsurgency Era*, 67.

137. See National security Action Memorandum No. 182, August 24, 1962, available at http://fas.org/irp/offdocs/nsam-jfk/nsam182.htm. Also see Shafer, *Deadly Paradigms*, 112.

138. Shafer, *Deadly Paradigms*, 114.

139. Blaufarb, *The Counterinsurgency Era*, 72.

140. Transcript, Walt W. Rostow Oral History II, 1/9/81, by Ted Gittinger, Internet Copy, LBJ Library, 2.

141. Quoted in Lodewijks, "Rostow, Developing Economies, and National Security Policy," 297.

142. Rostow, *View from the Seventh Floor*, 84–85.

143. Rostow Oral History II, 2.

144. Robin, *The Making of the Cold War Enemy*, 185.

145. Alfred Blumstein and Jesse Orlansky, *Behavioral, Political, and Operational Research Programs on Counterinsurgency Supported by the Department of Defense* [Study S-190] (Arlington, VA: Institute for Defense Analysis, 1965), 1.

146. Blumstein and Orlansky, *Behavioral, Political, and Operational Research Programs on Counterinsurgency Supported by the Department of Defense*, 5.

147. Ibid., 27–28.

148. Millikan comments recorded in Joint Seminar on Arms Control, Abstract of Discussion [JSAC/AD], May 22, 1961, UAV 462.1142.3, Harvard University Archives, 4.

149. Blumstein and Orlansky, *Behavioral, Political, and Operational Research Programs on Counterinsurgency Supported by the Department of Defense*, 27.

150. Ibid., 28–29, 33.

151. Ibid., 16, 26.

152. Michael Klare, Compiler, *The University-Military-Police Complex: A Directory and Related Documents* (New York: North American Congress on Latin America, 1970), 6.

153. Eugene J. Webb, "A Review of Social Science Research in Vietnam With Procedural Recommendations for Future Research in Insurgent Settings," *Research Paper P-450* (Arlington, VA: Institute for Defense Analyses, December 1968), 6. FOR OFFICIAL USE ONLY released to author under Freedom of Information Act request.

154. Ibid., 9.

155. Data calculated from "Alphabetical Listing of Symposium Registrants," in Lybrand, *Symposium Proceedings*, 367–93. If SORO and HumRRO attendees are included, the percentage increases to 26 percent.

156. Deitchman, *The Best-Laid Schemes*, 57, table 1.

157. Quoted in "Statement of Seymour J. Deitchman, Special Assistant for Counterinsurgency, Office of the Director of Defense Research and Engineering, Department of Defense," "Behavioral Sciences and the National Security, Subcommittee on International Organizations and Movements, Committee on Foreign Affairs, U.S. House, December 6, 1965, 72.

158. See "Document Number 2," in Irving Louis Horowitz, ed., *The Rise and Fall of Project Camelot: Studies in the Relationship Between Social Science and Practical Politics* (Cambridge, MA: MIT Press, 1967), 52.

159. Colin S. Gray, "What Rand Hath Wrought," *Foreign Policy* no. 4 (Autumn 1971): 122–25; and Bernard Brodie, "Why Were We So (Strategically) Wrong?" *Foreign Policy* no. 5 (Winter 1971–1972): 157–58.

160. Freedman, *Kennedy's Wars*, 40.

161. Boulding, "The Intellectual Framework of Bad Policy Advice," 607.

162. McGeorge Bundy, "Oral History [1964]," 26.

163. Robin, *The Making of the Cold War Enemy*, 55.

164. Westmoreland, *A Soldier Reports*, 120.

165. Richard Posner, *Public Intellectuals: A Study of Decline* (Cambridge, MA: Harvard University Press, 2003), 387.

166. Kattenburg, *The Vietnam Trauma in American Foreign Policy*, 310. Also see Kenneth T. Young, "United States Policy and Vietnamese Political Viability, 1954–1967," *Asian Survey* 7, no. 8 (August 1967): 508.

167. Bundy, "Foreward" to Blaufarb, *The Counterinsurgency Era*, xi.

168. Schelling in Stanley Hoffmann, Samuel P. Huntington, Ernest R. May, Richard Neustadt, and Thomas C. Schelling, "Vietnam Reappraised," *International Security* 6, no. 1 (Summer 1981): 13.

169. Thomson, "How Could Vietnam Happen?" 48. Emphasis in original.

170. McNamara with VanDeMark, *In Retrospect*, 32.

171. Quoted in Thies, *When Governments Collide*, 219.

172. Young, "United States Policy and Vietnamese Political Viability," 508.

173. Kattenburg, *The Vietnam Trauma in American Foreign Policy*, 179. Also see Ellsberg comments in Joint Harvard–MIT Arms Control Seminar, "Minutes of the Fourth Meeting," November 30, 1970, UAV 462.1142.3, Harvard University Archives, 7.

174. Daniel Ellsberg, *Secrets: A Memoir of Vietnam and the Pentagon Papers* (New York: Penguin, 2003), 278.

175. "Unclassified Personal Diary of John T. McNaughton," 5, 7–8. Also see McNamara with VanDeMark, *In Retrospect*, 74.

176. Bernard Brodie, *War and Politics* (New York: MacMillan, 1973), 214.

177. McNamara with VanDeMark, *In Retrospect*, 117.

178. Johnson, "Oral History," 59–60.

179. Packenham, *Liberal America and the Third World*, 184–85.

180. Samuel P. Huntington, "Introduction: Social Science and Vietnam," *Asian Survey* 7, no. 8 (August 1967): 504.

181. Ibid., 505.

182. Ibid., 505.

183. Kattenburg, *The Vietnam Trauma in American Foreign Policy*, 88.

184. Robin, *The Making of the Cold War Enemy*, 13.

185. Typical of this critique is Shafer, *Deadly Paradigms*, 240–41. Also see Kattenburg, *The Vietnam Trauma in American Foreign Policy*, 75.

186. Christoph Frei, *Hans J. Morgenthau: An Intellectual Biography* (Baton Rouge, LA: Louisiana State University Press, 2001), 217.

187. Logevall, *Choosing War*, 140.

188. Kenneth N. Waltz, "The Politics of Peace," *International Studies Quarterly* 11, no. 3 (September 1967): 199–211.

189. Milne, *America's Rasputin*, 114–15.

190. Ibid., 116–17.

191. Preston, *The War Council*, 199. Also see Gelb, "Vietnam," 161–62.

192. Hans J. Morgenthau, "We Are Deluding Ourselves in Vietnam," *New York Times Magazine*, April 18, 1965, 25, 8587.

193. Louis Menashe, ed., *Teach-ins, USA; Reports, Opinions, Documents* (New York: F. A. Praeger, 1967), 198–209.

194. Hans J. Morgenthau, *Scientific Man versus Power Politics* (1946; reprint Chicago, IL: Phoenix Books, 1965), 2.

195. See his comments at the Joint Seminar on Arms Control, Abstract of Discussion [JSAC/AD], April 13, 1964, UAV 462.1142.3, Harvard University Archives, 3–4.

196. Hans J. Morgenthau, "Area Studies and the Study of International Relations," *International Social Science Bulletin* 4, no. 45 (1952): 651–52.

197. Hans J. Morgenthau, "Reflections on the State of the Discipline," *Review of Politics* 17, no. 4 (October 1955): 448.

198. Morgenthau, "Reflections on the State of the Discipline," 455.

199. Robin, *The Making of the Cold War Enemy*, 196. Also see Latham, *Modernization as Ideology*, 152.

200. The key piece that critics point to is Samuel P. Huntington, "The Bases of Accommodation," *Foreign Affairs* 46, no. 4 (July 1968): 650, 652. See for instance Donal Cruise O'Brien, "Modernization, Order, and the Erosion of a Democratic Ideal," *Journal of Development Studies* 8, no. 4 (1972): 364.

201. Fisher, "The Illusion of Progress," 43–44.

202. Gilman, "Modernization Theory, the Highest Stage of American Intellectual History," 62–63. Also see Gilman, *Mandarins of the Future*, 229; Leys, *The Rise and Fall of Development Theory*, 76.

203. Samuel P. Huntington, *Political Order in Changing Societies* (New Haven: Yale University Press, 1968), 4, 6. Also see Tripps, "Modernization Theory and the Comparative Study of Societies," 215.

204. Berger, "Decolonization, Modernization, and Nation-Building," 442n57.

205. Fisher, "The Illusion of Progress," 50.

206. Ibid., 25–26.

207. Huntington, "The Bases of Accommodation," 642. Also see 643 and 653.

208. Samuel P. Huntington, "Strategic Planning and the Political Process," *Foreign Affairs* 38, no. 2 (January 1960): 289.

209. Personal conversation, Martha's Vinyard, MA, June 2005.

210. Milne, *America's Rasputin*, 66.

211. William R. Polk, "Problems of Government Utilization of Scholarly Research in International Affairs," in Horowitz, *The Rise and Fall of Project Camelot*, 260–61. Also see Christopher T. Fisher, "Nation Building and the Vietnam War," *Pacific Historical Review* 74, no. 3 (August 2005): 446.

212. Hilsman, *To Move a Nation*, 47.

213. Milne, *America's Rasputin*, 24–25.

214. Hilsman, *To Move a Nation*, 574.

215. Gilman, "Modernization Theory, the Highest Stage of American Intellectual History," 49. Also see Pearce, *Rostow, Kennedy, and the Rhetoric of Foreign Aid*, 35–36.

216. Milne, *America's Rasputin*, 113.

217. Hilsman, *To Move a Nation*, 568.

Chapter 8. The "Renaissance of Security" Languished until the Owl of Minerva Flew after 9/11

1. Stephen M. Walt, "The Renaissance of Security Studies," *International Studies Quarterly* 35, no. 2 (June 1991): 220; David A. Baldwin, "Review: Security Studies and End of the Cold War," *World Politics* 48, no. 1 (October 1995): 124; Marc Trachtenberg, *History and Strategy* (Princeton, NJ: Princeton University Press, 1991), 3; and Ido Oren, *Our Enemies and Us: America's Rivalries and the Making of Political Science* (Ithaca: Cornell University Press, 2003), 164–71.

2. Quoted in Gregg Herken, *Counsels of War* (New York: Knopf, 1985), 313.

3. Barry R. Posen to Derek Bok, October 11, 1989, 2 (copy in author's possession).

4. Hedley Bull, "Strategic Studies and Its Critics," *World Politics* 20, no. 4 (July 1968): 598.

5. Fred Kaplan, *Wizards of Armageddon* (Palo Alto: Stanford University Press, 1983), 336; Herken, *Counsels of War*, 220–21; and Colin S. Gray, "What Rand Hath Wrought," *Foreign Policy* 4 (Autumn 1971): 119.

6. Advisory Committee on the Management of Behavioral Science Research in the Department of Defense, Division of Behavioral Sciences, National Research Council, *Behavioral and Social Research in the Department of Defense: A Framework for Management* (Washington, DC: National Academy of Sciences, 1971), 2–3.

7. David Halberstam, *The Best and the Brightest* (1969, reprint New York: Ballentine, 1992), 496. For a sample of the voluminous literature lamenting the monolithically leftist tinge of the academy see, inter alia, Roger Kimbell, *Tenured Radicals: How Politics Has Corrupted Our Higher Education* (New York: Harper and Row, 1990); David Horowitz, *The Professor: The 101 Most Dangerous Academics in America* (Washington, DC: Regnery, 2006); and Horowitz and Jacob Laksin, *One Party Classroom: How Radical Professors at America's Top Colleges Indoctrinate Students and Undermine Our Democracy* (New York: Crown Forum, 2009).

8. Samuel P. Huntington, *The Soldier and the State: The Theory and Politics of Civil-Military Relations* (Cambridge, MA: The Belknap Press of Harvard University Press, 1957), chapter 6 on "The Ideological Constant: The Liberal Society Versus Military Professionalism." Also see Michael Howard, *War and the Liberal Conscience* (New Brunswick, NJ: Rutgers University Press 1978).

9. Wesley W. Posvar, "The Impact of Strategy Expertise on the National Security Policy of the United States," *Public Policy* No. 13 (1964): 46–47.

10. Bernard Brodie, "Scientific Progress and Political Science," *Scientific Monthly* 85, no. 6 (December 1957): 315–19. Also see Allen Whiting, "The Scholar and the Policy-maker," *World Politics* 24, Supplement (Spring 1972): 237.

11. Albert Somit and Joseph Tanenhaus, *The Development of Political Science: From Burgess to Behavioralism* (Boston: Allyn and Bacon, 1967), 205.

12. First three identified by John G. Gunnell, "Handbooks and History: Is It Still the American Science of Politics? *International Political Science Review* 23, no. 4 (October 2002): 351. Also see "Symposium in Qualitative and Multimethod Research," *Security Studies* 25, no. 1 (January-March 2016): 1–49.

13. Gary King, Robert O. Keohane, and Sidney Verba, *Designing Social Inquiry: Scientific Inference in Qualitative Research* (Princeton, NJ: Princeton University Press, 1994), 9. Emphasis added.

14. King, Keohane, and Verba, *Designing Social Inquiry*, 18. Emphasis in original.

15. The phrase comes from John Gerring, *Social Science Methodology: A Unified Framework* (Cambridge: Cambridge University Press, 2012), 398, but he is an optimist about rigor and relevance.

16. King, Keohane, and Verba, *Designing Social Inquiry*, 15–17. But for more nuanced views, see Arthur Lupia, "What Is the Value of Social Science? Challenges for Researchers and Government Funders," *PS: Politics Science and Politics* 47, no. 1 (January 2014): 1, 2; and Erik Gartzke, "Zombie Relevance," foreignpolicy.com, February 27, 2011, at http://foreignpolicy .com/2011/02/27/gartzke-on-policy-political-science-and-zombies/.

17. Jeffry A. Frieden and David A. Lake, "International Relations as a Social Science: Rigor and Relevance," *Annals of the American Academy of Political and Social Science* No. 600 (July 2005): 138 (emphasis added); also see 151.

18. Marc Lynch, "Political Science in Real Time: Engaging the Middle East Policy Public," *Perspectives on Politics* 14, no. 1 (March 2016): 128. Also see Daniel Drezner, "The American Foreign Policy Establishment is Getting More Comfortable with Numbers," *Washington Post*, July 6, 2016, at https://www.washingtonpost.com/posteverything/wp/2016/07/06/the -american-foreign-policy-establishment-is-getting-more-comfortable-with-numbers/.

19. Andrew Bennett and G. John Ikenberry, "*The Review*'s Evolving Relevance for U.S. Foreign Policy 1906–2006," *American Political Science Review* 100, no. 4 (November 2006): 656.

20. James Mulholland, "Academics: Forget About Public Engagement, Stay in Your Ivory Towers," *The Guardian*, December 10, 2015, at http://www.theguardian.com/higher-education-net-work/2015/dec/10/academics-forget-about-public-engagement-stay-in-your-ivory-towers.

21. "Report of the Defense Science Board Task Force on Basic Research" (Washington, DC: Office of the Under Secretary of Defense for Acquisition, Technology and Logistics, January 2012), 21.

22. David Collier, Henry E. Brady, and Jason Seawright, "Critiques, Responses, and Trade-offs: Drawing Together the Debate," in Henry E. Brady and David Collier, eds., *Rethinking Social Inquiry: Diverse Tools, Shared Standards* (Lanham, MD: Rowman and Littlefield, 2004), 198. Also see Peter C. Ordeshook, "Engineering or Science: What is the Study of Politics?" *Critical Review* 9, nos. 1–2 (1995): 187–88.

23. For further discussion of this approach, see Stephen Van Evera, *Guide to Methods for Students of Political Science* (Ithaca, NY: Cornell University Press, 1997), 64–67.

24. For more detailed discussion of this, see Stuart Glennan, "Rethinking Mechanistic Explanation," *Philosophy of Science* 69, no. S3 (September 2003): S342–53.

25. Gerring, *Social Science Methodology*, 257.

26. Paul W. Holland, "Statistics and Causal Inference," *Journal of the American Statistical Association* 81, no. 396 (December 1986): 947. Emphasis in original.

27. Stuart Glennan, "Mechanisms and the Nature of Causation," *Erkenntis* 44, no. 1 (January 1996): 49–71.

28. Zenonas Norkus, "Mechanisms as Miracle Makers? The Rise and Inconsistencies of the 'Mechanismic Approach' in Social Science and History," *History and Theory* 44, no. 3 (October 2005): 362.

29. John Gerring, "Causal Mechanisms: Yes, But . . ."*Comparative Political Studies* 43, no. 11 (November 2010): 1500.

30. Holland, "Statistics and Causal Inference," 954. Emphasis in original.

31. Nancy Cartwright, "Are RCTs the Gold Standard?" *BioSocieties* 2, no. 1 (March 2007): 11–20. Noting that these weaknesses in Randomized Controlled Trials (RCTs) will undermine their policy relevance is Angus S. Deaton, "Instruments of Development: Randomization in the Tropics, and the Search for the Elusive Keys to Economic Development," *National Bureau of Economic Research*, Working Paper No. 14690 (Cambridge, MA; NBER, 2009).

32. Holland, "Statistics and Causal Inference," 945.

33. David Collier, Henry E. Brady, and Jason Seawright, "Sources of Leverage in Causal Inference: Toward an Alternative View of Methodology," in Brady and Collier, eds., *Rethinking*

Social Inquiry, 255. Also see Alexander George and Andrew Bennett, *Case Studies and Theory Development in the Social Sciences* (Cambridge, MA: MIT Press, 2005), 177.

34. Daniel Schwartz and Joseph Lellouch, "Explanatory and Pragmatic Attitudes in Therapeutic Trials," *Journal of Clinical Epidemiology* 62, no. 5 (May 2009): 499–505; and Jeffrey M. Drazen et al., "Pragmatic Trials," *New England Journal of Medicine* 375, no. 5 (August 2016): 454–63.

35. On "process tracing" as a method of social science inquiry to establish causal inference, see George and Bennett, *Case Studies and Theory Development in the Social Sciences*, 205–32 and 263–85. For discussion of the need to bring research to bear on policy problems, see Alexander L. George, *Bridging the Gap: Theory and Practice in Foreign Policy* (Washington, DC: United States Institute of Peace, 1993).

36. See the comprehensive discussion of Easton's intellectual trajectory in John G. Gunnell, "The Reconstruction of Political Theory: David Easton, Behavioralism, and the Long Road to System," *Journal of the History of the Behavioral Sciences* 49, no. 2 (Spring 2013): 208–9.

37. David Easton, "The New Revolution in Political Science," *American Political Science Review* 63, no. 4 (December 1969): 1053.

38. Ibid., 1054 and 1057.

39. Also see James Farr, "Political Science," in Theodore M. Porter and Dorothy Ross, eds., *Cambridge History of Science*, vol. 7, *Modern Social Sciences* (New York: Cambridge University Press, 2003), 325.

40. Frieden and Lake, "International Relations as a Social Science," 137.

41. Gabriel A. Almond, "Separate Tables: Schools and Sects in Political Science," *PS: Political Science and Politics* 21, no. 4 (Fall 1988): 835. Also see Somit and Tanenhaus, *The Development of Political Science*, 184, 200.

42. "How Are We Doing? Assessments of APSA Programs by Members and Former Members," Report to the American Political Science Association Council, April 17, 1999, 4 (copy in author's possession). The idea of such a survey was apparently first bruited in Richard K. Betts to Sheilah Mann and Robert Hauck, "APSA Publications Committee Discussion of APSR," March 15, 1991 (copy in author's possession).

43. On the Perestroika movement, see Emily Eakin, "Think Tank; Political Scientists Leading a Revolution, Not Studying One," *New York Times*, November 4, 2000, at http://www.ny-times.com/2000/11/04/technology/04TANK.html; and D.W. Miller, "Storming the Palace in Political Science," *Chronicle of Higher Education*, September 21, 2001, at http://chronicle.com/free/v48/i04/04a01501.htm.

44. APSA Task Force on Graduate Education, "2004 Report to the Council," in Kristen Renwick Monroe, ed., *Perestroika!: The Raucous Rebellion in Political Science* (New Haven, CT: Yale University Press, 2005), 360–61.

45. Jennifer Hochschild, "Inventing *Perspectives on Politics*," in Monroe, ed., *Perestroika*, 332–33.

46. Richard K. Betts, "Should Strategic Studies Survive?" *World Politics* 50, no. 1 (October 1997): 25.

47. Baldwin, "Security Studies and End of the Cold War," 124.

48. Bruce M. Russett, "Warriors and Scholars: Fellow Professionals in Hard Times," *Naval War College Review* 28, no. 2 (Fall 1975): 89.

49. Morris Janowitz, "Toward a Redefinition of Military Strategy in International Relations," *World Politics* 26, no. 4 (July 1974): 484.

50. Raymond Tanter and Richard H. Ullman, "Theory and Policy in International Relations: Introduction," *World Politics* 24, Supplement (Spring 1972): 6.

51. David C. Engerman, *Know Your Enemy: The Rise and Fall of America's Soviet Experts* (New York: Oxford University Press, 2009), 261.

52. Paul C. Avey and Michael C. Desch, "What Do Policymakers Want From Us? Results of a Survey of Current and Former Senior National Security Decision-makers," *International Studies Quarterly* 58, no. 2 (June 2014): 227–46, table 4.

53. This program is described at https://www.cfr.org/fellowships/international-affairs -fellowship.

54. This was part of a larger resurgence of defense-related research across the board on campus in the late 1970s and early 1980s. See Roger L. Geiger, *Research and Relevant Knowledge: American Research Universities Since World War II* (New York: Oxford University Press, 1993), 311–14.

55. Walt, "The Renaissance of Security Studies," 220; and Steven E. Miller, "*International Security* at Twenty-five: From One World to Another," *International Security* 26, no. 1 (Summer 2001): 15.

56. Joseph Kruzel, "Review: More a Chasm Than a Gap, But Do Scholars Want to Bridge It?" *Mershon International Studies Review* 38, no. 1 (April 1994): 179–81.

57. Joseph S. Nye Jr., "Studying World Politics," in Joseph Kruzel and James N. Rosenau, eds., *Journeys through World Politics: Autobiographical Reflections of Thirty-four Academic Travelers* (Lexington, MA: Lexington Books, 1989), 208. Also see 206.

58. Miller, "*International Security* at Twenty-five," 6.

59. Charles S. Maier, with the assistance of Owen Cote, "Peace and Security Studies for the 1990s: An Assessment of the MacArthur-SSRC Fellowship Program in International Peace and Security" (Unpublished ms., Harvard University, June 12, 1990), 23 (copy in author's possession).

60. Ibid., 24.

61. Walt, "The Renaissance of Security Studies," 212, 217–19, and 221.

62. Ibid., 211 and 219. Also see his "Review: The Search for a Science of Strategy: A Review Essay," *International Security* 12, no. 1 (Summer 1987): 142.

63. Miller, "*International Security* at Twenty-five," 14.

64. Jack Snyder, "Richness, Rigor, and Relevance in the Study of Soviet Foreign Policy," *International Security* 9, no. 3 (Winter 1984–85): 90.

65. See Thomas C. Schelling, *The Strategy of Conflict* (Cambridge, Mass.: Harvard University Press, 1960; reprint New York: Oxford University Press, 1963), 8.

66. Walt, "The Search for a Science of Strategy," 144.

67. "Foreword," *International Security* 1, no. 1 (Summer 1976): 2.

68. Robert Jervis, "Security Studies: Ideas, Policy, and Politics," in Edward D. Mansfield and Richard Sisson, eds. *The Evolution of Political Knowledge* (Columbus: Ohio State University Press, 2004), 108.

69. Richard H. Ullman, "Redefining Security," *International Security* 8, no. 1 (Summer 1983): 129–53; and Carol Cohn, "Sex and Death in the Rational World of Defense Intellectuals," *Signs* 12, no. 4 (Summer 1987): 687–718.

70. Maier, "Peace and Security Studies for the 1990s," 31.

71. Ibid., 14.

72. Edited transcription of brief remarks by John Mearsheimer for Panel Discussion at SSRC Conference of MacArthur Foundation Fellows in International Security, Williamsburg, VA, 4 November 1986 (Copy in author's possession).

73. Robert Latham, "Moments of Transformation: The SSRC-MacArthur Foundation Program in International Peace and Security on the Eve of Its 10th Anniversary," *Items: Social Science Research Council* 48, no. 1 (March 1994): 3.

74. "Ruth Adams, 81, Editor of Atomic Bulletin, Dies," *New York Times*, March 14, 2005, at http://www.nytimes.com/2005/03/14/us/ruth-adams-81-editor-of-atomic-bulletin-dies.html? _r=0. On Katzenstein's involvement with SSRC, see his c.v. at http://www.pkatzenstein.org/site

/view/145. Latham acknowledged his input, along with that of SSRC staff, in his report. Katzenstein's particular approach to broadening security studies is evident in his edited volume *The Culture of National Security: Norms and Identity in World Politics* (New York: Columbia University Press, 1996).

75. Latham, "Moments of Transformation," 1, 2, 3. Emphasis added.

76. Ibid., 5 and 6.

77. "National Security, Redefined," *New York Times*, November 10, 1992, 14. Also see Philip Shabecoff, "Traditional Definitions of National Security Are Shaken by Global Environmental Threats," *New York Times*, May 29, 1989, 24; Thomas L. Friedman, "Today's Threat to Peace Is the Guy Down the Street," *New York Times* June 2, 1991, E3; and Jimmy Carter, "Armies Won't Win the Next War," *Los Angeles Times*, July 7, 1991, M5.

78. Jessica Tuchman Mathews, "Redefining Security," *Foreign Affairs* 68, no. 2 (Spring 1989): 162.

79. Steven E. Miller to Derek Bok, November 2, 1989, 2–3 (copy in author's possession).

80. "Rosen is First Kaneb Professor," *Harvard University Gazette*, March 21, 1996, at http://news.harvard.edu/gazette/1996/03.21/RosenisFirstKan.html.

81. Full disclosure: I was one of the junior scholars who interviewed at UCSD at this time. For an account of my experience, see Mike Desch to John Mearsheimer, February 24, 1994 (copy in author's possession).

82. David Lake to John Mearsheimer, September 20, 1993, 1 (copy in author's possession).

83. John Mearsheimer to David Lake, October 14, 1993, 1 and 3 (copy in author's possession).

84. Betts to Haggard, November 16, 1993, 3.

85. Stephan Haggard to John Mearsheimer, October 23, 1993, 3 (copy in author's possession).

86. Peter Gourevitch to Joe Grieco, November 23, 1993, 1. Also see Peter Gourevitch to John Mearsheimer, October 27, 1993, 2 (copies in author's possession).

87. Jack Snyder to David Lake, 26 October 1993, 1–2 (copy in author's possession). Also see Richard Betts to Stephan Haggard, November 16, 1993, 1 and 4 (copy in author's possession).

88. Stephan Haggard to Richard Betts, no date [circa November 30, 1993], 1 (copy in author's possession).

89. Richard Betts to John Mearsheimer, November 30, 1993, 2 (copy in author's possession). Also see Richard Betts to Stephan Haggard, December 2, 1993, 1 (copy in author's possession).

90. Robert O. Keohane to Stephen M. Walt, January 18, 1994, 2 (copy in author's possession).

91. Stephen Haggard to John Mearsheimer, February 1, [1994], 2 (copy in author's possession).

92. Stephen M. Walt to Robert O. Keohane, February 7, 1994, 2 (copy in author's possession).

93. Stephen M. Walt to Stephen Haggard, December 10, 1993, 1; and Peter J. Katzenstein to John Mearsheimer, December 16, 1993, 2 (copies in author's possession).

94. John Lodewijks, "Rostow, Developing Economies, and National Security Policy," in Crawford D. Goodwin, ed., *Economics and National Security* (Durham, NC: Duke University Press. 1991), 285.

95. Charles J. Hitch, "Commencement" (Santa Monica: The RAND Corporation Graduate Institute, October 29, 1974), 3.

96. Robert Jervis, "Change, Surprise, and the Hiding Hand," in Kruzel and Rosenau, eds., *Journeys Through World Politics*, 398–99.

97. Stephen M. Walt, "Rigor or Rigor Mortis? Rational Choice and Security Studies," *International Security* 23, no. 4 (Spring 1999): 46.

98. Stephen M. Walt, "A Model Disagreement," *International Security* 24, no. 2 (Fall 1999): 115; also see 126–28.

99. Bruce Bueno de Mesquita and James D. Morrow, "Sorting Through the Wealth of Notions," *International Security* 24, no. 2 (Fall 1999): 69, 71–72.

100. Lisa Martin, "The Contributions of Rational Choice: A Defense of Pluralism," *International Security* 24, no. 2 (Fall 1999): 78; and Emerson M.S. Niou and Peter C. Ordeshook, "Return of the Luddites," *International Security* 24, no. 2 (Fall 1999): 96.

101. David Baldwin, "Review: Security Studies and the End of the Cold War," *World Politics* 48, no. 1 (October 1995):" 126, 132, and 135–39.

102. Edward A. Kolodziej, "Renaissance in Security Studies? Caveat Lector!" *International Studies Quarterly* 36, no. 4 (December 1992): 424.

103. Ibid., 421.

104. Baldwin, "Security Studies and End of the Cold War," 124 and 125n29.

105. Kolodziej, "Renaissance in Security Studies?" 437.

106. Examples include Barbara F. Walter, "The Critical Barrier to Civil War Settlement," *International Organization* 51, no. 3 (Summer 1997): 335–64; and James D. Fearon and David Laitin, "Ethnicity, Insurgency, and Civil War," *American Political Science Review* 97, no. 1 (February 2003): 75–90.

107. Betts, "Should Strategic Studies Survive?" 9.

108. David Abel, "War's Fall From Grace," *Boston Globe*, January 30, 2001, C1 and C5.

109. Richards J. Heuer, Jr., "Adapting Academic Methods and Models to Government Needs," in Heuer, ed., *Quantitative Approaches to Political Intelligence: The CIA Experience* (Boulder, CO: Westview Press, 1978), 1–2.

110. Michael K. O'Leary, William D. Coplin, Howard B. Shapiro, and Dale Dean, "The Quest for Relevance: Quantitative International Relations Research and Government Foreign Affairs Analysis," *International Studies Quarterly* 18, no. 2 (June 1974): 230.

111. Judith Ayres Daly and Stephen J. Andriole, "The Use of Events/Interaction Research by the Intelligence Community," *Policy Sciences* 12, no. 2 (August 1980): 216–17.

112. Charles A. McClelland, "The Anticipation of International Crises: Prospects for Theory and Research," *International Studies Quarterly* 21, no. 1 (March 1977): 15.

113. Joy Rohde, "Pax Technologica: Computers, International Affairs, and Human Reason in the Age of American Hegemony," unpublished ms., University of Michigan, February 2017, 18.

114. Stephen J. Andriole and Robert A. Young, "Toward the Development of an Integrated Crisis Warning System," *International Security* 21, no. 1 (March 1977): 127n18.

115. Stephen J. Andriole and Gerald W. Hopple, "The Rise and Fall of Event Data: From Basic Research to Applied Use in the U.S. Department of Defense," *International Interactions* 10, nos. 3–4 (1984): 303.

116. Andriole and Young, "Toward the Development of an Integrated Crisis Warning System," 109n6.

117. Andriole and Hopple, "The Rise and Fall of Event Data," 304.

118. For examples, see Jon C. Pevehouse and Joshua S. Goldstein, "Serbian Compliance or Defiance in Kosovo? Statistical Analysis and Real-time Predictions," *Journal of Conflict Resolution* 43, no. 4 (August 1999): 538–46; and Sean P. O'Brien, "Anticipating the Good, the Bad, and the Ugly: An Early Warning Approach to Conflict Instability Analysis," *Journal of Conflict Resolution* 46, no. 6 (December 2002): 791–811.

119. Robert H. Bates, David Epstein, Jack A. Goldstone, Ted Robert Gurr, Barbara Harff, Colin Kahl, Kristen Knight, Marc Levy, Michael Lustik, Monty G. Marshall, Thomas Parris, Jay Ulfelder, and Mark Woodward, "Political Instability Task Force Report: Phase IV Findings," November 18, 2003, 1.

120. Cameron Evers, "The CIA Has a Team of Clairvoyants," *The Week*, July 14, 2016, at http://theweek.com/articles/635515/cia-team-clairvoyants.

121. Daniel C. Esty, Jack A. Goldstone, Ted Robert Gurr, Pamela T. Surko, and Alan N. Unger, "State Failure Task Force Report," November 30, 1995, iii. Also see Daniel C. Esty, Jack A.

Goldstone, Ted Robert Gurr, Barbara Harff, Pamela T. Surko, Alan N. Unger, and Robert Chen, "Failed States and International Security: Causes, Prospects, and Consequences," unpublished paper delivered at Purdue University, February 25–27, 1998, 1.

122. Esty et al., "State Failure Task Force Report," v.

123. Bates et al., "Political Instability Task Force Report," vii.

124. Jack A. Goldstone, Ted Robert Gurr, Barbara Harff, Marc A. Levy, Monty G. Marshall, Robert H. Bates, David L. Epstein, Colin H. Kahl, Pamela T. Surko, John C. Ulfelder, and Alan N. Unger, "State Failure Task Force Report: Phase III Findings," September 30, 2000, 3.

125. Jack A. Goldstone email comment to author, January 21, 2018.

126. Goldstone et al., "State Failure Task Force Report: Phase III Findings, iv.

127. Bates et al., "Political Instability Task Force Report," vii, 111, and 180.

128. Ibid., 1.

129. Esty et al., "Failed States and International Security," 3–4.

130. Goldstone et al., "State Failure Task Force Report: Phase III Findings," iv.

131. Esty et al., "Failed States and International Security," 3.

132. Bates et al., "Political Instability Task Force Report," 11. Also see Jack A. Goldstone, Robert H. Bates, David L. Epstein, Ted Robert Gurr, Michael B. Lustick, Monty G. Marshall, Jay Ulfelder, and Mark Woodward, " A Global Model for Forecasting Political Instability," *American Journal of Political Science* 54, no. 1 (January 2010): 192–93.

133. Daniel C. Esty, Jack A. Goldstone, Ted Robert Gurr, Barbara Harff, Marc Levy, Geoffrey D. Dabelko, Pamela T. Surko, and Alan N. Unger, "State Failure Task Force Report: Phase II Findings," *Environmental Change and Security Project Report* 5 (1999): 66; Marshall, "Fragility, Instability, and the Failure of States," 12; and Bates et al., "Political Instability Task Force Report," 32.

134. Esty et al., "State Failure Task Force Report," viii-ix and 11–12 and Esty et al., "Failed States and International Security,"4.

135. Esty et al., "State Failure Task Force Report: Phase II Findings," 49. Also see 53 and Goldstone et al., "State Failure Task Force Report: Phase III Findings, 14.

136. Bates et al., "Political Instability Task Force Report," vii and 35.

137. Tim Zimmermann, "Why Do Countries Fall Apart? Al Gore Wanted to Know," *U.S. News & World Report*, February 12, 1996, 46.

138. Esty et al., "Failed States and International Security," 8; and Goldstone et al., "State Failure Task Force Report: Phase III Findings, 25 and 61.

139. Esty et al., "State Failure Task Force Report," iii, 16–17, and 19; and Goldstone et al., "State Failure Task Force Report: Phase III Findings," 49 and 52.

140. Marshall, "Fragility, Instability, and the Failure of States," 21.

141. Jack A. Goldstone, "Using Quantitative and Qualitative Models to Forecast Instability," *United States Institute of Peace Special Report*, no. 204 (March 2008): 14.

142. Goldstone, "Using Quantitative and Qualitative Models to Forecast Instability," 4.

143. Goldstone email, July 17, 2017; Goldstone, "Expert Commentary: How Valuable are the Indicators?" *Cyberbrief*, August 18, 2016, at https://www.thecyberbrief.com/article/how-valuable-are-indicators-1091, 2; and Jonathan D. Moyer and Drew Bowlsby, "Do Failed States Fail for the Same Reasons? Tracking Dimensions in the drivers of Political Instability," Paper presented at the International Studies Association Annual Convention, Baltimore, MD, February 2017, 4 and 16.

144. Bates et al., "Political Instability Task Force Report," 2.

145. Goldstone et al., "A Global Model for Forecasting Political Instability," 190–208.

146. Bates et al., "Political Instability Task Force Report," 3–5.

147. Confidential email from PITF member to author, July 17, 2017. Emphasis added.

148. Confidential email from IC official, July 17, 2017.

149. Confidential email from former senior IC official, March 21, 2014.

150. Frederick Barton and Karin von Hippel with Sabina Sequeira and Mark Irvine, "Early Warning? A Review of Conflict Prediction Models and Systems," *PCR Project Special Briefing* (Washington, DC: Center for Strategic and International Studies, February 2008), 11.

151. Ibid., Barton and von Hippel, "Early Warning?" 11–12.

152. Sean P. O'Brien, "Crisis Early Warning and Decision Support: Contemporary Approaches and Thoughts on Future Research," *International Studies Review* 12, no. 1 (March 2010): 99.

153. Goldstone, comments on draft chapter, attached to email to author, January 21, 2018. For discussion of the most recent U.S. government-sponsored forecasting efforts in the national security realm, Zack Beauchamp, "This Study Tried to Improve Our Ability to Predict Major Geopolitical Events. It Worked," *Vox.com*, August 21, 2015, at https://www.vox.com/2015/8/20/9179657/tetlock-forecasting.

154. Heuer, "Adapting Academic Methods and Models to Government Needs," 8; also see 5–6.

155. Stanley A. Feder, "Forecasting for Policy Making in the Post–Cold War Period," *Annual Review of Political Science* 5 (2002): 119.

156. J. Eli Margolis, "Estimating State Instability," *Studies in Intelligence* 56, no. 1 (March 2012): 14.

157. Dr. William Forrest Crain, "The Global War on Terrorism: Analytical Support, Tools, and Metrics Assessment," (Alexandria, VA: Military Operations Research Society, 30 November-2 December 2004), 16.

158. Ibid., 3.

159. Margolis, "Estimating State Instability,"14.

160. Esty et al., "Failed States and International Security," 10.

161. Confidential email to author, July 18, 2017.

162. Goldstone, "Using Quantitative and Qualitative Models to Forecast Instability," 2.

163. Margolis, "Estimating State Instability,"15–16.

164. Cameron Keys, "Historical Perspectives: A Review and Evaluation of 76 Studies of the Defense Research Enterprise, 1945–2015," Undated Department of Defense Report, circa 2015, 28.

165. Richard P. Nathan, *Social Science in Government: Uses and Misuses* (New York: Basic Books, 1988), 14.

166. Eli Berman and Lawrence Freedman, "Transforming Security Research: Summary Report," (Arlington, VA, National Science Foundation, February 26–28, 2013), 8 (copy in author's possession).

167. Nicholas Lemann, "What Terrorists Want," *The New Yorker* October 29, 2001, at http://www.newyorker.com/magazine/2001/10/29/what-terrorists-wants; and Ushma Patel, "Shapiro Brings Scientific Analysis to Terrorism and Counterterrorism Research," *News at Princeton*, January 28, 2010 at https://www.princeton.edu/main/news/archive/S26/46/99M53/index.xml?section=featured.

168. Marc Lynch, "The Political Science of Syria's War," *Foreign Policy* (December 19, 2013), at http://foreignpolicy.com/2013/12/19/the-political-science-of-syrias-war/.

169. See, for example, "The Interpreter" column in *New York Times*, at http://www.nytimes.com/newsletters/the-interpreter?hp&action=click&pgtype=Homepage&clickSource=story-heading&module=second-column-region&region=top-news&WT.nav=top-news.

170. "A Social Contract," *Nature* 454, no. 7201 (July 2008): 138.

171. Defense Science Board, *21ˢᵗ Century Strategic Technology Vectors*, vol. 2, *Critical Capabilities and Enabling Technologies* (Washington, DC: Office of the Under- Secretary of Defense for Acquisition, Technology, and Logistics, February 2007), 27.

172. John Tirman, "Pentagon Priorities and the Minerva Program," *The Minerva Controversy* (New York, The Social Science Research Council, August 30, 2009), 1, 3 (copy in author's possession). Also see Alain Joxe, "Should the Social Sciences Contribute to the Art of War in the

Era of Securitization? Or to Crafting Peace?" *The Minerva Controversy* (New York, The Social Science Research Council, August 30, 2009), 4 (copy in author's possession).

173. Robert J. Art et al., "War with Iraq Is Not in America's National Interest," *New York Times*, September 26, 2002, http://mearsheimer.uchicago.edu/pdfs/P0012.pdf; and Patrick Thadeaus Jackson and Stuart J. Kaufman, "Security Scholars for a Sensible Foreign Policy: A Study in Weberian Activism," *Perspectives on Politics* 5, no. 1 (March 2007): 95–103.

174. Dr. Tom Mahnken, "Building Bridges and Communities," *The Minerva Controversy* (New York, The Social Science Research Council, August 30, 2009), 1, at http://essays.ssrc.org/minerva/2008/12/30/mahnken/.

175. Goldstone, comments on draft chapter.

176. David Rohde, "Army Enlists Anthropology in War Zones," *New York Times*, October 5, 2007, at http://www.nytimes.com/2007/10/05/world/asia/05afghan.html?_r=0.

177. Montgomery McFate, "Anthropology and Counterinsurgency: The Strange Story of Their Curious Relationship," *Military Review* 85, no. 2 (March/April 2005): 24.

178. Max Boot, "Navigating the 'Human Terrain,'" *Los Angeles Times*, December 7, 2005.

179. Jerrold M. Post and Raphael Ezekiel, "Worlds in Collision, Worlds in Collusion: The Uneasy Relationship Between the Counterterrorism Policy Community and the Academic Community," *Terrorism* 11, no. 6 (1988): 503.

180. Annie Jacobsen, "*The Pentagon's Brain: An Uncensored History of DARPA, America's Top Secret Military Research Agency* (New York: Back Bay Books, 2015), 360–63.

181. Crain, "The Global War on Terrorism: Analytical Support, Tools, and Metrics Assessment."

182. Kerry Fosher, "Foreword" to Seymour J. Deitchman, *The Best-Laid Schemes: A Tale of Social Research and Bureaucracy* (Quantico, VA: Marine Corps University Press, 2014), 2.

183. Defense Science Board, *21st Century Strategic Technology Vectors*, vol. 2, 28.

184. Defense Science Board, *21st Century Strategic Technology Vectors*, vol. 1, *Main Report* (Washington, DC: Office of the Under-Secretary of Defense for Acquisition, Technology, and Logistics, February 2007), iii.

185. Keys, "Historical Perspectives," 45.

186. Jeff Bearer, "Introduction" to Deitchman, *The Best-Laid* Schemes, 7–8.

187. Defense Science Board, *21st Century Strategic Technology Vectors*, vol. 1, xiii.

188. James J. Blascovich and Christine R. Hartel, eds., *Human Behavior in Military Contexts* (Washington, DC: The National Academies Press, 2008), 67.

189. Defense Science Board, *21st Century Strategic Technology Vectors*, vol. 2, 29 and 43; and Defense Science Board, *21st Century Strategic Technology Vectors*, vol. 1, 12.

190. "Statement of Dr. Jim Fearon," "Iraq: Democracy or Civil War?" Subcommittee on National Security, Emerging Threats, and International Relations, Committee on Government Reform, House, 109th Cong., 2nd sess., September 15, 2006, 54.

191. McFate, "Anthropology and Counterinsurgency," 28.

192. Dan Ephron and Silvia Spring, "A Gun in One Hand, A Pen in the Other," *Newsweek* April 21, 2008, 34.

193. See for example "Statement of Colonel Martin P. Schweitzer, Command, 4/82 Airborne Brigade Combat Team, United States Army Before the House Armed Services Committee, Terrorism & Unconventional Threats Sub-committee and the Research & Education Sub-committee of the Science & Technology Committee," United States House of representative, 110th Congress, 2nd Session, Hearings on the Role of the Social and Behavioral Science in National Security, 24 April 2008 (copy in author's possession).

194. Farah Stockman, "Anthropologist's War Death Reverberates," *Boston Globe*, February 12, 2009, A1. Also see Hugh Gusterson, "The U.S. Military's Quest to Weaponize Culture," *Bulletin of Atomic Scientists* 20 June 2008, at http://thebulletin.org/us-militarys-quest-to-weaponize

-culture; and Hugh Gusterson, "When Professors Go to War," foreignpolicy.com, July 2008, at http://foreignpolicy.com/2008/07/21/when-professors-go-to-war/.

195. "Failure in the Field," *Nature* 456, no. 7223 (December 2008): 676.

196. Defense Science Board, *21st Century Strategic Technology Vectors,* vol. 1, 13.

197. Crain, "The Global War on Terrorism," 1–2.

198. Ibid., 104.

199. Ibid., 68.

200. Ibid., 25.

201. Ibid., 3. Also cf. 10.

202. Copy of original Minerva Minerva Broad Agency Announcement in author's possession.

203. Ibid.

204. Patricia Cohen, "Pentagon to Consult Academics on Security," *New York Times*, June 18, 2008, at http://www.nytimes.com/2008/06/18/arts/18minerva.html.

205. Mahnken, "Building Bridges and Communities," 1.

206. Eric Edelman email to author, June 10, 2010. A trial balloon for this idea apparently floated in Jonathan Stevenson, "We Need a New Think Tank for the War on Terror," *Wall Street Journal*, August 7, 2008, A11.

207. Robert M. Gates email to author, June 13, 2010.

208. Robert M. Gates, "Speech Delivered to the Association of American Universities," Washington, D.C. Monday, April 14, 2008, at http://archive.defense.gov/Speeches/Speech .aspx?SpeechID=1228. Also see Catherine Lutz, "The Perils of Pentagon Funding for Anthropology and the Other Social Sciences," *The Minerva Controversy* (New York, The Social Science Research Council, August 30, 2009), 1 (copy in author's possession).

209. Dr. Setha Low, President of American Anthropological Association to Hon. Jim Nussle, Office of Management and Budget, May 28, 2008, 1 (copy in author's possession).

210. Cohen, "Pentagon to Consult Academics on Security."

211. Mahnken, "Building Bridges and Communities," 2. Also see Thomas Asher, "Making Sense of Minerva Controversy and NSCC," *The Minerva Controversy* (New York, The Social Science Research Council, August 30, 2009), 1 (copy in author's possession).

212. Dr. Mark L. Weiss, Division Director, Division of Behavioral and Cognitive Sciences, Directorate of Social, Behavioral and Economic Sciences, National Science Foundation, "Testimony Before the Committee on Armed Services Subcommittee on Terrorism, Unconventional Threats and Capabilities and Committee on Science and Technology Subcommittee on Research and Science Education United States House of Representatives," April 24, 2008, 1, at https://www.nsf.gov/about/congress/110/mweiss_natlsecurity_042408.jsp.

213. "Social and Behavioral Dimensions of National Security, Conflict, and Cooperation (NSCC)" at https://www.nsf.gov/funding/pgm_summ.jsp?pims_id=503294.

214. 2008 version of Program Solicitation, "Social and Behavioral Dimensions of National Security, Conflict, and Cooperation (NSC), NSF 08–594, Washington, DC, August 30, 2008, 9–10. (copy in author's possession).

215. Author interview with Dr. Thomas Mahnken, October 31, 2013, 1–2.

216. Mahnken, Building Bridges and Communities," 3. Emphasis added.

217. "NSF Signs Memorandum of Understanding with Department of Defense for National Security Research," Press Release 08–11, July 2, 2008 at https://www.nsf.gov/news/news _summ.jsp?cntn_id=111829. Emphasis added.

218. See discussion in "Hearing on National Defense Authorization Act for Fiscal Year 2009 and Oversight of Previously Authorized Programs," Committee on Armed Services, House, 110th Cong., 2nd sess., April 24, 2008, 19.

219. 2008 version of Program Solicitation, 4.

220. Office of the Under Secretary of Defense for Acquisition, Technology, and Logistics, "Report to the Armed Services Committees, Coordination of the Minerva Program, the Human Social Culture Behavior Modeling Program and Strategic Multi-Layer Assessment Efforts," (Washington, DC: OSD, August 1, 2015), 1. According to Russell Rumbaugh with John Cappel, "National Security Programs Supporting Social Science in Academia," (Washington, DC: The Stimson Center, January 2014), HSCB is slated to be phased out.

221. Yudhijit Bhattacharjee, "Pentagon Asks Academics for Help in Understanding Its Enemies," *Science* 316, no. 5824 (27 April 2007): 534–35.

222. David C. Engerman, "Jihadology: How the Creation of Sovietology Should Guide the Study of Today's Threats," *Foreign Affairs.com*, December 8, 2009. Also see HRG-2009-ASH-0102: Understanding Cyberspace as a Medium for Radicalization and Counter-Radicalization, Committee on Armed Services, House of Representatives, December 16, 2009, 20, Dr. Jarret Brachman, Author, "Global Jihadism: Theory and Practice," at http://congressional.proquest.com .proxy.library.nd.edu/congressional/docview/t29.d30.hrg-2009-ash-0102?accountid=12874.

223. Ron Robin, "The Minerva Controversy, A Cautionary Tale," *The Minerva Controversy* (New York, The Social Science Research Council, August 30, 2009), 1 (copy in author's possession).

224. Ron Krebs, "Minerva: Unclipping the Owl's Wings," *The Minerva Controversy* (New York, The Social Science Research Council, August 30, 2009), 2 (copy in author's possession).

225. Priya Satia, "The Forgotten History of Knowledge and Power in British Iraq, or Why Minerva's Owl Cannot Fly," *The Minerva Controversy* (New York, The Social Science Research Council, August 30, 2009), 4 (copy in author's possession).

226. Hugh Gusterson, "Unveiling Minerva," *The Minerva Controversy* (New York, The Social Science Research Council, August 30, 2009), 1 (copy in author's possession).

227. Joy Rohde, *Armed With Expertise: The Militarization of American Social Research During the Cold War* (Ithaca, NY: Cornell University Press, 2013), 153.

228. Thomas G. Mahnken, "Bridging the Gap Between the Worlds of Ideas and Action," *Orbis* 54, no. 1 (Winter 2010): 8.

229. This is also the retrospective judgment of Mahnken, one of the original proponents of Minerva. See his "The Military and the Academy: Overcoming the Divide," foreignaffairs.com, May 2016, at https://www.foreignaffairs.com/articles/2016-05-06/military-and-academy.

230. HRG-2011-TEC-0021: Social, Behavioral, and Economic Science Research: Oversight of the Need for Federal Investments and Priorities for Funding, Committee on Science, Space and Technology, House of Representatives, June 2, 2011, 67, Dr. Myron Gutmann, Assistant Director, Directorate for Social, Behavioral, and Economics Sciences, National Science Foundation, at http://congressional.proquest.com.proxy.library.nd.edu/congressional/docview/t29 .d30.hrg-2011-tec-0021/usgLogRstClick!!?accountid=12874.

231. Weiss, "Testimony Before the Committee on Armed Services Subcommittee on Terrorism," 3.

232. HRG-2015-HAP-0062: Department of Defense Appropriations for 2016, Part 2, Committee on Appropriations, House of Representatives, March 24, 26, April 14–15, 2015, 441–44, Prepared Statement of Heather O'Beirne Kelly, Ph.D., Lead Psychologist, Military and Veterans Policy, American Psychology Association, at http://congressional.proquest.com.proxy.library .nd.edu/congressional/docview/t29.d30.hrg-2015-hap-0062?accountid=12874.

233. Author interview with Anne Dreazen, OSD Policy Program Manager for Minerva from 2009–2011, October 28, 2013, 3.

234. Interview with Mahnken, 5–6. Also see interview with Dreazen, 1.

235. Geiger, *Research and Relevant Knowledge*, 28.

236. Erin Fitzgerald, Program Director, Minerva Research Initiative, ASD (R&E) Basic Research, email to author, November 7, 2013.

237. Erin Fitzgerald, "The Legislative History of the Minerva Research Initiative," Power Point slides, 24 October 2013, 3 and 8. Emphasis in original (copy in author's possession).

238. Interview with Mahnken, 4. Also see author interview with Interview with Dreazen, 1–2, and Fitzgerald, "The Legislative History of the Minerva Research Initiative," 2.

239. HRG-2009-SAS-0026: Nominations Before the Senate Armed Services Committee, First Session, 111th Congress, March 26, April 28, May 12, June 2, 11, July 9, 30, September 15, October 22, November 19, December 17, 2009, 141. Also see the exchange between Senator Jack Reed and Deputy Secretary of Defense Michele Flournoy, at http://congressional.proquest.com.proxy.library.nd.edu/congressional/docview/t29.d30.hrg-2009-sas-0026/usgLogRstClick!!?accountid=12874.

240. Mackenzie Eaglen, "Taking a Scalpel to the Defense Budget, *WebMemo*, no. 3132 (February 3, 2011): cited in HRG-2012-BGS-0002: Concurrent Resolution on the Budget Fiscal Year 2013, February 1–2, 7, 9, 14–16, 28, March 1, 6, 2012, 1089, at http://congressional.proquest.com.proxy.library.nd.edu/congressional/docview/t29.d30.hrg-2012-bgs-0002?accountid=12874.

241. Interview with Dreazen, 2.

242. Berman and Freedman, "Transforming Security Research," 7.

243. List available at http://www3.nd.edu/~carnrank/.

244. "Assessing China's Efforts to Become an 'Innovation Society'—A Progress Report," HRG-2012-ESR-0004, Hearing Before the U.S.-China Economic and Security Review Commission, 112th Congress, Second Session, Statement of Dr. Thomas Mahnken, Professor of Strategy, U.S. Naval War College, 143, at http://congressional.proquest.com.proxy.library.nd.edu/congressional/docview/t29.d30.hrg-2012-esr-0004?accountid=12874. Also see interview with Mahnken, 3.

245. "Department of Defense Authorization for Appropriations for Fiscal Year 2012 and the Future Years Defense Program, Part 1," HRG-2011-SAS-0020, Committee on Armed Services, Senate, March 1, 8, 17, 29, 31, April 5, 7, 12, May 19, 2011, 236, Admiral Eric T. Olson, USN, Commander, U.S. Special Operations Command, at http://congressional.proquest.com.proxy.library.nd.edu/congressional/docview/t29.d30.hrg-2011-sas-0020?accountid=12874.

246. Interview with Mahnken. 3.

247. After identifying the universe of Minerva-supported peer-reviewed articles, I had two research assistants code them in terms of whether they offered explicit policy recommendations. This follows the approach taken by the TRIP journal project. They came up with estimates of between 17 and 26 percent. I then looked at the articles where their coding was inconsistent and made my own assessment, which gave us a final figure of slightly more than 24 percent. This is better than the current 5 percent average for scholarly international relations journals but substantially less than the 36 percent of the leading security studies journals such as *International Security*. The list of articles and our codings are at http://www3.nd.edu/~carnrank/.

248. Berman and Freedman, "Transforming Security Research," 6.

249. See "Minerva-USIP Peace and security Collaboration," at http://minerva.defense.gov/Programs/US-Institute-of-Peace-Collaboration/.

250. Keys, "Historical Perspectives," 22, 24.

251. Deitchman, *The Best-Laid Schemes*, 175.

252. Alan Wolfe, "Academia (Kind of) Goes to War: Chomsky and His Children," *World Affairs* (Winter 2008), at http://www.worldaffairsjournal.org/article/academia-kind-goes-war-chomsky-and-his-children. Also see Joan Johnson-Freese and Thomas M. Nichols, "Academic Stovepipes Undermine U.S. Security," *World Politics Review* April 14, 2011, at, http://live.belfercenter.org/publication/20943/academic_stovepipes_undermine_us_security.html?breadcrumb=%2Fexperts%2F1818%2Fthomas_m_nichols.

Chapter 9. Conclusions, Responses to Objections, and Scholarly Recommendations

1. A good example is Edward D. Mansfield and Jack Snyder, *Electing to Fight: Why Emerging Democracies Go to War* (Cambridge: MIT Press, 2005), a précis of which was published as Edward Mansfield and Jack Snyder, "Democratization and War," *Foreign Affairs* 74, no. 3 (May/June 1995): 79–97. Their argument was picked up by the National Intelligence Council, *Global Trends: 2030* (Washington, DC: NIC, 2012). Also see Erik Gartzke's various Minerva-supported research projects at http://erikgartzke.com/projects.html.

2. For an embarrassing example of how postmodern flights of rhetorical fancy took in even other scholars, see Alan D. Sokal, "Transgressing the Boundaries—Toward a Transformative Hermeneutics of Quantum Gravity," *Social Text* 46/47 (1996): 217–52.

3. Roger Hilsman, Jr., "Intelligence and Policy-Making in Foreign Affairs," *World Politics* 5, no. 1 (October 1952): 13; and Klaus Knorr, "Failures in National Intelligence Estimates: The Case of the Cuban Missiles," *World Politics* Vol. 16, no. 3 (April 1964): 465–66. Also see Joseph Nye, "International Relations: The Relevance of Theory to Practice," *Oxford Handbook of International Relations*," in Christian Reus-Smit and Duncan Snidal, eds. (New York: Oxford University Press, 2008), 648.

4. Quoted in Nicolas Guilhot, ed., *The Invention of International Relations Theory: Realism, the Rockefeller Foundation, and the 1954 Conference on Theory* (New York: Columbia University Press, 2011), 258.

5. George F. Kennan, *American Diplomacy, 1900–1950* (Chicago: University of Chicago Press, 1951), 38.

6. Michael Maccoby, "Social Scientists on War and Peace: An Essay-Review," *Social Problems* 11, no. 1 (Summer 1963): 106–7. Also see Alain C. Enthoven and K. Wayne Smith, *How Much Is Enough? Shaping the Defense Program, 1961–1969* (Santa Monica: RAND, 2005), chapter 3.

7. "Remarks of Dr. Hans Speier," in William A. Lybrand, ed., *Symposium Proceedings: The U.S. Army's Limited-War Mission and Social Science Research* (Washington, DC: SORO, March 26–28, 1962), 292.

8. Michael Howard, "The Classical Strategists," *Adelphi Papers* 54 (London: IISS, 1969): 19.

9. Robert K. Merton, "Role of the Intellectual in Public Bureaucracy," *Social Forces* 23, no. 4 (May 1945): 412. Also see Maurice Matloff, Office of the Secretary of Defense, Oral History, Albert Wohlstetter, January 30, 1986, Los Angeles, 4 and 29.

10. On this last, see Robert Jervis, ed., ISSF Roundtable on "Politics and Scholarship," *H-Diplo/ISSF* on June 1, 2010, at http://www.h-net.org/~diplo/ISSF/PDF/ISSF-Roundtable-1-2.pdf.

11. David D. Newsome, "Foreign Policy and Academia," *Foreign Policy* 101 (Winter 1995–1996): 55.

12. Though he does not use the phrase "marketplace of ideas," John Stuart Mill, *On Liberty* (Indianapolis, IN: Bobbs-Merrill, 1956), 19–66, provides the rationale for it. The system of checks and balances in which "ambition must be made to counteract ambition" is famously outlined in "Federalist #51," in Alexander Hamilton, James Madison, and John Jay, *The Federalist Papers* (New York: Mentor, 1961), 322.

13. Chaim Kaufmann, "Threat Inflation and the Marketplace of Ideas: The Selling of the Iraq War," *International Security* 29, no. 1 (Summer 2004): 36; and Jon Western, "The War Over Iraq: Selling the War to the American Public," *Security Studies* 14, no. 1 (January–March 2005): 102.

14. Derek C. Bok, "The Federal Government and the University," *Public Interest* 58 (Winter 1980): 82. Also see Richard Hofstadter, *Anti-Intellectualism in American Life* (New York: Vintage), 429.

15. John Kenneth Galbraith, "Power and the Useful Economist," *American Economic Review* 63, no. 1 (March 1973): 2.

16. McGeorge Bundy, "The Battlefields of Power and the Searchlights of the Academy," in *The Dimensions of Diplomacy*, ed. E. A. J. Johnson (Baltimore, 1964), 15.

17. N. Gregory Mankiw, "A Quick Refresher Course in Macroeconomics," *Journal of Economic Literature* 28, no. 4 (December 1990): 1659.

18. Rodney W. Nichols, "Mission-Oriented R&D," *Science* 172, no. 3978 (2 April 1971): 34. More recently on this theme, see Emily J. Levine and Mitchell L. Stevens, "The Right Way to Fix Universities," *New York Times,* December 1, 2017, A25.

19. For an extreme example of initial optimism about the compatibility of cutting-edge social science and policy relevance soon souring when the tensions between them developed, see Dawn Rhodes, "Pearson Family Members Foundation Sues University of Chicago, Aiming to Revoke $100m Gift," *Chicago Tribune*, March 6, 2018 at http://www.chicagotribune.com/news/local/breaking/ct-met-university-of-chicago-donation-lawsuit-20180305-story.html.

20. Joseph Lepgold and Miroslav Nincic, *Beyond the Ivory Tower: International Relations Theory and the Issue of Policy Relevance* (New York: Columbia University Press, 2001), 108–37. Also see Joseph Lepgold, "Policy Relevance and Theoretical Development in International Relations," in Miroslav Nincic and Lepgold, eds., *Being Useful: The Policy Relevance of International Relations Theory* (Ann Arbor: University of Michigan Press, 2000), 364.

21. Jack Levy, "Domestic Politics and War," in *The Origin and Prevention of Major Wars*, ed. Robert I. Rotberg and Theodore K. Rabb (Cambridge: Cambridge University Press, 1988), 88. Also see Azar Gat, "The Democratic Peace Theory Reframed: The Impact of Modernity," *World Politics* 58, no. 1 (October 2005): 73.

22. Frieden and Lake, "International Relations as a Social Science: Rigor and Relevance," 142. Also see Bueno de Mesquita, "The Methodical Study of Politics," in Shapiro, Smith, and Masoud, *Problems and Methods in the Study of Politics*, 232.

23. A. Bennett and G. John Ikenberry, "The *Review's* Evolving Relevance for U.S. Foreign Policy," *American Political Science Review* 100, no. 4 (2006): 655–56.

24. Joseph Kruzel, "Review: More of a Chasm Than a Gap, But Do Scholars Want to Bridge It?" *Mershon International Studies Review* 38, no. 1 (1994): 180.

25. Michael W. Doyle, "Kant, Liberal Legacies and Foreign Affairs," *Philosophy and Public Affairs, I and II* 12, nos. 3 and 4 (1983): 205–235, and 323–353.

26. Inderjeet Parmar, "The 'Knowledge Politics' of Democratic Peace Theory," *International Politics* 50, no. 2 (2013): 234.

27. Anthony Lake, "From Containment to Enlargement," Johns Hopkins University, School of Advanced International Studies, September 21, 1993, 6. The oblique "waves" reference is clearly to Samuel P. Huntington, *The Third Wave: Democratization in the Late Twentieth Century* (Norman: University of Oklahoma Press, 1991).

28. Paul C. Avey and Michael C. Desch, "What Do Policymakers Want From Us? Results of a Survey of Current and Former Senior National Security Decision-makers," *International Studies Quarterly* 58, no. 2 (June 2014): table 6.

29. Michael Desch, "America's Liberal Illiberalism: The Ideological Origins of Overreaction in U.S. Foreign Policy," *International Security* 32, no. 3 (Winter 2007/08): 7–43.

30. Hal Brands, "Why Scholars and Policymakers Disagree," *American Interest* 13, no. 1 (June 2017), at https://www.the-american-interest.com/2017/06/05/why-scholars-and-policymakers-disagree/. Also see Hal Brands and Peter Feaver, "Saving Realism from the So-Called Realists," *Commentary*, August 14, 2017, at https://www.commentarymagazine.com/articles/saving-realism-called-realists/. The most influential statement of neorealism is Kenneth Waltz, *Theory of International Politics* (Reading, MA: Addison-Wesley, 1979).

31. Kenneth Waltz, "The Spread of Nuclear Weapons: More May Be Better," *Adelphi Papers* 171 (London: International Institute for Strategic Studies, 1981).

32. Peter D. Feaver, "Optimists, Pessimists, and Theories of Nuclear Proliferation: Debate," *Security Studies* 4, no. 4 (1995): 770; and Francis J. Gavin, "Politics, History, and the Ivory Tower-Policy Gap in the Nuclear Proliferation Debate," *Journal of Strategic Studies* 35, no. 4 (2012): 597.

33. Nicolas Guilhot, "The Realist Gambit: Post-war American Political Science and the Birth of IR Theory," *International Political Sociology* 2, no. 4 (2008): 282–83.

34. "Remarks of Dr. Daniel Lerner" and "Remarks of Dr. Leonard Doob," in William A. Lybrand, ed., *Symposium Proceedings: The U.S. Army's Limited-War Mission and Social Science Research* (Washington, DC: SORO, March 26–28, 1962), 236, 284.

35. Testimony of Prof. Kalman Silvert, President, Latin American Studies association, and Professor of Government, Dartmouth College," "Federal Support of International Social Science and Behavioral Research," Subcommittee on Government Research, Committee on Government Operations, U.S. Senate, 89th Cong., 2nd sess., June 27, 28; July 19, 20, 1966, 230. Also see Nathan, *Social Science in Government*.

36. Beate Jahn, "Theorizing the Political Relevance of International Relations Theory," *International Studies Quarterly* 61, no. 1 (March 2017): 64.

37. William A. Lybrand in Lybrand, *Symposium Proceedings*, xi.

38. Testimony of John K. Plank, Director of Political Development Studies, Brookings Institution, Washington, DC, "Federal Support of International Social Science and Behavioral Research," Subcommittee on Government Research, Committee on Government Operations, U.S. Senate, 89th Cong., 2nd sess., June 27, 28; July 19, 20, 1966, 260.

39. Daniel W. Drezner, "What Nick Kristof Doesn't Get About the Ivory Tower," *Politico*, February 21, 2014, at http://www.politico.com/magazine/story/2014/02/nick-kristof-academics-rebuttal-103786. Also see Henry Farrell and Daniel W. Drezner, "The Power and Politics of Blogs," *Public Choice* 134, nos. 1 and 2 (January 2008): 15–30; and John Sides, "The Political Scientist as a Blogger," *PS: Political Science and Politics* 44, no. 2 (April 2011): 267–71.

40. Marc Lynch, "Political Science in Real Time: Engaging the Middle East Policy Public," *Perspectives on Politics* 14, no. 1 (March 2016): 128. Also see Mark Lynch, "After the Political Science Relevance Revolution," *The Monkey Cage*, March 23, 2016, at https://www.washingtonpost.com/news/monkey-cage/wp/2016/03/23/after-the-political-science-relevance-revolution/; and Ezra Klein, "How Political Science Conquered Washington," *Vox*, September 14, 2014 at http://www.vox.com/2014/9/2/6088485/how-political-science-conquered-washington.

41. Bruce E. Cain and Lynn Vavreck, "Keeping It Contemporary: Report to the American Political Science Association of the Ad Hoc Committee on the Public Understanding of Political Science" (Washington, DC: APSA, 2014), 3.

42. Lynch, "Political Science in Real Time," 122.

43. A 2018 survey of senior national policymakers found that "blogs" (10.6 percent) and "social media" (2.5 percent) were far less often listed as "very important sources of information" than "classified reports" (81.7 percent) and "newspapers and magazines" (66.8 percent). Preliminary results of joint Notre Dame International Security Center/ TRIP Policymaker survey. Results available at http://www3.nd.edu/~carnrank/.

44. For evidence that only a handful of blogs associated with traditional media connections get much attention, see 2018 Policymaker Survey results. Even the *Washington Post*–affiliated "The Monkey Cage," the most prominent academic political science blog, has far less valence among policymakers than the blogs associated with foreignpolicy.com (about 18 percent of national security policymakers were familiar with the former, compared to 66 percent for the latter). Blogs like PoliticalViolence@aGlance, which tend to feature exclusively quantitative and formal political science research had even lower recognition among national security policy-

makers, with less than 3 percent noting familiarity with it. Again, full results at http://www3
.nd.edu/~carnrank/.

45. Craig Calhoun, "Word From the President: Toward a More Public Social Science," *Items
and Issues* 5, nos. 1–2 (2004): 12.

46. Michael C. Desch, "Results of a Survey of APSIA Deans and Chairs of Top 50 Political Science Departments," Webinar, Association of Professional School of International Affairs,
New York, NY, January 2017. Full results available at http://www3.nd.edu/~carnrank/.

47. Tanisha Fazal, "An Occult of Irrelevance? Multimethod Research and Engagement with
the Policy World," *Security Studies* 25, no. 1 (January–March 2016): 35.

48. David Hounshell, "The Cold War, RAND, and the Generation of Knowledge, 1946–
1962," *RAND History Project* [RP-729] (Santa Monica: RAND, 1998), 254–55.

49. Ibid., 253. Also see Michael Bernstein, "American Economics and the National Security
State," *Radical History Review* 63, no. 3 (Fall 1995): 14.

50. Quoted in Joseph Kraft, "RAND: Arsenal for Ideas," *Harper's Magazine* (July 1960): 76.

51. James Piereson, "The Problem With Public Policy Schools," *Washington Post*, December 6.

52. Chalmers Johnson, "To My Friends and Colleagues: A Note on the Crisis in Japanese
Studies at UCSD and My Position on It," February 20, 1994, 1 (copy in author's possession).
Also see Dan Hattis, "Toward a New Orthodoxy," *UCSD Guardian*, April 25, 1994, 5–6; Chalm-
ers Johnson, "Hurleyism Swamps Foggy Bottom," *Los Angeles Times*, February 3, 1994, http://
articles.latimes.com/1994-02-03/local/me-18414_1_u-s-foreign-policy; and Chalmers Johnson,
"Preconception vs. Observation, or the Contributions of Rational Choice Theory and Area
Studies to Contemporary Political Science," *PS: Political Science and Politics* 30, no. 2 (June
1997): 170.

53. Avey and Desch, "What Policy Makers Want from Us?" table 4.

54. Frieden and Lake, "International Relations as Social Science," 151.

55. Helga Nowotny, Peter Scott, and Michael Gibbins, "Introduction: 'Mode 2' Revisited:
The New Production of Knowledge," *Minerva* 41, no. 3 (2003): 179.

56. Richard P. Nathan, *Social Science in Government: Uses and Misuses* (New York: Basic
Books, Inc., 1988), xiii.

57. Richards J. Heuer, Jr., "Adapting Academic Methods and Models to Government Needs,"
in Heuer, ed., *Quantitative Approaches to Political Intelligence: The CIA Experience* (Boulder, CO:
Westview Press, 1978), 3.

58. See Laura Sjoberg, "Locating Relevance in Security Studies"; Helen Louis Turton,
"'Please Mind the Gap': Policy Relevance and British IR"; and Eric Voeten, "Rigor Is Not the
Enemy of Relevance," *Perspectives on Politics* 13, no. 2 (June 2015): 396–98, 399–401, and 402–3;
and Michael Horowitz, "What is Policy Relevance?" *War on the Rocks* June 17, 2015, at http://
warontherocks.com/2015/06/what-is-policy-relevance/.

59. This is an example of what John Gerring, *Case Study Research: Principles and Practices*
(New York: Cambridge University Press, 2007), 53–54, calls "strong causal strength."

60. Daniel W. Drezner, *The Ideas Industry: How Pessimists, Partisans, and Plutocrats Are
Transforming the Marketplace of Ideas* (New York: Oxford University Press, 2017), 104.

61. Abhijit Banerjee, Angus Deaton, Nora Lustig, and Ken Rogoff, "An Evaluation of World
Bank Research, 1998–2005," September 24, 2006, 7, at http://siteresources.worldbank.org
/DEC/Resources/84797-1109362238001/726454-1164121166494/RESEARCH-EVALUATION
-2006-Main-Report.pdf.

62. Ibid., 74. Emphasis in original.

63. Laying out, but not endorsing, this argument, is Peter deLeon, "The Influence of Analysis on U.S. Defense Policy," *Policy Sciences* 20, no. 2 (June 1987): 108–9.

64. Paul Romer, "The Trouble With Macroeconomics," Commons Memorial Lecture of the Omicron Delta Society, January 5, 2016, 13.

65. On this, see *Wall Street Journal* reporter Scott Patterson's, *The Quants: How a New Breed of Math Whizzes Conquered Wall Street and Nearly Destroyed It* (New York: Crown, 2010).

66. Paul Krugman, "How Did Economists Get It So Wrong?" *New York Times Magazine*, September 6, 2009, 37. Also see Neil Irwin, "Ask a Sociologist to Fix the Economy," *New York Times*, March 19, 2017, Week in Review, 7.

67. See Stephen Budiansky, *Blackett's War: The Men Who Defeated the Nazi U-boats and Brought Science to the Art of Warfare* (New York: Knopf, 2013), 147–49.

68. Robert Gilpin, *American Scientists and Nuclear Weapons Policy* (Princeton, NJ: Princeton University Press, 1962), 154, 166.

69. Quoted in James G. Hershberg, *James B. Conant: Harvard to Hiroshima and the Making of the Nuclear Age* (Palo Alto: Stanford University Press, 1993), 196.

70. "Not enough time to follow academic work" is the reason cited by 62 percent of national security policymakers as an obstacle to them using academic work in the 2018 Policymaker Survey.

71. Avey and Desch, "What Policy Makers Want from Us?" 228. Excellent advice about how learn these skills is available in Daniel Byman and Matthew Kroenig, "Reaching Beyond the Ivory Tower: A How to Manual," *Security Studies* 25, no. 2 (April–June 2016): 289–319; and through the various programs of "The Bridging the Gap" Project at http://bridgingthegap project.org/.

72. My thinking on these bigger issues owes much to Stephen Van Evera, "U.S. Social Science and International Relations," February 9, 2015, at https://warontherocks.com/2015 /02/u-s-social-science-and-international-relations/.

73. Hans Morgenthau, "The Purpose of Political Science," in James C. Charlesworth, ed., *A Design for Political Science; Scope, Objectives, and Methods* (Philadelphia, PA: American Academy of Political and Social Science, 1966), 79. Also see "Remarks of Dr. John W. Riley, Jr.," in William A. Lybrand, ed., *Symposium Proceedings: The U.S. Army's Limited-War Mission and Social Science Research* (Washington, DC: SORO, March 26–28, 1962), 155.

74. Rogers M. Smith, "Of Means and Meaning," in Kristen Renwick Monroe, ed., *Perestroika: The Raucous Rebellion in Political Science* (New Haven, CT: Yale University Press, 2005), 531.

75. Rogers M. Smith, "Still Blowing in the Wind: The American Quest for a Democratic, Scientific Political Science," *Daedalus* 126, no. 1 (Winter 1997): 275.

76. See his "The Implications of Theory for Practice in the Conduct of Foreign Affairs," in Guilhot, *The Invention of International Relations Theory*, 276.

77. Wohlstetter, Oral History, 2–3.

78. Bruce Kuklick, *Blind Oracles: Intellectuals and War from Kennan to Kissinger* (Princeton, NJ: Princeton University Press, 2006), 40–41.

79. For a general discussion of various facets of this phenomenon, see James A. Smith, *The Idea Brokers: Think Tanks and the Rise of the New Policy Elite* (New York: The Free Press, 1991); David M. Ricci, *The Transformation of American Politics: The New Washington and the Rise of Think Tanks* (New Haven: Yale University Press, 1993); Donald E. Abelson, *Do Think Tanks Matter? Assessing the Impact of Public Policy Institutes* (Montreal: McGill-Queens University Press, 2002); and Andrew Rich, *Think Tanks, Public Policy, and the Politics of Expertise* (New York: Cambridge University Press, 2004).

80. F. A. Hayek, "The Dilemma of Specialization," in Leonard D. White, ed., *The State of the Social Sciences* (Chicago: University of Chicago Press, 1956), 470.

81. Ernest J. Wilson III, "How Social Science Can Help Policymakers: The Relevance of Theory," in Nincic and Lepgold, eds., *Being Useful*, 118.

82. Bob Woodward, *Plan of Attack* (New York: Simon and Schuster, 2004), 88.

83. Bruce Russett, "Bushwhacking the Democratic Peace," *International Studies Perspectives* 6, no. 4 (2005): 395–408.

84. Miguel Angel Centano, "The New Leviathan: The Dynamics and Limits of Technocracy," *Theory and Society* 22, no. 3 (June 1993): 312. Also see the related discussion in Carl Kaysen, "Model-Makers and Decision-makers: Economists and the Policy Process," *The Public Interest* 12 (Summer 1968): 80–95.

85. Alexander L. George, *Bridging the Gap: Theory and Practice in Foreign Policy* (Washington, DC: U.S. Institute of Peace, 1993), 15.

86. Max Weber, "Politics As a Vocation," in H. H. Gerth and C. Wright Mills, eds., *From Max Weber: Essays in Sociology* (New York: Oxford University Press, 1946), 93–94.

87. Hilsman, "Intelligence and Policy-Making in Foreign Affairs," 22–24, 43.

88. Kruzel, "More of a Chasm Than a Gap," 180. See also, Stephen Krasner, "Garbage Cans and Policy Streams: How Academic Research Might Affect Foreign Policy," *Power, the State, and Sovereignty: Essays on International Relations* (London: Taylor and Francis, 2009), 259.

89. Allen E. Goodman, "Vietnam and the Limits of Scholarly Intervention," *Freedom at Issue* (1973): 17, who argued that scholars can only have influence through "advocacy" and not through "opposition."

90. Thomas C. Schelling, *The Strategy of Conflict* (Cambridge, Mass.: Harvard University Press, 1960; reprint New York: Oxford University Press, 1963), 10n4. Copyright © 1960, 1980 by the President and Fellows of Harvard College. Copyright renewed 1988 by Thomas C. Schelling.

91. Derek C. Bok, "The Federal Government and the University," *The Public Interest* 58 (Winter 1980): 83–84.

92. Quoted in Wesley W. Widmar, "Theory as a Factor and the Theorist as an Actor: The 'Pragmatist Constructivist' Lessons of John Dewey and John Kenneth Galbraith," *International Studies Review* 6, no. 3 (2004): 435.

93. Harry Kriesler, "Through the Realist Lens," *Conversations With History*, April 8, 2002, section 4, at http://globetrotter.berkeley.edu/people2/Mearsheimer/mearsheimer-con0.html.

94. Carol Gruber, *Mars and Minerva: World War I and the Uses of Higher Learning in America* (Baton Rogue: Louisiana State University Press, 1975), 5, 259.

95. Edward Shils, "Social Science and Social Policy," *Philosophy of Science* 16 (1949): 230.

96. Anne Norton, "Political Science as a Vocation," in Ian Shapiro, Rogers M. Smith, and Tarek E. Masoud, eds., *Problems and Methods in the Study of Politics* (New York: Cambridge University Press), 67–68.

97. David Easton, "Harold Lasswell: Policy Scientist for a Democratic Society," *Journal of Politics* 12, no. 3 (August 1950): 454.

98. Max Weber, "The Meaning of 'Ethical Neutrality' in Sociology and Economics," in Edward Shills and Henry A. Finch, eds. and trans., *The Methodology of the Social Sciences* (New York: The Free Press, 1949), 5.

99. Ibid., 6–7. Also see Max Weber, "Science As a Vocation," in Gerth and Mills, *From Max Weber*, 129–58.

100. This debate is beginning belatedly in economics, largely as a result not only of the intellectual failure of the discipline of economics to anticipate the Great Recession but also because of direct involvement of a large number of prominent economists in the governmental and business decisions that caused it. See "Dismal Ethics," *The Economist*, January 8, 2011, 76; and Sewall Chan, "Academic Economists to Consider Ethics Code," *New York Times*, December 20, 2010, at http://www.nytimes.com/2010/12/31/business/economy/31economists.html.

101. My attempt to provide it is "The Ethical Imperative for Some Scholars to Be Public Intellectuals: (And For the Rest to Let Them Do So)," in Michael C. Desch, ed., *Public Intellectuals*

in the Global Arena: Professors or Pundits? (Notre Dame, IN: University of Notre Dame Press, 2016), 349–72.

102. Samuel P. Huntington, "One Soul at a Time: Political Science and Political Reform," *American Political Science Review* 82, no. 1 (March 1988): 4.

103. Robert D. Putnam, "APSA Presidential Address: The Public Role of Political Science," *Perspectives on Politics* 1, no. 2 (June 2003): 250.

104. Richard Hofstadter, "A Note on Intellect and Power," *American Scholar* 30, no. 4 (Autumn 1961): 596.

INDEX

A NOTE ON THE TYPE

This book has been composed in Adobe Text and Gotham.
Adobe Text, designed by Robert Slimbach for Adobe,
bridges the gap between fifteenth- and sixteenth-century
calligraphic and eighteenth-century Modern styles.
Gotham, inspired by New York street signs, was designed
by Tobias Frere-Jones for Hoefler & Co.